My Great-Grandmothers

My Great-Grandmothers

Four Ordinary Women
Whose Stories Deserve to Be Told

Cora Huggins Springer (1852–1919)
Texanna Cantrell Heare (about 1861–1890)
Kate Kuhn Gabler (1866–1960)
Minnie Wohlfeil Hemsworth Olds (1891–1968)

Bonnie Randolph

My Great-Grandmothers: Four Women Whose Stories Deserve to Be Told

Copyright © 2025 by Bonnie Randolph. All rights reserved.

ISBN (paperback): 979-8-9935835-0-1
ISBN (ebook): 979-8-9935835-1-8

Library of Congress Control Number: 2026900568

No part of this work may be reproduced or transmitted in any form, or by any means, electronic or mechanical, including photocopying and records, or by any information storage or retrieval system without written permission from the author.

Disclaimer: The lives of my great-grandmothers are based on facts discovered through research of each woman's life and the historical context in which she lived. Few stories, diaries, or letters were passed down. If I have misinterpreted the records and gotten the story wrong, I meant not to offend but to understand.

Cover and interior designer: Olivia M. Hammerman, www.indigoediting.com

Dedicated to my parents:
Dan Springer (1922–2001)
Eleanor Katherine Gabler (1932–2020)

"Is it probable, that one hundred and fifty years hence, any one of our race will be able to trace his descent, in like degree, from four such women as these? A more pertinent question is, will any of the race be left to trace descent from anybody?"
    —Agnes Blake Poor, *My Four Great Grandmothers* (1919)

Her four great-grandmothers were born in Massachusetts in 1734, 1753, 1754, and 1748 and had large families who produced an astronomical 263 grandchildren.

Contents

Acknowledgments ix
What a Girl Should Know xi
Preface xiii
Cora Huggins Springer (1858–1924) 3
    Huggins Ancestors 4
    Robertson Ancestors 16
    Springer Ancestors 21
    Life in Gravel Hill 26
    Childhood during the Civil War and Reconstruction 31
    Marriage 41
    Texas 59
    Back in Gravel Hill 65
Texanna Cantrell Heare (about 1861–1890) 85
    Peters Colony 87
    Texas Frontier 91
    A Childhood Spent Circling Dallas 97
    1875 Court Cases 106
    Marriage 116
    Children 121
Catherine Kuhn Gabler (1866–1960) 141
    Sailing to America 151
    St. John the Baptist German Catholic Church 158
    Growing up with the Ebners 169
    Marriage 183
    Widowhood in St. Louis 193
Minnie Wohlfeil Hemsworth Olds (1891–1968) 215
    Visit to the Old Country 216
    Life in Marienwerder 221
    Immigration to Green Bay 225
    West to Oregon 236
    Birth of Minnie 243
    Frank Hemsworth 251
    Dellon Olds 269

Resurrecting My Great-Grandmothers 277
   Faith 278
   Legal Rights 279
   Marriage, Children, and Widowhood 281
   Legacies 284
Endnotes 289
Selected Bibliography 303
Index 307

Acknowledgments

Thank you to friends and family who took the time to read drafts: my cousin Sharon, my sister Brenda, my sister-in-law Sue, and friends Sigrid, Jenny, and April, and especially my niece Heather, who always encouraged me.

What a Girl Should Know

To sew
To cook
To mend
To be gentle
To value time
To dress neatly
To keep a secret
To be self-reliant
To avoid idleness
To mind the baby
To darn stockings
To respect old age
To make good bread
To keep a house tidy
To control her temper
To be above gossiping
To make a home happy
To humor a cross old man
To marry a man for his worth
To be a helpmate to a husband
To take plenty of active exercise
To see a mouse without screaming
To be light-hearted and fleet-footed
To wear shoes that don't cramp the feet
To be a womanly woman under all circumstances

Originally printed in the Springfield, Oregon, Union and reprinted in the Ashland Tidings and other newspapers in 1889.

Preface

Soft dust billowed over my bare toes as I walked in the dirt road that stretched beyond our farm in the Oregon Coast Range. I was struck with an uncanny feeling of déjà vu—the sun warm on my shoulders, dust swirling gently, and a memory of another little girl in a faded calico dress. I've always wondered who she was and why, in that moment, I felt a connection to her.

I loved reading novels with family trees printed on the inside cover. Maybe I didn't need to rely on fictional family charts or wonder about the meaning of déjà vu experiences; I could research and find my own ancestors. Now retired, I decided to write the stories of my great-grandmothers—four women I was most curious about and without whom I wouldn't exist. They were my "invisible ancestors," whose tangled branches in my family tree held mysteries and secrets I hoped would help me understand their lives. All of us have great-grandmothers. How much do we really know about them? Were they well-educated city-dwelling activists or sunbonnet-wearing country women with work-roughened hands?

I knew my paternal great-grandmothers were from Texas and Tennessee. Cora had many children, and Texanna was a framed photograph that my grandma displayed in her dining room. I knew much less about my mother's side of the family tree. I remembered my maternal great-grandmother, Minnie, who seemed stern and forbidding. I avoided her. I always knew about a Catholic great-grandmother named Catherine (Kate) in St. Louis, who had a daughter named Eleanor, whom no one in Oregon had ever met. Nonetheless, my mother, Eleanor Katherine, was named for them.

A myriad of societal reasons make unearthing the lost stories of women more challenging than those of men. Often neglected in official records and family histories, genealogists diligently seek to uncover maiden names and birth and death dates. Born in the nineteenth century, the mysterious lives of my great-grandmothers had to be pieced together from family stories, census reports, newspaper articles, and a handful of photographs. They turned out to be impoverished women who traveled light and did not keep diaries or letters, convinced that their activities and thoughts were not worth recording. Husbands and fathers overshadowed them by custom and law. They were born into an era when women seldom owned property, signed legal documents, or participated in politics. Men wrote the histories, paid the taxes, served in the military, and left wills.

I began my research journey years ago with my father's family, with whom I was closest. I knew the story of my father's parents catching the six o'clock train the morning after their wedding in West Texas for a grand adventure in Oregon. After exploring Oregon, they homesteaded in the Coast Range, their children settling on adjoining property. I grew up playing with cousins and sitting on my grandma's couch, looking through her photo albums of picnics in Texas, with women in long skirts on horseback in dry, dusty canyons without a tree in sight. How different it looked compared to the dripping, dense forest of brush and towering Douglas firs and cedars outside my grandma's vine-covered windows.

I naively thought my dad's oldest brother had free time to answer my questions since he was a bachelor. He mailed me his birthdate and his mother's, and asked his brother for his when he saw him on his way to collect the mail. That was it. My high hopes of filling in the blanks on the family tree were dashed. But then my dad suggested I write to a cousin in Tennessee who, unbeknownst to me, had corresponded with the family. She sent back shocking information: my grandfather's father was a Springer, and his mother was a Huggins. He married a girl whose father was a Huggins and whose mother was a Springer. What did that mean for my family tree?

Searching through the U.S. Census, books, military records, newspapers, and every conceivable source, aided by cousins and other researchers who generously contributed, I researched the lives of Kate, Minnie, Texanna, and Cora. I finally untangled the Huggins and Springer families in Gravel Hill, Tennessee. I traced my great-grandmother Kate back to her childhood home in Indiana, where I got stuck until I found the name of her father's village in Alsace in her youngest uncle's obituary. Knowing the village name allowed me to access French civil and older Catholic records to find her grandparents and their ancestors. I found her husband's family in the Catholic records of Koblenz, Germany. Minnie's family was Prussian. I had assumed their records had been destroyed during the World Wars or the Soviet occupation, until I learned about a website featuring German Lutheran records from what is now Poland. Fact by fact, I uncovered their stories. I trudge on; there is still more to discover and more to write about. One day, an obscure record will reveal the birthdate of my great-grandmother, Texanna, in frontier Texas, and provide information about her mother, only identified as Margaret.

How did my great-grandmothers live and think during the nineteenth and twentieth centuries? Against the backdrop of the Civil War, Reconstruction, economic depressions, and the Progressive Era's technological and transportation advances, I quickly realized how little I knew about women's lives. I also recognized that I had never taken the time to reflect on my own experiences. I audited an introductory women's studies class at a community college, where I discovered feminist history had expanded while I hadn't been paying attention.

I know that my life experiences are quite different from those of my great-grandmothers. I enjoy more freedom and leisure time. I travel alone easily. Religious faith doesn't motivate or comfort me. I remember getting my first credit card, wearing pants to class, and casting my first vote in a presidential election. Even though I strongly believe in equality, I have rarely marched for women's rights or burned my bra. Bras are too expensive, and I'm a very pragmatic woman.

Now in my 70s, was I the shining star in an orbit of conventional, passive women who left hardly a ripple, or part of a circle of strong women with vast continents of experience? I'm sure my female ancestors saw themselves as ordinary and would have been puzzled by anyone wanting to research their lives. They may have viewed their lives as a book with some chapters to share and some to conceal, just as I do.

My great-grandmothers spoke to me slowly about their lives. I hoped to find women resisting societal norms, customs, and laws, but I expected to meet conventional women who put on their aprons each morning and took them off at night. I am not a historian or a professional genealogist—just a woman researching the lost history of her great-grandmothers. I don't want to fade into faceless anonymity, a woman who wouldn't catch a moment's attention from anyone, either. All women deserve to have their stories told.

xvi *My Great-Grandmothers*

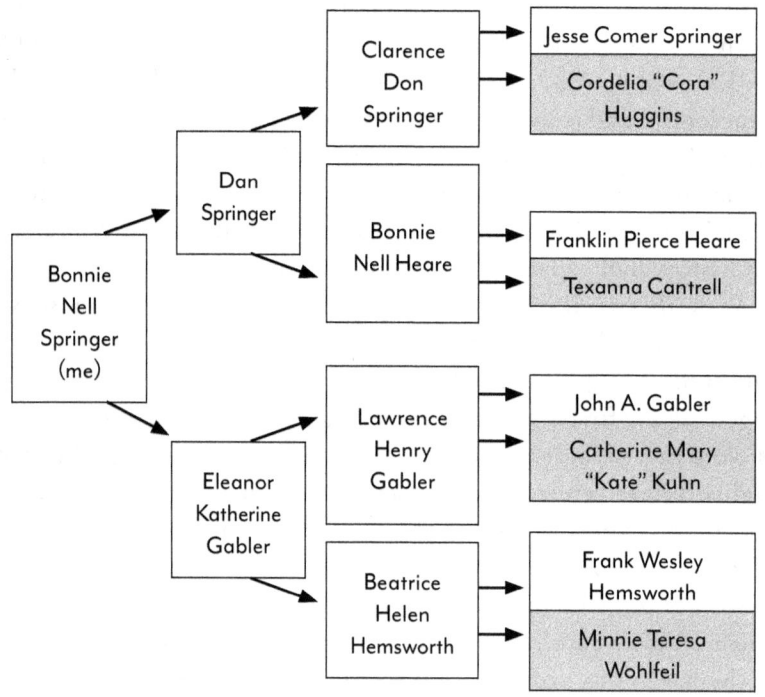

Cora's Family

James Monroe Huggins
born: June 9, 1832, Lauderdale County, Alabama
married: November 4, 1852, McNairy County, Tennessee
died: September 17, 1883, Gravel Hill, McNairy County, Tennessee
parents: Phillip Jasper Huggins (1809–1851) and Agnes Robertson (1812–1853)

Elizabeth Springer
born: May 13, 1835, Giles County, Tennessee
died: December 10, 1929, Gravel Hill, McNairy County, Tennessee
parents: Ezekiel Springer (1797–after 1860) and Hannah (1794–1856)

Children
Victoria, 1853–1883, m. John Walker Latta, 4 children
William Sampson, born in 1855, died as a baby
Balzoria, born in 1856, died as a baby
Cordelia "**Cora**," 1858–1924, m. Jesse Comer Springer, 12 children

> Herbert (1878–1878)
> Predetta (1880–1946)
> Clarence Don (1882–1953)
> Grover Cleveland (1884–1941)
> Hettie E. (1886–1915)
> Eupha Lucinda (1888–1975)
> Floy Ann (1890–1974)
> Claude Erby (1892–1974)
> Eldon Victoria (1895–1957)
> James Carl (1898–1980)
> Dora (1899–1940)
> John Monroe (1903–1983)

Monroe Dudley "Dud," 1859–1926, m. Margaret Nicey Elder, 7 children
Julia A., born in 1861, died as a baby
Julius Franklin, born in 1862, died as a baby
Zulah Bell, 1864–1955, m. Felix Grundy "Dink" Rasberry, 9 children
James Bryant, 1867–1952, m. Mary Ellen Prince, 10 children
Armanda, born in 1870, died as a baby
Alvirada R. "Rady" 1870–1929, m. Lillie McCoy, Martha Sullivan, 7 children
Hannah Agnes "Aggie" 1875–1901, m. Archibald W. Hamm, 2 children

Cora Huggins Springer
(1858–1924)

When my great-grandmother, Cora, married her cousin Jess, eyebrows were raised. Many cousins tied the knot in Gravel Hill, but these two were particularly close; their marriage considered immoral in most communities and outright illegal in others. The kinfolk of Gravel Hill surely had concerns about the health of Cora's children, but it wasn't proper to question His will. The Almighty would bless as He saw fit. God knew what to give and what to withhold.

Cora Huggins was born in 1858, three years before the outbreak of the American Civil War, in the small settlement of Gravel Hill, nestled among the rolling hills of oak and pine in McNairy County, western Tennessee. She was named Cordelia but always went by C.C. or Cora. As a child, she walked along dusty roads lined with scattered houses, her great-uncle's two-story brick store, a church, and two cemeteries—one for the Huggins family and the other for everyone else in Gravel Hill. At 19, she married a boy she had known her whole life. Cora's mother and Jesse's father were siblings, and Cora's father was a brother to Jesse's mother. These two double first cousins shared the same grandparents—a relationship referred to as a collapsed pedigree in genealogy.

A shy-looking teenage Cora gazes passively at the camera in an undated photograph. She wears a calf-length, opaque skirt over long dark stockings and a ruffled jacket, cinched with a white, tatted belt. Her lacy scarf is pinned with a cameo brooch. A black knit hat rests atop her long, dark blond hair that cascades down her back. Her future will consist of a farm life filled with children and work, enough to make her downturned mouth more pronounced as she ages.

Cora Huggins

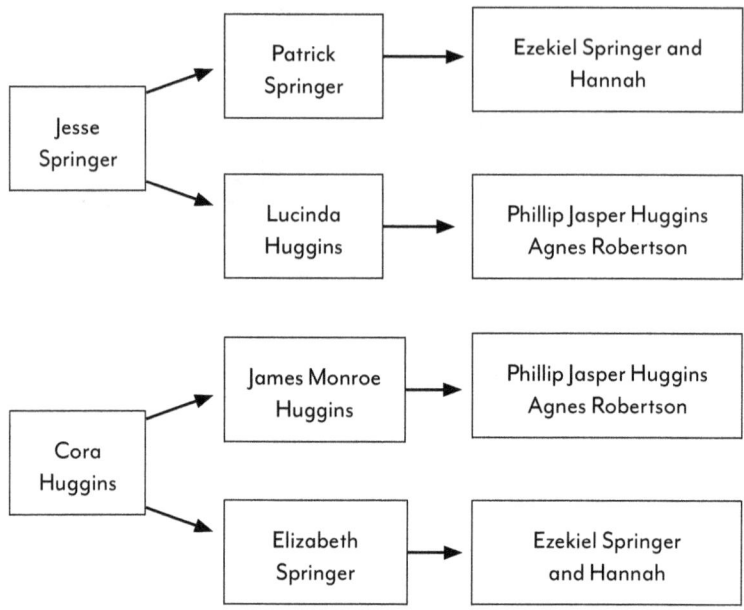

Cora was part of a clan of poor southern White women who were seldom sufficiently literate to leave behind a written legacy of personal diaries or correspondence for future generations to read. Uncovering the life of the "silent" female ancestor is not straightforward, as she rarely speaks. By researching the lives of the men in her life—grandfathers, father, husband, and sons—a slight crack opens to hear a whisper of her voice.

Cora's ancestors married unsociable men who quickly grew dissatisfied with their farms when they could see smoke rising from a neighbor's chimney. They became convinced that there was better farmland further west, out of sight of neighbors, complete with timber, flat ground for plowing, and a source of sweet, fresh water. Consequently, their wives packed up the households and children to move to another cramped one-room log cabin, where they faced the daily chores of caring for the children, fetching water from the creek, milking the cow, cooking meals over an open fireplace, washing clothes, spinning, sewing and mending, tending the garden, and doing it all over again the next day.

Huggins Ancestors

The origins of the Huggins family are murky. There is a tale of three Huggins brothers from London who immigrated during colonial times.

One brother settled in New York, another in Baltimore or Boston, and the third in North Carolina. Many stories have been passed down through families about three immigrant brothers, ancestors with royal blood, or an Indian princess in the family tree, but they remain just that—tales.

However, this tale contains some truth because Huggins did live in North Carolina. Cora's great-great-grandfather, Phillip Huggins, born around 1745, had a son named Phillip, born around 1765 in Maryland, who likely lived in Virginia before moving to the mountains of western North Carolina. He would have traveled south on the Great Wagon Road through the Shenandoah Valley to the Carolinas, drifting westward into the Great Smoky Mountains. His family likely trudged on foot, with their belongings strapped to their backs—the more fortunate rode on horseback or in a cart. Chickens were crammed into saddlebags with their legs bound together, while the cow trailed behind, tied by a rope to the saddle.[1] Travel was slow. Streams and rivers had to be crossed, and roads were little more than an Indian trading path or animal trail, not wide enough for a wagon.

In a pattern repeated during westward expansion, settlers were lured by the availability of cheap land on the frontier. There was a reason: frontier settlers were exploited and used as a buffer to protect the more established civilization along the coast from the Cherokees and other Native Americans. The inevitable land disputes fostered chilling tales of violence shared at corn shuckings, cabin raisings, funerals, and preachings.

By 1785, Phillip and Luke Huggins moved to Burke County, North Carolina, where Phillip sued a man.[2] Their land, where Phillip Senior and his sons lived in 1790, became part of Buncombe County in 1791. Three Huggins households were recorded in the 1800 Census: Phillip Senior and his sons, Phillip and Luke. The younger Phillip married Jane Morris on December 8, 1791.[3] Jane may have been the daughter of William Morris, a Revolutionary War veteran who had come to the Carolinas with the Huggins, possibly from Virginia. Phillip Huggins, Luke Huggins, and William Morris were listed on a 1782 Bedford County, Virginia tax list. Nine years after their 1791 marriage, Phillip and Jane Huggins had seven children under the age of ten, while his brother, Luke, had eight children.[4]

Phillip Huggins Senior and his sons accumulated over 400 acres in adjoining parcels along Little River in Buncombe County, North Carolina, between 1792 and 1800. Phillip, his son, obtained a land warrant from Thomas Davidson, one of the earliest settlers in the area. The warrant, dated April 18, 1792, was for 200 acres bordering the land he was already living on.[5] It took seven years and seven months for his patent to be issued, and then he paid thirty shillings per 100 acres. His father, Phillip Huggins, served as the witness. The patent read as follows:

> *State of North Carolina, No. 649. Know ye that we have granted unto Phillip Huggins two hundred acres of land in Buncombe County, lying on Little River. Beginning on the West side of said river on a black oak corner on Good's line ten poles from said river, and runs due North one hundred poles to a small hickory on McDowels & Millers line then east with said line sixty-eight poles crossing said River to McDowells and Millers Corner on a black oak, then due North with said line one hundred and fifty-six poles to a stake, then due East one hundred and twenty-eight poles to a stake, then due west sixty-eight poles To a corner on a small hickory, then due South one hundred poles To a post oak corner on William Goods line, then due West one hundred and twenty-eight poles crossing said river To the Beginning. To Hold to the said Phillip Huggins his heirs and assigns forever dated 26th day of November 1799.*

Phillip Huggins received a patent for another 100 acres on the east side of Little River in 1797, adjoining his and his brother Luke's land. He was also issued a warrant for 100 acres on Little River and 200 acres on Little Willow River; however, the patents were not recorded. Edward Huggins, possibly another brother, was granted a patent in 1799 for 150 acres at the headwaters of Little Willow and Crabtree Creek, for which he paid three pounds and 15 shillings. Today, the area where the Huggins family settled is approximately 30 miles south of Asheville, in Henderson County, North Carolina, just north of the South Carolina border.

Tucked away in the Blue Ridge Mountains, subsistence farmers like Huggins struggled to provide for their families. By the end of the Revolutionary War, government resources had been depleted. The Continental dollar was virtually worthless, so foreign coins like British or Spanish currency, referred to as "hard money," were favored. It wasn't until the Currency Act of 1792 that the dollar became America's standard legal currency. Huggins and his neighbors probably never saw a dollar. Instead, butter and homemade whiskey functioned as their currency. Butter could be traded for salt, coffee, sugar, ribbons, nails, needles, and candle molds—items they couldn't produce.

A supply of whiskey was essential, and every visitor was offered a drink. No one left a cabin without a trusty long rifle and a pouch packed with bullets, flint, and precious powder. Some settlers had old seven-day clocks, but as a rule, they learned to guess the time with some accuracy by watching the sun on clear days. With the Bible serving as their moral compass and guide, the independent Huggins and their distant neighbors distilled whiskey, played mournful tunes on their fiddles, and held a gloomy outlook on life. They earned a reputation for being stubborn, stoic, uneducated, crude, wild, suspicious, and explosive—and the devil to govern.

Even so, the newly formed Buncombe County required a court-house six to eight miles from home, allowing a man to walk there, attend to business, and return before dark. A single-story, one-room log courthouse was constructed. Such a large crowd assembled for the first session in April 1792 that the court had to reconvene in Colonel William Davidson's barn. Men were requested to remove their coonskin caps. A sheriff, a justice of the peace, a surveyor, and other officials were selected based on merit rather than social class. Only on the frontier could men from modest means rise above the stringent class system to become community leaders or the "Better Sort." Taxes were established at one shilling six pence per taxable person (defined as White and male). Orphaned children were assigned guardians, and the court approved the construction of grist mills. Livestock brands were registered to indicate ownership. Phillip Huggins' legal mark of notching his animals' ears in a specific pattern was "a Smooth Crap off the right Ear and a hale in the Left."[6]

All White males aged 16 to 50 (except those masters who owned two or more slaves) were required to build and maintain roads close to their homes. They had to clear brush, remove fallen timber, and construct or repair bridges. One such assignment was to "Mark and lay off a road the nearest and best way from the ford of Ben Davidson's creek to Green River Cove." Another task assigned involved overseeing a road from Ben Davidson's creek to Little River, near the Huggins' land. These roads were typically 12 feet wide, marked per mile, bridged where necessary, and, at a minimum, simply a path adequate for the passage of a single horse and rider.

Phillip and Luke began selling their land in Buncombe County between 1802 and 1805. Phillip moved to Tennessee, where he lost track of his brothers. His father may have already died. Phillip, Jane, and their children probably lived in the sparsely populated White County, Tennessee. A Phillip Huggins obtained a land grant of 117 acres on the south side of Calfkiller Fork in 1807, in a lowland that stretched four miles through mountainous caves, waterfalls, and coal fields of White County. One boundary of Phillip Huggins' land was a white oak carved with a "PH" on a bluff overlooking Calfkiller Fork.

The birthplaces of Phillip and Jane's children offer clues about their whereabouts. Their first ten children were born in North Carolina between 1792 and 1803, and the next two were born in Tennessee in 1807 and 1809. Their youngest daughter was born in Kentucky in 1811. In Kentucky, they might have lived near the confluence of the Tennessee and Ohio Rivers in Marshall County, where a daughter later settled. Some genealogical researchers suggest they resided alongside the Hamm, English, and Milton families in Warren County, Kentucky.

From December 1811 to March 1812, settlers were terrified by three powerful earthquakes, followed by thousands of aftershocks centered in New Madrid along the Mississippi River. The earthquakes caused the river to flow backward, changing its course. Trees snapped in half and toppled over, while a strange roar sent cows and horses darting into the woods, many of whom were never found. The shaking caused church bells to ring as far away as Charleston, South Carolina. Frontier settlers, lacking scientific training, believed that the end of the world was near. Churches and camp meetings were filled with people praying for divine help, a period later sarcastically referred to as "The Earthquake Revival."

Luke Huggins, the nineteen-year-old son of Phillip and Jane, enlisted in the War of 1812 in Kentucky. He was part of Andrew Jackson's ragtag army, which took pride in defeating the professional British army at the Battle of New Orleans on January 8, 1815. Luke was discharged in Pulaski, Giles County, Tennessee, where his parents may have moved with the Milton, English, and Hamm families, whose children later married into the Huggins family.

In 1805, Congress passed a law prohibiting White settlers from occupying Native American land, including the southern part of the Tennessee Valley. Speculators and squatters ignored this law. Some married into the Cherokee tribe and owned slaves while building houses, taverns, and cotton gins. Chief Doublehead, a feared yet enterprising Cherokee, illegally leased a thousand acres in northern Alabama and southern Tennessee through his Doublehead Company. He was killed when it was discovered that he had enriched himself through treaties with Whites without consulting the Cherokee Nation.

The United States government tried to force these squatters out by burning their homes, tearing down fences, and destroying crops. Soldiers even cut down the corn in the fields with butcher knives. One squatter was home alone with her children when federal troops arrived in the spring of 1811 with orders to evict settlers from Indian lands. She saved her home by cooking a lavish meal for the hungry troops. Although they set fire to her cabin, two well-fed soldiers came back to put out the flames.

The Cherokee and Chickasaw cessions of 1816 allowed for legal settlement by Whites. Cora's great-grandfather, Phillip Huggins, and his adult sons took advantage of public land sales in Lauderdale County in 1818, paying $2.00 per acre for 159.68 acres situated between the Natchez Trace and Jackson's Military Road. The Natchez Trace was an ancient Native American trail that originated in Natchez, on the Mississippi River, and extended northeast to Nashville. Jackson's Military Road, two hundred miles shorter than the Natchez Trace, was constructed during the War of 1812 to transport troops and supplies more speedily. This route quickly became heavily traveled by travelers and drovers with horses for sale, providing Huggins with a first-class road to the markets.

Phillip and his sons purchased additional parcels of land in Lauderdale County bordering Lawrence County and Wayne County, Tennessee, to the north, and the shoals of the Tennessee River, a day's walk to the south.[7] Native Americans had left piles of mussel shells along the riverbanks of the Tennessee River. Settlers used the natural pearls from the mussels as marbles and buttons, and fastened the shells to sticks to use as hoes until tools could be forged. A raw settlement quickly developed into Florence, the county seat. Large brick buildings, frame houses, and cotton mills were constructed. Steamboats brought luxuries, and cotton, corn, whiskey, and other goods were shipped back to New Orleans. But it was not without violence. In 1822, a river pilot was murdered at Muscle Shoals; his head was chopped off while he slept.

Irish immigrant James Jackson owned a 3,000-acre plantation called the Forks of Cypress, where he raised horses that became the bloodstock for Kentucky thoroughbreds. Alex Haley's enslaved ancestors worked in its cotton fields. Dred Scott was an enslaved hostler at Florence's Peter Blow Tavern in 1820. The 1830 Lauderdale County census recorded 7,960 white residents, 3,795 enslaved people, and 26 free people of color, resulting in a ratio of two whites to every Black.

Native Americans were not counted in the census. They faced expulsion due to President Andrew Jackson's Indian Removal Act. In May of 1838, the military forcibly removed over 17,000 Cherokees. The process was swift and brutal. Detachments of soldiers drove men, women, and children from their homes, some with only the clothes on their backs. Possibly more than four thousand perished. Ultimately, the Choctaw, Chickasaw, Creek, and Seminole Nations suffered the same fate as the Cherokees. Many were marched through Lauderdale County, passing Cora's great-grandparents' farm. The "Trail of Tears" was one of the darkest episodes of relations between the United States and Native Americans.

North of Florence, Huggins and their neighbors raised horses, mules, cattle, sheep, and hogs on hilly, wooded land, building cabins near springs scattered with arrowheads. Dense thickets of giant grasses called canebrakes reached twenty feet high on fertile ground and four to seven feet high on ridges and in thin soil. By cutting and digging out the canebrakes, the rich bottomland produced a little wheat, oats, tobacco, flax, and bushels of Indian corn. Neighbors worked together during harvest and hog butchering, using every part of the pig except the squeal. Fresh pork was seen as unwholesome and left for those "who had a mind to swallow or be swallowed by flies." If a family arrived with nothing, their neighbors helped them until they could grow a crop. If a man fell ill, they tended to his corn. A man without a horse could turn the earth in two-foot rows to plant corn and clear the weeds. Communities came together for foot races, horse races, cock fights, stickball, and bare-knuckle matches. "Bees" were popular gatherings: cabin-building bees, barn-raising bees, cornhusking bees, and quilting bees. Women swapped recipes and shared gossip they had picked up from the few travelers they saw. Strangers and foreigners were virtually unknown.

Cora's great-grandmother, Jane, and her numerous children likely lived in a primitive, 10-foot-by-10-foot one-room log cabin, chinked with mud, with a hard-packed dirt floor and no windows. A six-foot-wide chimney dominated the space, leaving little room to maneuver around a crude table and benches crafted from split logs, and a corner bedstead topped with a mattress resting on rawhide strips. Clothing was hung on pegs. The children spent their days outside, only coming inside to eat and sleep. Everyone used the smelly necessary house or visited the woods. Cabins faced east to catch the morning sun, but in winter they were drafty and dark. An old quilt or a handmade door hung on wooden hinges kept out the cold wind. Overnight guests were always welcome, regardless of the privacy we hold dear today.

Jane taught her daughters to churn butter, weave cloth, make tallow candles and soap, use herbs, roots, and plants to heal and comfort the sick, and care for the cows and chickens. They learned to preserve food for winter by drying fruits and vegetables in the sun, and salting and smoking meat. Soap was made after the fall hog-killin' using wood ash and fat. Old ashes and rancid cooking grease made a terrible-smelling soap, but it was still strong enough to peel the skin off your hands!

Children were encouraged to eat sulfur for its health benefits. Healing teas were brewed. Horseradish or lye poultices were considered the most effective treatments for bruises, boils, and rheumatism. Goldenseal (which the Cherokee used as an antiseptic) was used for nasal congestion, mouth sores, eye and ear infections. Lady's slipper orchids were used for nervousness, and butterfly roots caused heavy sweating in fever cases. Dittany tea, balm of Gilead, or pine buds steeped in whiskey were used for colds and lung problems. The seeds of Jerusalem oak, turned into candy, were a reliable treatment for intestinal worms.

Typhoid fever, intermittent fever, and pneumonia with chills were the most common diseases reported in Lauderdale County, along with whooping cough, scarlet fever, and brain congestion. People were burned alive, drowned, or killed when hunting or by getting kicked by a mule. Older folks succumbed to dropsy or what is now known as congestive heart failure. The good Lord knew that life could be short and brutal.

Corn was pounded, molded, ground, fried, boiled, baked, and distilled into whiskey or fed to animals. Hogs fattened on corn provided lard for cooking, lamp oil, and table meat. Deer, squirrels, rabbits, quail, wild turkey, and fish from the creeks supplemented their corn diet. There was often deer or bear meat in the smokehouse. Meals were prepared in an iron pot hung from bars and hooks in the fireplace or in a cast-iron Dutch oven (a heavy black kettle with an iron cover). After pouring the cooked meat into a large brown earthen platter, the Dutch oven was refilled with dough and placed on hot embers to bake into "corn pone." In the same kettle, spring water was heated for a hot drink using coffee or a substitute. The Dutch oven was one of the most essential tools for hearth cooking and eventually evolved into wood stoves.

Jane Huggins wore dresses that opened down the front to the waist, allowing her to nurse the baby. She never ventured into the sun without her sunbonnet, as pale complexions were seen as a sign of health and wealth. She crafted buckskin hunting shirts for her husband, along with breeches and gaiters made from home-dyed cloth. He wore a belt around his waist and carried a long, well-honed hunting knife and a shot pouch. His long hair was tied in a queue and covered by a fur cap made of mink or coonskin, with the tail dangling down the back. Adults wore boots or went barefoot, while the children rarely wore shoes.

Clothing was hand-stitched from a variety of fabrics, including wool, linen, cotton, and silk, with wool and linen being the most commonly used. England had prohibited the American colonies from producing cotton cloth, but even after the Revolution, cotton remained expensive, and silk was prohibitively costly. However, half an acre of cotton and an acre of flax provided enough linen and cotton clothing for a family each year, just as several sheep supplied ample wool. Men sheared the sheep while young children cleaned and carded the wool. Older girls, mothers, and grandmothers lucky enough to own a spinning wheel, flax wheel, and loom carded, spun, knitted, and dyed threads blue, butternut, or red using home-grown indigo, boiled hickory bark, and copperas. The indispensable loom was kept on the porch as the cabin was too small. Elias Howe didn't invent the sewing machine until 1846, and it was not until 1851 that Isaac Singer perfected a practical model. It's doubtful whether Cora's mother saw a sewing machine until long after the Civil War.

In the evenings, by candlelight or grease lamp, men crafted leather for bridles, harnesses, and shoes for the family while women sewed and enjoyed a pipe of tobacco. Cora's mother smoked a pipe for most of her life. Archaeologists identify remains by the distinctive, clean, round holes left by ceramic pipe stems in people's teeth, including those of very young children. As cigar smoking replaced pipes among men, women continued to smoke, prompting northerners to mock snuff-dipping and pipe-smoking women and girls from the South. Corncob pipes were easy to make: cut a cob in half and whittle the bowl with a knife, then insert a reed for the stem. Cobs caught fire easily, but since there was an endless supply, making new pipes was a simple process.

Snuff dipping persisted among rural Southern women into the 20th century. Women were described as relaxing in rocking chairs by the fireplace, usually chewing on a twig before dipping snuff. They would spit, skillfully using two fingers to purse their lips and direct the juice as accurately as possible. It was considered unladylike just to hawk and spit.

Husbands and wives worked daily in an agrarian farming society. Their relationship was typically more equal than that of city dwellers. Although milking cows was considered women's work, men helped with the milking; in turn, women assisted with plowing. It took both the husband's and the wife's perseverance, management, and labor to get by. Undoubtedly, it was a tough life, physically and emotionally, even for strong and healthy women.

The saying that a farm woman's work was never finished isn't an exaggeration. These women faced a never-ending cycle of cooking, cleaning, and caring for their children, often while pregnant or soon after giving birth. Under constant stress, some women became suicidal, manic, or fell into deep depression, struggling to manage their households. There was no tolerance for nervous disorders. For women who also endured domestic abuse, the situation was untenable. Resources were scarce, except for calling Granny. A more enlightened woman might have seen similarities between her situation and that of slaves. Since Cora's female ancestors left no written records of their lives, it's impossible to know whether they felt rebellious, complacent, or satisfied with their circumstances. Yet, after a long day of labor from first light to dusk, a country woman was known to dance on a puncheon floor until midnight to the music of a gourd banjo or fiddle.

Cora's great-grandfather, Phillip Huggins, served as the administrator of the estate of his neighbor and friend, Matthew English, when Matthew died at 45. Matthew had settled on the Chief Doublehead Reserve (illegally, as it turned out) and needed proof of land ownership and confirmation that loans had been repaid. In Graham vs. Huggins, William Graham claimed that Matthew English had borrowed $100 on November 30, 1819, from William Hickingbottom. Hickingbottom transferred the IOU slip to Graham in 1824. Graham produced a facsimile in court, testifying that the original IOU had burned. Phillip Huggins testified that he was well acquainted with his neighbor, Matthew English, and had discussed transactions and trades with him in detail. He had never heard of the alleged transaction mentioned. Graham was a liar, and the court agreed. Nevertheless, Phillip Huggins was forced to sell Matthew English's assets to settle his debts. Matthew's widow, Dicey, purchased from the estate the items she needed: 11 geese, four bee stands, a heifer, a pig, a mare, and a pot oven, skillet, and kettle—spelled pot ovin, skillit, and cittle. Phillip's sons bought a pair of adzes, five sheep, and an oven with a lid.[8] Although older than his neighbor Matthew, Phillip became his son-in-law when he married Matthew's daughter after Jane's death.

Phillip Huggins, the patriarch, fathered 19 children: 13 with Jane Morris and six more with his much younger second wife, Elizabeth English. He was about 27 when his first child was born and 73 when his last child was born. His older children began to marry. His daughter Rachel married in Lauderdale County in 1817. The following year, two of his daughters married in Giles County, Tennessee, and another daughter married in Kentucky. Two sons were married in Lauderdale County in 1819, followed by a daughter in 1820. There were four weddings in 1823: his son, James Montgomery Huggins, got married in January; his daughter Jenny married on February 14; eleven days later, Phillip married Elizabeth English on the same day his son Thomas married Elizabeth's sister Nancy. Daughters Rachel and Tabitha married Hamm brothers. Rachel gave birth to 17 children, the first at 20 and the last at 42, with no twins. James Montgomery officiated at many of these marriages. The children of Cora's great-grandfather spread west from Lauderdale County, Alabama, to McNairy County and Hardin County in Tennessee, Texas, Kentucky, and Arkansas.

James Montgomery Huggins emerged as the most prominent of Phillip's sons. He was active in politics and the Baptist Church and served as Constable of Lauderdale County and Justice of the Peace.[9] He also loaned John Liles $262, who offered as collateral a wagon and harness, one clock, six heads of sheep, one cow, two yearlings, two bedsteads, other furniture, and tools, including a log chain and a crosscut saw.[10]

James represented the 40-member Butler Creek Baptist congregation at the Shoal Creek Baptist Association meeting held at the Turkey Creek Meeting House in Hardin County, Tennessee, in 1829. The following year, the association gathered in Wayne County, Tennessee, where his neighbor and ordained minister, Elder Henry Garrard, delivered a sermon from Genesis, chapter 45, "See that you fall not out of the way." James wrote to the Muscle Shoal Church to extend the "left hand of fellowship," questioning whether the congregation was righteous enough to remain part of the Baptist association.

People were frightened in 1833 when a dramatic shower of 30,000 meteors fell in an hour, an event immortalized in the song "Stars Fell on Alabama." That year, the Lauderdale County Court ordered Henry Garrard, James Huggins, and Jesse Melton to form a company responsible for building and maintaining roads. This meant one man served as overseer, while another became the "apportioner" of hands (accountable for recruiting his neighbors). Road assignments for James and the crew included repairing sinkholes on Sinking Creek and marking a road to begin at Florence to join Chisholm's Road at the corner of the Tennessee State line on August 18, 1834. In 1839, James complained to the court about Butler Creek Road. In response, the court ordered six men to change the road near his place and intersect again at the most convenient point between the Thirteen Milepost and Hurricane. James served as County Commissioner of Roads and Revenues from February 1837 through 1839, which required quarterly trips to Florence when the court met.[11]

Church work and court duties kept James busy while his siblings worked on their farms, avoiding mention in court records. One exception was Phillip Jasper Huggins, Cora's grandfather, who served as the constable for Lauderdale County in 1839. He was appointed appraiser for estates and Assistant Marshal for the county, responsible for counting 14,484 people for the 1840 census. He was likely a member of the First Division, Second Brigade, 11th Regiment of the Alabama militia, as was his neighbor, Thomas McBride. Organized on July 20, 1820, Phillip Jasper served as lieutenant (with 12 others) on October 30, 1830; as a Captain on October 4, 1833; and as a Lieutenant Colonel in 1837.[12] He was a volunteer in the 1836 Indian War.[13] Cora's grandfather and his brother James were literate, respected, and trusted by their neighbors. They were "born mountain," men who paid their debts.

Cora's paternal ancestors:

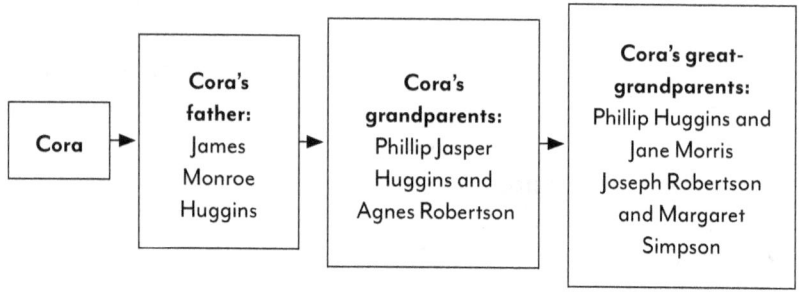

Phillip Jasper and his older brother James Montgomery Huggins married the Robertson sisters. James Montgomery married Elizabeth Robertson in 1823, while Phillip Jasper married Agnes in 1827. Both sisters were 15 years old when they married, at a time when most girls were older, allowing their mothers enough time to teach them the many skills they would need for their own households. Elizabeth and Agnes were the eldest daughters of Joseph Robertson and his wife, Margaret Simpson, who were probably born in North Carolina between 1780 and 1785 and married in 1804. Phillip Jasper and Agnes will become the shared grandparents of Cora Huggins and Jess Springer. Phillip Jasper's brother, James Montgomery, will raise the orphaned Jess in Gravel Hill, where Huggins will worship the Lord, marry, farm, and raise large families.

Robertson Ancestors

When Joseph Robertson, Cora's great-grandfather, died in 1828 in his late forties, he left his wife, Margaret, pregnant with their eighth child, five children at home, two married daughters, two sons-in-law, three grandchildren, land, livestock, household goods, and two slaves.

The slaves were a surprise. I assumed Cora's forebearers were either too poor or believed that owning humans was unscriptural. Still, the White Southern version of the American dream, which aimed to increase social and economic mobility, was rooted in slave ownership and land acquisition. Wealthy planters stood at the pinnacle of the social hierarchy in 19th-century Southern America. Below them were yeoman farmers, like Cora's ancestors, who owned land. At the bottom were the poor, landless Whites—the tenant farmers—a class my ancestors worked hard to escape. There were few differences between the lives of poor Whites and those of the enslaved, except for one significant distinction: Whites were legally allowed to improve their situation, make decisions for themselves, and, in short, be free.

Owning slaves was my ancestors' pathway to prosperity. In 1812, William Robertson, possibly Joseph's father, sold a girl named Hannah to Phillip Huggins in White County, Tennessee, for "the consideration of the sum of one hundred and fifty dollars."[14] Transactions involving the sale or purchase of slaves were recorded alongside land deeds; both acreage and slaves were treated as assets. The Huggins likely expected Hannah to care for their children, prepare meals, and bear children with a White or Black man—decisions that were seldom hers to make. Any children Hannah might have would then become financial assets for her White owners, much as a cow's calves.

Joseph Robertson's probate records detail how the two enslaved men were used. One man was named Jarman, and the other Shadrack. One was between 20 and 25 years old, while the other was between 25 and 30 years old. Jarman was valued at $500, while Shadrack was appraised at $450. Jarman may have been considered more valuable than Shadrack due to his age and skills, or he might have been younger and presumed to be stronger and healthier. The two enslaved individuals were undoubtedly the estate's most valuable assets. The best saddle horse was valued at $90.00. Thirty-one head of hogs were appraised at $40.00, whereas the two men totaled $950.00.

For the first few years after Joseph Robertson's death, Jarman and Shadrack were hired out for $80.00 a year—money that went to their owner, not to them. Then, in 1832, James Montgomery Huggins, the estate's appointed administrator, hired Jarman from the estate for $95.00 for the year, while Shadrack was assigned to the widow. Margaret's oldest son, Thomas, was in his early twenties. Shad, as he was often referred to in the probate records, likely worked alongside Thomas in the fields, just as he had with Thomas' father before he died. By December 1833, Jarman was sold to James Irvin, who lived far enough away that, as administrator, James Huggins billed the estate for travel expenses to deliver him to his new master. There is no record of what happened to Shad, but it is presumed he was sold as well. Like Margaret Robertson, Phillip Huggins owned slaves in 1830: two males under 10 years of age, and two males aged 10 to 23.

Under oath, Allen Wilson, Phillip Huggins, and Canner Coburn made a truthful and impartial appraisal of the property belonging to the estate of Joseph Robertson based on their skills and judgment. His estate included beds, a bookcase, tables, stone jugs, a tin trunk, crops in the fields, plows, hoes, axes, and other farm equipment; 16 head of cattle; 31 hogs; three horses; 24 geese; barrels of corn; three cowhides; a grindstone and other tools; bolts and hinges and other hardware; three guns; saddles; cooking pots; and a clock. A tin bank and a coffee mill were appraised at 50 cents, while a cupboard was valued at $15.00. His land was described as 160.26 acres in the northeast quarter of Section 17 in Township One of Range 10 West, Lauderdale County.

A public auction took place on December 13 and 16, 1828. The widow, Margaret, had to purchase her household goods from the estate, including two beds and furniture ($20.00), four chairs for $2.50, tables for $4.50, a bureau and bookcase for $15.00, and a stone jug for 25 cents. A neighbor bought her spindles. Perhaps Margaret felt that her survival, and that of her children, depended more on livestock and farming equipment than on spinning. She bought a gray horse for $50, a yoke of oxen for $25, 15 head of hogs for $12.00, a wagon for $40, and various tools. By law, her Widow's Allowance allowed her to keep a year's worth of food from the auction gavel. She kept 46 barrels of corn, 1200 pounds of pork, fifteen dollars' worth of sugar and coffee, two bushels of salt, eleven bushels of wheat, and two milk cows. Her oldest son, Thomas, purchased a bay horse for $25.00, a saddle for $3.12½, and a gun and shot pouch for $10.00.

Margaret received a life interest in one-third of the real property owned by her husband as her dower right—an absolute right derived from common law requiring a man to support his spouse. Although Margaret's husband had left assets, he had also lent money. As the administrator, James Huggins was responsible for collecting the loans. Some loans (principal plus interest) were repaid immediately, others took longer, and some were never collected. At the bottom of a probate page was a list of notes due from men believed to be insolvent.

The widow went to court in May 1832, unhappy with her son-in-law's management of her husband's estate. She stated under oath that two years before, "she loaned James Huggins a horse to ride and $5.00 to pay expenses in going to Kentucky to collect a debt due by Jesse Kirkland to the estate of Joseph Robertson," and further stated that the $5.00 belonged to the estate of her deceased husband. She complained that James M. Huggins had his own business to attend to in Kentucky, which included seeing his sister and collecting money owed to him by a man named Garrett. Mr. Huggins was gone for about 10 or 15 days. Margaret signed the statement with her mark. She could not read or write, but clearly wanted James to repay the $5.00 he borrowed for the Kentucky trip.[15]

The settlement of the estate dragged on. In 1840, twelve years after Joseph's death, James M. Huggins was appointed by the Orphans Court of Lauderdale County to sell a 160-acre parcel and a ten-acre parcel of land at public auction to the highest bidder. The widow emerged as the highest bidder at $800 for both parcels and requested that the title be transferred to her name. Twelve years later, Margaret finally lost patience and asked the court for a final decision. James promptly settled the estate. He paid the law firm of Kennedy and Simpson in Lauderdale County a 5 percent commission on the estate's receipts, paid the Circuit Court costs, and compensated the Sheriff. Ultimately, $5,890.24 was divided among nine heirs, including the widow, Margaret Robertson (who consented in a written statement to accept a child's part); her children Charles; Susan; William; Rebecca; Thomas S; Joseph; Phillip Huggins (now deceased) through his wife, Agnes; and James M. Huggins through his wife, Elizabeth. Each inherited $654.47. The final accounting for the Joseph Robertson estate was recorded on February 24, 1854, twenty-six years after Joseph's death. Did James have to wait until Margaret's youngest child turned 25? Court records indicate that Margaret only complained twice to the court regarding her son-in-law's performance as estate executor.

After 20 years in Lauderdale County, James Montgomery Huggins, his wife Elizabeth, and their children moved west to southern McNairy County, Tennessee, joining his older sister Tabitha, Thomas Hamm's wife. As in Lauderdale County, James was the most ambitious member of the family. He owned the first combined steam sawmill and cotton gin in McNairy County, and its cough-puff noise could be heard from his General Mercantile Store in Gravel Hill. He applied for a warrant for 200 acres of land on August 8, 1840, under an original University of North Carolina land grant, and received the patent on August 28, 1849. He sought additional grants of 37.5 acres in 1847, 427 acres in 1851, and 131 acres and 200 acres with his oldest son in 1854.[16] In 1850, his farm was one of the most profitable in Gravel Hill, with 150 improved acres out of 700, six horses, four mules, six oxen, 30 cows,

18 sheep, and 75 swine, producing 1,000 bushels of Indian corn, 100 bushels of sweet potatoes, 300 pounds of butter, and 100 pounds of honey. Huggins Creek was frequently mentioned in McNairy County deeds. There was even a Huggins Creek Post Office that operated from 1847 to 1854. Today, on Google Maps, Huggins Bottom Road crosses Muddy Creek, part of Muddy Bottom, known for its fertile farmland interspersed with swampy areas.

James partnered with his oldest son, Leroy, to buy land and lend money. Leroy continued the business as L.M. Huggins & Company, later rebranding it to L.M. Huggins and Brothers. Neighbors short on cash used their possessions and livestock as collateral, including horses, cows, sheep, hogs, saddles and bridles, beds, and bed coverings. The collateral stayed in the borrower's possession unless they defaulted, at which point Leroy had the right to advertise and sell the collateral to the highest bidder, often at the Gravel Hill Store. One individual borrowed $123.70 for a month in 1861, using his horses, cows, beds, and a desk as collateral. Another man used 16 head of sheep, 40 head of hogs, two men's saddles, one sidesaddle, and a sorrel mare. Leroy acquired two mares, five head of cattle, three sheep, and a clock when a loan for $35.91 wasn't repaid. He served as the postmaster of Gravel Hill from 1847 to 1869, likely keeping an eye out for future financial opportunities.

Tucked away in the deeds of McNairy County were bills of sale for individuals bought by James Montgomery and his son, Leroy Huggins. Slaves, like land, were considered property. These enslaved people worked where and when they were told—perhaps at the Huggins' cotton gin or sawmill, operating hand levers to grind corn into meal, gin cotton, or sawing trees into lumber. In 1854, Leroy purchased a female slave named Chart for $700. On Christmas Eve 1858, James paid $1650 for a man named Peyton, aged 25, whom the seller warranted as sound, sensible, and a slave for life. Leroy paid $1400 for a man named Jacob, also aged 25, whose bill of sale similarly guaranteed his health, sensibility, and status as a slave for life. The Huggins paid more for slaves than for land. Had they known the future, they would have realized that slaves were a poor investment for several compelling reasons, one being that in ten years, Chart, Jacob, and Peyton would be freed by President Abraham Lincoln and belong to no one.

Cora's grandfather, Phillip Jasper Huggins, and his family followed his brother James Montgomery to McNairy County. Phillip's move westward to Gravel Hill united him with several siblings, and his wife, Agnes, with her sister, Elizabeth, and brother, Thomas Simpson Robertson. Like his brother, James Montgomery, Phillip Jasper applied for a land grant of 176 acres, which he received on October 15, 1851.[17]

While his farm did not produce as much as his brother's, it outperformed many other farms in McNairy County. Phillip Jasper cultivated 90 acres from 206 acres and kept horses, mules, cattle, sheep, and hogs. He had four working oxen for plowing the fields to grow wheat, oats, and cotton, but primarily focused on Indian corn and sweet potatoes. In 1850, Phillip harvested 600 bushels of Indian corn, which was estimated to require 80 hours of labor per bushel for hand-planting, plowing, and harrowing.

Phillip Jasper Huggins died around 1851 in his early forties, followed by his wife Agnes two years later. They left behind a farm and up to ten children, two of whom may have died young. One daughter was married, a son married during the interval between his father's and mother's deaths, and the remaining six children were orphaned. Family legend states that a cedar tree marked the graves of Phillip Jasper and Agnes, its branches symbolizing everlasting life with God, the creator.

Springer Ancestors

The origin of the Springers in America is as mysterious as that of the Huggins. They didn't start a war, assassinate a president, become pirates, or write classic literature—and so were left out of history books. Instead, a little nest of Springers farmed in obscurity on Buffalo Creek in northwestern South Carolina. And unlike the Huggins, who reused New Testament names from generation to generation, such as Phillip, James, John, and Luke, the Springers seemed to favor Old Testament names like Ezekiel, Jonathan, Elijah, Uriah, and Aaron.

My ancestors probably arrived in this country as indentured servants. Between half and two-thirds of the population in the American colonies were indentured servants. Labor-intensive tobacco was the Virginia Company's dominant crop. As a result, convicts, political and religious prisoners, poor unwanted children snatched from the streets of London, kilt-wearing Scots caught speaking Gaelic, and laborers who dreamed of owning land were transported to be auctioned for cash or tobacco by ship captains to cover their passage. Rules varied by colony, but typically, those over 17 were indentured for 5 years, while children were required to serve until they reached 21. Convicts accused of capital crimes might serve 14 years, while those with less serious offenses could serve seven years. At the end of their term, they received freedom dues, including food, clothing, a headright of 50 acres, and/or money. Eventually, African slave labor replaced European-born servants.

Thousands of settlers seeking affordable land journeyed south to the Carolinas in the late 1700s, as westward migration was effectively blocked by the Appalachians' lack of passes, known as gaps. The Springer ancestors traveled south by sea or land to the fertile river valleys of the Cherokee Nation in the foothills of the Blue Ridge Mountains. During the French and Indian War (1754–1763), the Cherokees sought to drive out the settlers by destroying their farms and homes, forcing the White settlers to scramble for safety in forts, only to be inundated by more settlers once a fragile peace was established. Initially, the King's officials did little to interfere with the newcomers' clearing of land, building their churches, or protecting their crude homes from Indian attacks, which suited the Springers and their neighbors. They valued their religious and civil liberties and were relatively unconcerned when the War for Independence began on the seaboard. However, as the rebellion continued, their loyalties grew more complicated. Patriots opposed British rule, Loyalists refused to take the oath of allegiance, and others worried about clear land titles. Guerrilla warfare persisted after the Revolutionary War from those who couldn't move past the conflict.

Three-quarters of the early South Carolina settlers were Scots-Irish Presbyterians, joined by Quakers in the mid-1750s (who left by 1800 because of their opposition to slavery) and Baptists, who arrived in the back country in 1762. A preacher described the Baptists as a religiously destitute people in the wilderness. writing that there was a great need for God's word to be "preached to an ignorant people who had little or no preaching for a hundred miles and no established meeting. People were so eager to hear, they would come 40 miles to hear a sermon."[18] Springers were Baptists.

There is a caveat to the mystery of early Springer origins concerning Charles Christopher Springer, born in 1658 in Sweden and sent to London for his education. While there, he was kidnapped and shipped to Virginia, where he served five years as an indentured servant. After completing his term of indenture, Charles walked to the Swedish colony in Christiana Hundred, now northern Delaware. He wrote to his mother in 1693, eight years after he vanished from London, sharing his fate and informing her that he was married with three daughters and expecting a fourth child. Through two marriages, he fathered at least six sons and five daughters. He left an estate estimated at 1900 acres of land, of which 228 acres ran through the center of Wilmington, Delaware.

Jumping ahead about 200 years to 1882, an enterprising duo of George W. Ponton and Charles H. Bierce—both aliases, as it turned out—devised an inheritance scam in London, Ontario. They created documents stating that Charles Christopher Springer's estate was valued at $100 million. The city of Wilmington had agreed to pay his heirs $20 million to settle the claim. One of these men (Ponton) claimed to be an agent representing the Springer heirs, each of whom would receive $90,000; the other (Bierce) claimed to be an heir. The scheme to persuade people to buy shares in the "Springer Heirs Corporation" collapsed when it was exposed as a scam. Ponton and Bierce were arrested. Despite this, Springers from across the country rushed to prove they descended from Charles Springer to claim their inheritance. For years, the "Fabulous Springer Estate" has remained alive and well in the imagination of Springers everywhere, persisting even today despite being proven a hoax. Research, hindered by a lack of primary sources, has revealed no connection between the Springers of western South Carolina and those who settled in New Sweden (present-day Delaware).

My brother's Y-DNA is related to the Springers of Union County, South Carolina, and his Y-haplogroup, I-M253, is found everywhere the Norse invaded. His DNA, when compared to that of other male descendants, indicates that brothers Ezekiel, Aaron, John Jr., and Dennis Springer were likely sons of John Springer, born around 1730 in Virginia, who lived on Buffalo Creek in Union County, South Carolina, prior to 1764. It was good land, covered with luxuriant grass and wild pea-vines that made raising stock easy and profitable except for the Cherokees, who were reluctant to share their land.

Cora's Springer ancestors:

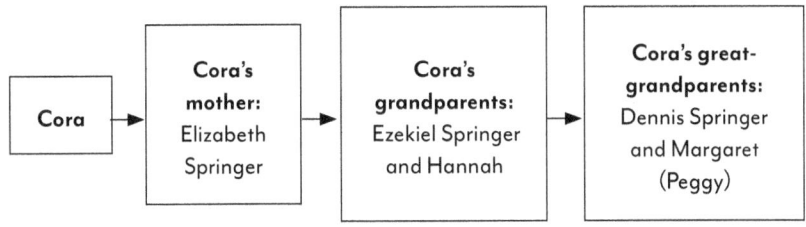

Dennis Springer (Cora's great-grandfather) was born in 1768 in South Carolina and married Margaret (Peggy) from Virginia around 1790. Some researchers believe her maiden name was Polk or Paulk. Dennis bought 125 acres for $500 on the waters of Buffalo Creek in Union County on December 5, 1808 (the date noted in the deed as the twenty-fourth year of America's Independence). The transaction was witnessed by John Springer (likely his father), who signed with an "x."[19] Dennis witnessed several deeds, bought a spade and a plow at an estate auction, appraised an estate, served on jury duty, and had children. After moving with other Springers to the southern part of the Tennessee Valley, he sold his 125 acres in Union County for $1,100. The land was described as:

"Where on I formerly lived" on the waters of Buffalo Creek, being half of a 250-acre tract granted to John Hays Senior August 16, 1774, and "lying on the east line of said tract which intersects with the Rocky Branch and Miry Branch." The deed was dated January 17, 1822, and was signed by Dines Springer and Peggy Springer.[20]

The nest of Springers in Union County, South Carolina, only expanded with another generation in the Tennessee Valley. The 1826 tax list for Lawrence County, Tennessee, alone listed numerous Springers, likely all related: two Ezekiels, two Aarons, one Jonathan, Elijah, John, William, Thomas, and Dennis. On October 10, 1825, Dennis was one of three men appointed to appraise the estate of John Masterson. He purchased 92 acres of land from his son-in-law, Raney Belew, near the Huggins property south of the Tennessee state line on August 11, 1827. The county court appointed Dennis and two others to oversee the election held on the first Monday of August 1832 to elect a senator, sheriff, lower house members, a tax collector, and other officials. He bought one cutting knife and sixteen ounces of indigo (a plant dye used to color cotton blue) from the estate of Guthridge Masterson on September 17, 1839. After leaving behind these bits and pieces in public records, Dennis Springer passed away in 1842 and was buried in Lexington, Lauderdale County, Alabama.

Dennis' son, Ezekiel, and his wife, Hannah (whose maiden name may have been Thomas), were founding members of the Second Creek Primitive Baptist Church, located just north of the Tennessee-Alabama state line. On June 26, 1830, church members entered into a Covenant Agreement with Jane Springer and a few others. Their church was a hand-hewn log building constructed in the early 1820s, which also served as a school. It likely had a dirt or "puncheon" floor (made of split-hewn logs) and few windows. Small, notched logs were stacked to form walls to a desired height or until the logs ran out. (In some cabins and churches, a tall man could not stand upright.) The congregation sat on backless benches made of split logs, mounted flat-side up on four legs driven into the ground. Pulpits were formed from two poles driven into the ground, with wooden pieces nailed about chest height, where the minister could lay his Bible and sermon notes, if he had any. Other denominations also used the church, as each faith met on a different Sunday each month. This arrangement enabled itinerant preachers traveling by horse to share the gospel with four dispersed congregations. When the crowd grew too large, services were held outdoors.

Minutes of the Second Creek Primitive Baptist Church record Ezekiel's appointment to speak with a wayward member. Ezekiel also volunteered with other men to draft a Bill of Discourse on July 4, 1830, for the church members' review. A month later, the Articles of Decorum, including the practice of foot washing, were read and approved. In November 1832, Brother Jones ordered, "Old Mrs. Springer out of the meeting house," and protested when he was censured.[21] Primitive Baptist services were known to be unruly, as parishioners jerked, barked, or rolled through the mud when filled with the Holy Spirit.[22]

In March 1839, a committee was formed that included Aaron Springer and another man from the Second Creek Primitive Baptist Church, along with two members from the Mill Creek Church—Dennis Springer and John Richardson—to investigate Robert Newton, who was accused of breaking a rule of conduct. Congregations were quick to report on each other and just as swift to enforce strict discipline, even over issues like clothing. Members were warned against fiddling and dancing. One preacher labeled playing marbles as worldly and wicked. He vividly described the fate of the players as "The whole couple will go to hell like a whirly gust of woodpeckers."[23]

Ezekiel and Hannah Springer requested their dismissal letter from the Second Creek Primitive Baptist Church in March 1834 when they moved east to Giles County, Tennessee, where their daughter, Elizabeth, was born. Before relocating, Ezekiel purchased a plough from an estate in Lawrence County on January 29, 1833. In 1836, Ezekiel and Elijah Springer (possibly Ezekiel's cousin) paid a poll tax in District 4 of Giles County. Ezekiel owned 130 taxable acres valued at $900. Taxes on land, slaves, or carriages differed from poll taxes, called "head taxes," and were paid by all adult White males. While living in Giles County, Ezekiel witnessed the will of David Hogan, who stated that his small estate wouldn't hold much value if divided among all his children, so he left his entire estate to his son, Wiley. Wiley married Ezekiel and Hannah's oldest daughter, Malinda, the following year.

Sometime before 1840, Ezekiel and Hannah moved again. This time, they left Giles County to settle west of the Tennessee River in McNairy County, bringing their baby Elizabeth, her seven siblings, and Ezekiel's mother, Margaret, known as Peggy. Peggy, the mother of eleven children, was buried in McNairy County when her long life ended there in 1851. In the future, Elizabeth Springer will marry James Monroe Huggins to become Cora's parents; Elizabeth's brother, Patrick Springer, will marry James' sister, Lucinda Huggins, to become the parents of Jess Springer, whom Cora will marry.

Life in Gravel Hill

McNairy County, Tennessee, was called "Old Snake" after a creek that wound its way into the Tennessee River. U.S. troops drove off White settlers who encroached on Chickasaw Nation land by burning their homes, destroying their fences, and treating them the same as the Whites who squatted on Cherokee land. After treaties were negotiated by Andrew Jackson and former Kentucky Governor Isaac Shelby in 1818, the Chickasaws surrendered 10,700 square miles of land between the Mississippi and Tennessee Rivers, opening it for white settlement.

Between 1830 and 1850, the Springers, Hamms, Robertsons, and Huggins settled in Gravel Hill, McNairy County. They were determined men with long beards, thin, worn women in homespun dresses and sunbonnets, and barefoot children so closely related that everyone was a cousin. Gravel Hill met the basic requirements for a community, including its proximity to a creek, a gristmill, a store, a blacksmith, a school, a church, a saloon, and a tannery. It lacked a saloon because it was a "dry" town, but plenty of people kept Gravel Hill supplied with whiskey anyway. In 1846, mail was delivered once a week. By 1854, mail service had increased to twice a week. The Gravel Hill doctor was compensated with a quarter of beef, or a 1,000-pound hog, or six chairs, or an offer to make door and window sashes. The McNairy County Court assigned road crews to maintain and construct new roads and bridges. In June 1858, a group of men, including James Huggins, was selected to build a road from the Houston Bridge Road near the Gravel Hill Post Office to establish the most practical and direct route to Corinth, Mississippi. Men could be excused from paying their poll tax if they worked on the roads.

A gossip-sharing peddler carried a large pack on his back, selling baking powder and vanilla; needles, thread, buttons, and thimbles; or an elixir to ease women's complaints—usually containing a shot of whiskey. Diseases of the womb were treated with a vegetable compound or magnetic foot batteries, which promised to help regulate disturbances and irregularities of monthly sickness, heal falling wombs, chronic inflammation, ulceration of the womb, incidental hemorrhages, painful and irregular menstruation, barrenness, or changes in life. Medicine for malaria fever was a top seller since it was a common ailment. A peddler on foot or horseback paid a fee of $7 per year to the McNairy County Court; a two-horse peddler paid $10 annually; and a peddler using a four-horse vehicle paid $20 each year. A wagon was equipped with drawers, cubbyholes, and baskets to hold more merchandise, such as rope, kettles, fabrics, ribbons, and farm tools.

Newly arrived in Gravel Hill, Ezekiel Springer signed a note for $200, pledging his personal property and livestock as collateral.

"Ezekiel Springer being justly indebted to Alston Hatley by a note of hand dated in March in the year 1839 and due 25th day of Dec 1839 for two hundred dollars and feeling anxious and desirous to Secure the A Hatley in the above named sum of money have this day bargained Sold & delivered unto the said Hatley the following property to wit Sixty barrels of Corn forty four head of hogs marked with a crap & under bit in each ear four fodder stacks One yoke of Oxen 3 Beds & furniture & 2 dozen chairs also Household & kitchen furniture To have and to hold the afore Said property to the only use and benefit of him the Said Hatley his heirs and assigns forever Nevertheless it is agreed between the parties that the property remains in the possession of said Ezekiel Springer until the 25th day of Dec 1843 and should he not pay fully satisfy the above named property is to be sold by the A Hatley to the highest bidder for cash after giving ten days' notice if the property brings more than the above amt Springer is to have it if less it goes to his credit In Testimony where of I have here unto set my hand and seal this the 14th day of Nov.1842."[24]

The Springers likely borrowed the money to buy seed, repaying it once the crop was sold. In 1850, their farm was valued at $350. They cultivated 60 of their 165 acres and owned three horses or mules, three milk cows, 13 sheep, and 18 swine. They harvested cotton, 65 bushels of wheat, 10 bushels each of oats and Irish potatoes, 100 bushels of sweet potatoes, and 400 bushels of Indian corn. Hannah made 50 pounds of butter and gathered 10 pounds of honey. Although she was illiterate, two of her four children living at home attended school during the year.

The family owned twenty-four chairs, three beds, probably a pine or oak table, one or two trunks for storing clothes, and a cupboard for dishes and pans. Cooking was done outside until they installed a chimney, or the cabin became too hot. The children slept on mattresses filled with corn husks in the loft. Owning twenty-four chairs was surprising, but Ezekiel might have preached as well as farmed. He donated two acres of land for the construction of the Primitive Baptist Church.

Besides their house, Ezekiel and Hannah likely had several outbuildings: a spring house, a smokehouse, a corn crib, a chicken coop, a cow stall, and, of course, the privy with a half-moon cut into the door. Milk, vegetables, and other perishable foods were lowered into the cold water of the spring house, while sacks of wheat and shelled corn ground into flour and meal were stored on an upper shelf. In the smokehouse, hams and smaller pieces of pork were smoked and seasoned over wood fires, then wrapped in linen or cotton bags and hung from the rafters to keep rats and mice away. Each year, they used a barrel of lard.

Hannah died at age 62 in 1856, leaving behind a married daughter in Lawrence County, Tennessee, a son in Texas, and seven children in Gravel Hill; four were alive, and three were buried. Ezekiel died in McNairy County about five years after Hannah; the location of his grave is unknown. Before he died, he sold some land: 64.5 acres for $387.00 and 154 acres with buildings for $600.13. His remaining property was valued at $150. Ezekiel and Hannah's son, Patrick, will have a son named Jess, while their daughter, Elizabeth, will have a daughter named Cora.

After marrying Lucinda Huggins, Patrick Springer bought unclaimed public lands, paying at least $1.25 per acre with his brother, Dennis. In June 1849, Dennis bought 200 acres, and Patrick acquired 89 acres that fall. A rush to apply for grants occurred when Tennessee's General Assembly opened more public land for sale in August 1849, causing McNairy County's clerk to suffer writer's cramp.

The future looked promising in 1850. Patrick and Lucinda owned a 65-acre farm, with 12 acres improved, valued at $150. They had one horse, two milk cows, four cattle, three sheep, ten pigs, and farm equipment worth $100. They grew 18 bushels of wheat, 200 bushels of Indian corn, two 400-pound bales of cotton, 10 pounds of wool, 5 bushels of Irish potatoes, and 10 bushels of sweet potatoes, and produced 30 pounds of butter. The young couple valued their homemade goods at $5.00 and estimated the value of the animals slaughtered during the year at $15.00. Patrick bought more land in 1852 for $75; months later, his brother, A.T. (Aaron Thomas), purchased 154 acres with buildings for $260—possibly the same place their father later sold.[25]

The future became much darker when Lucinda died six weeks after giving birth to her fourth son in 1854 at age 26. Patrick died two months later on January 3, 1855, at age 29, leaving four boys aged six, four, two, and an infant orphaned. According to family lore, Patrick and Lucinda died of pneumonia. They were buried side by side in Gravel Hill Cemetery. Patrick's mother, Hannah, was buried beside them. Homemade tombstones mark all three graves. The square lettering on the stones appears to have been engraved by the same person who neglected to plan letter spacing. Hannah's stone has Hannah S carefully carved, with W B for 'was born' and the dates of her birth and death. Lucinda's stone spells her name "Loucinda" with the final "r" in "Springer" on the line below, and Patrick's stone has "Spring" carved with "er" below. The three stones sat on a two-foot bank by Gravel Hill Road in 1978, but I understand they were moved when the road was widened.

Relatives took in the orphaned boys; otherwise, the court would have determined guardianship, often placing children in "Poor Houses," with others who could not care for themselves, or in county- or church-operated orphanages. In McNairy County, orphans were bound as apprentices to local families until they reached the age of 21. The guardians were responsible for teaching them spelling, reading, writing, and arithmetic. Males were taught a trade, such as farming or saddle making, and received a suit of clothes and a good saddle horse upon completing their apprenticeship. Girls were to be educated in the same subjects as boys and learn domestic skills. After finishing her apprenticeship, she could receive a good feather bed, a cow, and a calf.

Patrick's sister, Malinda, widow of Wiley Hogan and married to James Jefferson (J.J.) Hamm, took in the baby and the four-year-old, James Polk and Phillip Frank, also known as J.P. and Frank Springer. With Malinda's ten children from two marriages and two from J.J.'s first marriage, James Polk and Phillip Frank formed a household of fourteen children. Malinda gave birth to her last child in November 1861, and J.J. died the following month.

Patrick Springer's Headstone

A prosperous family raised six-year-old Alexander and two-year-old Jesse Springer. Heading the Huggins clan, James Montgomery Huggins Sr. was a successful farmer and owned the Gravel Hill store and mill.

While still a teenager, Alexander went missing during the Civil War. It's likely that he became one of the many unidentified bodies lost on the battlefield. The other three boys, J.P., Frank, and Jess, married and farmed around Gravel Hill.

Patrick's probate was complicated because he did not legally transfer the deeds for three tracts of land before his death. Witnesses attested that Patrick sold a 187-acre parcel for $230 to William English and then purchased 112 acres days after Lucinda's death for $90. Thomas Prather recalled that in March 1852, he paid Patrick $185 for 74.85 acres, including buildings that had been part of Patrick's grant, and Patrick executed the deed himself. Patrick's brother-in-law, J.J. Hamm, was appointed to oversee Patrick's estate. After J.J. died, Leroy Huggins took over as administrator. In 1862, Leroy paid $1.40 in taxes on acreage valued at $400, which the boys inherited. He continued to pay taxes yearly: J.P. Springer had 178 acres, Alex had 182 acres, and F.P. and Jesse each had 145 acres. Leroy also served as guardian for two Hamm children and three Farris children, paying taxes annually on their land. On August 1, 1870, even though Alex was missing, Leroy Huggins distributed the following from their father's estate to the boys:

- J.A. Springer (Alexander, who disappeared) $199.20
- Jesse C. Springer. $160.30
- P.F. (Frank) Springer $152.10
- J.P. Springer. $144.70

Childhood during the Civil War and Reconstruction

When Cora, my great-grandmother, was born, a new quilt square was added to the ancestral patchwork quilt of the Huggins, Robertson, and Springer families. Her daddy, James Monroe Huggins, added Junior to his name to distinguish himself from his uncle, James Montgomery Huggins, who added Senior. Although he signed documents as James M. Huggins Jr., he was known as Jim. He married Elizabeth Springer in 1852 and raised his three sisters and three brothers, who were orphaned after their parents' passing. He was granted guardianship of his four youngest siblings on September 6, 1858.

Cora was the heart of a vibrant flower, surrounded by petals of family and community when she was born on March 16, 1858. She joined her five-year-old sister, Victoria. Two babies born between Victoria and Cora had died—a boy named William Sampson and a girl named Balzoria—so Cora was especially precious to her parents, James Monroe and Elizabeth. Cora was treasured by the Springers, Huggins, Hogans, and Hamms, all of whom were connected through marriage and their Primitive Baptist faith. Her great-uncle, James Montgomery Huggins Sr., served as the family's head.

Abraham Lincoln was elected the 16th President of the United States two years after Cora was born. In 1860, Cora's father was 27, and her mother was 25. Living with them were her aunts and uncles: Cyrena, age 21; John Randolph, age 18; Phillip Jasper, age 13 (named after his father); and Thomas Jefferson, age 11. Victoria was seven, Cora was two, and her little brother, Monroe, was one. They owned a good farm valued at $2000 and a personal estate of $877, likely the farm that was part of Phillip Jasper Huggins' land grant. Cora's grandfather's eight surviving children inherited 1/8 of the 176 acres. In the years to come, John Randolph will purchase his sister Margaret's share from his brother-in-law, James McCoy, for $200. Cora's father will buy his sister Elizabeth's share from her husband, William Hogan, for $100, and acquire his sister Cyrena's share from her husband, Josiah Jordan, who owned their wives' shares by right of marriage.[26]

Cora was four years old when the Civil War broke out, with the North calling it "the War of the Rebellion" and the South referring to it as "The War Between the States." The war changed McNairy County in frightening ways and left a lasting impression on Cora and her family, which included her three teenage uncles and three aunts, two of whom were married with babies and lived next door to her farm. Victoria, Cora, and their little brother, Monroe (Dud), were joined by a sister and a brother born the following year, though neither baby survived. In total, her mother gave birth at least 12 times, with only seven children surviving.

Few men in Gravel Hill with farms to run and children to feed were eager to enlist in the Civil War. Newspapers, filled with battle reports and editorials depicting a fractured nation, were discussed at the Gravel Hill store. The more philosophical porch-sitters thought the nation resembled a person with two personalities, one insisting on union and the other on disintegration, like a chicken with its head chopped off yet still standing. Men who did not take sides "ought to be hung." The war divided McNairy County: 1,318 men voted for separation, and 586 voted against it.[27]

Huggins and Springers lived in the southern part of the county that supported the Confederacy. They strongly believed that the Federal government should be prevented from interfering with Southern policies and laws and taking away their God-given rights. In May 1861, the McNairy County Court authorized the formation of a Home Guard. Those who joined were responsible for arming and equipping themselves, receiving no compensation for their service. Additionally, the court appointed men to collect guns, reimbursing citizens three dollars per gun. Most farmers likely kept at least one gun hidden, despite the offer of three dollars. Everyone believed the war would end by Christmas, and they wanted a gun for protection and for hunting to feed their children.

Cora's daddy, James Monroe Huggins Jr., at three different ages.

James Montgomery Huggins Sr. was elected President of the Soldiers' Aid Society at its meeting at the Gravel Hill Baptist Church. He issued this statement: "Whereas, we are now engaged in an unholy war waged against us by our former sworn friends, for the purpose of subverting our institutions, usurping our liberties, and subjecting our country. And, whereas, we have hundreds of thousands of our relatives, friends, and fellow citizens in the armies of the South battling for our independence and suffering all the rigors and dangers of a soldier's life that we may remain free and enjoy the blessings of a bountiful providence and birthrights bequeathed to us by our fathers. And, whereas, it is the bound duty of every patriotic man and lady in the land to do all in his or her power to aid the glorious cause of the Southern Confederacy."[28] The Huggins patriarch strongly advocated secession, which in some eyes was treason.

Fielding Hurst was a prominent landowner loyal to the North. He organized a guerrilla force for the Union and remained its leader after it was officially recognized and incorporated into the regular Union Army as the 6th Tennessee Union Cavalry. But Hurst struggled to follow standard military procedures and lost the trust of the Union Army's commanders. He then commanded his regiment to harass Confederate-leaning neighbors like the Huggins and Springers. Nathan Bedford Forrest, a well-known Confederate general under whom Cora's father served, vowed revenge on Hurst after the war. Retaliation and reprisals continued for years. Forrest and Hurst remain controversial figures today.

Union and Confederate patrols searched McNairy County farms for men, food, or horses. More alarming and unpredictable were roving gangs of guerrillas, like Hurst's quasi-military force, or gangs of teenage boys who used the war as an excuse to terrorize and commit crimes with impunity. Guerrillas harassed families by stealing, looting, burning, and sometimes killing. They knew every road, trail, and creek in McNairy and Hardin Counties and followed the Tennessee River to prey on folks in Lauderdale County, Alabama. When Cora heard horses coming, she ran and warned her daddy and teenage uncles to hide in the woods, in hollow trees or thickets, under the house, in the barn, or in the cellar. It was worse in winter, when men had to hide out for sometimes weeks, with little food, water, or blankets, as they had to leave home so quickly. Fields were left unplowed, and church services were unattended as horses and mules were requisitioned by both sides. The bluebellies dug potatoes right out of gardens, the guerrillas took the sweet corn, and the rebs took everything left.

Some women had gumption and fought back. Four men on horseback threatened to burn down the house of a woman sympathetic to the Union if she didn't tell them where her husband was hiding. As one man got down on his knees to light a brush pile against the house, the woman reached inside the door, grabbed an ax, and split his head open like a pumpkin. Holding the bloody ax ready to strike again, the other men jumped on their horses and galloped away. Knowing they would be back, she ran into the burning house, grabbed the rifle and all the ammunition she could find, and escaped to the woods to find her husband.

A couple of Huggins were rumored to have hidden with their kin in Kentucky, while others joined the guerrillas. Thomas Huggins lived on Bumpass Creek, just over the line in Hardin County. His sons, Tom, John, and Leroy, joined Bert Hays' outlaw guerrilla gang, which sometimes numbered as many as 40 men. John married a 14-year-old girl whose guardian was James M. Huggins, Sr. His brother, Tom, stole his young wife before killing two men with a young man named Brance Davis. The families of the murdered men retaliated by killing Tom and Brance four days later. Their parents collected their bodies and buried them side by side. Brance had stolen 21 ladies' side saddles, which were hanging in his father's corn crib at the time of his death.

Another rebel gang led by George Owens spent a frigid winter night in 1864, gathered around a campfire in the woods, drinking stolen whiskey. In a fit of rage, Owens leaped up and killed one of his men, wounded another, shot two horses, and fired at a third gang member, clipping the lapel of his jacket. On another occasion, out of pure spite, Owens murdered a simple, childlike man who didn't respond quickly enough when Owens yelled at him to go home. Months later, twenty-four-year-old Owens was killed by the very people he had terrorized.

On an unusually warm Sunday in the spring of 1862, everyone in Gravel Hill could hear constant thunder. Big guns boomed for two days as 66,000 Union troops fought against 44,700 Rebels who had moved up from Corinth, Mississippi, in what became known as the Battle of Shiloh, also called the Battle of Pittsburg Landing. The brutal fighting near the Tennessee River caused a tragic loss of nearly 24,000 soldiers who were dead, wounded, or missing. James Hamm, a boy from Gravel Hill, had to carry wounded soldiers off the battlefield on his back. John Springer, home on sick leave from the 18th Tennessee Cavalry, heard gunfire early in the morning. He walked five miles from his home, only to be killed in the battle. His brother searched the orchards, fields, and woods until he finally found John's body among the bloated and decaying corpses and brought it home for burial in the Gravel Hill Cemetery. Another cousin was wounded by a Minié ball that passed through the ulna near his left wrist. He was sent to Tupelo, Mississippi, to recover, but his hand was never the same. Homes in McNairy County were turned into command posts. Some local women nursed the wounded, regardless of the color of their jackets. The bloody fighting, where men fought their own brothers, left people with little hope that the war would end soon.

During the war, railroads played a vital role in transporting troops, including the wounded, and delivering supplies. A regiment required

72 cows each day, along with feed for mules and horses. The North considered Corinth, Mississippi, and Richmond, Virginia, as the two most strategically important locations in the South because of their railroads. Just south of Gravel Hill, Corinth experienced more military action than any other community in the Confederate West. In spring 1862, the South lost control of Corinth to the Union; by October, 22,000 Rebels tried but failed to retake the town from 25,000 Union troops, 35% of whom were ill, leaving behind gray coats, blankets, guns, canteens, knapsacks, and broken wagons during their retreat. Wounded soldiers were left unprotected from insects and exposed to diseases like diarrhea, yellow fever, malaria, and influenza. A Confederate officer described Corinth as a "sickly, malarial pot, fit only for alligators and snakes."

The federal government enacted the Confiscation Acts of 1863 and 1864, authorizing the U.S. Treasury Department to seize rebels' real and personal property. Tax agents could take 10% of provisions from Gravel Hill farms to supply the Union troops. Cora's sister, ten-year-old Victoria, climbed into their corn crib to give Union soldiers their stored corn. The fields and woods near their house became infested with Union and Confederate patrols, roving guerrillas, escaped slaves, deserters, and outlaws searching for food and livestock. Families buried silverware and jewelry, and as the war continued, they also buried food. One family hastily buried a roasted pig when they heard horses approaching. One guerrilla accidentally stepped on the soft soil and uncovered the roasted pork. They had a feast while the family had none. Often, the guerrillas knew their victims their entire lives. When kinfolks were killed and livestock stolen, you knew exactly who did it—by sight and by name.

One woman kept a diary verifying the many killings done in the county by guerrillas, as well as the hardship the war brought to residents. Assisted by seven slaves, she lived in a house large enough to have 46 Northern men for supper. During the Battle of Shiloh, her home was "croded with citizens and wounded men." In an entry on November 11, 1862, she noted, "Northern Soldiers burned three houses for Mr. Huggins last sabbath morning disstoyed his property." She fed troops who repaid her by stealing her horses, hogs, mules, a grindstone, bundles of fodder, onions, salt, sweet potatoes, and corn. Her list continued until she wrote on April 11, 1864, "Our brown cow died last night with hungar."[29]

The year 1863 brought calamities to the South. Knoxville fell to General Burnside, and the Confederacy lost most of East Tennessee. By 1864, the war looked like a patchwork quilt, with a stitch for each man killed or wounded, each farm burned, each child orphaned, and each horse stolen. The Conscription Act of February 1864 required men aged 17 to 64 to enlist. Cora's daddy, along with her uncle Will Hogan, the Prather boys, A.T. Springer, brothers Levi and Giles Springer, and other Gravel Hill farm boys, enlisted in Company A of the 18th (Newsom's) Tennessee Cavalry Regiment—a consolidation of six companies of Newsom's Tennessee Cavalry and four companies led by Nathan Bedford Forrest. They were proud to serve under General Forrest, praising his unorthodox tactics of hitting hard and fast with his cavalry, even though he was chronically short of equipment and generally outnumbered.

James Monroe Jr. began a letter home to his wife, Elizabeth (whom he called Betty), on August 29, 1864, near Oxford, Mississippi, to answer her "kind letter which came to hand and read with the greatest of pleasure." He gave a small sketch of his travels as part of a Rebel cavalry chasing Yankees. He had ridden his poor horse 30 miles one night in the rain. At Memphis, his outfit attacked at daybreak, "and gave the Yanks such a scare that they did almost forget all they ever knew." His cousin, James Hamm, was slightly wounded when a "ball just skelped his thigh," but "he just went off the field by his self" and was almost well. Company A benefited from the battle, getting Union blankets, hats, oil cloths, and some shoes, although James only got a blanket, and "the boys holding the horses lost it." He heard they lost 23 men; the Yankees 500. But he was glad the battle was over and gave thanks to the all-wise creator. He had gone ten days without taking off his boots and almost had to split them open to get them off. He ended his letter with, "May the Lord bless you and the children with good health and plenty to eat in the prayers of your loving husband, James Monroe Huggins." He added a postscript later the same day when "the boys were drawing ten days rashings." The rumor was that the Yanks had returned, so there was a chance he might get close and hoped to hear from home again. He added

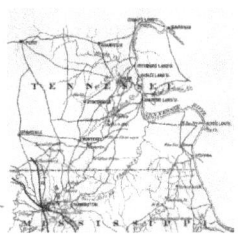

Gravel Hill is on the west, Corinth, Mississippi, lies in the southwest corner, and Pittsburg Landing is on the Tennessee River. 1862. Library of Congress

a message for C.C. (six-year-old Cora) that he had received her letter, read it with the greatest pleasure, and kept it in his pocket until he got close to Memphis, when he read it one more time and tore it up. He also wanted his wife to "tell Bud and Thomas (his younger brothers) that they must write to him and let him know how they are getting along and to bale and feed his horse good for the little mule can't stand to go without feed." He gave his love and respect to all inquiring friends and urged Betty to accept good praising. He added a few more lines the next day, reporting he was well and hardy. He had just returned from the country with clean clothes. There was no news in camp worth relating, so he ended by quoting General R.E. Lee, "By the Grace of God, I have gained a single Victory before Richmond."

Weeks after President Lincoln was shot, Cora's daddy became a prisoner of war when he surrendered on May 4, 1865, at Citronelle, Alabama. He was paroled a week later in Gainesville, Alabama. He had enlisted on December 1, 1863, as a private and left as a First Sergeant. A.T. Springer, S.S. Littlejohn, and Will Hogan stayed with him until the end. It was said that the Gravel Hill boys listened intently to Nathan Bedford Forrest's final farewell as he cut up their precious Confederate flag, giving a piece to each soldier who had fought on sheer blood and guts during the final months of the campaign. Forrest was quoted as saying, "Any man who is in favor of a further prosecution of this war is a fit subject for a lunatic asylum and ought to be sent there immediately."

Cora's daddy and the bedraggled, sick, and emaciated former Confederate soldiers of Gravel Hill, haunted by their experiences, headed home, many suffering from "soldier's heart," known today as PTSD. Infested with lice in dirty, threadbare clothes, they found fence rails down, weed-choked fields, broken or missing plows, and empty corn cribs. The corn left in the fields "was so rotten even the horses wouldn't eat it." Women wore their Sunday best because their everyday dresses were just rags. Salt, coffee, tea, soda, and medicine were in short supply. Families dug soil from the floors of their smokehouses to boil for salt. The county was described as so poor that a buzzard would starve flying over.[30]

Victoria was 12 years old at the end of the war, and Cora was seven. A few old hens still needed to be fed and watered, clothes had to be washed and mended, and food had to be found for supper. Yet, the sound of horses' hooves pounding the ground, dogs barking, or a stranger's voice yelling in the shadowy corners of the barn terrified the girls. So close to Shiloh and Corinth, they were haunted by memories of troops demanding livestock and food, and bushwhackers riding up to the house to threaten and steal. Victoria never forgot climbing into the corn crib and giving the Union troops their corn. Awful stories were shared: of homes burned, people starving, and men shot. Now, the girls were warned to avoid all strangers, especially ex-soldiers who had spent the war years killing and stealing and couldn't or wouldn't stop.

Former Gravel Hill soldiers returned to what they knew: growing corn, sweet potatoes, and cotton—if they could get the seed. Or raising hogs, sheep, and cattle—if they managed to find breeding stock. Some believed the land would not produce again because it was soaked with blood. Food was scarce, and life never improved much. President Andrew Johnson claimed to love 'those poor beaten rebs," but did little to show it. During Reconstruction, efforts were made to rebuild the South and address the inequities faced by 400,000 former slaves wandering northern Mississippi and southern Tennessee in search of food. The Freedman's Bureau, part of the War Department, was authorized to provide relief and guardianship for refugees, mostly former slaves. By January 1866, President Johnson appointed provisional civil governors in all states except Texas. Military rule replaced civil authorities in March 1867, and Federal troops were sent south to handle the unrest. Resentment among former white Confederate soldiers toward freed slaves deepened their hostility, as they believed Negroes were taking over the country. Northerners who came south to profit were seen as unscrupulous opportunists meddling in local politics and businesses, were called carpetbaggers. Southerners who supported the carpetbaggers and free Blacks were labeled as scallywags. This bitterness fueled the creation of Jim Crow laws and organizations like the Sons of the South and the Ku Klux Klan. Originating in Giles County, Tennessee, where Cora's mother was born, the KKK started as a small, harmless, fun-loving group that grew into one of the most violent secret organizations in American history. Wearing white masks, high-pointed hats, and long robes, they enforced white supremacy by keeping African Americans subservient and disenfranchised. Black schools were vandalized and destroyed. Negroes faced intimidation, attacks, torture, lynching, and eviction from their land. General Nathan Bedford Forrest became the first

Grand Wizard of the KKK (1867–1869), though he later disputed this, claiming to favor racial harmony. Still, it was inevitable that Cora would be influenced by racial prejudice from a young age.

The myth of the Lost Cause allowed Southerners to believe the Civil War was just, heroic, and had nothing to do with slavery. It helped them cope with the trauma of defeat and justify segregation. Former Confederate officers, like Robert E. Lee, were idolized, and monuments were erected in their honor. The Southern White woman was idealized as pure and saintly. She and her sisters had shown steadfast support throughout the war, sacrificing more men, time, and resources than Northern women ever considered. Memorial organizations nurtured the myth of glorifying the war and the men who fought in it. The Daughters of the Confederacy sponsored a $50,000 memorial in 1917 on the sacred soil of Shiloh as a tribute to the confederacy of patriotic Southern womanhood.

In 1870, James Monroe was 37; Elizabeth, 35; Victoria, 16; Cordelia, 12; Monroe (Dud), 10; Zula, 7; and James Bryant, 2. Two of James Monroe's brothers still lived with them: Phillip Jasper (Bud), age 23, and Thomas Jefferson, 20. An eight-year-old named Reynolds Woodville was also part of the household. Their farm was valued at $2,000, with a personal estate of $1,500. Cora helped with chores and looked after her younger siblings. Her mother had twins in June, but only the boy survived.

Like other families in Gravel Hill, Cora's family struggled to keep their land, pay taxes, and have enough to eat. There was a desperate need for credit. Little money was available for loans, and when offered, came with exorbitant interest rates. No Southern bank was solvent. Stores had nothing to sell. Farms were devalued. Rising costs, falling prices, and high interest rates after the Civil War were compounded by droughts, grasshopper plagues, and boll weevil infestations. Memphis suffered fearful epidemics, including yellow fever, smallpox, and cholera. Doctors in 1878 had no understanding of the cause of yellow fever. They only knew outbreaks happened when it was hot and muggy and seemed to be spread by riverboat and railroad passengers.

Since public schools in McNairy County were not mandatory until 1878, itinerant schoolmasters taught subscription schools for two or three months before moving on. Teachers usually sat near the fire, often with a couple of seasoned hickory switches they used freely and frequently. Paid by parents and the community, and sometimes supplemented by public funds, the schoolmaster (nearly all of whom were male) might earn as little as $25.00 per month, out of which he paid for board and lodging. One teacher received $52.50 for 35 instructional days, teaching 40 boys and 42 girls in 1876. In 1870, Victoria, Cora, and Dud attended school while the younger children stayed home. The Blue Back Speller, McGuffey's Reader, and Dilworth's Spelling Book taught students how to construct short sentences like: "No man may put off the law of God." McGuffey's Reader sold for 38 cents at the Gravel Hill store in 1861. Cora's mother and aunt, Elizabeth and Agnes Robertson, who married the Huggins brothers at 15, could neither read nor write.

When public schools were first established, they were typically one-room buildings that served up to 50 students and were taught by a single teacher. In 1881, McNairy County had 68 schools for White and 12 for Black children. Seven years later, there were 60 schools for White and 21 for Black students. Early schools included a brick school, 35 frame buildings, and 27 log structures, in contrast to the 1881 count of 2 brick buildings, 18 frame buildings, and 50 log cabins. School was sometimes held in a deserted tenant house in the middle of a field, a half mile from shade or water.[31] A few McNairy County school teachers or administrators were uneducated, or at least, not good spellers. One administrator submitted the following report: "G C Simmons, J A Plunke and P Massey were elected common school commissioners of the 20 colde distrate of Mcneary county the 2 saderday in June 1860 and after beinge qualifide as the law directs proceede to take the scholastic popuation and found it to beas folers to wit: Returned to the county courte clearke in Sexember in 1860."

Marriage

Cora Huggins married her double first cousin, Jesse Comer Springer, in 1877 when he was 25 and she was 19. In this complex DNA mixture from Huggins and Springers, Cora and Jess knew each other their whole lives, sharing the same grandparents and attending the same church picnics. His father was her mother's brother, and Cora's father was a brother of Jess's mother. The scientific term for cousin marriage, consanguinity, is a subset of endogamy, the practice of marrying within a close-knit group over generations. Children resulting from cousin marriages have a higher likelihood of inheriting recessive genes, which can lead to health risks. But in Gravel Hill, courting was limited by how far a young man could walk or ride a mule and still get his chores done. It was difficult to meet new girls and marry outside the community. Perhaps it was always understood that Jess would marry Cora. Maybe he started teasing her, trying to make her smile. Whatever the reason, the motivations for marriage differed from those today. Romance and passion were viewed as childish and unreliable motives; relying on logic and reason was preferable. Was Jess a good farmer? Was Cora respectful to her parents? Marriage was about duty and loyalty. Love was something else entirely. A girl hoped to marry someone she could learn to love.

Jess and Cora's wedding probably took place at her parents' house. Cora wore her best dress to enter a life where she had been taught the value of frugal management. Unmarried girls faced the risk of caring for aging parents and bachelor brothers. When one Gravel Hill girl grew old enough to marry, her brothers told her that if she stayed home and looked after Mama, they would give her a mare and a saddle. Her mother told her, "Do what you want, girl; horses die, and saddles get stolen."

Cora's first child was born after a yellow fever outbreak swept through Memphis and the towns and valleys of the Mississippi River, claiming an estimated 13,000 to 20,000 lives. Unfortunately, Jess and Cora's baby didn't survive either. Baby Herbert died in October after the wet, hot summer gave way to fall, and the epidemic in Memphis, 80 miles to the west, had subsided. Herbert was laid to rest in Gravel Hill Cemetery alongside his great-grandmother, Hannah Springer, and his grandparents, Patrick and Lucinda Springer. Unlike their homemade tombstones, the baby's grave was marked with a commercially made stone that read, "Herbert, son of Cora & Jess Springer, August 28, 1878, October 6, 1878." Herbert was buried with the Springers, even though he was both a Huggins and a Springer descendant. Years later, Jess and Cora will be buried across the road in the Huggins Cemetery.

In 1880, Jess was 27, Cora was 22, and their second child, Predetta, was 3 months old. Their family grew to include Predetta, Clarence Don (my grandfather) in 1882, Grover Cleveland in 1884, Hettie in 1886, Eupha in 1888, Floy in 1890, Claude in 1892, and Eldon in 1895. Three more children were yet to arrive.

Jess and Cora avoided using traditional names like Ezekiel, Phillip Jasper, James Monroe, or Elizabeth, which had been passed down for generations and complicate genealogy research. They named their second son Grover Cleveland Springer, shortened to Cleve, as was common with many other little boys named after prominent political figures. President Cleveland was the first Democrat to win a presidential election since 1856. Tennessee was predominantly Democratic and took pride in being home to Andrew Jackson and Davy Crockett. Jess no doubt voted for Cleveland; Cora wouldn't gain the right to vote until shortly before her death.

Prudish conventions of the nineteenth century made it impossible for husbands and wives to discuss sex, pregnancy, and childbirth. It was believed that the groom did not want his bride to possess any knowledge or desire for lovemaking. Sex was something he desired and would teach his new bride. Of course, sex usually leads to pregnancy. A young mother's only preparation for delivery involved helping another woman. Medical books rarely described pregnancy, and none mentioned childbirth or postpartum procedures. Doctors also had to learn through experience. Cora's mother or the local midwife may have helped in delivering her babies, but Jess could have helped in an emergency. Although sex, pregnancy, and childbirth were rarely discussed, Jess and Cora were raised in a farming community and certainly had a basic understanding.

Baby clothing was generic because the baby's sex was unimportant until the infant began to walk. Even after the baby started walking, some mothers continued to dress male babies in girls' clothing. With Cora's eleven babies reaching adulthood, ignoring gender made hand-me-downs more practical.

I imagine Cora's day began before dawn. Unbraiding her long hair to twist into a tight bun, she lit a fire in the cook stove and headed toward the barn to milk the cow and let the chickens out. Females had a gentle touch when milking, which cows appreciated. Males tended to be impatient, making the cows nervous and more likely to kick, thereby reducing milk volume. Hens laid more eggs when cared for by women.

She heard Jess out in the pasture, so she headed for the house, grabbing her apron to start cooking breakfast and heating water. Breakfast was a hearty meal of pork, eggs, fried potatoes, fruit pie, corn cakes, and coffee. While he ate, Jess instructed the boys on what needed to be done. At just 6 and 8 years old, they were told to check the fences, put out hay for the steers, slop the pigs, drive the cows to the lower pasture, make sure the livestock had enough water for the day, and then get to school on time. But it was more important to finish chores than attend school. In the afternoon, the boys would drive the cows home for milking, clean the leather tack, and feed the livestock. Cora had her ten-year-old daughter, Predetta, dress her little sisters and gather the eggs before leaving for school with the boys. Cradling her newborn daughter in the crook of her arm, Cora churned the butter, a process that took anywhere from thirty minutes to an hour and was almighty tedious, but it let her sit down. She stored the butter wrapped in linen in a wooden tub on the lowest shelf in the cool spring house until she had accumulated enough for trading at the Gravel Hill Mercantile. Hettie, age 4, and Eupha, age 2, filled the kindling box for the fire before playing outside. She cautioned them to avoid the puddles formed by wagon ruts. When harvest time arrived, there would be no time for playing as the family would work in the fields from dawn until dusk, the babies tucked under a shady tree.

Jess harnessed the mules to plow the lower field. He could plow until he couldn't see the furrows. Mid-morning, Cora took a moment to sit down and nurse the baby. Her large patch of Irish potatoes was coming up. Cora and the three oldest children had planted them early one morning before sunrise, just like her mama had done and her mama before her. Jess had planted a big field of sweet potatoes and sowed the west fields with Indian corn. She worried about having enough food preserved and smoked to last through the winter. She never forgot her hunger during the war or its aftermath.

After the children got home from school, Cora grabbed her sunbonnet off the peg by the back door and let it hang by its strings on her shoulders while milking the cow. The brim was so large that it hindered her from resting her forehead against the cow's warm flank as she filled the wooden bucket with the rhythmic swish-swish of milk. Her bonnet also blocked her from seeing what the children were up to behind her. Still, her sunbonnet was more Christian than frilly hats full of feathers, flowers, and whatnot. Knee-length drawers, a plain petticoat, and a loose-fitting Mother Hubbard dress that concealed her pregnancies suited her just fine. She was either nursing or pregnant throughout the first thirty years of her marriage.

With the ham sliced, the last of the sweet potatoes roasted in the coals, and the cornpone ready for the cast-iron skillet, supper was about ready. Predetta wiped the younger children's faces and supervised handwashing while Jess and the boys cleaned up outside. Sugar was scarce, so the cornpone was sweetened with sorghum syrup.

After the girls helped her clean up the kitchen, Cora relaxed. The kerosene lamp, its chimney carefully cleaned of soot, was bright enough for Cora to sew while listening to singing and stories told around the fireplace, where the dancing flames threw shadows on the wall. Jess repaired his boots, figured out the accounts, and planned field crops for next year.

Cora's heavy workload was assigned days for efficiency. Blue Monday was laundry day—a dreaded chore that required considerable time and effort. Amid the children's fussing, the smoke, cinders, and harsh weather, doing the wash was downright miserable. It required heating buckets of water in a copper pot over a wood stove or a smoky fire, a recipe for ruined health on a cold, windy day. Jess's filthy overalls were soaked, and then Cora boiled all the clothes, scrubbing them on a rough washboard or using a flat block—a wooden block 18 inches square, set on legs. One of the children beat the clothes with a paddle. She used lye soap, which severely irritated her hands, to wash the never-ending piles of diapers and scrub out the tough spots on clothes. It took her all day to do the washing: build a fire to heat water, fill the copper tub by the well, heat the water, scrub the clothes on a washboard, lift the wet clothes out of the tub with a wash stick to rinse them twice—once in plain water and once with bluing, wring out the clothes (perhaps using a hand-cranked wringer), and hang them out to dry on the clothesline, spreading the white items over the bushes to bleach in the sun.

Eventually, the women's workload at Gravel Hill eased. The hand-cranked wringer was replaced by an electric one, to be upgraded to a modern washer. Water flowed from the kitchen faucet instead of being pumped and hauled by hand to the house.

Cora never got to enjoy the benefits of electricity. Only one in ten farms had electricity as late as the 1930s. Then, every Gravel Hill household followed the progress of "Hook Up Day." Once connected, electric lights appeared everywhere: lamps, ceiling fixtures, porch lights, and even a pole light to light the way to the barn.

Jess and Cora with Predetta, Clarence, Cleveland, Hettie, and Eupha about 1889. The two boys are in the lower left and the lower right. The other three children are girls.

Tuesday was ironing day. Cora heated the heavy flatiron, which weighed between eight and ten pounds, being careful not to burn herself when she picked it up. The handles became as hot as the bottom of the iron. She used beeswax to smooth the iron's bottom so it would slide more easily over the fabric. Nearly every item was ironed: clothes, table linens, and bedding. Whatever was worth washing was worth ironing. Three models of folding ironing boards were featured in the 1894 Montgomery Ward catalog. Woolen clothing was spot-cleaned outside with a combustible cleaning fluid, which was too dangerous to use indoors.

Wednesday was baking day. On average, seven loaves of bread were needed each week. Cora used an astounding number of kitchen utensils: kettles for making preserves, wash tubs, crocks, pails, dippers, baskets, everyday pots, pans, and dishes. Her wood cook stove was a vast improvement over hearth cooking. The benefits were numerous: it produced more heat with less fuel, needed less tending, was less fascinating to her little ones, and was less likely to send out flying sparks and hot cinders. However, both a fireplace and a stove required chopped wood or shoveled coal to keep them going throughout the day. In six days, a coal stove was estimated to consume 292 pounds of coal, 14 pounds of kindling, and produce 27 pounds of ash. A housewife spent four hours each day removing ashes, adjusting dampers, lighting fires, carrying coal or wood, and rubbing the stove with thick black wax to prevent rusting. A hearth or stove fire warmed the house in the winter, but made it miserably hot in the summer.

I asked my mom if switching from a wood cook stove to an electric range was better. She looked at me like I was crazy and snapped, "Of course it was. No more filling the stove with wood and scraping out the ashes. You could control the heat better in an electric stove—there was no comparison!" She remembered a wood stove with a compartment to heat water, four burners, and warming shelves above the stovetop. Hot water!

Thursday was set aside for mending and sewing—something Cora likely dedicated every spare minute to throughout the week. She wished she could mend during church services, but knitting or stitching was prohibited. She considered making a new shirt for Jess from brown domestic cloth, using an old shirt as a pattern. At ten cents a yard, domestic cloth, known as slave cloth or poor man's cloth, bleached well in the sun and lasted longer than the pricier calico, making it suitable for backing a quilt as well. All she needed were her needle, thimble, and scissors. Cora learned to sew as soon as she was old enough to handle a needle. By the time she turned nine, she could hem, run, backstitch, gather, and sew an overhand stitch.

Nothing was wasted. Outgrown clothing was altered for the next child in line. Strips from old sheets and blankets were cut for the children to braid into doormats. Cora likely crocheted collars and cuffs, or tatted lace to decorate clothing and household linens, adding a ribbon here and there. Knitted shawls kept her shoulders warm on the way to church. Store-bought clothes in Montgomery Ward or Sears and Roebuck catalogs cost money, and money didn't grow on trees.

The house was cleaned on Friday. On Saturday, the family shed the clothes they had worn all week to take turns bathing. Water was heated in a long copper boiler on the wood stove and poured into a round washtub in the middle of the kitchen. One resourceful resident bored a hole through the floor and installed a three-inch pipe underneath his tub for drainage. The first person in line, usually Jess, enjoyed the cleanest and warmest bathwater.

Shoes were passed down from child to child and only worn when it was cold. Even Cora likely went barefoot, stopping before entering the church to put on her shoes. Sunday service began after a quick breakfast. After church, a cold supper awaited them.

It was a common practice to administer a mild laxative to children once a week. A teaspoon of a homemade mixture of prunes blended with senna pods was believed to help keep children healthy. My uncles complained that my grandma gave them cascara bark tea, which made them stay close to the outhouse the next day.

Jess and Cora's home was like a domestic factory where all family members contributed. Cora could handle a hundred tasks: smoke pork, make jams, jellies, chutneys, and pickles; churn butter, bake pies, cakes, and delicious bread; sew curtains and dresses for the girls and shirts for her sons; prepare home remedies to heal the sick; assist a neighbor in childbirth or solemnly close the eyes of the dead and wash the body for burial. The clothing and patchwork quilts she sewed, washed, and mended were essential goods, as were the grains and vegetables they grew, the meat they raised, and the foods they preserved. Jess and Cora worked together to survive. They tended crops, fixed fences, cared for livestock, cooked meals, and taught skills to their children. From a young age, they understood that a new calf or lamb meant food, an increase in the flock, and the possibility of wealth. Some animals were worked, some milked, some provided supper, and some were shot, and that was that.

In 1873, agricultural experts suggested that raising corn and livestock could yield more profit than cotton in McNairy County. "King Cotton's royal throne has been usurped and should be banished from Old Snake's fields. The heavy tribute paid to him made empty cribs, empty smokehouses, empty pocketbooks, empty dishes, and empty heads."[32]

Springers and Huggins paid attention to the advice. They were subsistence farmers who avoided planting a single crop, like cotton. Kinfolk typically produced 30 to 50 bushels of wheat, around the same amount of oats, one or two 400-pound bales of cotton, some Irish (white) potatoes, 50 to 100 bushels of sweet potatoes harvested before the first frost, and hundreds of bushels of Indian corn. Cora and Jess's grandfather, Phillip Jasper Huggins, grew 75 bushels of sweet potatoes in 1850, while their other grandfather, Ezekiel Springer, grew 100 bushels - a bushel equal to fifty-four pounds of sweet potatoes. Southerners would have starved without sweet potatoes before, during, and after the Civil War.

Multicolored ears of Indian corn are used to decorate our Thanksgiving table, but it was a staple back then. Hard-kernelled, less sweet, and starchier than sweet corn, it was fed to hogs, chickens, and cattle, distilled into corn whiskey, and ground into meal at the grist mill for numerous dishes, including cornpone, johnny cakes, hominy, mush, succotash, and popped in the fireplace for a popcorn treat. Fanny Farmer's 1896 Cookbook suggested cooking 1 cup of hominy with four cups of water for an hour, then packing the hominy (or cornmeal) mush into greased one-pound baking powder boxes or small bread pans. My mother made cornmeal mush, leaving it in a loaf pan overnight before slicing and frying it. We ate it with butter and syrup, making it one of my favorite meals. The first time I saw polenta served in a restaurant, I recognized it immediately.

Working from daylight to dusk in the fields was necessary for planting, thinning, weeding, and harvesting. Once a field was plowed and harrowed, corn was planted by hand and cultivated with a hoe or horse-pulled shovel plow in May and June. It was "laid by" or left to dry on the stalk in July and August, then harvested in early fall. Each ear, picked by hand, was husked and tossed into a wagon. The best corn picker could load 100 bushels per day. The ears were stored in the corn crib until the family needed them or sold them. Children were expected to pick 100 pounds of cotton by the time they were five years old. In the evenings, they shelled peas or helped their mother can produce from the garden in Mason jars. Oats and wheat were cut with scythes, shocked, and left standing in the field to dry during the hottest part of summer. It was hot, dirty work. Sheep herds provided 25 to 50 pounds of wool a year, and cows produced 50 to 300 pounds of butter. Bees yielded 30 to 100 pounds of beeswax. Everyone had hogs, which were ideal farm animals because they matured early and produced several large litters. Hogs were also efficient foragers when kept from rooting in fields and gardens. In 1848, Southerners consumed an average of 173 pounds of pork per year. The estimated population was 106 hogs per 100 people in 1860.[33]

The race to get the first bale of cotton to market in McNairy County continued a long-standing tradition. Before emancipation, slaves picked the cotton. After emancipation, White and Black sharecroppers harvested cotton for the landowners, who faced a risky trip back to Gravel Hill after selling their cotton for cash. The newspaper reported that three men robbed a farmer near Gravel Hill of $100 as he was returning from Corinth, where he had taken three bales of cotton. One man covered him with a revolver while the other two held his team by the bits. No one knew the robbers' identities, and no steps had been taken to identify the guilty parties.

Mules, horses, and oxen supplied the power needed for plowing, planting, cultivating, and harvesting crops. Oxen possessed the strength to pull tree stumps to clear a field. Cora's grandfather, Phillip Jasper, had four working oxen in 1850, and his brother, James Montgomery, had six. The Civil War had significantly reduced the number of horses, forcing farmers to rebuild their stock. When Cora was in her teens, her father had a horse, three mules, and two milk cows.

Cora's family was Primitive Baptist. The religious revival during the Second Great Awakening (1790 to 1830) transformed Protestant Christianity and led to the emergence of fundamentalist churches. Primitive Baptists developed from the "regular" Baptists in the 1820s over disagreements about missionary societies, Sunday Schools, and theological seminaries. The dissenters, also known as Hard Shell Baptists, believed that Sunday School interfered with parents' rights to teach their children in religion, that supporting missionaries lacked biblical support, and that theological seminaries did not follow the example of Christ or the apostles. They favored semi-educated, fiery, emotional lay preachers who emphasized faith over formal training. Sermons were delivered spontaneously in straightforward, vivid language, often with simple illustrations and analogies that made the congregation feel the heat of hell and the joy of heaven. The "singing clerk" recited each line of the hymns without instrumental accompaniment. It was believed that the Bible instructed worshipers to sing, but musical instruments were considered unscriptural.

Primitive Baptists emphasized the Calvinist doctrines of grace and predestination. Surprisingly democratic, both men and women (including Blacks and Whites) were seen as equal in God's eyes, although White males were favored. Still, sisters in good standing could expel a brother they found drunk at the horse races. Black and White congregants worshipped together based on these egalitarian practices, but those with darker skin knew to sit at the back.

The Primitive Baptist Church was established in 1832 in Gravel Hill. Cora's grandfather, Ezekiel "Zeke" Springer, donated 2 acres of land in 1841 for a permanent building to be shared with other congregations each weekend. Worshippers were encouraged to seek salvation, speak the truth, and shame the devil. No aspect of life went unnoticed as members quickly accused others of rule infractions. Church minutes reveal that Brothers and Sisters in Christ disciplined one another for drinking and swearing, adultery, fornication, dancing, gambling, non-attendance at church, or propagating heretical doctrine—accusations that threatened the removal of the accused from church membership. Once removed, the church ceased to be responsible for the sinner's conduct. One man was admonished to quit drinking to avoid drunkenness. Another man was charged with lying about the soundness and age of a mule to deceive the purchaser. He refused to admit he lied, so the church withdrew his membership. In October 1868, a member was accused of joining the Methodist Church. He was excluded the following month. He probably had already joined the Methodists.

Three ordinances were practiced: believer's baptism by immersion, communion, and foot washing. The Primitive Baptist Church held its annual Foot Washing Day on the second Sunday of May beginning in 1844. The ordinance followed the example of Jesus, who washed his disciples' feet on the night before the Passover Feast. It taught believers to love one another through sacrificial, humble service. In a simple yet moving ritual performed in silence, men and women lined up separately as church deacons poured water into shallow wash basins. A woman washed another woman's feet, dried them with a long white towel, then switched positions. Only baptized Primitive Baptists participated in the ceremony and observed the Lord's Supper.[34] However, people traveled from miles away by wagon, buggy, or mule, bringing covered dishes for a day of preaching, singing, and fellowship, even if they weren't members.

Decoration Day, a tradition brought from Appalachia, was also well-loved. Families and relatives from afar gathered at the burial grounds to clear brush, remove weeds and litter, and decorate graves. Blankets were spread on the ground for singing, visiting, and potluck (known as dinner on the ground).

Revivals and camp meetings were quite popular, marked by passionate preaching from itinerant preachers standing on stumps or in wagon beds. Scheduled from Sunday to Friday, it wasn't unusual for a camp meeting to last three or four weeks, especially if folks were baptized in Huggins Pond. Baptismal candidates followed the preacher, who held his Bible high, as they waded into the muddy water, while the congregation sang hymns on the bank.

Revivals usually took place in August, a busy time for women since it was also canning season, but there was nothing quite like a revival for singing praises to the Lord and shouting some good old hallelujahs. By the 1920s, the large crowds had begun to dwindle, but Gravel Hill remained known as the place for old-time preaching. Women tried to outdo each other by preparing suppers for the preacher, though they were careful to downplay their efforts: "Oh lordy, too much salt," or "It was just a little thing, didn't take no time at all." Boys gallantly fanned girls with palm-leaf fans in the heat, while the little ones napped in the shade. Shenanigans also occurred. One year, around dusk, some boys swapped babies sleeping in wagons. Parents got all the way home only to discover they had the wrong baby. It took the whole night to sort out the little ones.

Primitive Baptists condemned such worldly amusements as gambling, dancing, fishing on the Sabbath, and joining secret orders like the Masons. When James Montgomery Huggins Sr. became a founding member of the Gravel Hill Masonic Lodge, he faced a choice between the Masons and the church. A long-time Primitive Baptist minister, well known in the community, experienced the same dilemma in 1850 and switched denominations. To resolve his issue, James founded the Missionary Baptist Church of Jesus Christ of Gravel Hill. The Rules of Decorum were adopted in October 1867. The congregation met in homes until 1874, when James donated an acre of land to build a log building for worship. Potential members of the new church needed a unanimous vote from all members present to join, but only men held leadership positions. Women were judged as too emotional and lacking in rational ability to discuss religion, politics, or business. Brother J.C. Springer and his wife, C.C. Springer, were accepted into membership by experience in 1883 when Cora's father died.

When I saw the two churches in Gravel Hill in 1978, I was told they were once one church but split years ago (more than 100 years) over the doctrine of foot washing. The split probably occurred not only because of foot washing but also because James M. Huggins Sr. joined the Masons, an organization to which Cora's father also belonged. Beside the "new" church was the Huggins Cemetery, the perfect place for couples "sparkin" sitting on the benches shaded by cedars.

When Cora's father died, she had been married for six years, had buried one child, and had two healthy children. Everyone knew that life and death were a hair's breadth apart, just as they recognized the devil was busy pulling brothers and sisters from the path of righteousness. Cora's daddy, James Monroe Huggins Jr., passed on to his eternal reward on September 17, 1883, deeply in debt. By December, his son-in-law, J.C. (Jess) Springer, and his son, M.D. (Dud) Huggins, were appointed administrators of his estate by the McNairy County Court. James Monroe Jr. owned a steam mill that functioned as a combination saw mill, grist mill, and cotton gin—likely the same mill his uncle, James Sr., had operated 40 years earlier—but James Monroe Jr. had a lien against the cotton gin for $200 and another lien against the steam engine and boiler for $328.50. He also owed taxes on his land. A notice was published in the newspaper for all persons holding claims against the estate to step forward. The administrators collected money owed, ranging from $1 to $58, for services such as cutting lumber or grinding corn. But it wasn't enough. The mill and fixtures were sold for $740.10, two engines for $20.25, a wagon for $50, and two yokes of oxen brought $118.90. His debts outweighed his assets, and the estate was declared insolvent. James M. Huggins Jr. left unpaid loans, including interest, totaling $2,302.83, prorated to $396.41, or 0.1722 cents on the dollar. By February 4, 1893, his debts had all been paid, except for $13.83 owed to three men.[35]

Cora must have been appalled by how her father's death left her mother in a purgatory of poverty and destitution. Her mother had two married daughters and five children still at home. She owned nothing from her thirty-year marriage except the dower portion of her husband's land.

Three commissioners were appointed by the McNairy County Court, all of whom were freeholders (residents who held title to property), to determine her Widow's Allowance: a reasonable amount of money and food protected from creditors from her husband's estate to support her and her family for one year from his death. Elizabeth and her children were allowed to keep 60 barrels of corn, 30 bushels of wheat, 1200 pounds of pork, 75 pounds of sugar, 60 pounds of coffee, 2.8 pounds of salt, 100 pounds of lard, 40 gallons of molasses, 10 pounds of soda, 4 pounds of pepper, 4 pounds of spice, 2 pounds of ginger, and $36.58 to buy articles not on hand.

Widow's Allowances varied. Cora and Jess's Aunt Malinda had three children with her first husband and seven more children with her second husband while raising two children from her first husband's first marriage, plus two of Jess's orphaned brothers. When her second husband, J.J. Hamm, died in December of 1861, probably of malaria, she was taking care of at least a dozen children, the youngest a month old. In the settlement of her husband's estate, a list of purchases from L.H. Huggins & Brothers' store in Gravel Hill was included. Besides whiskey (a gallon for fifty cents), tobacco, nails, and hardware, fabric was also purchased, including calico, linsey-woolsey, and brown domestic, which Malinda dyed with indigo, madder, and Venetian red. On December 18, 1861, she bought 26 yards of brown domestic, a spool of thread for ten cents, five yards of black serge, and seven yards of black lace, likely for her funeral clothing. Her Widow's Allowance reflected the value of her husband's estate: 25 barrels of corn or what was on hand, 1200 pounds of pork (250 pounds on hand), one-half barrel of molasses, $2.00 worth of sugar, one sack of salt, two pounds of soda, one pound of pepper, and one pound of spice. Her Widow's Support was calculated as $115.35.[36]

When Giles Springer died in 1910, his wife, Lizzie, was granted her dower portion of land and a year's support, as mandated by law. Jess was one of three commissioners appointed by the court to set aside a Widow's Allowance for her and her four children. Since she was left with "no crops or provisions of any kind," her only asset being cash, she was allocated $100. Auctioneers sold everything: tools, household furniture, the milk cow, mules, and a wagon. Jess bought a crosscut saw from his cousin's estate for $1.75 and a corn sheller for $1.50.[37]

Widows knew all about the evils of alcohol. A movement to limit alcohol consumption evolved into a moral and political crusade. A four-mile law enacted in 1887 banned the sale of whiskey within four miles of a school or church. That left two places to drink in the county: Hendrix's saloon, located five miles north of Purdy, and John Hickey Swain's saloon in the northeast. These establishments became a haven for all the drunkards in McNairy County and were known for shootings, fights, and murders. Both saloons required a long horse ride from Gravel Hill and cash in the pocket.

Tennessee became a "dry" state in 1909 and remained so until the repeal of Prohibition in 1933. Cora's brother, J.B. Huggins, noted that even though Gravel Hill was bone dry, some men claimed there was more drinking now than when whiskey could be purchased legally. When officers took several quarts of whiskey from back pockets on a Sunday and poured it on the ground, the "boys" were surprised to be summoned to appear before Esquire J.B. Huggins on Monday morning. Two months later, the actions of some boys made it seem like a bootlegger was still at large.

Cora's granddaughter, Liz, shared a story about a neighbor in Gravel Hill who operated a still when she was a child. Liz and her brother returned one of his stray hens—or simply found a hen—and, in return, he gave each child a dime, by which everyone understood that no one would report his still to the authorities.

The Women's Christian Temperance Union and Murphys for Men supported the temperance movement in McNairy County. Murphy meetings were held at the old Presbyterian Church in Purdy. Each Murphy pledged to abstain from all intoxicating liquors and wear a blue ribbon. The church ladies were delighted; their men would be in church instead of fooling around behind the church. As all women know, drunkenness is especially harmful to women.

The famous boneyard at Purdy, the county seat of McNairy County, was a horse-swapping area where horse racing and other mischiefs took place, often flavored by whiskey. Boys dreamed of riding a winning horse at the Purdy fairgrounds.

Purdy was a lovely oval of two streets spanning half a mile, connected at both ends, with the courthouse at its northern end. The bustling town included general merchandise stores, saloons, livery stables, eateries, hotels, a theater, a Masonic lodge, and a Male and Female Academy (akin to a private high school today), along with two newspapers and offices for lawyers and doctors. Although the town was nearly destroyed during the Civil War, many saloons survived, equipped with back rooms for gambling and prostitution. Gamblers bet on everything from horse races to their cotton crops. Behavior deteriorated to such an extent that women were barred from Purdy on Saturdays due to the prevalent drunkenness, lest they be insulted by profanity. Cursing was an arrestable offense.

Towns that adapted to the times thrived, while those that did not began to decline. Purdy's leading taxpayers opposed the Mobile and Ohio Railroad laying tracks in their town, which led to its gradual decline and calls to relocate the county seat. A long, contentious struggle ensued, with at least twelve attempts to legally transfer the county seat from Purdy to a town closer to the tracks. The controversy intensified when the McNairy Courthouse in Purdy burned in 1881, destroying all records except for some deeds. Between forty and three hundred masked men (depending on who was telling the story) rode into Purdy one night to warn the contractor rebuilding the courthouse to stop work, leave the area, or be ridden out of town on a rail. A splinter faction of the mob set fire to a carload of lumber intended for the courthouse. The contractor halted construction. In 1884, the town of Falcon won an election to become the county seat, but the Supreme Court refused to accept the results. Three years later, a valid vote approved moving the county seat from Purdy to a new location called New South. Postal officials in Washington changed the name to Selma, which they spelled Selmer in the acceptance document. Jess voted in the divisive decision to move the county seat from Purdy to Selmer on July 26, 1890. Cora likely grew tired of hearing about the entire controversy.

Gravel Hill was bypassed by both the Mobile and Ohio Railroad and the highway, marking the beginning of its slow and inevitable decline. In 1890, the nearest railroad station was seven miles away—a large wooden building featuring platforms on all sides and two passenger waiting rooms, one for Whites and one for Blacks.

The name of Gravel Hill was briefly changed to Gravelburgh during the 1880s before reverting to Gravel Hill (sometimes spelled as one word or as two). The 1900 business directory listed two general stores, a grist mill, a cotton gin, a Masonic Lodge, a school, two Baptist churches, a blacksmith shop, a doctor's office, and a pharmacy. The lodge was likely located on the upper level of the Gravel Hill Mercantile (once owned by James M. Huggins Sr.). The store, in its heyday, had served as the post office, polling station, and site of casket-making upstairs. On Saturdays, the yard of the mercantile bustled with wagons and folks exchanging gossip and news. Old men sat on the porch, reminiscing about the war and days gone by, regardless of the weather. Folks traded chickens, hides, cotton, or country hams for groceries and seed. At least six clerks were busy helping customers needing flour, sugar, salt, plows, or coffins.[38]

Far from an idealized, harmonious community, feuds, insults, and unresolved arguments persisted. When trouble arose, a name could be attached to it. Everyone was kin, a friend, a neighbor, or an acquaintance. They shared the same past, repeated the same stories, read the same newspapers, relied on the same doctors, traveled the same dirt roads, and planted similar crops. A few men occasionally drank themselves into oblivion, and a few hotheads were likely to get into fights. There might be a dishonest Bible salesman or outright chicanery to avoid. Tales of drama and humor, scandals, and misfortunes were part of the ancient recollections of a small community. Jess and Cora kept an eye on their neighbors, and the neighbors returned the favor. In times of trouble, people supported one another, keeping their heads down and their mouths shut.

As the postmaster of Gravel Hill from 1886 to 1890, Jess earned an annual salary of $37.35. He delivered the mail to its 90 residents twice a week in a mule-drawn mail buggy. This gave him a front-row seat to observe the comings and goings, as well as the gossip, of an endogamous community where every family was related.

Springers raised their children and paid their taxes. Before Jess married Cora, he bought 1/8 of 180 acres from the estate of James Jefferson and Malinda Hamm for $75. Five years later, he sold the land to his cousin, Will Hogan, for the same price he had paid: $75. In the spring of 1878, Jess bought 170 acres from a Huggins cousin for $275. He must have sold some land, as he was taxed on 60 acres assessed at $250 the following year. In 1881, Jess purchased additional land for $110. By 1882, he owned 120 acres assessed at $250. In 1886, Jess sold two parcels of land, 54 and 92 acres, for $300 to his brother Frank. James M. Huggins Sr., who raised Jess, deeded Jess 69 3/8 acres on the west bank of Muddy Creek for $640. That same day, Jess sold the land to J.W. Emmons for the same amount. As part of the property transaction and to protect her dower rights, Cora was privately interviewed, separately from her husband, to acknowledge that she freely and voluntarily agreed to the deed, without any pressure or constraints from her husband. Wives were only questioned in land transactions involving the property on which they lived; otherwise, men were free to sell property without their wives' consent.

I met May Huggins Hamm, a cousin of the Springer children, during my 1978 visit to Gravel Hill. She was 98 years old, a tiny lady with white hair, wearing a white blouse with a lacy Peter Pan collar, lying quietly in a hospital bed in the former dining room of her home. She told me that when she was a girl, Jess had picked her up in their wagon and taken her to his house to play with his children. When they arrived, the family was out in the fields. Jess asked if she was hungry and cut her a large slice of bread. She remembered Jess, Cora, and their children sitting on the porch at night and singing together. Jess loved to sing.

Singing schools, established to improve congregational singing, were popular in McNairy County and early America. Itinerant schoolmasters taught basic music theory and harmony for a small fee, typically in ten-day sessions that included both sacred and secular music, with an emphasis on hymns. Using the shape-note singing system, which simplified sight-reading by assigning a unique name and shape to each degree of the standard musical scale, singers memorized the shapes and their corresponding intervals. This innovation allowed for singing and reading music in any key. Singing schools were seen as wholesome places for young people to court, too.

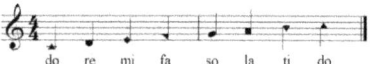

Singing conventions were held quarterly in communities or at the courthouse, attracting singers from all over to perform shape-note gospel singing. Jess's brother-in-law (and cousin) claimed that when J.C. Springer felt blue, he would go sing anywhere in the county. In 1914, a crowd of 1200 gathered to hear 316 singers and enjoy a basket dinner. Jess represented Gravel Hill at the Singing Convention held in Adamsville the following year.[39] Gravel Hill hosted the McNairy County Singing Convention in 1915, when singers from three counties filled two churches.[40] A large crowd also attended the McNairy County Singing Convention in 1921 for two days.

Jess and Cora's family around 1897. The youngest is Eldon, born on August 2, 1895. Cora likely made the girls' dresses as they have cape collars and gathered waists. Her dress has leg-o'-mutton sleeves. My grandfather, Clarence, is at the center of the back row.

My dad loved singing and yodeling while milking the cow. After retiring, he enjoyed listening to musical jam sessions around Corvallis, Oregon. Musicians with fiddles, guitars, and sometimes even a mandolin created melodies reminiscent of plaintive Scottish ballads. To my surprise, my dad recognized many of the songs. They were tunes his dad used to play on the fiddle. I suspect my grandad learned the old ballads by singing with his family on the front porch in Gravel Hill.

Texas

The Panic of 1893, a severe economic depression in the United States, lasted four years and profoundly impacted the prices farmers in McNairy County received for wheat, corn, and other commodities. It led to their inability to make mortgage payments, purchase seed for the following spring's planting, or buy winter supplies. It prompted them to question their definition of independence, which included being debt-free and free from government control. The stock market crashed, railroads failed, and numerous banks closed across the nation. President Grover Cleveland, reelected to his second term, preached self-reliance and frugality while enjoying cigars and beer and weighing 280 pounds. The functions of government, he sonorously pronounced, "do not include the support of the people."[41]

Excited conversations at the Gravel Hill Mercantile and after church revolved around Texas. Circulars proclaiming, "Find a home in Texas where the big crops are," sparked an exodus of residents to Fannin County, Texas, where wildflowers bloomed in the spring and the wind ruffled the tips of native grasses. Farmers arrived, often with 13 children—the kind of family Theodore Roosevelt promoted—to rent farms in the Red River Valley that included a cistern, a storm cellar, and fields for planting cotton and corn. By 1890, the largest town, Windom, was a thriving community of one hundred residents, with a post office, a lumberyard, cotton gins and grist mills, a doctor, a blacksmith, a wagon maker, a grocery store, and most importantly, the Texas and Pacific Railroad depot, where farmers brought cakes and pies to sell to passengers.

One can only imagine Cora's reaction to the idea of moving to Texas with children, aged three to eighteen, and pregnant to boot. Cora likely had never ventured more than ten miles from Gravel Hill. Ephesians

5:22–24 echoed in her head. "Wives, submit to your own husbands, as to the Lord. For the husband is the head of the wife even as Christ is the head of the church, his body, and is himself its Savior. As the church submits to Christ, wives should also submit everything to their husbands." Cora probably took a deep breath and followed Jess. Her sister, Victoria, and her cousins had already moved to Fannin County: Margaret Lou in 1891 and Laura in 1896. Her Uncle Tom moved by wagon in 1895 to Cooke County, Texas. More like a big brother than an uncle, Thomas Jefferson Huggins was raised in the same household as Cora.

Likely in the summer of 1898, Cora and Jess moved to Fannin County by wagon or train, after selling their 150-acre Gravel Hill property. In July, the Missionary Baptist Church of Gravel Hill issued a letter of dismissal to J.C. Springer and C.C. Springer. By November, Cora had given birth to her tenth child in Texas. Cora's brothers, Rady and Dud, joined them in Texas two years later, followed by her sister, Zulah, the next year. By 1901, all of Cora's siblings and their families had relocated to Fannin County, except for their dear mother, brother James Bryant (J.B.), and youngest sister Aggie, who passed away in November 1901 in McNairy County at the age of 26. Texas neighbors didn't have to ask, "Who are your people?"

By wagon, tightly packed with belongings, the children would have enjoyed camping when the weather was good. The boys herded the livestock and slept under the wagon with the dog to keep snakes and critters away. Diaries mention families eating squirrels and pecans, along with tasty quail and rabbit stews. Still, they could survive for weeks on a 100-pound sack of shelled, cracked, or ground corn. Their journey required learning unique skills and making countless adjustments over bumpy, deeply rutted roads. Stops were made to repair broken wagons. A large can of grease was essential, as the axles and other parts needed frequent lubrication. A shovel and a pry bar provided leverage when stuck in mud or sand. When the rivers rose, mules had to be double-teamed to ford. Oxen or mules pulling heavy loads developed sore, tender hooves and had to be rested. The pace was painfully slow. Springers likely sang songs, recited poetry, and told stories to pass the time. They sought campsites with plenty of grass for the mules, located on high ground to avoid flooding and mosquitoes. If they arrived at a camp after dark, they shouted "hello" to announce themselves so they wouldn't be greeted by gunfire.

A train might have gotten them to Texas faster, but cost more. They could rent a freight car for their livestock, farm tools, and household items that they couldn't sell or give away in Gravel Hill. Some cars even had a stove at one end, allowing families to cook meals while traveling with their livestock and belongings. Second-class passengers sat on benches arranged in rows like crowded church pews—first-class passengers paid for a private compartment. Cora had probably never ridden a train before; she usually walked or rode in a wagon wherever she needed to go. She could likely count the number of carriage rides on one hand.

By train, Cora may have glimpsed the mighty Mississippi River and the delta land of cotton fields through a grimy window. Well-dressed ladies and gentlemen strolled to the station in Memphis, their Black servants following closely behind with luggage. She may have noticed tall boarding houses, storefronts displaying dry goods, hand-scrawled menus at eateries, and beef carcasses swinging in the wind at the butcher shop. Wind gusts swirled dust and offal, along with hawkers' bills, sheets of newsprint, and a stove-in derby hat down the street. She may have worried about her egg money, pinned securely inside her dress. Her children pressed so close to her side she couldn't move. Never before had they seen so many strangers. They looked like country bumpkins, vulnerable to flimflammers: pickpockets, sneak thieves, and confidence men. The air, thick with the smells of leather, sawdust, roasting meats, tobacco smoke, stale beer, and horse manure, was sweetened by the scent of new hay in a wagon. Bankers walked by in their Sunday go-to-meeting suits, workmen bent over in leather aprons, and a printer's devil clutching a stack of freshly inked advertisement bills. Small shops stretched on forever: grocers, butchers, hardware stores, drapers, pharmacies, and undertakers. A man rolled a keg of whiskey, boys played with hoops and leather balls, idlers lounged in straw hats, and women and girls carried packages of brown paper tied with string and watched where they stepped. And what a racket it was from the clip-clop of horses, the rumble of steel wagon wheels rolling on cobblestones, and peddlers shouting. A pitiful family huddled in a doorway, dressed in rags, dirty and unkempt, beneath a gaslight.

Jess rented a farm in Fannin County near Dodd City, five miles east of Bonham. The family moved into a house likely equipped with a wood stove, a large rainwater tank since local wells had hard water that stained everything, and a two-hole outhouse a short distance away, well-stocked with a Sears and Roebuck or Montgomery Ward catalog.

After James Carl was born in 1898, Cora gave birth to Dora in 1900. Six children, from Clarence to six-year-old Claude, attended school during its four-month session. The oldest daughter stayed home to help Cora. The education of the Springer children was inconsistent—they attended school only when their labor wasn't needed at home or in the fields; perfect attendance was unheard of. Most schools held a two-month summer session and operated for three to four months in the winter. Clarence was still attending school at 17 but reported finishing only eighth grade. Eupha and Hettie were students until the ages of 21 and 19, respectively, although Eldon was the only child to complete a year of high school. High schools developed late and faced strong resistance from working-class parents, who considered them frivolous. It was important for their children to learn to read and write, but education beyond that wasn't considered essential. Children's main responsibility was to help at home and send their wages to their parents.

In Fannin County, Clarence and Cleve attended school with Sam Rayburn, who would later become well-known as the Speaker of the U.S. House of Representatives for 17 years and a staunch advocate of agricultural initiatives. Like the Springers, Sam spent his childhood on a 40-acre cotton farm near Windom. He was the same age as Clarence, while Cleve was two years younger.

Jess and Cora's marriage would become illegal in Texas because they were first cousins with shared grandparents. First-degree cousin marriages, once valued for political alliances and consolidating social and economic power within families, came to be seen as a social stigma and taboo. In the twenty-first century, marrying a cousin is viewed as misguided, since inbreeding increases the risk of stillbirths and miscarriages. The chance of children inheriting recessive disorders like cystic fibrosis, sickle cell anemia, and speech and language problems, along with other health issues, also rises. Currently, twenty-four states prohibit marriages between first cousins, mainly due to concerns about their children's health. Family lore suggests Jess and Cora moved to Texas and advised their children against marrying kin.

Huggins and Springers brought their traditions, customs, prejudices, and beliefs to Texas. They worked during the week and attended church on Sundays. The dead were buried in the graveyard with as firm a faith in their final awakening on resurrection day as back home. Springers looked, dressed, and acted like everyone else. However, they may have been secretly amused by the Texas cowboys who wore two-inch high-heeled boots.

when Cora or her mother was ill. Jess received more attention in late July 1915 when J.B. reported Jess had strained a tendon in one of his legs. But after ten days of confinement, he was up again.

The McNairy County Independent newspaper covered national news, farming updates, community events, local entertainment, and recipes. Articles from the National Woman's Christian Temperance Union and Sunday School lessons were also included. Advertisements for patent medicines for constipation and indigestion, as well as ads for tobacco products like Prince Albert Tobacco and Lucky Strike cigarettes, were sprinkled throughout. Traveling optometrists and dentists announced their visits. A Chattanooga doctor conducted eye exams, prescribed treatments, and took orders for spectacles. Cora began wearing glasses.

The McNairy County Fair in 1916 offered a $5.00 premium to the farmer with the best agricultural display. Winners of the Fiddlers Contest and Singing Contest each received $2.50 in cash prizes. Everyone attended ball games and enjoyed the popular horse races. In 1918, one farmer butchered 38 hogs, totaling 9,861 pounds. A farmer from Gravel Hill sold two 300-pound hogs, while another grew a 54-pound watermelon. Grass was set on fire to drive the rabbits overrunning the fields toward waiting hunters. In less than three hours, 75 rabbits were killed, while about 100 escaped to live another day. That was until a week later, when some boys shot ten rabbits in an hour.

Jess left for Texas in August 1916 with his cousin J.R. Huggins and the local doctor. The doctor was looking for a new practice farther west, while Jess and his cousin planned to visit relatives. Jess returned home, saying that he had almost decided that Gravel Hill "was about as good a country as can be found anywhere." Cora's brother, two sisters, and her daughter Predetta came from Texas to visit in August 1918. They enjoyed the shady oaks where they had played as children, a welcome relief from the scorching sun of Fannin County. Claude and Carl registered for the World War I draft, alongside other farm boys, who listed Jess Springer as their employer. Claude later served under Colonel Harry S. Berry in France, traveling farther from Gravel Hill than anyone in the family had ever imagined—the only child of Cora's to go off to war. Her memories of the Civil War—the booming echo of guns from Shiloh and the fleeting shadows in the woods—made her anxious. Then, word came of a Gravel Hill boy who died shortly after landing in France from bronchial pneumonia.

During the war and the Spanish flu epidemic, Cora's daughter, Floy, became one of the 74 members of the newly organized Red Cross Chapter on November 1, 1918. Not all deaths were caused by the flu. Cora was summoned to the bedside of her little grandson, Byron Smith, who had pneumonia. Hardly two months old, he did not survive, and his spirit returned to God. A young boy was carried to Memphis and operated on for appendicitis. He was brought back a corpse and laid to rest in Gravel Hill Cemetery. The newspaper reported that this was the saddest burial ever witnessed, not only because of the death of the child but because of the deep sympathy for the heartbroken mother, who had more than her share of trouble in her married life, having lost seven of her children. A runaway mule had recently killed her husband, and her oldest son had died about six months earlier in France. Her father had also passed away the previous August.

Outsiders considered Gravel Hill folk as poor but law-abiding and productive. There were always a few bad characters: shiftless thieves or downright dangerous men. A man returning from Corinth in 1915 passed a rider on a mule who warned him to hide his money because robbers were down the road. He stashed his $30 in his shoe, and sure enough, robbers were waiting in a dark ravine. One of the robbers held his horse while the other pointed a revolver at him. They were described as young men, one tall and slim, the other short and stout. Highway robberies had been reported in the ravine for several years.

That same year, the son of the local doctor, home for Christmas, was found riddled with bullets, with $60 taken from his pockets. Another murder occurred in May 1919. Two neighbors, Archer and Cross, got into an argument about Archer's hogs getting into Cross's field. The reporter wrote, "Soon Cross applied the vilest epithet to Archer with all its blasphemous attachments and started towards Archer with a knife in his hand, when Mr. Archer threw his double-barrel shotgun on him and fired, killing Cross instantly." The defendant was described as a model citizen, while the deceased, according to his neighbors, was an overbearing, bulldozing character who had a habit of bullying people. Being a large, muscular man, he often got his way with ordinary men. The defendant, slender and delicate, exhibited a 'gritty' resolve. The jury returned a verdict of not guilty.

J.B. Huggins reported that he had a fine sow break out and stray from home. He found his hog in a log stable early Sunday morning, more than a mile away, nailed hard and fast. Tongue in cheek, he wrote in the McNairy County Independent, "Nothing would draw the nails except two bucks, which were displayed, and the sow was freed from its prison and struck the road for home, with her owner in close pursuit, with the experience and satisfaction of knowing that not every man is his brother's keeper."[46]

On January 31, 1919, Jess was confined to his bed with the flu but was slowly improving. Then the doctor diagnosed him with stomach cancer. The local newspaper reported on February 28, 1919, that Mrs. Predetta Emmons, Cleveland, and Clarence Springer were called to their father's bedside due to his serious illness. Cleve and Predetta returned to their homes in Texas, but Clarence, whose home was in Oregon, planned to stay in Gravel Hill until his father's condition improved. It was the first time Clarence had seen his father since his wedding in Texas in December 1906. Unfortunately, Jess did not improve. The death angel hovered. There wasn't anything Cora could do. Jess died on March 15, 1919, from stomach cancer.

Cora's brother, J.B. Huggins, wrote his obituary. "J.C. Springer, one of our best citizens, died at the home Saturday morning at 4 o'clock, at the age of 66. His remains were laid to rest in the family cemetery Saturday evening. Reverend Carmack conducted the funeral services. He leaves a wife and ten children to mourn his loss, five of whom are married, four at home, and one in the army; the youngest child is 15 years old. He has been a faithful member of the Missionary Baptist church for twenty-six years. His life has been one of honesty and uprightness, always holding up for the right. Many young men will long remember his good advice, and such men as he will be sadly missed. Our hearts go out in sympathy to the bereaved family, may each of them be made to realize that their loss is his eternal gain." Obituaries for Jess appeared in the Commercial Appeal newspaper in Memphis and the Honey Grove Signal in Texas, each stating, "A member of a prominent pioneer family in McNairy County, he was a fine man in every way, and his passing brought deep sorrow."[47]

J.B. Huggins was appointed to administer his estate. The estate totaled assets of $1,688.54, consisting of $1,265.18 in the First National Bank of Selmer, $3.08 in bond interest, $74.28 from the corn crop, two government bonds valued at $150, loans to two sons totaling $86, a war savings certificate of $100, and $10 collected from Ella South. Jess was careful with his money. He was conspicuously absent from the McNairy County records as either a loaner or a borrower. His estate paid out these expenses:

- Burial expenses to J.R. Gooch 83.20
- Suit of clothes 25.00
- Paid A.B. Hamm for wire 20.40
- shop work 2.00
- Doctor bill 73.00
- Paid Mrs. C.C. Springer for a year's support 635.00
- Paid Claude Springer 246.00
- Paid John Springer. 2.00
- Difference in war stamps from face to cash value 11.80
- Paid to each child of Jess and Cora's:
    Eupha Latta 47.02
    Eldon Smith 47.02
    Claude Springer 47.02
    Carl Springer 47.02
    Floy Springer 47.02
    Predetta Emmons 47.02
    C.D. Springer 47.02
    Cleveland Springer 47.02
    Guardian of John Springer 47.02
    Guardian of Dora Springer 47.02
- Difference in note allowed 10.00
- Difference in $100 bond, face value to cash value 13.50
- Difference in $50 bond, face value to cash value 5.70
- Paid for Tomb Rock 50.00
- Paid for hauling same 5.00
- Paid Administrator for his services 32.90
- Paid Clerk for inventory, settlements, etc. 2.75
- Difference in fractional parts of cents in divide 09

Total . . . . $1688.54[48]

Cora heard a story about a widow who cried and worried about what she would do. Her farm went to rack and ruin, and her children turned out poorly. Another widow gathered herself, managed the farm, and her boys grew up to be steady, hardworking men; her girls became good mothers. Cora probably muttered to herself, "The good Lord helps those who help themselves," and got busy cooking and taking care of her mother and children, as she had always done.

Legal documents referred to her as the generic "wife," such as J.C. Springer and wife, or occasionally as Mrs. J.C. Springer. After becoming a widow, her brother, writing in the Gravel Hill newspaper, began referring to her as Mrs. Cora Springer or Mrs. C.C. Springer. In Gravel Hill, women were addressed with respect as "Miss" or "Aunt," like "Aunt Sis." People became so used to calling one woman Aunt Sis that they forgot her birth name was Quintina Huggins.

Automobiles and trucks were rare on the potholed dirt roads around Gravel Hill. Arthur Huggins and a friend drove his car into a mud hole in a low spot and had to walk home to bring a team and wagon to pull it out. Tractors proved to be more useful. They began replacing mules in crop farming, reducing the hours families spent hoeing. In 1921, the cash crops were cotton, hogs, and cattle. Farmers were advised to plant less cotton because of the boll weevil threat. Corn and eggs were seen as safer choices. The corn crop was excellent, providing plenty of feed for hogs, but farmers were warned to cull their hogs since hogs were selling in St. Louis for little more than their freight costs. Telephones were promoted as a way to call friends, neighbors, and relatives, as well as to get accurate weather reports. However, electricity and telephones arrived slowly in Gravel Hill. One man fell and broke his arm trying to string a telephone wire to his house.

Neighbors gathered in the evenings to play games, pop popcorn, or make candy. Claude Springer and other young people sang their hearts out at a New Year's party in 1920. A large crowd gathered to enjoy the evening entertainment at the McCoy home in 1921. When the crowd dispersed, a 100-pound hog was accidentally run over and badly crippled. Guests quickly got busy, put on their overalls, heated water, and butchered the hog by 11 pm.

Liz, Cora's granddaughter, remembered church dinners on the grounds of Gravel Hill Church and wearing new "Sunday" shoes that gave her blisters. She enjoyed biscuits and gravy with fried rabbit, drizzled with molasses, at her grandparents' house. Her grandmother always had teacakes in the middle drawer of her pie safe, and Granddad Jess had a cistern with a tin lid. The kids would holler down to the bottom to hear their voices echo.

Without Jess, Cora's children helped manage the farm. Floy was 29; Claude, fresh from the Army and about to marry, was 27; Carl was 22; Dora was 19; and John was 17. Claude, Carl, and John provided the labor for the farm. Floy and Eldon helped their mother and 84-year-old grandmother with household chores, cooking, gardening, and caring for the poultry. Dora and John went to school. Claude and his bride,

Mollie, lived with Cora for three weeks after their October wedding until their home was ready. Mollie remembered her new mother-in-law as very sweet and kind.

Cora and Her Mother

Cora's brother, J.B. Huggins, was appointed guardian of Dora and John in July 1921, even though Dora was 19 and John was 17. Was there a need to protect their inheritance, or did Dora and John have health issues caused by genetic disorders from their parents' cousin marriage? Liz, my first cousin once removed, grew up in Gravel Hill. During a family fish fry in Corinth, with my usual lack of tact, I asked if marriage between cousins in Gravel Hill resulted in people with genetic defects. Liz, her brother, and her sister-in-law were surprised to realize during a long conversation that many of their relatives had never had children despite wanting them. Although Cora had 12 children, she had few grandchildren. Jess and Cora's first child died as a baby; their oldest daughter, Predetta, had one child who died young; my grandfather Clarence had five children; Cleve had one son; Hettie had none; Eupha had five children, but one died at birth; Floy had one son; Claude had one child and fostered four brothers; Eldon had three children, one of whom died as a baby; James had one; Dora had none, being the only child who did not marry; and John had one. Liz and her brother remembered an albino brother and sister from a previous generation who wore sunglasses to church to protect their sensitive eyes from the sun. A year after this conversation, Liz called me from her home in

Florida. She found out that not only did her mother's parents, Jess and Cora, share the same grandparents, but her father's grandmother was a sister of her maternal grandparents. In other words, she descended from two Springer siblings and three Huggins siblings.

Burton Springer, Cleve's son, grew up in Texas and visited his grandparents in Gravel Hill. In the early 1980s, he wrote about his memories of these visits. He remembered Elizabeth, his great-grandmother, as a tall, lean woman. Her rocking chair was placed on the left side of the fireplace in the living room. Blinded by cataracts, her sight partially returned in the 1920s, allowing her to read newspaper headlines and recognize people's faces.

Sal and Puss

Burton's memory was hazy, but he recalled that Granny sometimes smoked a small cob or clay pipe. Someone would light it by taking a lump of live coal from the fireplace to ignite the tobacco in her pipe. Behind a curtain hung diagonally across a corner of the room was her portable toilet, which, as a visiting child, he was lucky enough to share. The fireplace served as the social center of the house, and the furniture was arranged around it. Burton remembered a group of old men sitting before the fire, sharing stories. One of them was Uncle Will Hogan, who stroked his long white beard while he spoke. The old men chuckled over an oft-told tale about a prominent Union General (they said Grant) who commandeered temporary headquarters in the area during the Civil War. Using his knowledge of the fields and woods, a local intrepid sneak slipped up to the back of the corral, gently let down the fence rails, and took the general's horse.

Burton also remembered a corn-cob fight held by the neighborhood boys in the barn and corral, just down a gentle slope from his grandparents' house. There were stalls and pig pens in the lower part of the barn, with a hayloft above. Since the livestock were fed corn, there was plenty of ammunition for the fight. Teams were formed. Burton discovered that a wet, well-thrown corn cob was an effective missile. He also had a chance to join the boys on their hunts. The Gravel Hill boys went rabbit hunting during the day and coon hunting at night. They were reluctant to accept Burton until he borrowed a 20-gauge shotgun and shot a cottontail rabbit running through the underbrush.

Jess and Cora's home featured a veranda that faced the road. An abandoned log cabin sat slightly to the side, near the road. One day, Burton sat on the steps of this cabin and watched a funeral pass, made up entirely of horse- and mule-drawn wagons and buggies. The mourners were Black, except for a few White families. He was told it was the funeral of Sal and Puss's brother. Sallie F. Ray (Sal) was actually the mother of Martha Ann Ray (Puss) and was esteemed by the Springers. Three generations of women—Sarah, her daughter Sal, and her granddaughter Puss—were born into slavery and may have been enslaved by R.B. Wray, James M. Huggins Sr., or his oldest son Leroy. James Sr. had three slaves in 1850: a 28-year-old female, a 19-year-old male, and a four-year-old male.[49] In 1860, he owned a 38-year-old female, two 26-year-old males, one 26-year-old female, and a 15-year-old male. Leroy also owned a family of slaves: a 26-year-old male, a 20-year-old female, and a one-year-old baby.

Sal and Puss worked for the Springers and other families, washing clothes and helping during hog-killing for almost nothing except for their supper. In 1920, Sal reported being 90 years old and Puss, 62. Sal's mother, Sarah, probably lived past 100; Sal lived to 103, and Puss passed away in 1947 at 88. During Burton's visit, some children took him to their log cabin deep in the woods. Once Puss realized that Burton was Cleve's boy (and Jess and Cora's grandson), she pulled an orange from a hidden spot in the wall that she had saved from Christmas.[50]

At the far end of their cabin, canning jars filled with vegetables lined the shelves on either side of the fireplace to prevent them from freezing. Before leaving for World War I, two Latta boys and Claude Springer chopped and hauled firewood for Sal and Puss. Puss said they would visit the stump and pray for the boys every day until they returned safe and sound.[51]

Their little old shack was about to fall down when Sal died. After her death, a one-room cabin was built in the yard of the Latta homeplace, where Puss lived the rest of her life and helped Mrs. Latta. A cousin told me she loved sitting in Puss's little cabin, watching her stir a pot of stew hanging in the fireplace or rock quietly in her chair. Puss was always pleased to see her.

Racism was ubiquitous. The local newspaper in 1913 used derogatory language in referring to Negroes, Mexicans, and Japanese. Young Negroes who went "around with a gun hunting should be arrested for vagrancy and put to work on county roads." The newspaper column, "Among the Negroes" congratulated those Negroes who knew their place. "A better class of Negroes is not to be found anywhere than those residing in McNairy County; all are industrious, law-abiding, and most of them can read and write."[52]

Cora was a part of the segregated South. White teachers instructed White children, while African American teachers taught students of their own race. The White Teacher's Institute was held in Selmer during the summer, and a week later, the Colored Teacher's Institute met. Black and White people could not ride in the same train car, drink from the same water fountain, eat at the same lunch counter, or use the same bathroom. Incredibly, these practices persisted until after the passage of the 1964 Civil Rights Act. Today, people use the terms "before Segregation" or "after Segregation" to determine the dates of old classroom photos posted on Facebook.

Women were denied the right to vote regardless of their race. In 1913, a suffragist in Tennessee offered three reasons for granting women the right to vote: it was in women's interests to vote; women were performing their civic duties despite restrictions; and citizenship was a human right, not a male privilege. However, progress toward women's voting rights was slower in the South than in the Western states or New England. Its strong ties to its Confederate past, along with discriminatory Jim Crow laws and Ku Klux Klan violence, caused some Southern White women to fear that their right to vote might also be extended to Black women.

Tennessee became the 36th state to ratify the Nineteenth Amendment to the U.S. Constitution, granting women the right to vote in 1920. A young state representative cast the deciding vote after his mother urged him to support ratification. Before the turn of the century, Wyoming, Utah, Colorado, and Idaho had already granted women the right to vote, followed by Washington, California, Arizona, Kansas, and Oregon between 1910 and 1912. The intelligence and capabilities of women were finally acknowledged after they replaced thousands of men called into military service during World War I. In the remote area of Gravel Hill, where women still wore sunbonnets to fetch a bucket of water, some women exercised their right to vote, while others did not. Those who did not were content to leave such matters to men. But when interviewed at 96 in 1931, Cynthia Ann Hamm, whose long life had spanned twenty-four presidencies, said, "I've voted every time but one since they let women vote. Democrat, of course. Kept up with the papers, too. A body has to know what's going on."

If Cora voted for a political candidate, it probably felt like stepping into a public realm she had avoided all her life. Raised in the shadow of the Confederacy, indoctrinated by her church to believe women took a back seat to men, and baffled by women who engaged in the seedy game of politics, her days were consumed by farm chores and family demands. I suspect Cora ignored the suffragettes' voices. She recognized injustice but bore it in silence. She had much to lose by outright rebellion: her standing in the church, her place in the community, and her husband's respect. Throughout her life, she was taught her primary duty was to God and to "submit to her husband in all things." Her daily responsibilities were her burden, strengthening her courage and faith. Voting and politics had always been the domain of men. Jess had served on juries and monitored elections—not her. Voting was for a raucous, strident, unnatural class of women; respectable women stayed clear of the polls. Her brain would shatter like fractured glass if she read about politics, crime, and wars. Her daughters could handle the new-fangled future. It was bad enough that they cut their hair (their crowning glory to God, she probably believed), shortened their skirts, wore face paint, and even learned to drive cars. Cora likely had never even ridden in an automobile unless her brother gave her a ride in his new Dodge. A wagon pulled by a reliable team would have sufficed to get her to church.

Cora's first opportunity to vote came on November 3, 1920, when she was in Texas visiting her daughter and other relatives. She returned home in January. That fall, she was called to the bedside of a sick daughter in McNairy County. However, by the following February, Cora herself fell ill. After suffering a mild stroke of apoplexy, she was temporarily unable to speak. She recovered enough to visit her daughter, Eupha, in August, taking her son, John, along with her. Then, in September, Cora experienced a slight stroke of paralysis. Her brother reported that she was improving at home.

During the Christmas season of 1923, the newspaper reported on the comings and goings of Cora's family. Arthur Huggins of Memphis and Edgar Huggins of Corinth visited relatives and friends in Gravel Hill on Christmas Day. Laurence Hewitt spent the holidays with his father there and returned to Memphis on Sunday. Mrs. Tommie Smith of Corinth spent the weekend with her mother, Mrs. J. C. Springer. Roy and Clyde Huggins returned to their work in Memphis. In February, Cora had many visitors: J. N. Hamm, Mrs. Elsie Farris, J. B. Huggins, and Wylie Randolph of Gravel Hill; children Cleve Springer and wife, James Carl and wife, Mrs. R.T. Emmons, and M.D. Huggins of Texas. Cora was reported to have suffered another mild stroke of apoplexy. Some visitors returned to their homes as Cora seemed to rally, but she unexpectedly passed away on the morning of February 19, 1924, her passage between life and death barely a flutter. Her brother, M.D. Huggins and her daughter, Predetta, received telegrams in Texas to hurry back to Gravel Hill.

Her obituary read, "Mrs. Cora Springer, aged 67 years, the widow of J.C. Springer, who died five years ago, died at her home near Gravel Hill after 10 days of illness with paralysis. She was the sister of Esquire J.B. Huggins and the daughter of Mrs. Elizabeth Huggins. She leaves a broken-hearted mother, Mrs. Elizabeth Huggins, who is nearing her 89th birthday, two sisters, three brothers, and ten children (five sons and five daughters) to mourn her loss. Her children were all present when the end came, except the oldest boy, who lives in Oregon, who was prevented on account of sickness in his home. She is survived by the following children: Cleveland, Clarence, Claude, Carl, Mesdames Emmons, Latta, McBride, and Smith, and Miss Dora Springer. The remains were laid to rest beside her husband in the old burying grounds of the family. Reverend Hammond, her pastor, preached the funeral, and R.B. Gooch was the undertaker in charge."[53]

Cora was buried in the Huggins Cemetery next to Jess and her father, across the road from her first child, her grandmother Hannah, and Jess's parents. Her life was a quilt of light and dark, worrisome in one way and uplifting in another. She rested in the hallowed ground with those who came before her and in sight of the church where she had worshipped, waiting for Judgement Day. Perhaps the minister eulogized her by saying, "It seems hard for us to part with her; her sweet voice cannot be heard on this earth again, but she will remain in the memory of those who loved her. It was God's will to call her home."

After Cora's funeral, her brother M.D. returned to Fannin County, Texas, with Cora's oldest daughter, Predetta, who took her youngest siblings, John and Dora, to live with her. John married in Texas in 1931. Dora never married and died of cancer at age 40. Cleve traveled to Oregon to visit Clarence before either of them had children, but his wife didn't care for Oregon, so they returned to Texas. Hettie married in 1912 and died of uremic poisoning three years later in Windom, Texas. Eupha married a cousin from the Huggins side in 1908. Floy impulsively hopped on a log truck owned by a widowed truck driver working for the day in Gravel Hill. She was 32 years old. They married in his home in Chester County, Tennessee. They had one son, who told me he grew up sleeping with his mom while his half-brother from his dad's first marriage slept with him. He became a successful bank president, and it wasn't until his father's death that he realized his mother had loved his dad. Floy's husband gave away what little they had to people he deemed worse off. A cousin remembered always bringing Sunday dinner with them when they visited because they had nothing. Claude settled down with Molly in Gravel Hill. Eldon married in 1916. Carl married in 1922, moved to West Texas in 1924, and later to Memphis. Three children—Clarence in Harlan, Oregon; Cleve in Miami, Texas; and Predetta in Honey Grove, Texas—subscribed to the McNairy County Independent newspaper to keep up with the news from home.

Elizabeth outlived her daughter Cora by five years. She came to Gravel Hill as a child with her parents, Ezekiel and Hannah Springer, and grew up to marry James Monroe Huggins Jr. at age 17, then spent 46 years as a widow. Like many women, her life resembled an old quilt with patches of family—her parents, her husband, her life with Cora and Jess, extended visits with her other children, and, after Cora's death, living with her son, Bryant (J.B.). The frayed seams between the quilt patches tug at memories of church revivals, ruined crops, wars, picking cotton, and the heartbreak of losing babies. She spent most of her marriage living in a two-story log house. When a new home was built in 1916, the old log house was rolled down the hill and incorporated into the barn, a testament to a life where nothing was wasted. Cora's mother died on December 10, 1929, of senility at the age of 94 years, 6 months, and 27 days. Her granddaughter-in-law, Molly, was with her when she died at Uncle Bryant's and wrote, "She went so easy." She had outlived all but Victoria, Zulah Bell, and James Bryant (J.B.).

Cora and Her Mother

A memorial was erected to Cora's father, James Monroe Huggins Jr., for his part in the Civil War, in the Huggins Cemetery in 1994. The dedication was read as a light rain fell on the burial grounds. "Not for fame or fortune. Not for place of rank. Not lured by ambition, but in simple obedience to duty as they understood it: This man suffered all. Sacrificed all. Dared all and died." A Confederate flag was placed on the grave.[54]

My grandfather visited Gravel Hill twice: once when his father died and again from October 15 to December 6, 1940, just before World War II broke out. During his second visit, a niece took him to meet the daughter of Nathan Bedford Forrest to discuss Civil War history. When I visited south of the Mason-Dixon Line in 1978, I saw two men in bib overalls leaning on the fence at the Huggins Cemetery. When I introduced myself as Clarence Springer's granddaughter from Oregon, they nodded slowly, grinning, and recalled his visit in 1940, as if it had just happened yesterday. I was also shown the old "home place" where Jess and Cora lived. The house was gone, but the land where it once stood was surrounded by gently rolling ground of scrub oaks broken up by fields.

Women received little recognition for their personality or significance, except in relation to men. Jess managed the family, while Cora held it together with sheer will, faith in the good Lord, and her love. After Jess passed away, Cora continued caring for her mother and children. She may have harbored rebellious dreams and desires or unchristian thoughts in her youth, but she had been taught that too much passion was perilous and that rebellion was the work of the devil. She was not so discriminated against as overlooked. Her strength came from her faith in the Almighty.

Texanna's Family

Barch Cantrell
born: 1817, Warren County, Tennessee, died before January 1, 1875, Texas
Married:
1) Nancy Ann Hughes, June 9, 1844, Jerseyville, Jersey County, Illinois. Nancy was born in 1820 in Tennessee, died April 24, 1859, in Parker County, Texas, and was buried at Veal Station, Parker County, Texas.
2) Margaret died before 1870 in Texas

Children with Nancy
Mary Jane, 1846, Illinois—1902, Oklahoma, married James Blackburn, 7 children
Tillman Henderson, 1850, Texas—1886, Texas, married Josephine Tomlinson, 2 children
William Alexander, 1852, Texas—1936, Texas, married Martha Jane Ballard, 3 children
Charlsilla Elizabeth, 1855, Texas—after 1900, Oklahoma, married Zachariah Roberts, 6 children; married Ellis Waddington, 1 child
George Washington, 1859 Texas—1944 Texas, married Sarah Frances Hardwick, 6 children

Children with Margaret
Texanna, born about 1861, possibly in Collin County, Texas, died February 7, 1890, Gainesville, Cooke County, Texas, married Franklin Pierce Heare, 3 children.
    Bonnie Nell Heare, 1885–1971, married Clarence Don Springer, 5 children
    Isaac Wesley Heare, 1886–1953, married Olive Irene Reid, 2 children
    Texas Anna Heare, 1889–1972, married Clifton Claude McMullen, 5 children

Texanna Cantrell Heare
(about 1861–1890)

Texanna was a girl of the Texas frontier; her life shrouded in the mist of 19th-century history. She left no letters, diaries, or memoirs. Yet, she likely grew up as a scrappy little girl in a faded calico dress, able to load and fire a gun, and taught to fear marauding outlaws. She was my great-grandmother, whom I knew nothing about. Even my grandmother—her daughter—never talked about her, except to say of the one photo she had, "Oh, my poor little mama."

Females become less ghostly by magnifying the records of males. Her father, Barch Cantrell, left only a faint trail to illuminate his daughter's history. Similarly, her husband, Franklin Pierce Heare, left few traces of his brief time with her.

This is the only photograph of Texanna, likely taken in Gainesville, Texas, in 1887 with her husband and children. Their oldest child, my grandmother, peers at the photographer, distrustful of the mysterious process of having her picture taken. Texanna is dressed in a tightly buttoned jacket with a small nosegay of flowers at her throat, her eyes modestly downcast, her long, tapered fingers relaxed; her dark hair stylishly curled by a Victorian curling iron. Her flawless, alabaster skin resembles that of a porcelain doll.

Barch Cantrell was part of a community of Tennesseans who moved from southern Illinois to northern Texas. He had five children with his first wife, Nancy. After her death, he quickly married Margaret, who gave birth to Texanna, born in Texas around 1861. Nothing is known about Margaret except for her first name. Nor is much known about her daughter's given name or birthdate. Her name was listed as Texanna, Texas Anna, Texas, Texana (with one "n"), and Texa in the records in which she is mentioned. I think of her as Texanna because I like the name.

Texanna, her husband, Frank, and children, Bonnie and Ike

Texanna came from a long line of Cantrells who likely originated in Derbyshire, England, and settled in colonial Philadelphia. Then, eerily, like the Springers and Huggins, they traveled south to the Carolinas. Texanna's grandfather, William, was born in Orange County, North Carolina, in 1769 and moved to Tennessee in 1806. He fathered fourteen children in two marriages, including ten sons to carry the Cantrell surname far and wide. His ninth son was Barch, Texanna's father. Barch married Nancy Ann Hughes in Jersey County, Illinois, on June 9, 1844.[55] After the birth of their first child, they headed to Texas with kinfolk, joining a crowd of land speculators, slave-owning planters, merchants, lawless adventurers, luckless debtors one jump ahead of the sheriff, and salt-of-the-earth farmers, all with Texas fever and high expectations for cheap land capable of producing bumper crops. Many scrawled G.T.T. on cabin doors and fences to let their neighbors know they had "gone to Texas." The promise of Texas meant starting a new life without having to die.

From southern Illinois, wagon caravans plodded down the Texas Road through Indian Territory (present-day eastern Oklahoma) across the Red River. In the spring of 1845, a thousand white-topped wagons crossed the river during a six-week journey. Families bound by kinship and dreams forded rivers and struggled over rough roads that became quagmires in the spring and were filled with choking dust throughout the summer and fall. In wagons packed tightly with essentials—a coffee pot and skillet, bedding, a bag of meal, a gun, and an ax protected by a heavy canvas cover—they hid the money they received from selling their farm back home. Water barrels, tools, spare wheels, and furniture were lashed to the wagon's exterior.

Disasters were common. People drowned, suffered from sunstroke, and were bitten by poisonous spiders and snakes. Women died in childbirth, and infants struggled to thrive. Children were jostled off wagon seats and run over. The long skirts and petticoats of women and girls became caught in the spokes of the wagon wheels, pulling them to a gruesome death. Newspapers of the day quoted one lad bawling beside his family's wagon. Asked about his trouble, the boy shouted: "Fire and damnation, stranger! Don't you see mammy there shaking with the ager! Daddy's gone a-fishing! Jim's got every cent of our money there is playing poker! Sal's so corned she don't know that stick of wood from seven dollars and a half! Every one of the horses is loose! There's no meal in the wagon! The skillet's broke! The baby's in a bad fix, and it's a half mile to the creek. I don't give a damn if I never see Texas!!"

Peters Colony

Barch and his first wife, Nancy, arrived in November 1846 to settle in Peters Colony, Texas, with their three-month-old daughter, Mary Jane. Five years earlier, the Republic of Texas contracted with eleven Englishmen from London and nine Americans from Louisville to establish a large reservation of land in the north-central part of the Republic. Peters Colony hoped to attract at least 600 families a year to farm land inhabited by inhospitable Indians but featuring water, grasslands, and rich soil. Married men would receive 640 acres, while single men over the age of 17 could claim 320 acres, provided they built a cabin and cultivated at least 15 acres of land. Peters Colony promised to survey the land but, more often than not, failed to do so. Disputed land titles clogged the courts for years.

Peters Colony eventually expanded to encompass all or portions of Denton, Collin, Dallas, and 24 other Texas counties, covering the area surrounding and including the cities of Dallas and Fort Worth and extending north to the Oklahoma border, or most of the land between the Red and Trinity Rivers. It consisted of open rolling plains, covered by prairie grass as high as the stirrups, and a ten-to-twenty-mile-wide band of mostly dense scrub oaks known as Cross Timbers, all watered by 20 to 30 inches of rain annually in a land prone to fierce tornadoes. Cantrells and their kinfolk brought dogs, guns, and the Methodist religion. When Nancy's aunt was asked how she liked her new home on the Texas frontier, she replied, "Oh, it's great for men and dogs but hell on women and ponies."[56]

As a married colonist, Barch Cantrell received a Third-Class Certificate for 640 acres (a square mile), comprising two surveys: one for 557 acres and the other for 83 acres in the Nacogdoches District, Texas. His application was officially approved on April 29, 1850. Interestingly, the two parcels were 13 miles apart; the 83-acre parcel was located on White Rock Creek near the settlement of Dallas, whereas the 557-acre parcel was situated on Duck Creek south of Plano, Collin County, Texas. Barch and his family may have lived briefly on either piece or not at all. His grant was noted as not being located, so he may have lived in a more settled area, such as Plano, where he had ties. Attorney L.L. Marshall sold Barch's two Peters Colony parcels, totaling 640 acres, in March 1851 for $500. The sales were recorded on November 15, 1853, the same day Barch revoked his power of attorney by signing his mark.[57]

The Baurch Cantrell Survey has been cited in Texas land transactions and lawsuits throughout the 19th and 20th centuries. It has been sold and resold, divided, and classified many times: James Thomas bought the 557-acre parcel in 1851 for $250; Abraham Hart paid the same amount for the 83-acre parcel. Thomas sold the 557-acre parcel on Duck Creek to Jacob Clemons (Clem) Skiles, who retained about 260 acres of this land at the junction of Plano and Arapaho Roads. Two hundred eighty acres of the survey sold for $3600, and 6½ acres of the smaller parcel, three miles east of the Dallas County Courthouse, sold for $700 in 1883.[58] The location of a corner of the Cantrell Survey was settled on appeal by the high court in 1884 (the only proof was a man who testified his father had told him it was a stone in the prairie), and in another case, the survey itself was questioned.[59] Four acres were sold for $1600 in 1887; a tract of 117 acres was involved in a 1925 divorce proceeding; and 110 acres purchased in 1933 were sold in 1957 as part of an estate settlement. A series of zoning ordinances passed by the City of Richardson in 1960 changed part of the survey to industrial zoning. This zoning was amended in 1965 to require improvements, leading to Dallas County's successful establishment of the Richardson

Industrial Park on April 20, 1981. Richardson, now known as Telecom Corridor for its high concentration of telecommunications companies, is home to the University of Texas at Dallas. Oh, the value of Barch's 640 acres today!

Barch left few records: some land deeds, tax records, and a census report. He appears on the 1848 through 1852 tax rolls of Dallas County, the 1853 tax roll of Anderson County, the 1858 and 1859 tax rolls of Parker County, and the 1869 tax roll of Brazos County. Unable to read and write, he signed legal documents with an "X." His name appeared as Baurch, Barch, or simply as B. Cantrell. Barch was likely the correct spelling, as his son William named his son Reuben Barch, and several other descendants carried Barch as a middle name.

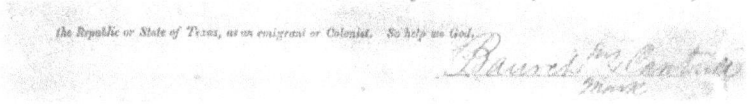

In the early tax records of Dallas County, Barch paid the minimum tax, claiming no personal property, including Negroes, horses, mules, cattle, and various items such as books, clocks, wagons, sheep, hogs, and guns. The only year his land was taxed was in 1849, when 320 acres were assessed at $160. Other colonists had improved 15 to 45 acres of their original 640-acre land grants and owned horses, cows, oxen, and hogs, harvesting at least 100 bushels of Indian corn each year. Thomas Vance, who witnessed Barch's Peters Colony land grant, owned 320 acres valued at a dollar an acre (the standard assessment), two mules worth $100, and nine cattle valued at $71. William Hughes—likely Barch's brother-in-law—had 38 acres improved from a total of 602 acres. He owned nine horses, 14 cattle, 12 sheep, and 20 hogs, and harvested 600 bushels of corn. In 1858, he paid taxes on two enslaved individuals, valued at $2,000; 28 horses, worth $1,450; and 25 cows, sheep, and a wagon. Two years later, he paid taxes on 35 horses, nine cows, and 40 sheep.

While Barch's brother-in-law and other property owners were called for jury duty in the sparsely populated Dallas County, Barch was not. The jury heard cases involving murder and divorce, disruptions of religious worship, and the malicious shooting of hogs, cattle, or horses. The most common charge was gaming. Men wagered on anything: card games, dice, horse racing, or crop yields.

Perhaps Barch was the quintessential frontier Texan—a rawboned man in worn clothes, an experienced horseman armed with a flintlock rifle and a Bowie knife. He tried running a small herd of cattle and may have driven a freight wagon for wages, likely in exchange for goods rather than cash, since currency was scarce. Texas's bounty included herds of wild horses—free transportation or valuable merchandise for anyone capable of roping and breaking them—as well as a market for cowhides and deerskins. Or he may have been a soldier. Men from Fannin, Collin, and Dallas counties joined military units to protect settlers and fight in the Mexican War. Jack Hays, a Tennessean the same age as Barch, organized a mounted regiment in 1847, eventually known as the fabled Texas Rangers. Hays studied the methods of Indian warfare as a surveyor and was skilled at protecting his men in skirmishes. His regiment wore no uniform or rank insignia and paid little attention to military regulations, but they were brutal guerrilla fighters. "They certainly were an odd-looking set of fellows," observed an officer, "and it seemed to be their aim to dress as outlandishly as possible." Dust coated their bushy beards and their mélange of garb and headgear. They rode every variety of mount, from little Mustangs to big American horses. Each carried a rifle, a pair of pistols, and one or two Colt revolvers. However, there is no record of Barch having been a soldier.

Instead, he had children. Mary Jane Cantrell was born in 1846 in Illinois, before the family moved to Peters Colony. Tilman Henderson Cantrell was born in 1850, and William A. Cantrell was born in 1852, likely in Dallas County or Collin County.[60] His fourth child, a daughter named Charlsilla Elizabeth Cantrell, was probably born in 1855 in Anderson County, Texas.

The Cantrells moved to Anderson County, located southeast of Dallas, by wagon, on foot, or horseback, along roads that were barely wide enough for a wagon. Crude "hotels" offered overnight accommodations along the way. One hotel measured 25 feet by 35 feet with a single door, two windows, and "rooms" divided by canvas wagon covers. Travelers paid to sleep on the dirt floor next to strangers. Barch and his family likely preferred camping under the stars rather than staying in a "hotel" or sailing down the river. The poorly navigable Trinity River, filled with snags, sandbars, and low water, endangered the lives of passengers, deckhands, and toiling slaves, making it a risky choice.

Barch bought 93 acres in Anderson County along Brushy Creek, a tributary of the Neches River, on August 26, 1854, from William R. Payne.[61] He shared a property line with his brother Elisha's 320 acres, which were also purchased from William Payne. At least six Cantrell men and three women, along with their families, lived in Anderson County. Two of them were Barch's brothers, while the others were his nephews and nieces, the children of his oldest half-brother, Stephen, who was 30 years his senior. Some Cantrells had settled as early as 1846 when they paid a poll tax.[62] In 1853, B. Cantrell paid the minimum of a 50-cent poll tax, a 50-cent state tax, and a 25-cent county tax, claiming to own no horses, cattle, or Negroes.

Anderson County was part of the Piney Woods region of East Texas, characterized by a cotton and slave economy reminiscent of the Deep South. However, the Cantrells lived fifteen miles northwest of Palestine, the county seat, in an area of fertile valleys rich in timber and water, ideal for growing corn and raising swine. Outsiders referred to Texas as the kingdom of Porkdom. One of the Cantrell brothers owned 125 hogs in 1850. A diet of acorns produced healthy hogs and quality bacon, and Indians did not steal hogs. Hogs also provided recreation. Young hogs released in the spring bred with wild hogs, making the fall hunt more thrilling and much more enjoyable.

After four months in Anderson County, Barch sold his 93 acres on Bushy Creek for $280 and moved to the true frontier of Texas.[63] The Comanche and Kiowa hunting grounds, located 60 miles west of Dallas, began to attract White settlers. Grassy valleys stretched for miles, and beautiful post-oak timber clustered around the creeks. Deer, turkey, antelope, and buffalo were abundant. The excellent grazing land fattened wild-range cattle with horns as thick as wagon axles for lucrative markets in the California gold fields. Cattle worth $5 to $10 a head in Texas fetched five to twenty times that amount in San Francisco.

Texas Frontier

Frontier life was a dangerous dance of alliances and betrayals, marked by intense bloodshed and threats of violence, punctuated by brutality. Men with quick tempers could be friendly one moment and brutal the next. It was hard to tell who was worse, the Anglos or the "savages." Few roads existed; there were no bridges, and isolated log cabins dotted the gently rolling plains. Sugar, tobacco, coffee, flour, shoes, firearms, gunpowder, and harnesses were considered luxuries. Itinerant circuit-riding preachers carried the Gospel in their saddlebags and preached with six-shooters beside their Bible—the Bible to save souls and the guns to save their scalps. Men in the congregation rested their rifles across their knees as a precaution against a surprise attack.

In diaries and letters, women feared the country would drive them mad. Mothers lost sleep, protecting their children from rumors of Indian raids. Women plowed or had their oldest sons plow the tough prairie sod for corn fields so they wouldn't starve through the winter. Men were gone for weeks, driving cattle or fetching supplies. A mother, nurse, and teacher to her little ones, a woman learned to mend a fence, shoot a rifle, and dress a deer. She could kill a rattlesnake if it got in the cabin too close to the cradle. Loneliness weighed heavily when neighbors were miles away. Faith in the Good Lord provided comfort.

Leah See had settled 160 acres of land in Parker County before selling it to Thomas Riley. Riley sold it as a pre-emption claim to Barch Cantrell for $150 on February 2, 1858, who received the patent on September 15, 1859.[64] In 1858, Barch paid taxes on 50 head of cattle, valued at $225. A year later, he had a cattle herd of 55 assessed at $274.

Nearly a hundred years later, a dispute arose over the exact boundaries of what became known as the Leah See property, initially surveyed by John See (presumably her son), for which Barch received the patent.[65] The 160-acre parcel was located on Ash Creek, a tributary of the West Fork of the Trinity River, straddling the county line between Parker County and Tarrant County. In 1944, Lola Pickens Carter, from Azle, Parker County, Texas, purchased two acres of the Leah See Survey, patented to 'Burch' Cantrell, and complained the survey was wrong. Her neighbor, Wayne Dunaway, also requested corrections for his four tracts of land. Early surveys, notoriously inaccurate, burdened Texas courts for years as they relied on physical features like post-oak or blackjack trees that had vanished by the twentieth century. The requested corrections resulted in the 1965 Tarrant–Parker Survey, which encompasses the town of Azle today.

In 1859, the closest town to Barch's land was Veal Station, a Methodist town, and Cantrells leaned toward Methodism. It was named after William G. Veal, the first postmaster, a minister and Mason, yet ultimately a flawed man. Veal was shot in the head by a doctor at the 1892 Confederate Veteran Reunion headquarters in Dallas, Texas. The doctor claimed that Veal had wronged his wife twenty-eight years before. It came to light that this wasn't the first report of Veal abusing women. He had been charged with improper conduct toward a woman in 1876 but was vindicated, then charged again in 1878 for an attempted seduction. He defended himself by claiming his victim was temporarily insane and hallucinated the entire incident. However, the jury found Veal guilty and fined him $500. He was suspended indefinitely from the Methodist Church and the Masonic Brotherhood.[66] An editor of the Fort Worth Journal wrote that Veal was "one of the vilest, most corrupt, and most abominable men that Texas ever knew."[67]

A hand-planed plank meeting hall was built in Veal Station using lumber hauled 200 miles by ox teams from sawmills in East Texas or transported 280 miles from Houston. The hall was large enough to accommodate a school and worship services, with a Masonic Lodge upstairs. Masons were quite popular. Rather than being viewed as a secret heretical sect filled with obscure symbols, they were seen as a mainstay of early Texas, rivaling the church in importance, reinforced by preachers who praised their Christian principles. Lodges organized New Year parties, plays, and patriotic dinners, and supported the only education many children received. A massive bronze bell hung above the Meeting Hall, audible three miles away to warn settlers of imminent Indian attacks—a bell that was melted down to support the Confederacy during the Civil War, an act regretted by the citizens.

On a Sabbath morning in 1859, the peaceful town of Weatherford, 15 miles southeast of Veal Station, received word that 250 Indians were coming to destroy the town and kill all its residents. The preacher jumped down from the pulpit and ran to the town square to ring the warning bell, yelling at the top of his lungs that the Indians were coming. Men, women, and children ran in every direction: the country folks to horses, mules, or buggies, or on foot. Some fell to their knees and began to pray, believing their day of judgment had come. Several families harnessed their teams and headed east toward Fort Worth, while other men jumped astride their ponies with their wives clinging behind and a child or two in front, while others hid in the ravines and thickets. No Indians came. After a while, the bravest of the frightened folks began asking questions, and it was discovered that the big scare had resulted from a bit of fun by some boys.[68]

Whites feared an Indian attack at any moment, to the point of hysteria, although a few tolerated them but were annoyed by their insatiable curiosity. Fears of Kiowa and Comanche raids were exceptionally high during a full moon, the so-called Comanche moon, when rivers and creeks offered cover and shelter, especially after trees leafed out along the creeks. When the grass was lush, horses on the range would congregate in large bunches, making stealing them easier. Indians left a rancher "killed, scalped, his nose cut off, and lanced in every part of the body" while stealing horses. The same day, Indians stole more horses and "whipped a woman severely, shot her through the arm, offered her other heart-rending indignities, scalped her and left her to die." Her friends found her, but she did not survive. In the spring of 1861, Indians killed and scalped a man named William Youngblood while he cut and split fence rails near his cabin. Texas Rangers overtook the Indians, recovered Youngblood's scalp from the leader's shot pouch, and galloped home in time to place the scalp on Youngblood's head a moment before he was lowered into his grave. One old timer recalled, "The Comanches were as brave a race as ever trod the soil or straddled a horse. They would rise from the death agony of a mortal wound to take one last shot or pass with a knife."[69]

Newspaper accounts of Indian massacres with gruesome descriptions became the stuff of legend. Nevertheless, attacks resulting in death or injury to settlers were rare occurrences. Indians targeted horses and cattle, particularly horses. They seldom took women and children, although they valued the scalps of women with long, thick hair, which they used as padding for their shields. Cautious settlers never left home without a Bowie knife, a shotgun, and a six-shooter tucked into their belts, even while plowing. However, when no Indian troubles had been reported for a while, settlers grew careless and ventured far from their cabins to work or visit neighbors unarmed—often to their regret. It was death-defying to outrun Indian ponies to safety.

Anglos held deep prejudices against Indians, Mexicans, and Negroes, justified in their minds by biblically inspired convictions of the superiority of the European race and the doctrine of Manifest Destiny. Fort Worth had a newspaper called *Whiteman*, dedicated to eradicating Negroes, Indians, abolitionists, and horse thieves.

The "Texas Troubles" began when a fire destroyed the business section of Dallas, leaving only the courthouse standing in July 1860. The fire was likely started by the new and volatile phosphorus matches found in stores, but vigilantes blamed Negroes and northern abolitionists. Two preachers from Iowa were beaten and expelled. Wagons were stopped and searched for firearms and ammunition. But when three Blacks were hanged on the banks of the Trinity River, the sheriff worried that if more were hanged, the loss of property would be too significant.[70]

In this atmosphere of fear and violence, Barch's wife, Nancy, gave birth to George Washington Cantrell on April 15, 1859. Tragically, she died nine days later, probably from complications of childbirth. Neighboring women likely gathered to lay out her body, covering her face with a cloth moistened with vinegar to delay mortification. They stitched her shroud, sewing through the night. The men dug a six-foot-deep grave in Veal Station Cemetery. She was 39 years old and likely skilled with a gun, capable of skinning and butchering just about anything edible, and managing a team and wagon competently. Her death would have been a catastrophe for her family. Mary Jane was 13, Tilman was 9, William was 7, Charlsilla Elizabeth was around four, and George was a newborn. Men who thought of Texas as an earthly paradise were warned that although a poor man could obtain land in Texas, he had better take care of his women. Females would suffer if proper shelters were not built, leading to calamity. Single parenting was considered nearly impossible, especially on a farm. Widowed men remarried quickly or sent children, particularly infants, to live with relatives. One man lost his wife in childbirth on a Sunday and remarried the following Wednesday. He had small children, including a newborn.

Barch's brothers and nephews apparently did not volunteer to take in his children. An older half-brother raised livestock with his two sons in sparsely populated Buchanan County, but the county's ten to fifteen White families faced even greater risks from Indian attacks. Two other brothers, Elisha and Hazel Green, lived closer. Hazel Green Cantrell moved to Parker County around 1855 and served as the County Assessor and Collector in 1856. Obviously, he could read and write, unlike his brother Barch. Hazel Green settled a claim on Ash Creek near Barch but sold the property for $400 on April 14, 1859, to buy land about a day's walk from Barch. His new farm was 160 acres in size, of which 14 acres were improved, valued at $300. He owned five horses, cattle, 25 hogs, and $10 worth of farm equipment. Hazel Green already had a full house with four children and would eventually have four more.

Barch chose to remarry instead. Since Nancy died in April 1859 and Texanna is believed to have been born in 1861, he didn't waste any time. Margaret, his second wife, remains a mystery except for two facts: she gave birth to Texanna around 1861 and died before 1870. She likely took on most of the housekeeping and child-rearing duties from 13-year-old Mary Jane, washing clothes and bathing children when the creek wasn't dry, and preparing a meager menu of wild game, fried salt pork, biscuits, or cornbread. The younger children may have gathered corn kernels where horses had been fed in abandoned Army camps—kernels that could be washed, ground, and eaten. Or they helped neighbors grind sugar cane in exchange for a gallon of molasses. No one complained about meals, least of all Barch. Only a fool argued with a skunk, a mule, or a cook.

Some children developed pellagra, which later became a symbol of "white trash," because of a diet reliant on corn. Epidemics of dysentery or "bloody flux" swept through Texan communities, and people succumbed to typhoid, malaria, lung fever, croup, whooping cough, pneumonia, and smallpox. Frequent prayers were offered for God's blessing for good health.

It seems unlikely that Barch stayed in Parker County. Before the Civil War, Parker County had a population of 4,213 people, including 222 slaves, on 397 farms, with 14,000 cattle, 4,000 sheep, and numerous swine. It was far less populated than Anderson or Dallas County due to the fear of Indian raids. Nevertheless, farmers produced over 79,000 bushels of corn, nearly 22,000 bushels of wheat, as well as rye, Irish potatoes, and sweet potatoes. A visitor to the 1860 Parker County Fair described exhibits of cabbage, beets, sweet potatoes, melons, pumpkins, butter, jeans cloth, bedspreads, embroidery, and other handiwork.

The fragile nerves of Whites during the Civil War in largely unprotected Parker County were heightened by fears of slave insurrections, Comanche raids, and a mistrust of their neighbors' political leanings. Confederate vigilantes attacked Unionists, calling them "God damned Union dogs" and stoning their houses. Riders fired their pistols through the streets of Weatherford, searching for Union men. In the fall of 1861, rumors circulated about a midnight raid to seize the federal arsenals in Sherman and Gainesville. Alarmed secessionists in Gainesville hanged forty suspected Union sympathizers accused of treason or insurrection. They shot two others as they tried to escape—an event that came to be known as the Great Hanging. Few of the dead had conspired against the Confederacy, and many were innocent of the abolitionist sentiments for which they were tried. Tragically, the Great Hanging is believed to be the most significant single incident of vigilante violence in U.S. history.

A Childhood Spent Circling Dallas

Barch likely fled the frontier for the relative safety of Collin County, close to family and fellow Peters Colonists. His second wife, Margaret, gave birth to Texanna—perhaps in Collin County. Years later, when Texanna's daughter applied for a delayed birth certificate, she stated that her mother was born in Collin County.

Margaret may have died in childbirth, but certainly before Texanna turned 9. Once again, Barch was left to raise his children alone, especially after his oldest daughter, Mary Jane, married James Blackburn in Collin County in 1866. John Beverly, a circuit-riding Methodist minister who occasionally preached at the Spring Creek Meeting Hall, officiated at their wedding. A local woman recorded in her diary that John Beverly cut his own throat in 1872 in a fit of insanity. He was not expected to live, but did.

Texans faced relentless, dusty winds that shattered their hopes and dreams during the war. Women plowed fields, drove freight wagons, operated hospitals and sick wards, and made bandages while the men were away. They helped the families of Confederate soldiers in need. Medicine, pins, needles, candles, clothing, shoes, paper, and salt were scarce. Women patched, improvised, or went without. They spun and wove more cloth than ever. Husbands' clothing was cut down for their sons. Dresses, coats, and underwear were sewn from whatever fabric they could find. Most farms were in disrepair. Fences were down, fields had grown wild, and houses needed repair. At the end of the war, it was said a man could make his fortune by rounding up all the stray cows that had multiplied during the war, as farming shifted from crops to cattle.

Many in Collin County sought to heal after the war, including the Blackburns, Vances, Beverlys (who lost five sons in the Civil War), Becks, and Kleppers, all of whom were Peters Colonists. Former soldiers returned damaged in mind and body. Accustomed to fighting, stealing, and killing, Texas was filled with profane men wearing spurs, six-shooters at their hips, sharp Bowie knives, and lariats tied to their saddles. Former secessionists, including Texas's governor, were seen as obstacles to Reconstruction and were removed from office, replaced by so-called carpetbaggers. Although most Texans accepted the indivisibility of the Union and the legal emancipation of the slaves, they rejected the notion of Negro equality. The Klan intimidated Blacks and supported White conservatives. Four years after Mary Jane married, the first Negro school was set ablaze at midnight in Collin County. Negroes, denied land ownership, farmed for White landowners on fractions: halves if the owner provided the farm equipment, thirds for grain crops, and fourths for cotton.[71] The number of murders doubled in Texas from 1866 to 1867. No decent woman or girl dared to go out alone after dark for fear of road agents or bushwhackers. Texanna's sisters knew to steer clear of renegade Indians, gamblers, cattle thieves, desperadoes, and men accused of murder back home.

On October 10, 1864, B. Cantrell purchased seventy acres of land in Johnson County, Texas, from Abraham and Amelia Onstatt for $250.[72] This may have been Barch, because he bought properties four years later under the name B. Cantrell in Bryan, Brazos County, Texas, where Texanna spent a few years of her childhood before her dad moved on again. Brazos County, 100 miles southwest of Anderson County on the rolling prairie, became prosperous after the Civil War when the railroad arrived.

Barch's first purchase in Brazos County was a 1½-acre lot from J.C. and Hanna Ross, Isaac Ross, and William McMurray, facing Port Sullivan Road near the Bryan train depot.[73] It was likely a commercial property, as the seller had been a blacksmith. Perhaps Barch earned a living as a trader or by running a livery stable that rented out horses and buggies to passengers arriving from the train—an occupation that did not require literacy. Texanna likely played nearby with her stick doll, whose eyes, nose, mouth, and hair were drawn on a scrap of calico. She may have watched women on the covered boardwalks as they shopped, protected from the weather and the mud and manure of oxen, horses, and mules. Main Street was wide enough for three to five yokes of oxen to turn and unload without the bullwhackers using words she wasn't allowed to say.

Texanna may have dreamed of riding the train, even though smoke and ash drifted through open windows, and the aisles were littered with disgusting spittoons. Railroads brought diseases like yellow fever (which broke out in Bryan in 1867) and a transient population of adventurers and those of unsettled habits, causing Bryan's moral reputation to deteriorate. Wagons of cotton and other goods were constantly loaded or unloaded around the clock, stores stayed open on the Sabbath, federal troops arrived to quell race riots, and unscrupulous carpetbaggers came with intentions of influencing local elections. Rowdy railroad workers visited gambling halls and saloons filled with armed patrons.

Strong opinions, combined with heavy drinking, led to trouble at all hours: gunfights, knife fights, and murders. Two gamblers in a Bryan gambling den started a gunfight that spilled over into a grocery, where an Irishman was killed by a stray bullet, along with one of the gamblers. Offenders were taken to the Brazos County Jail, known as the "Bryan Sky Parlor." It was fifteen feet above the ground and accessed by a removable ladder. No wonder Texanna likely did not wander around town.

In July 1868, a young White man named Holliday was accused of hanging a Black man at Brazos Bottom. In retaliation, the Negroes marched through nearby Milligan to hang Holliday. The Deputy Sheriff assembled a 20-man posse. Gunfire was exchanged, resulting in Blacks killed and wounded. White fears escalated. Seventy-five White men caught the train from Bryan to Milligan. The Blacks backed down, and most of the men went home. Trouble flared again the following day, and 150 angry men full of bravado left Bryan by train to confront the Negroes. Federal troops arrived to put down the riot. Some Whites claimed the Blacks had guns, although most were only armed with hoes, sticks, and a few old guns. The conflict only increased the distrust and hatred between the two races. Blacks felt frustrated with White justice, while the Whites wanted Blacks to stay in their place. The Milligan Massacre made news in papers across the country.

In December of 1868, B. Cantrell paid J.W. Bone, his wife, and his brother $200 for the east half of Lot 4, Block 2, which consisted of two acres. In March 1869, B. Cantrell bought the west half of the same lot from E.L. Bone. The following month, B. Cantrell paid Thompson M. Prince $100 for half of five acres near Bryan. Barch sold 1.5 acres to Susan Ware for $200, including a promissory note of $40 due on the first of December at 10% interest from maturity until paid.[74] This was the same 1.5-acre lot on Fort Sullivan Road he had purchased from Ross and W.H. McMurry the year before. By November, Susan Ware had sold this property to Middleton M. Harrison for $100.

In this flurry of real estate deals, B. Cantrell purchased the northwest half of a 10-acre lot for $75 on June 5, 1869. This lot was split between J.T. Lake, including where he lived, and Barch. Each owner's land fronted the railroad. The following month, B. Cantrell paid J.J. Stovall $50 for a lot fronting the tracks in Block 9. In September 1869, Barch sold to Catherine Bishop (whose husband was a trader) a 20-foot-wide strip running the length of Block 9 for $75.00.[75] B. Cantrell paid a tax of $1.98 on Lots 9 and 10, totaling 11 acres, valued at $655 in 1869. He also had a $30 horse and $75 of miscellaneous property. But Barch was ready to move again. Brazos County didn't suit.

Texanna moved with her father and brother to Henderson County, Texas, 120 miles northeast of Bryan. After the Civil War, the county's population increased as Whites and former slaves migrated from the South. Enslaved individuals had been the most valuable assets owned by Whites, far surpassing the value of purebred horses. In 1855, 411 slaves were valued at $196,000, nearly matching Henderson County's taxable land value. However, during the post-war depression, Blacks struggled alongside their former masters. Farm values plummeted by almost half, while the prices of imported goods, ranging from plows to fabric, remained high. Yet, money was needed for tobacco. Texans were known for their tobacco addiction, whether smoked, chewed, or sniffed. Women used snuff and smoked pipes. Girls believed that tobacco helped preserve their teeth. An English visitor claimed he saw a Texan teaching a two-year-old child how to chew tobacco and wrote in his diary around 1840: "High & low, rich & poor, young & old, chew, chew, chew & spit, spit, spit, all the blessed day & most of the night."

Barch traded unspecified lands for a hundred-acre parcel owned by B.G. Pippin on February 8, 1870, in Henderson County, and sold the 100 acres five months later to T. Flynn for $200.[76] He registered both deeds in July, signing with an X. There is no record of him paying taxes based on the value of animals and acreage; taxes allocated to the state and county to support roads, bridges, and schools. Their farm, located six miles from the county seat of Athens, was valued at $250, with their personal property valued at $225. Barch was 53, Texanna was nine, and her half-brother William was 17.[77]

Texanna's older half-siblings were scattered. Mary Jane lived in Dallas County with her husband, James Blackburn, their children, and her 14-year-old sister, Charlsilla Elizabeth. Their brother, Tillman, worked as a farm laborer for Elizabeth Klepper in Collin County. Elizabeth had six boys, aged one to thirteen, a missing husband, and land valued at $2,500 with a personal estate of $1,200. "Tillman" was another family name, like Barch, passed down in the Cantrell family, spelled as Tillman, Tilmon, or Tilghman.

Each decade, U.S. Marshals or their assistants were ordered to record the names, ages, places of birth, and other details of household members for the United States Census. With settlers scattered across the Texas countryside, with few trails and no maps, census takers simply waited in community stores for people to come in for supplies. But by 1860, this practice was frowned upon. The census takers were to visit every household. If a family was not home, the officials were to return three times and then ask neighbors for information. This may explain why the Cantrells were listed at the bottom of the last page of the 1870 U.S. Census for Henderson County, Texas. A family might be skipped in one census report or recorded twice if it is transient, but I have never found a family omitted from three consecutive censuses. Barch and his family were missing from the 1850 and 1860 censuses, and Texanna was not listed in the 1880 Census. Her half-brother, George Washington Cantrell, wasn't found in any census until he reached adulthood.

Barch's 100-acre farm in Henderson County probably had an old cabin, possibly with wooden boards nailed to the walls as shelves for Texanna's few dishes and pans. Some settlers camped in wagons and tents for up to two years before constructing a cabin. The best location was near timber and a water source. Since trees typically lined creeks, building a cabin by a creek gave settlers access to both building materials and water. Early cabins were small and had no windows (an open door provided light). A slab roof was made of split logs, with a puncheon or dirt floor, and a chimney built from mud and grass, homemade bricks, or rock. Later, a "lean-to" could be added to the cabin for a summer kitchen and dining area. These early cabins evolved into dog-run or dog-trot cabins, which were essentially twin log houses separated by a ten to fifteen-foot open-ended passageway that provided breezes and shade for both dogs and humans. By 1870, amenities such as bedroom partitions and exterior weatherproofing planks had become standard features. Most people owned a trunk for clothes, a bedstead, a simple table, and a couple of chairs. Well-off Texans had a parlor with a wood stove, a rocking chair, a looking glass, and a clock. Water closets, also known as outhouses, were constructed over holes dug in the earth, with seats built two feet above ground level. When a one-and-a-half-story house made of lumber and shingles was built south of Weatherford in 1860, people traveled from miles around to marvel at the pine floors and genuine glass windows.

Regardless of how much Texans owned or the size of their cabins, they were famous for their hospitality. Beds were arranged on pallets spread across puncheon floors or in the dogtrot between the two sections of a double log cabin. One owner of a one-room cabin with a large family welcomed everyone who dropped by. His cabin served not only as his home but also as a tavern and a place of worship, depending on the day of the week. A writer wrote in 1850, "The uncouthness of the settlers of Texas is greatly modified by their kindness of manner … and cannot fail of striking the stranger with the impression of its being a more perfect specimen of politeness than refined society's false show of affection." The only expectation of guests was proper conduct. No one wanted their freely given hospitality to turn into violence and gunplay. Texans were known to hold grudges for years.

Hounds and chickens kept the vegetation around the cabins worn down, creating a fire barrier. Settlers feared prairie fires more than they feared Indians. Chickens roosted in trees or wherever the hay was stored. Varmints killed hens, and snakes swallowed every egg. Dogs were trained to kill egg-stealing snakes, or the snakes had their head cut off with a butcher knife, or were shot. Children were taught to give a rattler a hard lick in its middle to break the snake's back so they couldn't coil and strike, then kill it. It was best to take a long stick and poke around before moving something or sitting down. Tarantulas and centipedes had stings or bites that could prove fatal. Every blade of grass was infested with pesky seed ticks and chiggers.

Nine-year-old Texanna was likely responsible for cooking and washing her father's and brother's clothes. Cook stoves became available after the Civil War, so perhaps she didn't have to bend over a smoky hearth to stir the stew or bake biscuits in a Dutch oven by laying hot coals on top of the lid, allowing the biscuits to brown on both sides. Meals were supplemented with game: venison, duck, squirrel, wild turkey, prairie chickens, and quail. She may have dried pumpkins and gathered pecans, walnuts, hickory nuts, wild grapes, and persimmons. Most settlers used a barrel of molasses made from sugarcane each year. The cane was fed between two wooden rollers, and the squeezed juice was boiled to form an unrefined syrup. The best coffee came green in large sacks to be roasted and ground at home as needed. Parched corn, rye, wheat, or oat bran crushed with a crude stone mortar and pestle, or ground in a coffee mill, was used as a substitute for coffee. One or two teaspoons of this mixture were added to each cup of water, then boiled or steeped for five minutes. Molasses was added as a sweetener. Authentic coffee, sugar, and lead were scarce and had to be bought or traded.

A free public school had not yet been built in Brazos County, so Barch may have paid tuition for Texanna. Education in rural Texas was a hodgepodge of institutes, academies, and Masonic-sponsored schools. During the Civil War, two-thirds of Texas schools closed. Some reopened after the war, but there was little accountability. Attendance was voluntary, the terms were short, and education was generally not a top priority. One-room schoolhouses had two or three windows on each long side and a single door at one end. A cast-iron stove provided heat in winter, while sunlight provided light. At recess, pupils carried fresh water from a nearby spring. Lunch consisted of a biscuit or cornbread dipped in molasses.

School days often started with prayer, a scripture reading, and a patriotic song. Textbooks, like Noah Webster's "blue-back" Speller and McGuffey's Reader, were in short supply. Since many rural schools lacked writing paper, blackboards, maps, and globes, students learned facts such as multiplication tables, the states of the Union, and capitals by singing in verse. This approach became known as the "blab" school, where students recited aloud. Some students were very young, while others were older than the teacher, and in some cases, better educated. One teacher applicant got the job because he could spell "scissors." Discipline was freely used to maintain order.

Texanna may have walked to and from school across the prairie in Henderson County. With few landmarks, children got lost and were taught to be cautious of wild cattle on unfenced ranges. Accustomed to being approached by cowboys on horseback, cattle sometimes chased children on foot with harmful intent, especially if the children found themselves between a cow and her calf or an aggressive bull. Texanna learned to stand perfectly still to avoid spooking the cattle until they lost interest in her.

She could also listen for the blast of the stagecoach horn as it thundered wildly into town to aid her sense of direction. One man recalled, "As often as not, the mules hitched to a stagecoach were as wild as the prairie flower and about as gentle as a wildcat with the toothache." Wild mules were mixed in with tame ones to make two or three spans. When the stagecoach took off from a station in a cloud of dust, the passengers had to hold on for dear life with the wild mules kicking, pitching, and running like the devil. Stages tended to use mules because no self-respecting Comanche would ride the darn things, and teams could be turned loose during the night without fear of the Indians running off with them. Stages roared into settlements at full speed, whip cracking, passengers waving handkerchiefs, and the driver shouting. Folks gathered to watch the spectacle of teams reined to a stop on their hind legs, rearing and plunging.

Texanna might have been invited to parties with girls from town, all dressed in their finest frocks with ribbons tying back their long ringlets. More likely, she was needed at home. She washed her father's and brother's clothes whenever enough water had collected in the rain barrel or well. After being worn for a week or two, their clothes became stiff with sweat and dust, making them heavy and awkward to wash. She loosened the caked-on dirt on a rough washboard in a wooden tub before laundering the wet garments in a large kettle over a fire. The clothes were rinsed and dried on a clothesline or tree branches. A simple bar of soap required hours of hard work. If the hogs didn't fatten enough to produce soap grease, she had to gather dry cattle bones, place them in a big kettle with lye, and, after boiling for a long time, secure a quantity of good, clean grease. By adding more lye to the grease, she could make decent soap. Everyone had ash hoppers, short logs hewn into troughs with holes drilled in the bottom, or large V-shaped boxes for making lye. Water was poured over ashes, preferably oak, every few days, and stirred. Folks expecting trouble kept a pot of lye behind the door; as a weapon, it could be as deadly as a gun, causing horrible, deep-pitted flesh wounds.

Bonnie, Texanna's daughter in the Oregon Cascades, 1907.

Men wore sweat-stained vests over loose-fitting shirts and pants made from wool, buckskin, or denim, over ankle-length drawers closed in the front with buttons. Rough buckskin, when made into pants and shirts, stained easily and was prone to shrinking if dried too quickly. If her father's buckskins got wet, he had to endure the discomfort and wear them until they dried, or he would never be able to get them on again. By the mid-1870s, the Levi Strauss Company made popular copper-riveted, rugged blue denim pants. All men wore hats and held up their pants with wide leather belts. Hat styles varied from broad-brimmed "slouch" hats to bowlers and derby hats. In Texas, a broad-brimmed hat adapted from the Mexican sombrero protected Texans' faces and shaded their eyes from the glaring sun. Summer hats were woven from corn shucks or wheat straw, while old jeans were made into winter head coverings.

When the dogs started barking, Texanna may have peeked out the cabin's doorway to see horses approaching, ridden by dusty, bearded men. Grabbing a gun that hung from pegs, she would have known how to use it to protect herself. Ammunition was scarce, so she had been taught to aim well. Her daughter, Bonnie, was a good shot with her .22 rifle and once shot a wolverine in Oregon. But perhaps this time, Texanna saw her father greeting the riders, and she relaxed, lowering the gun.

After Barch sold his land in Henderson County in 1870, he probably moved to Plano, Collin County, where he died before January 1, 1875, near his original land grant and people with whom he was related by history and kinship. A granddaughter, Maude Cantrell Bounds, age 91, reported in 1973 that Barch owned property in Collin County, where he died. It is believed he was buried in Plano's Old City Cemetery, a graveyard initially part of the Peters Colony Grant of Joseph Klepper and adjacent to the Methodist Church. The records were lost when a tornado destroyed the church on April 30, 1880. Other Colonists buried in the same cemetery include William Beverly, his son Reverend John Beverly (who officiated at Mary Jane's wedding), R.H. Brown, Joseph Klepper, and Fountain Vance, all of whom were possibly related or old neighbors from Illinois and Tennessee.

Using scattered land records from early Texas as sources, Barch lived in northern Dallas County, then moved southeast to Anderson County, and then to Parker County, west of Dallas. He may have lived in Collin County when Texanna was born, then moved to Johnson County, and returned to Collin County when his oldest daughter married. Next, he moved to Brazos County, then to Henderson County in 1870 with at least two of his children, Texanna and William, ultimately returning to Collin County. These Texas counties surround the city of Dallas, part of the Dallas-Fort Worth Metroplex (commonly referred to as the Metroplex), which is the economic and cultural hub of North Central Texas, boasting a population of over seven million.

Despite all his efforts, Barch never improved his economic condition. He may have helped break an unforgiving land for settlement, but he paid a heavy price, never rising above poor Whites on the Texas frontier. He probably saw himself as equal to any man and might have looked down on working for wages or being another man's tenant. That pride may have kept him poor, working harder and gaining less with a rifle or a plow than others.

1875 Court Cases

In July 1875, Barch's children gathered at the office of Ira C. Mitchell, an attorney in Plano, Texas, to pursue two cases. The first case involved the children from his first marriage who had "lawfully seized and possessed" their father's Peters Colony homestead in January. The current residents had ejected them. The plaintiffs were the heirs of the late Barch Cantrell and the late Nancy Ann Cantrell. J.E. and Mary Jane Blackburn, T.H. Cantrell, William A. Cantrell, Z.R. and Charlsilla Roberts, and George Cantrell sought $20,000 in damages and title to the land. All lived in Collin County except for William, who resided in Dallas County, and George, who lived in Parker County. The land in question was 557 acres, issued to Barch Cantrell by Peters Colony, certificate #433, located in Section 9, Township 2N, Range 2E, on the headwaters of Duck Creek in the northern part of Dallas County.

The defendants were David Bowser, Peter Sandifer, T. J. Malone, Mrs. Mary C. Drake, Samuel Drake, Susan Drake, Montgomery Drake, Robert Drake, and Josephine Parks, formerly Drake (wife of Henry Parks). They lived in Dallas County, except for Samuel and Josephine Parks, who resided in Limestone County. Mary Drake was the widow of George W. Drake, who owned 178 acres on Rowlett's Creek and a 360-acre homestead on Duck Creek, part of Barch's original grant. The Drakes and their neighbors all ran profitable farms for at least a decade, partially carved from Barch's original Peters Colony grant: Mary Drake (360 acres), David Bowser (160 acres), Peter Sandifer (207 acres), and Thomas Malone (119 acres). Mary Drake's was especially profitable. She had petitioned the court in September 1869 for the return of her husband's property after his death: 26 stock horses, 6 work horses, 2 unbroke mules, 23 stock cattle, 13 head sheep, 11 head hogs, wagon, buggy, farm equipment, and household furniture.[78] The defendants received a summons to appear in court on October 1, 1875. Through their attorneys, Peter Sandifer, Mrs. Mary Drake, and her children, Josephine Parks, Susan Drake, and Montgomery Drake, claimed there wasn't enough legal framework to require them to respond. The court ruled against the plaintiffs, Barch and Nancy's children. Texanna's half-siblings were ordered to pay court fees, which increased over time: $40.05 on May 16, 1878; $41.95 on July 12, 1878; and $43.45 on July 29, 1879. They dropped their suit on April 13, 1878.[79] It's hard to understand why Barch's children trespassed on land their father sold years earlier, thinking it still belonged to them.

In the second case, Barch's children, including Texanna, wanted to sell their father's property in Brazos County. Specifically listed (with the following spellings) were: J. E. Blackburn and Mary Jane Blackburn, his wife formerly Mary Jane Cantrell; Tigheman H. Cantrell; William Alexander Cantrell; Z.R. Roberts and Charlsilla Elizabeth Roberts, formerly Charlsilla Elizabeth Cantrell; George Carter Cantrell; children and heirs of Baurch Cantrell, late of Collin County, State of Texas, deceased, and Nancy Ann Cantrell, deceased, the first wife of said Burch Cantrell. Included was Texas Cantrell, the only child of Baurch Cantrell by his second and last wife, Margaret Cantrell, who was also deceased. All six of Barch's children signed a power of attorney; Mary Jane and Texanna signed with an "X." This case was more successful. Tillman went to Brazos County and sold their father's property to two men for $200, to be split equally among the six children.[80]

This court case was the first and only mention of Margaret, Texanna's mother. It also helped narrow down the date of her father's death in Collin County. After his death, Texanna probably lived with her half-sisters. Mary Jane and James Blackburn's first four children were born in Plano, with a brief move to Dallas County in between. By 1880, they had six children and were living in Cooke County. Texanna's other half-sister, Charlsilla Elizabeth (Ella), lived in Plano with her husband, Zachariah Roberts, who worked as a miller. Ella was only 16 when she married 24-year-old Zach. Their assets decreased with each new baby. According to Collin County tax records, they started their married life on a half-acre lot worth $300, which they bought from Joe Klepper. The next year, they owned a $60 wagon, three horses, four cattle, and $140 worth of miscellaneous property. In 1880, they lived next to Thomas Blalack, owner of Plano's Mill and Gin on Mechanic Street, where he and Zack worked as millers amid the noise, dust, and debris. Mechanic Street was once a footpath between the original boundaries of Joe Klepper's land grant and Sanford Beck's, who were old neighbors of their father in Illinois. Charlsilla Elizabeth had several variations of her name, just as Texanna did. She was identified as Elizabeth, Ella, Charles Elizabeth, Charles Ella, and even Charity.

Ella wasn't satisfied with the outcome of the 1875 case regarding the 557 acres she believed still belonged to her father. In another decade, she will go back to court and challenge the ownership of the 83-acre parcel of the Baurch Cantrell Survey three miles from the Dallas County Courthouse. This time, her siblings won't join her.

In 1880, five years after the court cases, Texanna's half-brother, Tillman, was 29, single, and herding cattle for John Ligon in Stephens County; William was 27 and married, with three stepdaughters and a daughter of his own in Dallas County. George, only two years older than Texanna, lived in Parker County in 1875 and remained there for the rest of his life. As Barch's only unmarried daughter, she was free from the responsibility of caring for her father, but how would she support herself?

Approximately 12 percent of women in Texas were employed in 1880, mostly in agriculture, followed by domestic work and teaching. The remaining minority were laborers, dressmakers, hotel or restaurant workers, or boarding-house owners. There were 5,000 laundresses, the majority of whom were African American. One option for 19-year-old Texanna was to teach school in Plano. Considering that her father and four of her half-siblings were illiterate, her educational status was uncertain. Only the youngest children, George and Texanna, were reported on the census as able to read and write. A Cantrell cousin in Anderson County finally learned his letters by attending school with his son.

Maybe Texanna owned a farm, which seems even less likely. During the Texas homesteading period from 1845 to 1898, men became homesteaders, with women supporting them. But a few brave or desperate women homesteaded alone. Not Texanna. That would have created such a family story that it would have been passed down and shared repeatedly.

A saddle horse would have allowed her to visit relatives and neighbors for Sunday dinner after church, giving her some independence. Nearly all women in Texas were skilled riders. Respectable women rode sidesaddle, slipping a leg over the horn's prong to avoid tangling in their voluminous skirts while keeping their ankles covered. Women who defied convention wore their husbands' jeans or overalls and rode astride.

Traveling by train to Dallas—or anywhere—without an escort required courage. Worries about Texanna's moral purity, fueled by fear of being approached by drunken cowboys, outlaws, rowdy locals, or other troublemakers, probably kept her close to home despite lawmen with six-shooters on their hips. In the 1880s, public intoxication was the leading cause of arrests in Plano, resulting in a $2.00 fine plus a $1.00 marshal fee. Fewer arrests were made for disturbing the peace (like using obscene language or shouting within town limits), assault and battery, fighting, public prostitution, or firing Roman candles.

In March 1880, citizens of Plano organized a Temperance Society to protest saloons that offered gambling, drinking, and occasionally a dance hall girl or two. Most saloons had a pool table, a few stools, tables, chairs, and swinging coal-oil lamps that lit the bar. Customers enjoyed whiskey in various flavors, including white corn, bourbon, and sour mash. Fruit brandy, wine, and absinthe could also be sipped. A cigar paired well with a glass of Old Tom Gin. Beer was scarce. Keeping it cold was difficult to prevent it from going flat.

Men might drink, gamble, or sit at the train depot gossiping and wear the same suit year after year, but women needed a dress to wear and a dress to wash. Texanna probably had an everyday calico dress and a nicer dress for church and parties, along with aprons, two petticoats trimmed with lace at the hem, a chemise, a shawl, one bonnet, and a straw hat. She may have purchased a corset she saw advertised in the Fort Worth Daily Democrat. She could dream of a new bonnet, but she could embellish her old one with flowers, feathers, beads, ribbons of velvet, silk, or satin, or even paper birds. A breast pin, ear drops, a lace or linen collar, and gloves made from cotton, kid leather, or silk could complete her ensemble. A box of hairpins helped secure her long hair coiled into a loose bun at the nape of her neck. Hair was styled using crimpers or curling irons warmed on the stove or over a lamp chimney. Crimpers created a shallow wave; curling irons produced a tight wave. Short hair was considered a disgrace. Smoothing buttermilk on her face at night was believed to lighten any suntan that crept past her bonnet brim. Faces painted with cosmetics were judged too risqué for backwater evangelical churches and conservative little towns. Long skirts were cumbersome but expected, reflecting strong notions about what was fitting for women.

Weaving cloth was a particularly labor-intensive task. All women learned to card and spin when they were girls. Before gin mills were established, women and children piled a large heap of cotton by the fire to warm before picking out the seeds. Two "carders," made of wood thick enough to hold metal teeth, about nine inches long and three inches wide, broke down wool or cotton fibers until they resembled cobwebs. This was spun on the spinning wheel and wound onto bobbins. The yarn, dyed with moss, minerals, berries, or nuts, was used to knit socks and stockings for the family or woven on a loom to create new dresses and underclothes. Women spent each day weaving and every night knitting. Buying a bolt of calico at the local mercantile was far easier.

Texanna would have understood the difference between utilitarian and decorative sewing. A simple everyday dress with a long, full skirt, whether attached to the bodice or made separately, became more feminine with the addition of fancy stitches or lace. Middle- and upper-class women were encouraged to engage in intricate needlework as a symbol of their leisurely status and were judged based on their ability to produce tiny stitches. Hand-sewing a dress from eight yards of calico (a plain cotton printed fabric favored for its practicality and comfort) or linsey-woolsey (which many women found coarse and heavy) took two weeks. Fine cotton muslin or imported silk became available only after the railroad system was established in the post-Civil War era. One woman wrote in her diary in 1871 that she had made 115 garments for the year (shirts, pants, dresses, underskirts, drawers, chemises, and other clothing), knitted 12 pairs of socks and stockings, pieced and quilted three quilts, cut rags for 20 yards of carpet, and patched a lot while giving thanks to the Good Lord in his wisdom and mercy. She also wrote that she hired Blacks to help with housework and cooking.

Quilt pieces came from old clothes and fabric scraps collected throughout the year. Popular patterns included Log Cabin, Lone

Star, Texas Tears, and Texas Sunshine. Sugar or "Bull Durham" sacks were torn apart and sewn together to hold carded cotton for batting. Neighbors gathered to hand quilt on a frame that could be lowered from the ceiling and pulled back up when not in use. The host provided dinner for everyone. With many hands working, three or four quilts could be finished in a day. Texanna's daughter, my grandma, found a dead sheep near her front gate and insisted that the wool not be wasted despite my dad's objections. She cut off the wool with scissors and carded it for quilt batting, making quilts for many of her grandchildren. Sixty years later, my sister-in-law reused the wool batting from their quilt to make pincushions for the women in the family.

No matter where she lived or with whom, Texanna wasn't idle. Kerosene lamps, brighter than candles, helped her see at night to mend and knit. Meals were prepared daily, with bread and pies baked for the week, and food preserved for winter by canning and drying. The smokehouse had to be kept clean, and oh, keep those mangy dogs and pesky peddlers out of the house. The sheep were sheared in May, wheat was cut in June, ears of corn roasted in July, peaches dried in August, cotton picked in the fall, pecans gathered in October, and the first hard frost signaled hog-killin' time. An immense log fire was built to heat water in a large barrel. Hogs were killed and "stuck" (bled by sticking long knives down the throat). Two strong men would plunge each hog into the barrel of boiling water, twisting and turning it until the hair would "slip". The carcass was removed, cut, washed, and scraped down. The entrails were removed, and once cooled, the carcass was cut into pieces for hams, shoulders, and middlings. Fat was rendered and stewed into lard or made into soap. The cracklings from the fat were considered a delicacy and relished by all. Children competed for the hog bladder, blowing it up with air and tying it so the air wouldn't escape. The bladder was saved to be popped at Christmas, making a loud noise.

By December 1880, Plano had shipped 3,000 bales of cotton by rail, and the streets were filled with wagons waiting to unload. The town expected to ship a record 4,000 bales of cotton. The Methodist Episcopal Church had a Christmas tree, and the newspaper published a lengthy list of lost and found horses and mules: one flea-bitten roan mare, 4 or 5 years old; a black mare, ten years old, branded 4J on her left hip and shoulder, and wearing a bell; and one dark bay stud colt, with no brands.

A fire destroyed over 50 buildings in Plano on August 27, 1881, resulting in the loss of many court records. The town was rebuilt, adding boardwalks that allowed Texanna to run errands without trudging through mud and manure. A new city ordinance prohibited cowhands from riding their horses and merchants from displaying wares on the boardwalks. Texanna could buy household items from the general store, including brooms, wash basins, washboards, blacking, bottles of bluing, cakes of soap, and clothespins, as well as tins of oysters, salmon, mackerel, and sardines, along with a required bottle of pepper sauce. There were gallons of molasses and vinegar for sale, along with ginger schnapps, parched coffee, tea, crackers, ground allspice, pickles, sulfur matches, beans, rice, cans of blackberries, peaches, cherries, and baking powder—not to mention wax dolls and candy for the children. The store stocked tin plates, cigars, snuff, pistols, tobacco knives, butcher knives, pocketknives, tape measures, steel pens, slate pencils, spectacle cases, and shaving brushes and razors. For ladies, calico and gingham dress goods were offered alongside fancy hats or bonnets. Furniture and hardware were rarely sold, as men made their own. Guns and ammunition filled one store counter, although farm families almost always owned an old percussion rifle or shotgun for which they crafted their own bullets. There were even harmonicas. Old men huddled around the woodstove or leaned on the porch railing, spitting tobacco juice and sharing minor incidents that turned into tales to be told slowly and savored. Time seemed endless, and stories continued without end.

Churches emerged in postwar Texas as the most significant cultural and social influence. Families of different faiths traveled 50 miles to revival meetings in wagons loaded with provisions, quilts, lanterns, dogs, and children, with the milk cow tied behind, to praise the Lord and hear fine gospel singing. Local members hosted a big barbecue on Friday night, and afterward everyone slept in their wagons or on the ground. Women and girls, craving female companionship, gossiped while men discussed crops and politics, leaving their guns stacked against tree trunks. Dressed in their Sunday best, they listened to a harsh, unforgiving Christianity characterized by hellfire-and-brimstone sermons that set moral standards for the community. To make up for the lack of hymn books, the preacher read two lines of a hymn for the congregation to sing. When a sinner came to Jesus, loved ones echoed the joy of his salvation, and soon, everyone was shouting and singing.

The famous Texas barbecues that started at revival meetings became a tradition for Fourth of July celebrations, often held in the courthouse square. Ranchers donated fat calves, and women shared their best recipes. Large communities added a brass band, dancing, horse racing, shooting contests, and pink lemonade. Folks shot off Roman candles and celebrated with a double blast from the old shotgun.

The threat of Indian raids diminished. The U.S. government made efforts to relocate all Indians from Texas to designated reservations in Indian Territory. In response, Indians raided south into Texas, fighting for their freedom and way of life. The state legislature authorized a militia company in each county to defend against "the invasion of hostile Indians, or other marauding or thieving parties." Texanna's uncle, Hazel Green Cantrell, and two of his sons, aged 19 and 23, enlisted in what was known as the Indian Wars, serving to protect the frontier for White settlers. They served for 90 days between September 10, 1872, and August 18, 1873, in Company P, Minute Men of Parker County. Upon reenlisting, they served an additional 90 days, from December 24, 1873, to March 29, 1874. Hazel Green served as a sergeant. One Comanche raid reached as far as Veal Station on August 16, 1874, where a White man was killed. Two more Whites were killed on the Weatherford and Jacksboro Road. Whites chased Indians to the Red River, the southern boundary of Indian Territory, but it was illegal to pursue them further. Ironically, it was also unlawful for Indians to plunder and raid Texas. In the end, however, Indian resistance on the frontier became a grim record of failure. Indians may have won battles, but ultimately lost the war, resulting in Whites taking their land and confining them to reservations.

On the Texas prairies, where bad news spread like chaff in the wind, Texanna probably heard about her cousins, Newt and Rube Cantrell, in Jack County. In April 1878, the brothers were arrested for carrying firearms and fined $25 plus court costs. Newton appealed, and his case was dismissed. But soon after, the brothers were caught with stolen cattle. The sheriff found them in the Corsicana, Texas, jail in August and shackled them together for the wagon ride home. The boys managed to escape.[81]

More sobering was the news of the murders of her uncle and cousin in Parker County in 1881. Hazel Green Cantrell, nicknamed Doc, had been involved in the second court case of the new Parker County, Dr. H.G. Cantrell vs. William Reynolds. Reynolds sought damages for Doc killing his son. Thirty years later, Doc had built a thriving ranch with cattle, 30 hogs, 18 horses, 30 chickens, and an orchard of 60 peach trees. He grew Indian corn, oats, and wheat, harvesting 25 bushels of Irish potatoes and 25 bushels of sweet potatoes from 230 acres. With his sons' help, he had cut and stacked 15 cords of firewood for the winter. But the family, like most Texans, was never far from their guns. On September 13, 1881, Doc and his oldest son were shot and killed, while his youngest son, Hazel Grant, was wounded on their farm on Silver Creek, fifteen miles northeast of Weatherford. J.W. Cox had rented a field from Doc to grow corn, but argued about the rent. Doc Cantrell, his two sons, and four hired men began gathering the corn Cox had planted. Objecting, Cox took his Winchester rifle and a double-barreled shotgun and went to the field. He asked if they had the authority to gather his corn. A son replied, "We have." Cox then demanded the authority, and the oldest son, William, raised his gun and fired, striking Cox in the shoulder, neck, and near his left ear. Cox returned fire twice, hitting both times, the last shot causing William's instant death. Doc Cantrell rushed to his fallen son for his gun when Cox fired his Winchester twice again, missing with the first shot but killing the old man instantly with the second. The four hired men ran off immediately. Cox's wounds were severe but not considered dangerous. He sent word to the sheriff, who immediately set out. Of the dead, Doc Cantrell, a well-known citizen of Parker County, was about 65 years old, and his son was nearly 30. Their most significant fault was an inclination to disregard their neighbors' rights, preferring "might to right." Cox had been in the country for less than 3 years, was about 35 years old, and had no family. The affair was deeply regretted.

The reporter had just written this when a friend of the Cantrells rushed in to report the Cantrells' side of the incident. According to the friend, Cox went to the field armed and began cursing and abusing Cantrells. They feared an attack and, being unarmed, did nothing to provoke him. The oldest son went home for his gun, and upon his return, Cox fired, striking him in the right shoulder. He returned fire. Cox's second shot struck him in the heart and head, killing him instantly. Doc Cantrell then ran to his son and, while turning him over, was shot in the shoulder by Cox. As he turned to run, Cox shot again, the bullet passing through his body and coming out at his stomach.

Cantrell's youngest son, fifteen-year-old Bud, died three months later, on December 26, 1881. Their killer, Joe Cox, immediately turned himself in, but a grand jury failed to find sufficient cause. Released on a writ of habeas corpus, Cox left the state. But the grand jury reconvened, charging Cox with two counts of murder: one for killing H.G. Cantrell and the other for killing his son, William. Cox was arrested in September 1884 in Delta County, Texas, by the Parker County Sheriff and brought back to Weatherford. In February 1885, the district court declared a mistrial; four jurors voted for conviction and eight for acquittal. Cox remained in jail until that fall, when he was released on bail to cheering, sympathetic citizens who believed the Cantrells' killings were acts of self-defense. Almost everyone who knew the circumstances thought the killings were perfectly justifiable.[82] Cox was considered a hero.

Texanna's uncle left behind a wife and five children. Doc's oldest son, who was also killed, lived on an adjoining farm and left a pregnant wife and baby. Hazel Green (Doc) and his sons William and Hazel Grant (Bud) were buried in the Veal Station Cemetery beside his daughter Margaret (who had died in 1876 at the age of 18), the same cemetery as Barch's first wife, Nancy. Doc's widow, Cynthia, asked the court to appoint appraisers for his estate, despite her inability to read or write. Her oldest surviving son, Cicero Marion, purchased their homestead on Silver Creek from his mother and three married sisters. He later sold this land in May 1884 to a cousin for $900, including $600 in cash and a $300 note due in October after the harvest.

After the murders, Texanna's aunt moved to Jack County, Texas, and stubbornly fought for what was hers. With her son, Cicero, she became embroiled in a long-running court battle over the ownership of a cow held as collateral for an alleged debt. The case of Cintha Cantrell vs. J.W. Motley and L.L. Picket of Jack County was brought before the Justice of the Peace, who dismissed it. She appealed the case to the County Court, which denied it, and subsequently to the Texas Supreme Court.[83] After enduring the violence of Parker County for twenty-five years, Cynthia spent her final years with her oldest daughter in Comanche, Stephens County, Oklahoma, far from the memories of Parker County, Texas.

Texanna's relationship with her half-sisters remained close. However, it's impossible to determine her relationship with her Cantrell cousins or even her half-brothers. Her half-brother, William, married a widow four years his senior with three daughters in 1877. Before their marriage, his wife had signed a promissory note for $125 as partial payment on

50 acres in Dallas County. She was unable to pay the note. Combined with court costs, the $125 grew to $197.25. The court issued an Order for Sale in July 1880. The property sold for $210.50 at the courthouse door to the highest bidder.[84] In a second case, William asked the court for permission to sell property belonging to his three stepdaughters, as they had no personal property or income other than five pieces of land inherited from their father, valued at $489 in 1883. William submitted undocumented expenses of $545 for tuition, clothing, food, and his labor costs for fencing a 14-acre tract and digging a well. He told the court that he planned to move to Duck Creek in Dallas County for better schools and opportunities for his stepdaughters and his own three children.[85] After living in Tarrant County, Texas, for 45 years, he passed away there in 1936.

Texanna's half-brother, Tillman, herded cattle in Stephens County until he bought a 40-acre ranch, where he kept two horses, four cattle, and attempted to raise hogs, but was also delinquent on his taxes. He married in 1881 and died five years later at age 35, leaving a wife and two young children, aged two and four. He was buried in Gunsight Cemetery in Stephens County, Texas. Their youngest brother, George Washington Cantrell, who was never found on a U.S. census until the 1910 Parker County Census, became a farmer, married, and had four sons and two daughters. After he died in 1944, he was buried in Peaster Cemetery near Weatherford, Texas.

Marriage

Lively jigs and four-handed reels were popular for courting when not forbidden by religious scruples, especially by Baptists, who frowned upon dancing. People traveled fifty miles to attend a dance in a large room above the livery stable or in a courtroom with all the chairs removed, the floor swept, the dogs chased out, and a bottle passed around discreetly. Local musicians were eager to play the fiddle, harmonica, Jew's harp, banjo, or whatever instrument was available. They played tunes like "Sallie Goodin," "Cotton Eye Joe," "Mississippi Sawyer," "Hell Broke Loose in Georgia," "Soap Suds Over the Fence," and "Arkansas Traveler." If a fiddler wasn't available, couples made music by clapping a rhythm to their dance steps. At dawn, everyone walked home or rode horseback.

The entire community eagerly watched the bidding at box socials. Young women spent weeks planning and decorating boxes filled with fried chicken, pickled peaches, deviled eggs, fancy cakes, and pies. Men placed bids on the boxes, and the winner got to have a meal with the young lady. Spelling contests, picnics, debates, and Shakespeare readings offered more entertainment, which, like dancing, often ended with singing hymns and ballads. The Farmers' Wives Society requested women wear simple home dresses to ensure performances at the Gainesville Opera House wouldn't become advertisements for the latest fashions.

Texanna, who called herself Texa, was approaching 24 years of age. She married Franklin Pierce Heare in Gainesville, Cooke County, Texas, on May 22, 1884. Franklin Pierce (Frank or F.P.) was a 30-year-old importer and breeder of Norman horses. Frank enjoyed an excellent reputation in the community and was well-educated. Perhaps Texanna met Frank at a taffy-pulling party, or enjoyed a buggy ride with her beau for an afternoon picnic or one in the moonlight. Frank did not enjoy robust health, but Texanna was not deterred. And as it turned out, neither one was particularly healthy.

Texanna wore her best dress on her wedding day. She became Mrs. Franklin Pierce Heare, probably in Mary Jane's parlor, with her nieces and nephews peeking around the corner at their aunt all dressed up, nervously smoothing her hair and smiling shyly. Vows could be exchanged on the front porch if the house couldn't hold all the guests. Or they could have had a buggy wedding, where Frank and Texanna sat in a buggy with their friends standing nearby, allowing the happy couple to drive away immediately after the ceremony.

Mary Jane's brother-in-law, Reverend M.C. (Melville Campbell) Blackburn, officiated the ceremony. Like his father, he was a Methodist circuit-riding preacher. This also marked the last time in Texanna's life that she would be formally addressed by her first name or her maiden name, Cantrell. From then on, she was known as Mrs. Frank Heare; her identity shaped by her husband's life, career, hardships, and pleasures.

Franklin Pierce Heare was the grandson of a Presbyterian Scotch-Irish immigrant from Ireland. Adam Heare arrived in 1776 at the age of 16, and today, "Adam Heare" is inscribed on the Wall of Honor at the Ellis Island National Museum of Immigration.[86] Adam married Margaret Todd (purported to be related to Mary Todd Lincoln, the wife of Abraham Lincoln). They raised their family of seven children in Hampshire County, Virginia, which became part of West Virginia during the Civil War. Their youngest son, John Lyle Heare, became a blacksmith in Hampshire County and had ten children with Eliza Ann Powelson, a descendant of Dutch settlers from colonial New York and New Jersey.[87] John Lyle died from pneumonia, likely exacerbated by the fumes from his forge, when his youngest child, Frank, was just a year old.

After his father's death, Frank's mother and his oldest sister, who was also a widow, loaded their children and belongings into two wagons and moved to Illinois to join Frank's oldest brother, James Todd Heare, who worked as a blacksmith like their father. Frank grew up in Mercer County, Illinois, near the Mississippi River. As he got older, he bred Norman horses to sell in Gainesville, Texas, in Cooke County. The demand for Normans exceeded the supply, making them undoubtedly the most profitable stock to raise. The large, strong horses were ready for light farm work by two years of age. By the time they reached 4 or 5 years old, they were well-prepared for more challenging tasks.

In 1875, at the age of 21, he lived near Gainesville with two brothers. John William, 38, was married with three children, and Lewis Cass, 27, got married that summer. John owned four horses valued at $160 and four cattle worth $20; Lewis had two horses worth $75 and two cows valued at $40; and Frank had two horses appraised at $200. Frank's horses were likely Normans, as they were far more valuable than his brothers' horses. The next year, Frank sold 160 acres for $480, located about 12 miles southwest of Gainesville, after signing a quitclaim deed for the property the year before. He may also have purchased two parcels of land totaling 178 acres in Grayson County, located east of Cooke County, as evidenced by his $8.20 tax payment. In 1880, he briefly returned to Illinois to live with his mother and raise more Norman horses for the Texas market. A neighbor Texan advertised a horse for sale in 1890, stating, "I have Ned French for sale, the noted draft stallion brought from Illinois by Frank Heare. He has proved himself to be one of the greatest breeders of any horse that has ever been in this country."[88]

A third brother, Isaac Wesley (Ike), settled near Gainesville and married in 1873. By 1879, he owned 185 acres, six horses, a dozen cows, and a wagon. Sadly, Ike died in 1883 at the age of 39 from typhoid. Brother John moved to Livingston County, Missouri, while Lewis Cass (L.C.) headed to the arid region of west Texas, where he eventually became the first judge of Wilbarger County. Frank's eight surviving siblings and a brother-in-law spread out across the country in Oregon, Iowa, Illinois, Missouri, and Texas. They shared Ike's estate of 185 acres, each receiving $100 from the buyer, Dr. G.L. Spurlock, in 1889, who married Ike's widow in 1885.[89]

Gainesville, flanked by the Chisholm Trail, became the financial capital of several counties across North Central Texas as a cattle town and an excellent horse market. Located seven miles south of the Red River and seventy-one miles north of Dallas, Gainesville served as a supply point for cowboys herding cattle north to Kansas. Hotels catered to cattle owners and buyers who exchanged vast sums of money for cattle and grazing rights. Cattle money generated tax revenue to fund a new county courthouse in 1878 and support for local schools and public roads. But cattle drives also brought endless lines of bellowing, bawling longhorns and their rowdy drivers, who were hot, tired, thirsty, and on the lookout for poker games, whiskey, and barroom girls (the soiled doves).

Barbed wire, windmills, and railroads changed all of this. Barbed wire, also known as the Devil's Hatband, was initially distributed by merchants in Gainesville and Sherman in 1875, sparking a debate over barbed wire versus free grass. Over the next decade, this controversial wire transformed the open prairies of North Texas into fields, enclosing most of the grazing land and forever changing stock raising and farming. Fence-cutting became so problematic that the Texas Legislature passed a law in 1884 that made it a felony. While barbed wire revolutionized grazing practices, windmills pumped water from underground, converting inhospitable land into fertile farmland and attracting more settlers.

Railroads could establish a town, prompt a town to relocate, or destroy a town, depending on where the tracks were laid. They transported crops, supplies, and mail more efficiently and at a lower cost than freight wagons, which were slowed by muddy roads in winter, dust in summer, and delays caused by poorly constructed bridges. Relatives in the east received letters by rail more quickly; letters expressing gratitude for God's blessings and good health, along with descriptions of the country, crop updates, water availability, and family news. Shadowing the tracks were telegraph poles strung with wire.

On November 7, 1879, people from all corners of the county gathered to witness the arrival of the first smoking, screaming, fire-belching locomotive in Gainesville, complete with its large cowcatcher. By 1890, Gainesville had seven trains running daily. Frank and Texanna could have purchased a round-trip ticket to Fort Worth for $1.95 per person, provided they returned the same day. Elegant Pullman sleeping cars with comfortable reclining seats were available for longer trips to destinations such as Kansas City, St. Louis, and Chicago. Nearly every train had a smoking car for the enjoyment of male passengers. The ladies' car allowed women traveling alone to avoid mixed—and occasionally bothersome—company.

Train depots were loud, bustling places, filled with milling wagons and buggies pulled by skittish horses, boys running about, women in silk dresses with large hats shading their faces, and men dressed in wool suits or long, dusty coats. Drovers snapped long whips to load cattle and horses into livestock cars from pens near the station. Country folks gawked at sights they had never imagined. In small towns, the depot became the main entertainment with the arrival of the train. It was the gathering place and social center where friends and family would meet, look over the peddlers and drummers with their large suitcases of new items for merchants, gossip about new arrivals, and exchange the latest news.

The Gainesville newspaper reported on the progress of a new horse racing track that promised a $3,000 purse. Texans had a particular passion for horse racing, with every village and town boasting a racetrack. The U.S. government was purchasing cavalry horses aged 4 to 8 years; no painted, white, dun, or light-gray horses accepted. The Red River had ice thick enough for a team and a heavily loaded wagon to cross. A cattleman reported seeing 15 wolves gnawing on a cow carcass that had frozen to death. A man fell on the ice and broke his leg below the knee. Another Gainesville citizen fell, striking his head on some building stones. Initially reported dead, he was later confirmed to be alive but gravely injured. The Knights of Pythias hosted a grand ball and banquet, a funeral was held for a Presbyterian minister, and a merchant was dangerously ill with typhoid. The mayor, serving as judge, fined several "drunk and troublesome" cowboys $10.70 for riding too fast. A Gainesville man was held up by two men who robbed him of his money. The robbers had six shooters and wore handkerchiefs over their faces. The police officers who pursued them had a good idea of their identities.[90]

The Deputy Marshal was on the lookout for train robbers, and the chain gang was producing effective labor. The court docket listed arrests for selling liquor to minors or for selling liquor on Sundays. Arrests were also made for vagrancy, maintaining a disorderly house (commonly known as a brothel), aggravated assault, cattle theft, burglary, and carrying a pistol. John Wilson, a prisoner in the Gainesville jail, threw a paper of pepper into the jailer's eyes and attempted to escape. Although blinded, the jailer pulled his pistol and fired in Wilson's direction with such accuracy that the fleeing man fell with a bullet through his heart.[91]

Children

Frank and Texanna welcomed their first child, Bonnie Nell Heare, on March 3, 1885. My grandmother wrote, "It must have been a dark and stormy day when I sent forth my wailing protests in the little log cabin on my Uncle Ike's farm." She recalled that three sides of the farm on Spring Creek were bordered by a young Osage orange hedge, which, by the time she turned 12, had joined the neighbor's hedge and created a cool, leafy tunnel for one-eighth of a mile. At the time of Bonnie's birth, Ike's widow owned 61 horses and acreage, offering an explanation why Frank and Texanna were living on Ike's farm after his death. Frank's sister-in-law needed help.

Five months later, Frank purchased 100 acres for $1,200, paying $200 in cash and issuing three promissory notes at 10 percent interest. The first note, due on January 15, 1886, was for $200; the second, for $400, was due a year later; and the third, also for $400, was due the following year. The notes were paid by January 31, 1891, when the seller, who lived in the Choctaw Nation, Indian Territory, canceled the lien. Frank owned a wagon valued at $40 and five horses appraised at $150. The next year, he paid taxes on eight horses, two cows, and a wagon appraised at $20. His farm was valued at $400 and doubled in value over the next six years. In 1887, he had four horses appraised at $60, a $10 cow, and a $50 mule, but the old wagon had depreciated to $10.

Their second child, Isaac Wesley Heare, was born on August 24, 1886, during threshing season on their 100-acre farm, two miles from where Bonnie was born. As Bonnie later described, "Ike checked in with baggage and two dogs in the old house on the place. His head was covered with red curls. The day after we threshed wheat." Bonnie got stuck under the old house while chasing a little dog. Her father had to lift the floorboards to get her and found a nest of eggs. She was also told she took her baby brother's bottle away from him in his cradle and hid under the bed to finish it.

Frank built a new house, painted white with brown trim, to replace the old one. The window shades featured a landscape pattern along the borders. Bonnie remembered sitting on the floor joists of the half-finished house, playing "church" and giggling behind her palm-leaf fan, just like she had seen older girls do. Across the flat prairie, she could see trains passing to the east, half a mile away. Beyond the wooden Elm Station, the eastern Cross Timbers stretched to the horizon. Three miles south, a few buildings in the town of Valley View were visible.

Lees had been the first White settlers in Valley View, part of the old Peters Colony. Mrs. Lee recounted, "There was not even a path, and the grass was as high as a man's head. Mr. Lee said we were coming to the frontier. I remarked that it looked very much like the back tier to me... no neighbors, no schools, no churches, no sustenance for soul or body, a veritable wilderness."[92] By 1881, Valley View had grown to about 250 residents, with three steam gristmills, cotton gins, and three general stores. The Gulf, Colorado, and Santa Fe Railway transported cotton, livestock, and wheat for local farmers. The first icehouse was built after the blizzard of 1889, when a lake froze solid enough to support a man on horseback. Mr. Lee had Negroes cut the ice into squares and store it in cottonseed hulls in a pit dug on the south side of the lake's bank.

To the west, the country was broken by Spring Creek and its tributaries, lined with timber. At least a dozen cattle rustlers were hanged from an old oak tree at Hangman's Grove, leading to the formation of the precursor to the Texas Cattle Raisers Association. To the north lay Gainesville, the commercial and railroad shipping hub for ranchers and farmers, nestled among shade trees. In 1888, the town featured a telegraph, telephones, gas heating, concrete sidewalks, and electric lighting. By 1890, Cooke County had a population of 25,000, along with 40,000 cattle, 14,000 horses and mules, and 15,000 hogs. The county also had 42,000 acres planted in corn, 21,000 acres in oats, and 37,000 acres in cotton, producing 24,000 bales.[93] Growth was, however, offset by the Panic of 1893, when 500 banks closed nationwide, 15,000 businesses failed, and many farms ceased operations.

Bonnie was allowed to carry a fancy bottle of vinegar when they moved into their new house, but she drank some on the way and had to be carried and laid on the sofa. She remembered crossing a river and seeing boats on the water in the spring when she traveled to Bonham, Texas, on the train with her mother and baby brother. When they returned home, they discovered Frank had shot a crow and hung it in the cherry tree. Laundry was taken to "Aunt Lina," a Negro woman. A girl from Valley View helped with the housework as her mother was not strong.

One Sunday, Frank took Texanna and the two children in their two-horse buggy to spend the day at Dr. Drayton's ranch, which was about three miles away. After dinner, Bonnie followed the big Drayton boys to the orchard, but they headed for the barn and didn't notice her. When it was time to go home, Bonnie couldn't be found. The men saddled their horses and searched the sprawling ranch. Her father rode toward Elm, a stream that flowed through the oak, hickory, and elm timber. He spotted a herd of cattle gathered around something. As he rode closer, he saw Bonnie's white head and heard her saying in a discouraged tone, "Go 'way tows." Once she was safely mounted in front of him on the horse, he asked her where she was going. "Home," she replied. By then, the sun had set, and the coyotes were yapping in the timber.

Frank renewed his subscription to the Gainesville Daily Hesperian newspaper for the 20th time in 1888, having been a subscriber for 19 years. When asked for his opinion on a political race between Davis and Bell (both running for the Texas State Senate), Frank was quoted as saying, "I live six miles south of town. I am for Davis. My impression is that Davis will carry my settlement." He was also called to serve on a jury in 1889. Of course, Texanna wasn't asked to serve on a jury or express her political opinion. She didn't have the right to vote, which wasn't a popular subject. The local chapter of the Texas Women's Christian Temperance Union became the first to endorse women's suffrage, but lost members because of its stance.

Texanna and Frank Heare welcomed their third child on October 31, 1889, in the new house on Heare Hill, naming her Texas Anna. They had named their son after Frank's brother, Issac Wesley. I would love to know if their oldest child, Bonnie Nell, was named for anyone, since I am named after her.

As Christmas 1889 approached, the newspaper advertised potted ham, deviled ham, and potted turkey for sale. An express wagon with four wheels, a very pretty toy for a child, was being given away with each purchase of a can of baking powder. Wool dress goods ranged from eight to ten cents per yard, but ready-made clothing was advertised as being just as good in quality as tailor-made. The new bookstore in town offered a complete set of classics, including works by William Shakespeare, George Eliot, Lord Alfred Tennyson, and Sir Walter Scott.

Frank took his family to a circus in Gainesville. Bonnie wore a bright red dress and told her daddy, "People will think I was afire," to which her daddy laughed. On Christmas morning, a small cedar tree stood on a stand, and under it was a doll in a buggy for Bonnie. The doll had a china head, hands, and feet with painted black hair. She named her Maggie.

Despite the season's festivities, the Heare house was quiet. Frank and Texanna were ill. A Heare cousin came down from Illinois to help. "Nigger Bill" was hired to do the outside work. He had to rescue Bonnie's two-year-old brother from wandering into the dangerous corral more than once. Bill claimed he caught the toddler hanging onto a wild horse's tail. Bonnie also recalled that Bill left the team and the wagon at the front of the house while he went to get the sideboards. The team spooked and ran away.

During their parents' illness, visitors described the children as naughty. Their daddy reassured them that they were good. However, Bonnie remembered hiding the rolling pin from the hired girl, who had to work without it. She showed a neighbor she liked where she had hidden it in the clothes closet. Bonnie and Ike did another disgraceful thing. "Brother and I were in our highchairs and reached into the rice dish with our hands. Of course, the grown folks at the table were shocked and tried to make us behave." Bonnie told her brother to throw his fork at one guest, and she threw her knife at another.

Bonnie remembered her mother lying in a high bed, covered with many quilts because she was so cold. Texanna passed away on February 7, 1890. Whether she had time to remind her children to be good, read the Bible, and resist temptation, words her mother may have whispered to her before dying, is unknown. "Mrs. Frank Heare died at her home, six miles south of Gainesville, last Friday of pneumonia, superinduced by La Grippe. The deceased leaves a devoted husband and two small children. The remains were interred in the Barnhart graveyard last Saturday."[94] Texanna was buried in the same cemetery as Frank's brother, Ike. Her obituary neglected to mention her three-month-old baby. Frank found himself widowed with three children: four-year-old Bonnie, three-year-old Ike, and the infant Texas Anna.

Texas reported hundreds of cases of La Grippe in 1890, also known as Russian influenza, similar to the Spanish flu epidemic of 1918–1919 and the COVID pandemic. The day after Texanna died, a minister in the eastern part of the county died of pneumonia caused by La Grippe.

Whether Texanna died from complications of childbirth or influenza, the Gainesville newspaper reported two weeks after her death: "We are glad that our friend Frank Heare has recovered from his recent illness. He leaves for Vernon, Wilbarger County," and an "Oklahoma Boomer" had returned and planned to rent Frank Heare's farm.[95]

After Texanna's mother died, Texanna was likely raised by her father with help from her older half-sisters. When Texanna died at age 29, her husband relied on his siblings to look after his children until he remarried five years later. Their daughter, Bonnie, left a written account of her first seven years. Frank's brother, Lewis Cass (L.C.), arrived shortly before her mother's death and took Bonnie west to his home in Vernon, Texas, two weeks later. They stayed overnight with a friend along the way. The first snow she ever saw covered the ground the next morning. The newspaper reported that the season's first genuine blizzard raged for 24 hours, damaging peaches and gardens. Bonnie was thrilled to find three little cousins to play with in her uncle's dugout. On her fifth birthday on March 3, her aunt baked her a cake, and they picked wild purple hollyhocks to decorate the center.

A friend of Texanna took the baby to her home in Ardmore, Chickasaw Nation, Indian Territory. The Atchison, Topeka, and Santa Fe Railway tracks ran north from Gainesville to Ardmore. To avoid hefty fines for bringing liquor into Indian Territory, Ardmore's upstanding citizens rode the train to Gainesville and returned with a bottle in a shoebox. On Sunday afternoons, town folk passed the time at the railroad station, counting debarking passengers carrying "Gainesville shoeboxes" under their arms.

After Frank's health improved, his sister, Mary, and his brother, L.C., helped Frank and his son move to Vernon to reunite with Bonnie. Frank traveled for several weeks through the Panhandle, into Indian Territory, and down to Grayson and Collin counties, likely searching for a home. A newspaper reported that Frank also shared his knowledge of the Hessian fly, a pest devastating wheat fields.[96] During his absence, Mary took Bonnie and Ike to her home in Graham, Young County, to pack up her household. They traveled part of the way by stagecoach. Bonnie remembered her first hotel lunch of hard-boiled eggs and dried figs. She thought Young County was the prettiest place in Texas, with beautiful mossy rocks and large oak and pecan trees. A neighbor boy showed Bonnie and her brother how to step on young thistles barefoot without getting hurt. Bonnie, following Mary to the attic to pack belongings, dove to one side to investigate something fascinating, and fell through the paper ceiling, narrowly missing the corner of the marble-topped dresser below. Her alarmed aunt hurried down the outside ladder, fearing Bonnie had been killed.

Bonnie had no memory of how they returned to Vernon, but she discovered that her father had purchased a house near the grain elevators and a wagon yard uptown. Mary's husband, Walter, found a job as a bookkeeper at the flour mill. Walter and Mary were then in their forties and had no children. Texanna's death pushed them into a new role of moving their household, taking in boarders, and helping Frank with his motherless children, including an adventurous, strong-willed five-year-old girl. One day, Bonnie demonstrated her bravery to her brother and two neighbor boys by hanging by her hands inside a well. The boys' mother saw her and informed Aunt Mary. Bonnie got a switching.

In the fall, Frank brought home smashed watermelons from the wagon yard for the cow to eat. The watermelons soon attracted flies and tasty butterflies, which Bonnie and her brother ate. Their frightened uncle threatened to switch them if they got sick, but Bonnie left the next morning on the train with her father to fetch her baby sister. And she didn't get sick anyway. At the Fort Worth depot, she saw a blind girl about ten years old with a card naming her destination. Bonnie gave her some of her candy popcorn.

They got off the train at Valley View and spent the night with friends. All the girls in the family gathered around a large pile of shelled corn in the back room. The next morning, Bonnie and her dad hitched a ride to their farm on the load of shelled corn heading to Gainesville to be ground. Bonnie ate something and lost her dinner in the backyard. Afterward, they visited the Gordon ranch, where Miss Olivia (whom Frank will marry) made a new outfit for her doll, Maggie. The dress was dark red and trimmed with a narrow red ribbon. Frank left that night, and Bonnie refused to go to bed without him. The youngest Gordon boy, about 16, held Bonnie on his lap on the doorstep until she fell asleep.

When they reached Ardmore, a boy driving a pretty dapple-gray horse pulling a cart met them at the station. A tall girl came out of a house carrying her baby sister on her shoulder when they drove up that evening. There were piles of burning logs and brush, and the children played hide-and-seek in the twilight. Frank got off the train at a stop on the way home to talk to someone. Bonnie didn't see him get back on and was about to jump from the bottom step when the conductor caught her. Behind him was her daddy! They returned to Vernon by a shorter route, and kind women helped with the baby. Texas Anna, nicknamed Sis, did not walk by her first birthday, so Bonnie and Ike pulled her over the carpet in a dishpan. She had a cute little round face, bright eyes, and pretty curls.

Their home in Vernon, next to the railroad tracks, had no trees, flowers, or grass—only a yard of hard-packed sand. The only wildflowers Bonnie remembered were small purple wild onions. Where the yard wasn't compacted from constant trampling, it blew into drifts. Their father planted a big patch of sweet potatoes between the yard and the railroad tracks. The vines grew so thick that the children hid beneath the leaves while playing hide-and-seek. Her brother tried to milk his pet calf, Buttercup, until the calf kicked him backward into a five-gallon bucket of cold water. When one of the boarders asked him what he would take for the calf, he replied disgustedly, "Fifteen cents." Later, Buttercup was tied on the railroad right-of-way to graze and was killed by a train.

Bonnie's most cherished memories involved time spent with her daddy. They rode in his buggy, pulled by his matched light gray team, Gyp and Dot, to see a train engine wrecked after a severe storm. He also let her pick up rabbits and birds he shot from the buggy. One evening, Frank had just pulled up next to the house with a wagon loaded with wood. As Bonnie climbed onto the wagon, they saw the passenger train pulling out and a man running to catch the last car. He missed the steps and fell beneath the train. Frank quickly handed Bonnie the reins and rushed to help another man carry the victim into the station. A few days later, a doctor had to amputate his leg at the knee.

Her daddy took her to Barnum and Bailey's big animal tent when it was in town, but she couldn't see much because there were so many adults, and she was too big to be carried. During Bonnie's second winter in Vernon, she earned her first dime. Her father gave her the dime to keep the flies off a freshly butchered hog while he went to dinner. It was the easiest money she had ever made. He let her sit on his lap and braid his beard into two neat plaits one evening when there was a knock at the door. Frank opened it without thinking, only to find an important businessman. Never again did he wear whiskers.

Swarms of Indians came down from the Territory and camped with their ponies and dogs in front of the house. An old, gray-haired Indian came begging for food. Uncle Walter told Bonnie to give her a cup of water and a few crackers. He knew she had plenty to eat. Sometimes the family attended their "war dances." The Indians set fire to a large pile of pine boxes and joined hands, circling the fire with a shuffling sidestep and a monotonous chant, moving closer and closer to the flames. Some would sit down and wipe their streaming faces. As the fire died, they would pass a hat through the crowd. They came to trade horses and get supplies.

During Christmas in 1891, another sister of her father visited from Illinois. She brought some fine horses in a boxcar, along with barrels of apples, cider, and two young daughters about Bonnie's age. The house was bursting with four Heare siblings and their families as they celebrated Christmas. Bonnie noticed that Santa wore a fur-trimmed overcoat like her daddy's, and his hat looked like Aunt Mary's dust cap, turned inside out. Santa brought Bonnie a little gay tin kitchen and goods for a dress. And her father got home late! Later, they planted the Christmas tree in the garden.

The following spring, the children had whooping cough and measles. Frank suffered from a "slow fever" for quite some time. The doctor suggested that the well water was contaminated. They cleaned it out and discovered the remains of dead gophers.

Often, turtledoves could be heard calling along the river, which remained dry all summer. Roadrunners ran by—long-legged, long-tailed, dull-colored birds. Her brother sat for hours in his little rocking chair on the front porch, watching loads of wheat being delivered to the elevator, until he knew most of the oxen by name. The children also kept themselves entertained by playing with terrapins and horned toads.

One of Bonnie's chores was to take a basket and fetch ice from the ice plant. One trip, she dropped her dime through a crack in the platform and feared she was ruined. After dinner one night, Bonnie wanted to join her family and their boarder in looking at a new house being built, but she had to wash the dishes first. She came up with the clever idea to wipe the plates with the dishrag, straighten the knives, forks, and spoons, and cover everything (they always set the table and covered it after meals). Then, she dashed off to the new house. But, alas, when Aunt Mary uncovered the table for breakfast, Bonnie got another switching.

Aunt Mary was getting Bonnie ready to start school when the men of the family decided to move to Greer County, which was then claimed by both Texas and the Indian Territory. Bonnie's daddy and uncle built a general merchandise store 50 miles north of Vernon and stocked it with dry goods and groceries as the county was quickly settling. Most settlers squatted on land until they could pay the filing fee and obtain a clear title. The general store could grubstake a newcomer until he harvested his first crop.

On a rainy December day, a cousin took Aunt Mary, the baby, and Bonnie in a covered buggy to Doan's Crossing on the Red River, where they stayed overnight with another cousin. The river was so high the next day that a cowboy had to ride ahead of the team to ensure they stayed on the proper crossing. The buggy box floated on the water while Bonnie sat in front. Even though she wore her pretty red padded velvet hood, she had a terrible earache that night.

The marble-like gypsum hills shimmered in the morning sun to the west in Greer County, overlooking a large prairie dog town. The Wichita Mountains loomed far to the northeast. They lived in the back room of the new store until their dugout was finished. Bonnie slept in the attic with her father. Aunt Mary helped Bonnie get ready for bed by the stove, and Bonnie would climb up the ladder behind her father. One night, she pretended to be asleep, and Frank had to carry her up the ladder.

Before the dugout was halfway finished, a storm filled it with snow. Aunt Mary melted the snow for wash water, saving them the trouble of fetching water from a neighbor's windmill. Since there was no school nearby, Bonnie had to write lines every day in her copybook. On nice days, she and her brother ran wild through the prairie dog town and beyond. Her brother was her horse, with lines tied to his arms. Then the roles reversed, and Bonnie became the horse. She tried to run off with him.

Frank paid $6.57 in taxes in 1893 in Greer County, which included five horses and two cows. The following year, he had five horses assessed at $85.00, along with $150 in merchandise and $100 in miscellaneous property, paying $4.25 in taxes. His brother-in-law's tax bill was considerably lower.

When Bonnie turned seven, Frank took his son Ike with him to Vernon for supplies, stopping overnight at Doan's Crossing. He watched a fierce lightning storm in the direction of the store uneasily. Hurrying home with his four-horse load, he met a cowboy who told him that a ranch house five miles west of the store "was blown all to hell." They later learned that the boys of the family had carried their mother and baby to safety under a grain separator, but their father had been killed. At the store, Bonnie's uncle and aunt had put the children to bed in the back room since the dugout wasn't floored yet. The adults moved bolts of dry goods and other merchandise off the shelves because rain was blowing in through the cracks. Aunt Mary heard a dreadful roar like she had heard in Missouri. Walter snatched up Sis and headed for the dugout, which was about six feet from the store's back door. Mary held Bonnie's hand until Bonnie felt the dugout door jamb. A strong gust of wind made Mary return to the store, where she extinguished the last lamp and headed toward the dugout's steps to find Bonnie missing. They heard her yelling. The wind had carried Bonnie about twelve feet to a chopping block by the woodpile at the side of the store. She remembered trying to hang on to short grass and chips while lying on the ground. The tornado shifted the store about eighteen feet and tipped it against a huge pile of hackberry logs.

Afterward, the store was a mess. On the grocery side, many small items were scattered on the floor. Bonnie remembered a ticking alarm clock splashed with bluing. In the back room, the tall black walnut wardrobe had tipped halfway over, held in place by two chains supporting tobacco caddies filled with cabbage and tomato plants. But the strangest thing of all was that a hen sitting on eggs on a nail keg remained undisturbed and later hatched her eggs. The building was straightened up, but was never returned to its original position. Neighbors shared the dugout for three weeks while their homes were being rebuilt.

Mary and the baby were alone in the store on a hot afternoon. Walter had gone to salt the livestock, Frank had taken Ike in the wagon to get supplies in Vernon, and Bonnie had gone to fetch fresh drinking water from the windmill. Two men stopped to ask about the distance to town, bought some tobacco, and rode away. Once home, Walter locked the store since Frank hadn't returned yet and came down to supper in their finished dugout. The two men who had purchased tobacco returned and shouted hello. Uncle Walter went to help them while Aunt Mary put the children to bed. When Walter reappeared in the dugout, he asked Mary to untie his hands. She thought he was joking until he turned around. Sure enough, his hands were tied with a grass hobble made from binder twine. Imagine the excitement! About that time, Frank arrived with a four-horse load of supplies. It was starting to rain, and his saddle was elsewhere, so all they could do was unload the wagon and wait for morning. The men who had tied Walter's hands made him lie down while they helped themselves to what little money was in the Post Office and on the dry goods side of the store, since Frank had taken the cash from the grocery side to buy supplies. Walter's good gold watch was hanging in plain sight beside the reflector lamp on the back wall, but the thieves did not notice it. They stole slickers, socks, and not much else. They dropped two boxes of children's black stockings outside when they discovered they were not men's socks. Tracks showed they had cut across the prairie to a road further west. The next morning, Frank got an officer and, along with neighbors, followed the tracks as best they could down into the breaks of the Red River. There was some excitement, but nothing came of it. Frank always carried his big .45 Colt revolver when he went for supplies. Bonnie couldn't imagine anyone robbing her father or her uncle.

My grandmother recounted stories of twisters, dust storms, and brutal winters filled with heavy snow and cold winds, when the snow drifted and cattle bunched in draws for protection. Due to a "herd law" in Oklahoma, many small cattlemen moved their herds through Greer County to seek cheaper pastures in New Mexico and Texas. Several families with their herds camped on Turkey Creek, just a mile away. One family stayed by the store for a few days, and while the children were fun to play with, the boy and girl had thick lips. Bonnie and Ike believed it was a consequence of making faces at their mother. My grandma also shared stories about the "darkies" who assisted families with laundry and butchering. At that time, I was reading Grimm's fairy tales and thought the darkies were little benevolent fairies. It wasn't until I was older that I understood who the "darkies" were.

Bonnie's father was feeling well again, and her aunt and uncle wanted to return to their home in Young County, located on the Brazos River. They sold their fine Jersey milk cow and the store. Bonnie had just started school in a nearby dugout. Most of the pupils were much older and had never gone to school before, but Bonnie's uncle had taught her at home the previous winter. When they left Greer County, Bonnie rode in the wagon, pulled by a team of mules, accompanied by her father, brother, and a hired boy to help. Holding Sis, Bonnie's aunt and uncle rode in a two-horse buggy with the saddle horses tied behind. They traveled 150 miles and encountered a storm that flooded their tent; still, they enjoyed camping on the Wichita River. Oh, the joy of returning to Aunt Mary's house, surrounded by oak and pecan trees! That winter, Bonnie lay on the rug by the big fireplace and listened to her uncle read—politics and all. Parts of "Pilgrim's Progress" made her cover her head when she went to bed. He taught Bonnie and Ike their multiplication tables before they started school that fall.

In December 1894, Frank returned to Gainesville to marry Susan Olivia Gordon, collecting Bonnie and Ike the following spring. However, he couldn't take Sis away from her devoted aunt and uncle. Sis grew up with Walter and Mary in Peaster, near Fort Worth, close to Texanna's brother, George Washington Cantrell. Although Texanna's children might have known some of her Cantrell relatives through George's family, it is more likely that Texanna's death severed that connection. My grandmother's memories centered around her father's relatives and her stepmother's younger brothers: Wesley, Fredrick, and Ernest Gordon. Fred even named a daughter, Bonnie Nell, after my grandmother.

Workers drilling for fresh water discovered oil southeast of Fort Worth, and Texas suddenly became oil country. My grandmother received a small royalty check each year from a 99-year mineral lease that her father had held. However, no significant oil strikes benefited the Heare descendants. Best Petroleum Explorations Inc. explored for oil on the H.G. Cantrell (Barch's brother) Survey in Parker County in 1983, but by then, the land was owned by others.[97]

A Category Four hurricane that destroyed Galveston and left 8,000 dead, cut a wide swath through Gainesville in September 1900. Frank and Susan sold their 100-acre farm, located six miles southwest of Gainesville, for $1,200. Frank created a Guardians Deed of Land for his three children. He named his children Bonnie, Isaac, and "Mary" in the document, rather than Texas Anna.[98] He probably meant his sister Mary, who was Texas Anna's guardian.

Isaac Wesley Heare

Frank and Susan, along with Bonnie and Ike, left Cooke County for Vernon, Texas, on August 1, 1900, arriving on August 15. Bonnie was 15. The Heares later moved to Mobeetie in the tornado-prone Texas Panhandle, an inhospitable, arid, barren, and flat land plagued by dust storms, grasshoppers, and summers as hot as the final resting place of the sinful, while winters were so cold that cattle froze to death. Settlers lived in sod houses until they could build wooden ones and prayed for rain for their thirsty cattle. The farther west one traveled in Texas, the drier it became. Once the home of buffalo until they were hunted nearly to extinction, this area of the Great Plains required miles of grazing land to keep cows alive. Newspapers reported that one tornado blew houses several feet off their foundations and destroyed a granary and storehouse. A fine stallion was killed, and eight other horses were badly injured. A family of six was injured, with the oldest boy not expected to survive. Help arrived with wagonloads of flour, meat, other provisions, and, most importantly, two doctors.

Limbs were added to the family tree by Texanna's children. Her daughter Bonnie married Clarence Don Springer in 1906. The next morning, they caught the 6 a.m. train for a grand adventure in Oregon. During their first decade in Oregon, Bonnie's father and stepmother visited them in the Cascade Mountains and rode the train to see the ocean.

Frank and Texanna's son, Isaac Wesley, married in 1919 in Pampa, Gray County, Texas. Texas Anna married around the same time. In January

1943, she filed for a delayed birth certificate in Dallas County for her 1889 birth in Cooke County, Texas.[99] She stated that at the time of her birth, her father was Franklin Pierce Heare, age 34, a rancher born in Hampshire County, West Virginia, and her mother was Texanna, age 30, born in Collin County, Texas, providing a possible location for her birth.

The history of the Cantrells and Texanna has been forgotten. Barch was in his fifties when he died. His oldest daughter, Mary Jane, passed away at 56; Tillman died at 36; Charlsilla Elizabeth (Ella) was in her 50s; and Texanna was about 27 years old. Two sons lived to be old men: William died at age 84, and George Washington Cantrell at 85. Texanna's half-brothers stayed in Texas, while her half-sisters moved into the Chickasaw Nation, Indian Territory (today's Oklahoma). Indian Territory offered free land but was also a popular hideout for Texas outlaws, bootleggers, cattle thieves, and gamblers.

Despite losing a case in 1875 to regain 557 acres of her father's Peters Colony grant, Charlsilla Elizabeth (Ella) tried again. This time for the 83-acre portion. She was ejected by a deputy in 1888 from the smaller portion of the Baurch Cantrell Survey in Dallas County. Ella, joined by her husband, sued Abraham Hart, who owned 76.5 acres, and three other men who owned parts of 6.5 acres, in Dallas County Court in July 1889. Unlike in the 1875 court case, she went to court by herself, apparently not convincing her siblings to join her. The 83 acres were described as being north of the Texas and Pacific Railroad and three miles northeast of the Dallas Courthouse. The defendants testified that their title to the land was good and valid. The court agreed, and the plaintiffs "took nothing" on December 2, 1889.[100] By that time, Ella's husband, Zach Roberts, had been dead for three months.

Zachariah Roberts passed away on September 6, 1889, in Perkins County, Indian Territory, just months before Texanna's death. Zach's only asset was a $2,000 insurance policy issued by the Knights of Honor through Lodge Number 977 in Plano, Collin County, Texas. For the next eight years, Frank assumed guardianship of Ella's minor children, although Ella's children continued to live with her in Indian Territory. He periodically submitted accounts of Zach Roberts' estate to the court. Charles Ella (as she was named in the probate) received $1000. Each child received $250 (after adjustments for disbursements and interest) upon reaching age 21. Ella requested money from the estate a couple of times for school clothing and when there was "much sickness in the family." When her youngest child turned 21 in 1907, he received $193.43, closing the case.[101] Five months after Zach's death, Ella married A.G. Waddington on April 3, 1890, in Cooke County and gave birth to a daughter nine months later, only to be widowed again. By 1900, Texanna's half-sisters, Mary Jane and Ella, lived as next-door neighbors in Elmore, Chickasaw Nation, Indian Territory.

Bonnie's father and stepmother spent the rest of their lives in Wheeler County, Texas.

In 1908, F.P. Heare owned 320 acres valued at $800, along with seven horses, two cows, and a carriage or wagon worth $20. A year later, he was taxed on these same assets, plus a lot in town assessed at $400. By 1910, the value of his acreage had increased to $1000. He still had five horses, two buggies or wagons, and his house in town. Frank supported himself through the income generated by his land, while Susan gave music lessons. They never had any children of their own. Local newspapers reported on their visits to Ike and Texas Anna, Frank's children in Texas.

Texanna's daughters, Bonnie and Texas, reunited after 50 years

Bonnie's younger sister, now known as Texas, visited Oregon after a fifty-year separation. The sisters were quite different. Texas had grown up in dry West Texas; Bonnie had lived in the Cascade Mountains and on hilly farms in the Oregon Coast Range among thick forests of Douglas firs, nestled in steep canyons filled with ferns, vine maples, and moss, drenched by rain. I wonder if they talked about Texanna, their mother. My grandmother wore her usual long-sleeved blouse and ankle-length skirt, paired with high-top Converse tennis shoes, to the family backyard dinner celebrating the reunion. Her sister wore a suit with a small straw hat. She seemed very refined to Bonnie's country grandchildren. At the children's table that day, I nearly fell out of my chair laughing at my cousin's antics. We got many adult frowns because we had been told to behave for Grandma.

I adored my grandma. Staying at her little house was heavenly. I begged my dad to please let me visit Grandma instead of chasing sheep through the cold, wet Oregon fields. Her home was always warm and cozy. Grandma would fix tea kettle tea—a soothing concoction of hot water, canned milk, and sugar. She patiently played games such as Authors, Dominoes, or, my favorite, Chinese Checkers. She told stories about Texas twisters, horny toads, and real cowboys. We looked at photo albums filled with pictures she had taken in Texas using a Brownie camera her father gave her. There were photographs of huge mule teams pulling harvesters, picnics in dusty dry canyons, and young people on a hayride, the men in their best clothes and the girls in pretty dresses. In a photograph my grandmother likely took, my grandfather (whom my grandmother will soon marry) sits in the middle of the wagon, wearing a dark suit and hat. Her brother, Ike, stands at the back with his jacket open. Although she was willing to take pictures of others, my grandmother refused to pose for photographs. She would throw her apron over her face or cut her image out of photos with scissors.

Researching Texanna's story was hindered by a lack of documentation. She was mentioned by name in only five records: the 1870 Henderson County Census listing her as a nine-year-old named Texana; an 1875 power of attorney identifying her as Texas, the daughter of Barch and his second wife Margaret; her 1884 marriage certificate naming her as Texa; her youngest daughter's delayed birth certificate listing her as Texas Anna; and as Texanna in my grandmother's voter registration from 1920. Still, she lived, gave birth to three children. For a long time, I doubted whether her father was truly Barch, but my DNA connects me to a great-granddaughter of Mary Jane, confirming our common ancestor was Barch Cantrell. Discovering ancestors in cemeteries, deeds, church registers, and in the DNA of people sitting across the dinner table will always fascinate me.

I can only imagine Texanna's memories: a broken fence, a clearing by the creek, and a dusty corral filled with horses. A dirt-floored cabin where she slept, the calico dress she wore until it became a faded rag, cowboys spitting tobacco, hellfire preachers, her father, and her older half-sisters and brothers, as well as her wedding; memories woven into stories only she could share. I wish I could have the gift of time travel—to discover where she lived as a child, her memories of her parents and her husband, and, especially, to hear her voice. But the reality of life in early Texas would disgust me: untreated diseases, filth, and a low hum of violence. I would balk at any expectation that my life's purpose was to provide a retreat for men to heal their troubled souls and restore their well-being.

I wondered whether my grandmother remembered her mother. She was not quite five years old when Texanna died. I found a note she wrote in 1942, reminding her brother that on February 7, 1890, "Our young mother passed on." At age 76, she made the following diary entry from her farm in the Oregon Coast Range, written in her spidery handwriting.

> February 7, 1961. My mother died on this day in 1890. This has been a dark mild day—raining slightly tonight—frogs singing.

Ironed and mended. Cecil going with Thad and Company to a basketball game at 2. Dan home after cleanup ...

She had written her mother's year of death as 1889, crossed it out, and then wrote 1890. Nowhere else in the diary did she cross out anything. She knew she had lost her mother on February 7, but had to think for a moment to recall the year. Texanna was remembered. I have tried to tell her story.

Kate's Family

Andrew Kuhn
born: November 9, 1819, Furchhausen, Bas–Rhin, Alsace, France
married: October 21, 1856, Vincennes, Knox County, Indiana
died: February 26, 1893, St. Meinrad, Spencer County, Indiana
parents: Andrew Kuhn (1790–1870); Catherine Brucker (1793–1855)

Mary Maschino
born: May 20, 1830, Liederschiedt, Lorraine, France
died: September 19, 1869, Vincennes, Knox County, Indiana
parents: Peter Maschino (1798–1869); Magdalena Clauss (1805–1843)

Children
Victoria Josephina Rosalia (Sister Laura), 1858–1939
Julia, 1860–1861
Mary Catherine, 1861–1938, m. Gerhard G. Recker, 6 children
Catherine Mary "**Kate**," 1866–1960, m. John A. Gabler, 4 children
    Lawrence Henry (1894–1971)
    Eleanor Frances (1897–1995)
    Joseph Anthony (1902–1938)
    Johanne (1905–1905)
Joseph, 1869–1869

Catherine Kuhn Gabler
(1866–1960)

When I was 13, standing under the shady maple trees in my grandma's front yard, I overheard my grandma and great-grandmother snickering. My great-grandmother whispered, "That old witch is dead." It dawned on me that they were talking about my mysterious St. Louis great-grandmother, whom no one in Oregon had ever met. All I knew was that her name was Catherine, and her daughter was Eleanor, which is why my mother was named Eleanor Katherine. I hoped my grandma and great-grandma would gossip more about "that old witch," but their eyes cut to me, and with their lips pressed together, they frowned in unison, not saying another word.

It was years before I began researching the so-called "witch of St. Louis." I discovered that she was born Catherine Mary Kuhn in 1866 in Vincennes, Indiana, to Andrew Kuhn and Mary Maschino, Catholic immigrants from Alsace-Lorraine, which is now part of France. She was called Kate. She wasn't a witch at all, just a deeply religious woman who chose to have nothing to do with her son living in Oregon. In retaliation, his Oregon family had nothing good to say about her.

I finally traveled to Vincennes in 2014 to delve deeper into the life of Catherine Mary Kuhn. I met her grandson, who had lived with Kate while growing up in St. Louis. Jim Hogan drove up from St. Louis with his longtime neighbor and friend, Polly Willard, to meet me in Vincennes. For the first time, I saw photographs of my great-grandmother Kate, who bore a striking resemblance to my mother with the same large brown eyes. I regret that they never met.

My great-grandmother Kate

My mother Eleanor

I found Vincennes, one of the oldest settlements west of the Appalachians, seemingly tattered and worn out, with its charming neo-classical architecture in need of restoration. Spread out in a crescent shape along the banks of the winding Wabash River in southwest Indiana, the town was dotted with historic sites: the William Henry Harrison mansion, Vincennes University established in 1801, the Old French House built in 1809, St. Francis Xavier Church, and the Red Skelton Museum and Performing Arts Center in honor of a more recent native son.

I struggled to navigate the city's narrow, potholed streets. Ironically, the cemeteries were located right across from the hospital. I couldn't tell where one cemetery ended and another began, but I finally spotted the sign for Mt. Calvary Cemetery. Walking through the cemetery on a cold, windy day, I alternated between reading the headstones with names familiar from my research and sitting in my blessedly warm rental car, the heater turned on full blast.

George Rogers Clark Memorial

As I turned a street corner looking for someplace warm, I was surprised to see the largest federal monument west of Washington, D.C., sitting on a slight bluff above the Wabash River. Resembling a giant birthday cake, the granite memorial marked the site of a British fort captured by Lt. Col. George Rogers Clark and a group of Frenchmen and frontiersmen in 1779. Jesuit missionary priests built a church with upright posts fixed in the ground. A bark roof supported a small belfry and an equally small bell. The dead were buried beneath the pews and earthen floor, as was the custom.[102] As the community of motley fur traders and Indians grew around the fort, so did St. Francis Xavier Catholic Church.

Next to the monument, I saw the Old Cathedral (Basilica of St. Francis Xavier Catholic Church), its library housing ten thousand rare volumes and documents, and a forlorn cemetery with headstones bearing barely legible French names. Fortunately, the cathedral was unlocked and slightly warm. Its foundation, measuring 60 feet by 115 feet, was laid on March 30, 1826. Inside, the pillars were made of giant yellow poplar trees. It was in this cathedral that my great-grandmother's parents were married. After hours of struggling through extremely hard-to-read microfilmed church records written by a long-ago priest in Latin, I expected goosebumps. However, the only goosebumps I felt were from being half-frozen. After visiting cathedrals in Europe, this one seemed disappointingly short and squat. Although I found the interior ornate, I felt no emotional connection to a family wedding long ago.

On October 21, 1856, another day bright with fall leaves, Andrew Kuhn married Miss Mary Maschino at St. Francis Xavier Catholic Church. When I revisited the Cathedral with Jim and Polly the next day, Jim looked stunned to stand in the same church where his great-grandparents married. Polly offered me a brief, insightful lesson on church architecture, opening my eyes to the beauty of the Gothic elements in the stained-glass windows, the gilt paint atop the columns, and the intricately carved pulpit. I began to envision a bride and groom.

The bride's family, the Maschinos, emigrated from Lorraine in 1853, while the groom's family arrived from Furchhausen, Alsace, in 1855. The French priest who married them (who was not a precise speller) recorded their names as Andre Kuhn and Marie Maugenau. The groom's parents were Andre Kuhn and Catherine Brock, and the bride's parents were Peter Maugenau and Helen Clauss.[103]

Alsace-Lorraine, situated in northeastern France, encompasses the Vosges Mountains and borders Germany to the north and east, and Switzerland to the south. The Rhine River forms its eastern boundary as it flows north. The region has been part of Germany, France, or Prussia, or has existed as an independent entity. A map of the area resembles a "7"; the upper part reflects the Lorraine region, while the vertical line of the "7" represents the Alsace region. The earliest known member of the Maschino family, Voir Maschino, was born in 1607 in Haspelschiedt, Lorraine. Descendants of Voir lived in a hilltop village called Liederschiedt, located half a mile south of the French-German border.[104] Both villages are in the Moselle region, known as Pays de Bitche. In 2021, the town of Bitche (pronounced with a silent e) made headlines when its Facebook account was shut down. Facebook's algorithm mistakenly identified the town's name as an English insult. Consequently, the town's authorities had to establish a new Facebook page named after the town's postcode, "Mairie 57230," to maintain communication with residents.[105]

The Kuhns and Maschinos recorded their places of birth on U.S. records as Elass-Lothringen, Germany, Alsace, France, or Prussia, depending on the year they were asked. For nearly seven centuries,

Alsace-Lorraine was part of the fiercely Germanic Holy Roman Empire, which named towns using the evolving German language. The Maschinos came from Lorraine, and the Kuhns came from Bas-Rhin (Lower Rhine), the northern part of Alsace.

Alsace-Lorraine has long been a troubled and vulnerable part of Europe. Cursed by its strategic location along the Rhine River and the high ground of the Vosges Mountains, our ancestors faced a relentless cycle of starvation, epidemics, and war. They struggled through cold, icy winters and cool, wet summers during the Little Ice Age, which lasted from roughly 1300 to 1850. Crop failures led to famine, which, in turn, drove up food prices. When crops were abundant, the population grew rapidly until there were too many mouths to feed, leading to recurrent famines. Epidemics were always a constant threat.

The roads of Alsace-Lorraine endured the marching feet of Roman, Vandal, French, Swedish, and Germanic soldiers. Caught in battles and forced to supply troops with shelter and food, our ancestors faced a precarious situation. Citizens perished during the Thirty Years' War (1618–1648) as the fertile lands of Alsace were transformed into battlefields. Further suffering was inflicted during the French Revolution and its factions of French soldiers fighting against Austrian and Prussian armies until Napoleon's final defeat in 1815. The failed 1848 German Revolution briefly offered a sense of freedom; however, with streets barricaded, cavalry charging citizens, and soldiers billeted in homes, life quickly returned to oppression and economic stagnation. The Treaty of Frankfurt ended the Franco-Prussian War of 1870–1871, permitting the German Empire to annex most of Alsace and Moselle. Thousands of men were drafted into the German Army during World War I, until Alsace-Lorraine was ceded back to France at the war's end. Germany occupied Alsace again in 1940 and forcefully conscripted men from Alsace into the Wehrmacht. Over the centuries, generations of Alsatians could boast of living on the same farm while being citizens of different countries.

Neither French nor German, Alsatians considered themselves distinct, as evidenced by large, ribbon-bonneted women, their exceptional beer, and their unique cuisine. The dress and headdress indicate women's marital status, religion, and even their village. Alsatian beer is primarily lager, known by its seasonal names: March beer was brewed from the new barley crop, while Christmas beer was slightly darker.

Alsatian Dress

I made two trips to Alsace. (I love to travel). On my first trip, I visited Saverne, nestled among the mountains to the north and bordered by small villages to the south. I didn't know the ancestral village of the Kuhns, so I wandered around Saverne, getting soaked in a steady downpour. By my second trip, I found the name of the ancestral village, allowing me to research the family online using records organized by village. I found handwritten civil records in French from the 1800s and older Catholic Church records in Latin dating back to the 1500s. I imagine the priests who carefully recorded these births, deaths, and marriages four hundred years ago would be speechless to know that I tried to decipher their squiggles (with much difficulty) using my home computer in my pajamas.

The earliest known ancestor, Jacob Kuhn, was born in 1690 in Westhausen, a village now called Westhouse-Marmoutier. Several generations later, Kate's grandfather, Andrew Kuhn, left Westhausen for the nearby village of Furchhausen to marry Catherine Brucker in 1814 and settle in Number 11, the Brucker family home and the eleventh house built in the village. Andrew worked as a journalier, or day laborer and farmworker, and owned no land.[106] However, he knew how to brew beer and distill whiskey, and used these skills in Vincennes, Indiana.

Like all the villages near Saverne, Furchhausen was densely packed with ancient half-timbered houses clustered around the Catholic church, where villagers organized their lives according to the church calendar and saints' days. Here, children dodged chickens, geese, pigs, and dogs in the rutted dirt streets crisscrossed by muddy paths.

Example of half-timbered wall. *Author's photo.*

In 2018, I visited Nicole Hornecker in Furchhausen. She lived in a late seventeenth-century half-timbered house. Her property formed a square around a central courtyard, with the house, barn, and sheds creating three sides; the fourth side was a wall with an entrance gate flush with the street. Nicole's workshop had replaced the barn but still formed three sides, with her doorbell located across the courtyard at the gate. Originally, homes were built so that the barn doors were at a 90-degree angle from the front doors. The manure pile outside the barn door also ended up near the front door. Villagers believed planting a walnut tree kept flies out of the house that swarmed around the manure pile.

Half-timbered village farmhouses were built from oak, with walls filled in with woven branches, mud, and straw, designed to shelter a family for at least a hundred years. Typically, the multigenerational family occupied two rooms: one with an open hearth for cooking and the other for sleeping. Lacking a chimney for ventilation, the walls were blackened with soot. There was little fresh air, even if the door was left open, but the trapped smoke seasoned the meat hanging from hooks above the fire and dried the bundles of rye stored in the attic. The grandparents slept at the head of the bed, while the father and mother rested upright, back-to-back, at the foot on a mattress made of linen sacks filled with wheat chaff from the harvest. Other family members slept leaning against the wall on benches or sat on the floor. It was believed that sleeping in an upright position protected people from the devil as well as nightmares. The German word for "nightmare" originates from a mythical creature in Germanic folklore, resembling a demon or goblin, which was thought to press down on people's chests as they slept. The dense, low-hanging smoke in the room probably caused their breathing problems and nightmares. Yet this gave rise to the saying, "You only lie flat once in your life."

The businessmen of Saverne lived in homes that were quite different from the village farmhouses. Family businesses occupied the ground floor, while living spaces for grandparents, parents, and children were on the second and third floors. These homes were usually U-shaped. The bottom of the U, facing the street, had wide doors that allowed wagons to enter the courtyard for unloading into a large cellar. The stairways and balconies leading to the living areas were attached to the inner sides of the U. In the event of a fire, they could be cut away (after the family had evacuated, of course).

Catherine Kuhn Gabler (1866–1960) 149

Furchhausen, Alsace, France

Nicole's neighbor took me on a wagon ride through the village and the surrounding fields of Furchhausen. From a low hill, I could see the next village. Like Furchhausen, it once was a community where every person, every house, and every field had a known history. Eccentricities were tolerated and grudges remembered for a lifetime. Most people now speak French, but Nicole's neighbor also spoke Alsatian, a German dialect. His surname was Kuhn, but he realized we were unrelated once he learned that my Kuhns had come to Furchhausen from Westhausen 200 years ago.

The Maschino and Kuhn families had many reasons to emigrate to America. Between 1848 and 1858, over one million Germans and French moved to the United States and other lands. They were lured by shipping agents and flyers that seemed to drift through the air. Railroads made the journey from eastern France to the Port of Le Havre quicker and easier than traveling by wagon or boat. As an added incentive, rail lines reduced fares to Le Havre and other ports by half to a third for emigrants. Some agencies even operated special trains in the spring to attract travelers to a port. Local newspapers advertised dockside rooming houses and provided schedules for ship departures. Letters from family or friends who had already settled in America offered the strongest motivation—letters that exaggerated America as a paradise where jobs and land were plentiful. It didn't matter. Even a slight chance to improve one's economic and social standing was a powerful motivator to leave. Kate's grandparents decided to emigrate.

Since government regulations controlled every aspect of citizens' lives, legal permission was required to emigrate. An application required two witnesses and a down payment to cover travel costs. The priest announced to the parish that a family was leaving so debts could be settled with neighbors. Women made clothing and harvested food, while children helped their parents, getting time to play only on Sunday afternoons. Families bid farewell to the village square where the old men gathered to talk and smoke their pipes; the familiar church spire piercing the sky, the distinctly long Catholic skirts decorated with velvet at the hem, and the resting benches along the market paths where women rested their necks from the strain of carrying baskets of goods balanced on their heads. They kissed friends and family goodbye, knowing they would never see each other again, except in heaven.

Sailing to America

To sail to America in the 1850s, the Maschinos and Kuhns likely traveled across France, utilizing the recently expanded rail system to reach the port of Le Havre. At the dockside, travelers had to present their official emigration papers, pay a fee of roughly 50 to 100 francs per adult, and wait for a ship with available space. A few arrived in Le Havre with barely enough time to board a ship, but most waited from a week to a month before departing. Renting rooms and buying food could quickly deplete their cash, so they traded precious family heirlooms for necessities. Some had to camp out on the street and seek temporary work. During this enforced delay, families were besieged by tavern keepers, ship brokers, and, worst of all, land agents, whom the emigrants regarded as villains fleecing the innocent. Most agents, however, were honest and served an indispensable role as middlemen between shipowners and prospective passengers.

In the early 1800s, passengers were required to bring enough provisions to last the six- to eight-week Atlantic crossing, such as barrels of home-brewed beer, smoked pork, and choucroute, a local type of sauerkraut. They also needed to buy an "emigrant kit" from a provision store near the docks, which included a thin straw mattress, a pot, a tin plate, a fork, a spoon, and a provision box built to resist rat gnawing, along with hooks and nails for hanging cheeses and clothing on the ship's beams. On board, passengers had access to one or two basic kitchens. Many German-speaking travelers from various regions were unimpressed by unfamiliar foods, such as herring, and preferred to bring their own. However, the bring-your-own-food system had problems. Fights broke out in the small cooking areas over who would cook next. A more serious concern was passengers who were too poor to bring enough food or who failed to bring any at all. Laws were passed to improve and regulate steerage conditions. Starting in 1848, ships were required to furnish each passenger with sixty gallons of water, thirty-five pounds of flour, fifteen pounds of ship's biscuits, and ten pounds each of oatmeal, rice, salt pork, peas, and beans. This did not alleviate the crowd in the galley kitchen, so many tried to mix their flour with water and eat it raw. Later, some ships found it easier to feed steerage passengers from a large pot: porridge with molasses or salt fish for breakfast, boiled beef and potatoes for lunch, and bread or biscuits for supper.

Peter Maschino and his family sailed from Le Havre, France, aboard the SS Württemberg and arrived in New Orleans on March 18, 1853, probably on a cotton ship. Owners of vessels with bales of raw cotton bound for the cotton mills in Alsace did not want to return their ships empty to New Orleans, so they offered reduced rates to immigrants. Ships departing from Baltimore for Bremen, the leading European port for tobacco, filled their empty holds with immigrants as shipowners looked to make money sailing back to Baltimore.

Clipper Ship. *Library of Congress.*

Between 1830 and 1860, approximately 15% of immigrants to the United States chose New Orleans over New York City as their destination. This golden era reached its peak in 1854, just before the outbreak of the American Civil War. In the next decade, that percentage dropped significantly to around 1%. But by then, rail transportation to the west from New York had improved. Immigrants became wary of New Orleans because of its ongoing health problems, like insect-borne diseases such as malaria and yellow fever. Travelers also sought to avoid getting caught up in the Union and Confederate military conflicts while sailing up the Mississippi River to destinations such as St. Louis, Cincinnati, and other inland cities. During the Civil War, less cotton was shipped because of Union blockades, which also reduced the number of "cotton" ships offering cheaper fares to New Orleans.

The ship's manifest listed Pierre, his second wife Marie, and, amazingly, seven children from his first marriage, along with three children from his second marriage. His daughter, Mary (who later married Andrew Kuhn), was the oldest at 21 years of age. She was followed by six siblings aged 19 to 7, plus three half-siblings. The two youngest boys with nearly identical names, Jean Nicholas, age two, and Nicholas, age one, were not required to be listed on the ship's manifest. Most shipping companies offered free passage to children under three, which led to family stories of thrifty parents attempting to claim a four-year-old as a two-year-old. Joseph Balthazar Maschino, the children's uncle, was also aboard. The captain of the Württemberg noted that out of 359 passengers, two adults and one child died during the voyage.[107] Listed as Manginot on the ship's manifest, their name became Maschino. After a couple of decades of living in Vincennes, some descendants changed the spelling to Marchino. Contrary to popular belief, immigration officials never altered or anglicized surnames or first names—the immigrants did so themselves. Andre became Andrew, Jean became John, Marie became Mary, Catherina became Catherine, and Laurent became Lawrence or Laurence. It was also common in the old country for parents to reuse a name after a baby died. For example, the Kuhns had two sons named Laurent. The first Laurent died as a baby, so they used the same name for the next son. In America, that practice seemed to die away.

Louisa Maschino celebrated her fifth birthday during the crossing. She recalled the three-month voyage to America, which began in January in northern France. They traveled up the Mississippi and Ohio Rivers from New Orleans to the Wabash River. The Wabash was too shallow for them to continue to Vincennes, so they disembarked in St. Francisville, Illinois, located 10 miles south, and continued the rest of the journey by wagon.

The Kuhns immigrated two years later. They were lucky to find passage on the Gosport, a sleek new 170-foot clipper ship. Built in Virginia on June 3, 1854, the Gosport carried 900 tons of coal to sell in Quebec City on its maiden voyage. After unloading the coal in Quebec City, she was loaded with timber bound for London. After the lumber was sold, the Gosport's hull was sheathed in copper in preparation for emigrants. Three hundred eighty-three passengers, including the Kuhns, faced a two-day delay in Le Havre before departing for New Orleans aboard the Gosport on December 4, 1854.

Captain Strickland was offered a bonus to deliver healthy passengers to New Orleans. In an unusual move, the captain had his crew construct animal pens aboard the ship to house a cow, goats, chickens, ducks, pigs, and sheep, ensuring a steady supply of fresh meat, milk, and eggs. The death of an immigrant meant a deduction from his bonus. Alternatively, the entire bonus could be withheld if the ship's doctor determined that Captain Strickland treated his passengers harshly or neglectfully. According to his crew of veteran sailors, whalers, portside bums, and a good number of ex-slaves, the captain treated the passengers far better than he treated them.

The ship was also crammed with consignments of wine, fortified spirits, cloth, hardware, cheeses, and machinery, all destined for sale in America. When the ship encountered the infamous headwinds of the Atlantic, both cargo and immigrants suffered. The vessel crested roiling waves only to drop abruptly into troughs, rolling from side to side and up and down. Crews were ordered to batten down the hatches, trapping passengers in the stifling confines below deck that soon reeked of sweat, waste, and vomit. There was no privacy. Toilets were screened buckets without lids that could not be emptied when the hatches were closed. The Kuhns, who likely considered themselves fortunate to be on a new ship despite its prior use in shipping coal and lumber, found themselves in dark, small, and poorly ventilated steerage accommodations. Men and women were separated; older boys bunked with their fathers, while teenage girls and younger children stayed with their mothers. Passengers were packed into triple decker bunks, just a few feet wide, with flimsy curtains dividing their sleeping quarters from those of their neighbors. Toward the stern, a single hatchway provided scant light and fresh air when open. There was a 3' by 4' space for cooking, 10 to 12 pot hooks, and two water closets for everyone.

The weather soon improved. A very German Yuletide Christmas was celebrated as the Gosport escaped the winter storms to sail south, reaching the mouth of the Mississippi River on January 8, 1855. Pilot boats guided the Gosport the last hundred and ten miles from the sea to New Orleans, through brackish mud, rotten fish odors, and swarms of bugs, past the huts of small fishing villages, swamps, and bayous, amid low land barely distinguishable from the gulf waters. Landfall materialized in a record-setting 32-day trip from Le Havre. Unfortunately, the excited passengers could not disembark until January

15, after health inspectors granted clearance and Captain Strickland had completed the Customs Passenger List.

The only occupation listed for passengers was "farmer." They hailed from Switzerland, Bavaria, Hesse, Württemberg, Baden, France, Prussia, and Saxony, including three passengers returning to "Amerika." The common language was German. The quick trip with no deaths on board earned Captain Strickland a bonus of over a thousand dollars.[108]

If medical examinations and questioning of steerage passengers revealed any of the diseases specified in immigration laws, or if they were deemed unable to support themselves, they were sent back. If a child was deported and younger than twelve, they had to be accompanied back to Europe by their parents. Usually, passengers had to show they had about $20. Despite the arduous process, only about two percent of immigrants were returned.

I love to travel, but I don't enjoy flying. As I thread myself to the back of the plane, past shoulders and knees, hugging my bags to my body, I always feel like I am in steerage. However, I only have to deal with being squeezed into a small space and my seatmate's behavior for a short time. Our ancestors had to face much more for much longer: a stewpot of seasick, frightened, drunk, and bored travelers, with babies crying and children quarreling. Some passengers entertained themselves by singing, playing musical instruments, and dancing. But even under the best conditions, the risks of cholera, smallpox, dysentery, measles, typhoid, lice, spoiled food, and seasickness took their toll. Amid the discomforts of overcrowding, a lack of sanitary facilities, contaminated food, and scarce water supplies, there were frequent fights, threats of women being harmed, and the constant fear of bad weather or worse—shipwreck.

The Maschinos and Kuhns were dismayed by the utter chaos of New Orleans and its population of over 100,000. The wharves echoed with the shouts of bare-chested men loading massive cotton bales onto masted ships and the ear-piercing whistles of steamships. Rivermen shouted prices for barrels of corn whiskey, sides of dried beef, and ham. Streets were filled with hawkers and their handcarts, chained Blacks headed for the slave market, Haitians in colorful clothing, elegantly dressed mulatto women followed by their servants, and poor, ragged Irish families, all amid the buzz of languages: French, Creole, Spanish, German, and English. The new arrivals tried to avoid the slave depot advertised in a New Orleans newspaper as one of the most spacious and well-ventilated depots around, offering 300 enslaved people. Alsatians found the odor of the inefficient sanitary system likewise appalling. During wet weather, the contents of the sewers flooded the streets. Equally disgusting was the New Orleans custom of burying the dead in vaults above the ground, like ovens baking rotten bread in the hot sun.

The Kuhns may have been welcomed by members of Die Deutsche Gesellschaft (The German Society), which was formed to provide newcomers with information and protect immigrants from dishonest 'runners' who allegedly acted as agents for boarding houses and riverboats. Members also assisted in securing food and shelter for immigrants and sometimes gave small sums of money for passage on a riverboat up the Mississippi River. The first page of the Daily True Delta newspaper listed nearly two full columns of steamboat departures for the upper Mississippi River and the Ohio River on January 16, 1855, which cost $4.00, excluding provisions. The Mississippi-Ohio-Missouri River system was the country's only major transportation network before the expansion of the railroads.

Some immigrants found work in New Orleans to earn enough money to continue north. I suspect the Maschino and Kuhn families left the city as soon as possible to avoid what they likely regarded as a disease-plagued and depraved city. Yellow fever, cholera, and typhus were common. In the summer of 1853, 8,000 residents of New Orleans died of yellow fever. Immigrants were blamed.

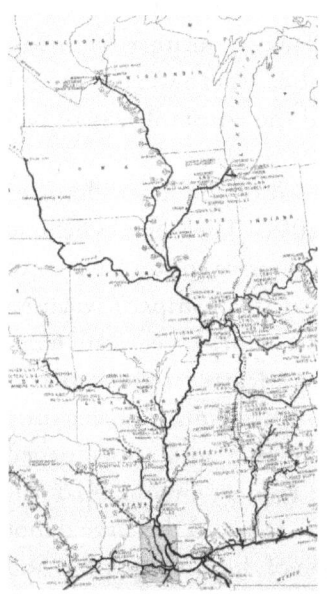

New dangers loomed on the Mississippi River: snags, sandbars, collisions, boiler explosions, and floods. With luck, their steamboat faced no difficulties beyond stopping periodically to take on more firewood for the boilers, allowing it to sail up the Mississippi River, onto the Ohio River, and up the Wabash River to Vincennes, Indiana.

A German immigrant recalled traveling north by steamboat from New Orleans on the Mississippi River to the Ohio River, as far as Evansville, then by train to board the stage for Vincennes, using the last of his money to pay a 50-cent fare. Taken in by the Catholic community in Vincennes, he became the organist for St. John's Catholic Church and began teaching the boys of the congregation. As there was no school building, he taught his twenty scholars in a building near St. Francis Xavier Cathedral. During his journey from New Orleans, people warned him not to go to Vincennes with its ponds and frogs, as he would die of chills and fever. When he arrived, he found the frogs made such a noise that he could hardly sleep.[109] The fertile bottomland experienced seasonal flooding, leaving behind swamps and causing people to fall ill with what was known as summer complaints or winter chills. Waterborne infections, such as typhoid fever and dysentery, were common.

Settling a few miles from Vincennes, Pierre Maschino, who quickly became Peter, utilized his workforce of sons and daughters to farm. Of his 16 children from two marriages, eleven married and remained near Vincennes. Seven years later, Peter's four youngest sons were helping on the farm in 1860. Daughters Magdalena, Anna, and Louisa worked as domestic servants in Knox County homes; Louisa was just 13. Sons were expected to farm or start apprenticeships, while daughters were expected to serve as housemaids as preparation for marriage and running their own homes. Wages were sent to their parents, helping support the family budget until they married. After marriage, a woman did not work outside her home; her place was at her husband's fireside, caring for him. It was considered an insult for a man's wife to have paid employment, as if he could not provide for his own family.

In early spring of 1855, the Kuhns arrived in Vincennes, Indiana. The family joined the eldest son, Jacob, who had lived in Vincennes for ten years. He had sailed from Le Havre on March 22 and arrived in New Orleans on August 5, 1845. Jacob established himself as a grocer and saloon keeper, and married the year before his parents and siblings arrived. His name was frequently listed in newspapers for renewing his liquor license. In 1867, he requested a permit to sell intoxicating liquors in quantities less than a quart from his premises between 3rd Street and 4th Street, previously known as the Farmer's Saloon. His name also appeared in the newspaper when a thief broke into his bedroom and stole a small amount of money from his pockets, while his neighbor, Frank Schaller, had a pair of pants taken.

Jacob's brothers, Andrew, Michael, and John, filed their intent to become American citizens shortly after arriving. Their sister, Catherine, married John Ebner, a widower with two daughters, fifteen years her senior, five months later. Because John Ebner had become a citizen, Catherine was too, though she could not, of course, vote.[110]

A month after Catherine's marriage, her mother, also named Catherine, died at age 62. She had spent six months in America. Although she gave birth to at least ten children, she was survived by her husband, Andrew, four adult sons, and one daughter. After her death, her husband lived with his daughter, Catherine, and son-in-law, John Ebner, a successful businessman. The Kuhn brothers, Jacob and John, also fared well financially, while Michael and Andrew (Kate's father) were less successful.

St. John the Baptist German Catholic Church

When the Roman Catholic Alsatians began arriving in Vincennes in 1840, they sought their own parish, rather than attending St. Francis Xavier Catholic Church alongside the French. Sermons were given in English or French, not German. And the Alsatians considered the French "loafers" who spent too much time enjoying life.

The Alsatians petitioned the Catholic Bishop for permission to build a church. The bishop initially denied their request, believing that the German community of Vincennes was too poor to support a separate parish. However, once permission was granted, the immigrants quickly built St. John the Baptist German Catholic Church.

The church's cornerstone was laid on June 17, 1851. Although most of the labor was donated by parishioners, carpenters were paid $2 per day, day laborers received $0.62 per day, and hauling by a two-horse team cost $1.25 per day. Jacob Kautz was paid $1.00 per barrel of beer for the workers. The sturdy brick church, measuring 40 feet by 80 feet, featured an altar and a cross at one end, with the pulpit tucked in a corner. It was completed in July 1852 at a cost of $5,060. Four years later, the cross was placed on the steeple, witnessed by many spectators. The church preserved the German language for Kuhns and Maschinos, enabling them to forge close relationships with fellow countrymen. It provided a cornerstone of emotional stability, spiritual guidance, and, at times, economic support. St. John's German Catholic Church was a credit to Vincennes.

The Sisters of Providence taught the girls, while laymen instructed the boys at St. John's School. Initially, students gathered in private homes or small buildings for lessons in both English and German. Some nuns even taught in the public schools when they opened in 1855. Over time, St. John's School expanded into an elementary school, a female academy, and a male college. A Catholic education emphasized the core beliefs of the Catholic faith and was considered crucial for children to learn cherished Christian virtues—qualities that did not develop naturally in the soul and could not be left to chance.

The annual church picnic, costing 50 cents, allowed guests to win handsome prizes at Freiz's Garden in 1870. Attendees were promised an excellent program of drama, singing, card games, and displays from trade and craft organizations. The Saint Ann's Altar Society, possibly dating back to the construction of St. John's, provided support for the sanctuary and altar needs. The St. John Benevolent Society was organized in 1866 with 88 charter members. Founded in 1889, the Teutonic Club offered young men a place for "innocent and legitimate amusement." When men left to defeat the Kaiser in World War I, the Teutonic Club changed its name to the Men's Dramatic Club. As a legacy to his father, John Ebner Jr. (my great-grandmother's cousin) donated a set of 5,000-pound bells to the church in 1889, which required a larger belfry but by then, the St. John's congregation had grown to 350 families. In 1902, the Golden Jubilee was celebrated with a procession led by boys wearing white shirts and gold sashes. Many priests and the bishop attended, delivering sermons in English and German. German Catholics were willing to help the less fortunate, provided the less fortunate were willing to work in exchange. Homeless people and deadbeats were not tolerated.

Reverend Aegidius Merz, responsible for enlarging the church and school, served St. John's for 34 years, from 1863 through 1897. He guided Kate through her childhood into adulthood, even officiating at her marriage. He was described as a very able man, strict and gruff, but with a heart of gold and a sincerely spiritual man. A priest who did more than one man's share of good. His handwritten entries of baptisms, marriages, and deaths in Latin sprawl across the pages. Once I got used to his handwriting, I could almost decipher it with Google Translate.

Jim, Polly, and I attended Mass at St. John the Baptist German Catholic Church. After the service, we admired the stained-glass windows. To my surprise, the four windows in the transept were dedicated to names I recognized from my research. The first window depicted

Pentecost and was donated in memory of Jacob Kuhn (Kate's uncle); the second represented the Resurrection, given in memory of the family of John Ebner Sr. (Kate's uncle in whose home she was raised); the third window illustrated the birth of Jesus and was dedicated to Anton Simon (John Ebner's son-in-law); and the last window portrayed the Annunciation, in memory of John and Rosalia Froelke. Each window cost $350.00 in 1908 and was made in Munich, Germany.

Mary Maschino's death record in Father Merz's handwriting. Mary was the widow of Peter Maschino and step-grandmother of Kate.

Despite language barriers and new ways of doing things, the Alsatians thrived with support from the large German Catholic community. They utilized skills learned in the Old Country in occupations such as baking, carpentry, and brewing. They made sausages and potato pancakes, and served bread at every meal. They spoke the Alsatian dialect of German, practiced Catholicism, made barrels of sauerkraut, and opened saloons to sell their beer. Saloon customers relished the fall batch of sauerkraut with their sausage and beer.

The growing number of immigrants began to alarm some Americans. By the 1850s, immigrants, many of them Catholic, outnumbered native-born Americans in Chicago, Milwaukee, and St. Louis. They were often stereotyped as paupers, criminals, and drunks. Nativists promoted conspiracy theories suggesting that Catholics could never be good U.S. citizens because of their allegiance to the Pope. The immigrants also tended to vote as a bloc, changing traditional voting patterns. As a result, anti-foreign sentiment crystallized into the Know-Nothing Party, a xenophobic and anti-immigrant faction that despised "dirty and lazy" German and Irish immigrants for taking jobs from real Americans. The Know-Nothings, known for replying "I know nothing" to questions, nominated former President Fillmore for President of the United States in 1856 (who was defeated by James Buchanan).

Perhaps the three Kuhn brothers filed their intent to become citizens quickly so they could vote against the growing Nativist Anti-Catholic movement that peaked in 1854 and 1855.

The Kuhns, engaged in business, and the Maschinos, primarily engaged in farming, quickly embraced their status as "American" while honoring their roots to Alsace-Lorraine, along with their culture, faith, and language. Twenty years after arriving, the Alsatians appeared less like newly arrived immigrants and more like an established community of locals.

In 1855, Vincennes was divided into three sections: Frenchtown, Dutch Flats (a predominantly German-speaking community that included the parish of St. John the Baptist), and an American Protestant area north of Main Street. An estimated 2,000 people celebrated the Fourth of July in 1859. A parade commenced with the Vincennes firemen and the Turner German clubs dressed in uniforms.[111] The Declaration of Independence was read first in German, then in English, followed by a speech delivered in German. An Indian skeleton and some relics, including a stone hatchet, were exhumed when a street was leveled in the upper part of the city.[112]

By 1860, Vincennes had a population of 6,000 (the population in 2024 was 16,500); hogs sold for $6.00 per 100 pounds; the post office listed lost letters (when addressees could not be found) in two separate lists, one for letters written in German and another for letters written in French. Vincennes thrived with two fire companies, two newspapers, a Knox County Agricultural Society organized in 1853, a 2,000-volume library, three musical bands, the Medical Society, a bank, St. Vincent Orphan Asylum for Boys, St. Mary Orphan Asylum for Girls, two railroads, a tri-weekly stage route, five hotels, 17 boarding houses, two ice cream parlors, 11 saloons, a vinegar manufacturer, and ten blacksmiths. New gas lamps were installed on Main Street. Buckley's circus came to town on August 3, when the temperature was 94 degrees in the shade. A month later, the circus returned. A great many people looked forward to seeing the elephant but were disappointed to learn she had died of lung fever the preceding Tuesday. And to top it off, several people had their pockets picked.[113]

After their marriage in 1856, Kate's parents moved to St. Louis, Missouri, with Andrew's younger brother, Michael. Andrew was 36, Mary was 26, and Michael was 28. St. Louis was a diverse city, home to descendants of French colonists, Native Americans, free Blacks, East

Coast Americans, Southerners, and immigrants. In 1850, 43% of the population was born in either Ireland or a German-speaking region. St. Louis was expected to become the hub of U.S. commerce and attract a flood of wealth by rail. Instead, Chicago emerged as the hub. The Kuhns faced more setbacks in St. Louis, including the Panic of 1857, clashes between pro-slavery and anti-slavery groups, and confrontations with the Nativists determined to make life difficult for Germans, Irish, and Catholics. In 1854, three days of rioting erupted, marked by gunfire, looting, and arson involving the Nativists and German and Irish immigrants. The riots caused deaths and serious injuries, damaged Catholic churches, broke windows of German-language newspaper offices, and destroyed Irish and German saloons. Under pressure from Nativists and with increased police presence, beer gardens where German Americans gathered and sang on Sunday afternoons were closed down. Mobs targeted Catholic churches, taunting, harassing, and insulting priests and nuns. Even as the Nativists and the Know Nothing Party faded, anti-Catholic bigotry persisted.

Andrew and Mary's first two daughters were born in St. Louis and baptized at St. Joseph German Catholic Church. Victoria Josephina Rosalia was born on May 30, 1858, and baptized on June 27; her godparents were Joseph Simon and Rosalia Muller, neighbors. Julia, their second daughter, was born in May 1860 and baptized on June 24, 1860; her godparents were Eugenio Kuhn (who may have been her uncle Michael) and Emelia Ruthlof.[114] But Julia died when she was 14 months old on July 26, 1861.[115] Mary Catherine, their third daughter, was born five months later on December 31, 1861. She was baptized on January 12, 1862, as the daughter of Andrea Kuhn and Maria Maschinau; her godparents were Juliana Dollis and Michael Kuhn. Juliana was the wife of Joseph Dollis, a dray driver in 1860 and a teamster for a liquor house in 1880. He, too, was from Alsace, while his wife was from Hanover, and their daughters were the same age as Andrew and Mary's. The historic church of St. Joseph's still stands proudly at 11th and Biddle, but its name was changed to the Shrine of St. Joseph in 1864 when a German immigrant who suffered an injury while working at a soap factory was healed after stumbling into Mass.

Andrew and Mary lived in a working-class neighborhood populated by Germans and Irish, at the rear of 168 North 12th, within walking distance of the church.[116] They likely resided in crowded tenements built two to three stories high. Andrew and Michael worked as porters or laborers amid the noise of piercing steamboat whistles, the snap of long whips over the backs of oxen, and the clatter of iron shoes on cobblestones. Near the river was a jumble of craft shops, tall warehouses, and cheap saloons—all covered in black soot from coal stoves and wood smoke. Politics were discussed more often in German than in English. Vendors shouted out lunch specials or patent medicine cures. Men scooped up stinky, slimy mud and manure from the streets into wagons and tossed the mess into the Mississippi River. All social classes carried a Bowie knife or a revolver.

St. Louis was deeply divided after the Confederate bombardment of Fort Sumter on April 12, 1861. Pro-slavery, native-born Missourians harbored a deep distrust of immigrants. Alsatian Catholics generally supported the Union and hated slavery and opposed secession, but that did not mean they were free from prejudice against dark-skinned people.

Union Army Volunteer Regiments (of which 80% were estimated to be German) were practicing maneuvers at Camp Jackson when news came that pro-confederate forces were planning to capture the St. Louis Arsenal. The arsenal was a significant prize, containing 60,000 Springfield and Enfield rifles, 1.5 million cartridges, and 90,000 pounds of powder. On the way to defend the arsenal, someone in the crowd yelled at the Union troops, "Damn the Dutch." Riots broke out. Gunfire echoed off the tenements. The rampage killed 28 civilians and injured many more. It continued for three days. Some Volunteer Regiment officers let their men go home and check on their families. Most returned to camp bruised and bloody. Two men never returned and were never found. Saloons were closed, and martial law was declared. Atrocities perpetrated by Rebels were reported: a boy was hanged to force him to tell where the family's guns were hidden, an old man was beaten with a rifle barrel and marched to Springfield, and rebels shot 60 balls into a Union man.[117]

Andrew, 43, and Michael Kuhn, 34, enlisted as privates in the 17th Regiment Missouri Militia, Company E, led by Captain Klagen, in St. Louis on September 1, 1862. Known as the Millers' Regiment because so many of its soldiers worked in the St. Louis flour mills, the regiment was never called up for active duty during the Civil War and disbanded on April 12, 1864. Militia units, raised from the civilian population to supplement the regular army in the event of an emergency, were akin to the modern National Guard system.

President Abraham Lincoln signed the country's first mandatory conscription law to raise more troops for the Civil War on March 3, 1863. All able-bodied men between 20 and 45 were required to enroll, and those inducted were to serve for three years. By July 1863, the conscription included alien males aged 20 to 45, regardless of whether they had declared their intention to become naturalized citizens. The pressure increased in October 1864, when scores of men were called up to replace Union soldiers who had completed their three-year enlistment period and were not eager to continue. Andrew registered in July 1863. He worked as a laborer and lived on 12th Street in the 5th Ward of St. Louis.[118]

Driving wagons loaded with barrels of flour, the brothers worked as teamsters for T.A. Buckland, a wholesaler, manufacturer, and owner of Park Mill, a flour mill located at the corner of 13th and Market, which probably explains why Andrew and Michael joined the Millers' Regiment. Buckland paid taxes on vehicle gross receipts, repairs, and cooperage. His property in 1864 was valued $84,280, far higher than that of his neighbors. Michael lived at the business, while Andrew resided with his wife and daughters two blocks away at 15th and Market.[119]

Tragedy struck. Just days after the Confederate surrender, Michael died on May 17, 1865, at age 35, and was buried in St. Joseph's Catholic Cemetery, also known as the Poor Man's Catholic Cemetery, where his niece Julia was also laid to rest. Whether Michael died from injury or disease remains unknown. He was not listed as a patient at St. Louis City Hospital from February through May 1865, nor was any coroner's report filed. Coroners documented deaths caused by accidents or murders. Common causes of death included beatings by husbands, drownings, gunshots, intemperance, suicides, or sunstroke. One young woman collapsed at her wash tub and died of sunstroke. A man was caught in a cogwheel while oiling machinery. People also died of lockjaw, consumption, scarlet fever, cholera, blood poisoning, brain fever, and being in the wrong place at the wrong time.

After Michael's death, Andrew and Mary moved back to Vincennes, Indiana, with their two daughters, Victoria and Mary, leaving behind the graves of Michael and their daughter Julia. They narrowly missed a cholera epidemic that swept through St. Louis in 1866, killing 140 people daily. There were twenty burials a day in the St. Joseph parish alone. Mary was expecting another baby.

My great-grandmother, Catherine Mary (Kate), was born in Vincennes on November 7, 1866. Two days later, she was baptized at St. John the Baptist German Catholic Church. Her uncle, John Kuhn, and her aunt, Catherine Ebner, were her godparents.[120] Andrew and Mary had named their previous daughter Mary Catherine and reversed the name for their new daughter to Catherine Mary. The Catholic Alsatians preferred to name their babies after a saint. The first name was the spiritual name, while the second was the secular or "call name."

The Kuhn brothers, along with their brother-in-law, John Ebner, registered to vote in Vincennes in 1867. Jacob, John Kuhn, and John Ebner's families and businesses continued to prosper. But for Andrew's family, hopes for financial improvement and good health did not materialize. Andrew was delinquent on his 1868 taxes, owing Knox County $4.60 for personal property worth $140. In July 1869, Mary gave birth to a son they named Joseph. His godparents were family members Balthasar Maschino and Magdalena Ebner. But just two months after their son's birth, Mary died. Baby Joseph's baptism was delayed until October 10, just before he also died. With the loss of his wife and son, Andrew became a widower and the sole parent of three young girls—Victoria, Mary, and Catherine—changing their lives forever.

The previous spring, the girls' maternal grandfather, Peter Maschino, had died. Each of his ten children received $11.07 from his estate, except for his daughter Mary, who was listed as deceased. Andrew Kuhn, through his wife's rights, received $3.69, and his three minor daughters, Victoria, Catherine, and Mary, each received $2.46. It appears Victoria signed her first name; her father signed her last name and signed for her younger sisters.[121]

For whatever reason, Andrew chose not to raise his daughters. The girls were separated. Newly married relatives of John Ebner took in eleven-year-old Victoria. Seven-year-old Mary went to live with Andrew's brother, John Kuhn, who brewed lager and manufactured yeast and later owned the St. John Hotel and Saloon. Kate, who was almost three, joined the household of her father's sister and brother-in-law,

Catherine and John Ebner, who ran several business enterprises. Growing up with relatives was the best solution for the girls. Otherwise, they would have been placed at St. Ann's Orphan Asylum, where they would have resided until age ten, then been boarded out or adopted. Farm families needed extra hands and were eager to accept orphaned children as workers. How they were treated is another matter.

Their father seemed to be in and out of their lives. In 1870, 50-year-old Andrew worked as a carpenter in Pekin, Tazewell County, Illinois, boarding at the home of Charles Bross. By 1873, he returned to Vincennes and paid $850.00 for Lot 36 on Water and Church Streets, a 35' by 135' plot. His younger brother, John, advertised a first-class boarding house at the corner of Water and Church, which included a good wagon yard for farmers and a grocery store selling cigars, tobacco, and high-quality liquors. The brothers may have shared a business arrangement that apparently ended when Andrew sold his property to John for a substantial loss of $235 two years later.

I wonder if Kate dropped by to visit her father, although her Aunt Catherine might have objected to his neighbors. Andrew lived in a small house behind Jennie Stanley's brothel, known as the "Carpenter Shop." A fire broke out at the brothel at 3 a.m. on January 13, 1876, forcing Jennie's half-naked girls out into the cold, much to the amusement of onlookers. Unfortunately, the fire also spread to Andrew's house, destroying it completely. Andrew's loss was covered by insurance, but the brothel sustained an uninsured loss of $4,000. Jennie managed to survive financially despite receiving numerous fines for intoxication, assault, battery, and operating a house of ill repute over the years. She turned a flatboat into a floating palace and earned more than ever by taking her girls up and down the river, moving her brothel whenever the law showed up.[122]

By 1880, Andrew was living and working as a laborer at St. Vincent Male Orphan Asylum, a Catholic home where over 150 boys prayed in the chapel and learned to farm its 300 acres. Proud that only four boys died in three years, the orphanage was housed in a three-story brick building overlooking landscaped grounds three miles from Vincennes.[123] Three years later, Andrew traveled with alms and gifts to St. Benedict's Indian Mission at the Standing Rock Indian Agency in Fort Yates. He stayed with Reverend Claude Ebner, a priest of the Order of Saint Benedict (O.S.B.) who was well known in Vincennes and a relative of John Ebner. In a letter dated June 22, 1883, Father Claude wrote about visiting Sitting Bull, as he only lived 15 miles away, and Andrew Kuhn was as cheerful and healthy as ever and was working hard for the Indian Mission's benefit. Two years later, Andrew visited friends and family in Vincennes with Brother Jamar Huber, a member of the Order of St. Dominic from Yankton, South Dakota. However, nearly a decade after that visit, Andrew died at 73 years and 6 months from complications related to asthma and old age. At the time of his death, he was part of the Benedictine community of St. Meinrad in Spencer County, Indiana, living among men dedicated to prayer and work.[124]

Anton and Caroline Simon were newlyweds when Victoria came to live with them after the death of her mother and baby brother. Caroline was John Ebner's daughter from his first marriage and, therefore, Victoria's stepcousin. However, Caroline died in childbirth two years later, when Victoria was just 13. It's unclear with whom Victoria lived afterward, but she soon dedicated her life to the church.

Sister Laura

Sister Laura of Mary (born Victoria Kuhn) received the habit and entered the Novitiate on October 15, 1881, with the Sisters of St. Joseph of Carondelet in Indianapolis. Her profession of vows occurred on October 15, 1883, in St. Louis, Missouri. The Sisters of St. Joseph of Carondelet managed St. Anthony School, but it would be years before Victoria, now known as Sister Laura, began teaching. She spent the first eighteen years of her religious life ill at Nazareth Convent in St.

Louis. She suffered from constant stomach pains until a running sore developed, "spreading rapidly over the entire breast," according to a letter she wrote. Three physicians diagnosed it as cancer and said there was no hope for a cure. She received the Last Sacraments several times. Her suffering was so intense, and death seemed so slow in coming, that she decided to make a novena of Holy Communion in honor of Saint Joseph. On the ninth day of the novena, March 18, 1901, she lay down exhausted on her bed after Mass. When she awoke, her bandages were dry, and only faint scars remained from her wound. She drove herself three miles to the doctor's office the next morning after her miraculous cure, needing no assistance to step down from the high-seated vehicle. When Dr. Samuel Will examined her, he found absolutely no discharge and a complete absence of pain. He certified that he had cared for Sister Laura for about two years. She had received treatment for epithelioma, during which time she suffered great pain; the discharge from the wound in her breast was sometimes profuse.[125] Word slowly leaked from the convent, and newspapers around the county picked up the story.[126] Thirty years later, Doctor Will re-examined Sister Laura and wrote that the sudden disappearance of the disease and its failure to return could not be explained scientifically. The miracle occurred on the feast of Saint Joseph, after whom the order was named. Sister Laura's healing is considered a divine gift. She is listed for beatification and, once confirmed as 'Blessed', can be officially recognized as a saint by the Catholic Church.

After a twenty-year absence from Vincennes, Sister Laura visited her sister, Mrs. Gerard G. Recker (Mary), her aunt, Mrs. Catherine Ebner, and other relatives and friends during a five-day trip in 1905, accompanied by her Sister's Companion—a nun she traveled with to deflect unfriendly attention. Nuns could face hostility when they traveled away from their convents by non-Catholics who dreamed up lurid tales and conspiracy theories about communities of unmarried women supervised by unmarried priests.

Relatives in Vincennes discovered Sister Laura to be in perfect health, without a trace of her former illness. She left Vincennes for Indianapolis, anticipating an assignment in West Superior, Wisconsin, where she had taught for two years. Later, she was assigned to St. Joseph Orphan Girls' Home in Kansas City. There, she taught sewing and household arts and oversaw a girls' dormitory for many years. Sister Laura was 72 years old and a retired teacher, still living at the St. Joseph Orphan Home in 1930. Her cousin, Ella M. Ulrich, had bequeathed her $200 the year before. She died at the Nazareth Convent in St. Louis on February 4, 1939, and shares the same tombstone with others of her religious community who died that same year. On a stone near a statue of the Sisters of St. Joseph of Carondelet, Resurrection Cemetery, her name appears as Laura of Mary Kuhn, 1859–1939.[127]

Kate's other sister, Mary Catherine, was raised by their Uncle John and Aunt Caroline Kuhn, who owned a boarding house that later became St. John's Hotel in Vincennes. Mary was listed in the 1883 city directory as a domestic worker at a hotel. Two years later, at the age of 25, Mary married Gerhard Recker. After their 8 a.m. wedding at St. John's German Catholic Church, followed by their wedding breakfast, they departed on the afternoon train for St. Louis. They were accompanied by Mary's 20-year-old sister, Kate, who planned to visit friends in St. Louis for a fortnight.[128] There was no indication of whether Gerhard and Mary were pleased to have Kate accompany them on their honeymoon.

Gerhard and Mary had six children in Vincennes, of whom four survived to adulthood. When their oldest son, Andy, was 18, he drove a horse-drawn delivery wagon across the railroad tracks and was struck so hard by a speeding B & O train that his brains were exposed and his neck was broken. The news spread like wildfire through town, and a large crowd gathered for a sight most would never forget. Andy's employer, Brokhage and Sons Delivery, sued the railroad on September 4, 1910, on behalf of Andy's parents, receiving a settlement of $1,250 to $1,500, estimated as Andy's lifetime earning power.[129]

Mary died in 1938 at her daughter's home in Kansas. Her body was transported by train to Vincennes to be buried in Mt. Calvary Cemetery following her funeral Mass at St. John Catholic Church.[130] In a burial plot for which her husband paid $45.00 in 1910 lie Mary, her husband, her son Andy, and her son-in-law, William H. Stein.

Growing up with the Ebners

Catherine Mary (Kate) grew up in the affluent John Ebner household, one of the wealthiest families in Vincennes. She likely was a replacement child for their daughter, who died a month after Kate's mother passed away. Kate fit near the middle of her Ebner cousins. Unsurprisingly, Kate was much closer to her Ebner cousins than her sisters.

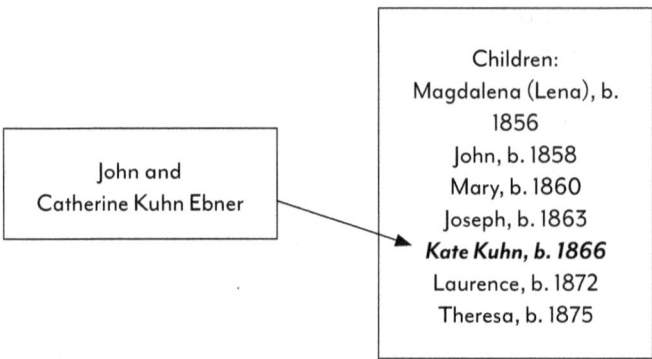

The Ebner house was always full of people. In 1860, John and Catherine's household included two daughters from his first marriage, their two children, Catherine's father, and two teenage relatives of John. By the next decade, the household had grown to 12 members. In 1880, their household consisted of five children and a niece, Katie (my great-grandmother), who was listed on the census as 'one of the family.' Even after Kate married, the Ebner home still was crowded, with her widowed aunt, two widowed cousins with five children, and a servant. Until 1914, the two-story brick house at the corner of 5th and Vigo Street (428 Vigo) was the Ebner family home.

The family home changed from 428 Vigo to 404 North Fourth when Kate's cousin, Laurence, purchased a house for $12,000.[131] Former residents remembered Ebner Ice Company iceboxes left in the basement. The house was built by William J. Wise in May 1859 and had cast-iron window caps. It was the first house in Vincennes to feature hollow brick walls with a dead air space between the inner and outer walls, instead of the traditional three-brick-thick construction. It also had five bedrooms, two baths, and three parlors. Although the porch is no longer enclosed and the chimneys and turret have been removed, the house still exists. Kate's grandson, Jim, thought the small figure at the corner of the mansion was Kate.

Kate's uncle and guardian, John Ebner, emigrated from Alsace in 1846 after receiving a German and French education. He mastered the miller's trade by age fifteen and enlisted in the regular French Army at twenty-one, serving six years in Africa, five of which he spent as a baker. He continued baking bread in New Orleans for three months before moving to Cincinnati, Ohio. In the spring of 1849, he relocated to Vincennes to work as a grocer until a fire destroyed his liquor and grocery business five years later. Undaunted, he opened a coffee house and, by 1860, was operating a saloon and had built a "well-known brewery at the upper end of town." Despite the Panic of 1857, which led to a decline in land prices and market deflation, exacerbated by the Crimean War in Europe, he also constructed a public hall. On September 11, 1860, the newspaper reported, "The German ball last night at Ebner's Hall was well attended and passed off very pleasantly."

Kate's uncles, Jacob Kuhn, John Kuhn, and John Ebner, were successful in the brewing and selling of beer and other spirits. However, tax laws and government revenue agents were a thorn in their side. In 1867, Jacob Kuntz and John Kuhn's breweries were seized for violating revenue laws. The owners were ordered to appear in Indianapolis.

John Ebner was suspected of a more serious crime than simply brewing beer. A search of his brewery for a whiskey still in 1866 was unsuccessful, but the next year, authorities found a still hidden behind the brewery's engine room. Ebner had been producing so much whiskey that his first still had worn out and needed to be replaced by one transported on a railcar full of coal. It is estimated that he made about 45 gallons of whiskey each month, which he sold through Ebner's Saloon in Vincennes. His father-in-law (Kate's grandfather) was the distiller. The government seized the still, valued at $10,000, imposed fines, and assessed Ebner $2,800 for unpaid taxes on distilled spirits. He was convicted in the U.S. District Court of Indiana of running an illicit distillery based on the "sin tax." On July 1, 1862, Congress passed excise taxes on items such as playing cards, gunpowder, feathers, telegrams, iron, leather, pianos, yachts, billiard tables, drugs, patent medicines, and whiskey to generate additional revenue to support the Civil War. Ebner appealed his conviction. He offered $10,000 to pay his fines and enlisted the help of Thomas Hendricks, a U.S. Senator from Indiana. He was pardoned by President Andrew Johnson in February of 1868, just before Johnson faced his own impeachment.[132]

John Ebner's presidential pardon was unpopular. A newspaper editor wrote, "Democracy is pretty low down when [a senator] plays the role of pardon broker to obtain a presidential pardon for a man who had been convicted of the most atrocious frauds upon the revenue." The whiskey tax supporters alleged that Ebner made more in a week by cheating the government than the average honest farmer earned in a year!¹³³

428 Vigo
The woman may be Kate's aunt Catherine.

404 North Fourth
The woman on the walk may be Kate.

Some of John Ebner's other problems were relatively minor. Reverend Gillespie of Vincennes bought a dozen bottles of port in a box for a lady relative from John Ebner. The Reverend failed to return the empty bottles and used the box as a flower box. John took him to court in the case of John Ebner vs. Reverend Gillespie for the value of a dozen port bottles (80 cents). A sympathetic reporter wrote of the decision, "Through some inexplicable technicality of the law," the jury ruled in favor of the defendant.[134] Then Ebner's Saloon was robbed of $70. At the time, Kate was too young to know what was happening, but it must have added tension to the household.

A week after her fourth birthday, her grandfather, the whiskey distiller, died after attending morning Mass at St. John's on November 14, 1870.[135] Andrew Kuhn had lived in the Ebner household for 15 years since his wife's death. A large monument in Mt. Calvary Cemetery was erected for Andrew Kuhn, John and Catherine Ebner, John's two daughters from his first marriage, their son Laurence Ebner, and Laurence's two wives. The newspaper announced Andrew's death as "Death of an Old Citizen":

> *Mr. Andrew Kuhn, father-in-law of our fellow-citizen John Ebner, died suddenly Tuesday morning. He had been attending service at St. John's Church and shortly after his return home, was stricken with apoplexy. Mr. Kuhn was well-known in the city, where he has lived for a number of years. He was born in Alsace, France and was in his 84th year.*

Ebner attempted to sell his brewery several times but took it back each time due to poor management. The brewery was described as a brick building, three stories high, 110 feet long, and 65 feet wide, with good cellars underneath: one for lager beer, two for gerring, one for schank beer, one for common beer, and one large malt cellar. Above the lager beer cellar was a beer saloon, malt kiln, kettle, machinery, oven, and other equipment. Ebner also ventured into the ice business, which naturally appealed to brewers, who needed ice to keep their products cold. In 1860, he constructed four large icehouses near the river with a capacity of 13,000 tons of ice. The ice plant evolved into the Ebner Ice and Cold Storage Company, with ice plants in other Indiana cities and across the river in Illinois, making the name Ebner synonymous with ice. Five wagons and 12 horses delivered ice to Vincennes homes when they displayed cards in their windows for ice deliveries of 25, 50, or 75 pounds.

John Ebner probably contributed as much toward Vincennes's growth and prosperity as any other city citizen. He first arrived in America with

$139 and, by 1873, was worth $50,000, paying $900 annually in taxes. "He is a clever old Teuton—full of mirth and jolly."[136] German-speaking immigrants were stereotyped as either good-natured, pipe-smoking Santa Clauses or aloof, correct, cold, and unforgiving Prussian types. It seems John Ebner was of the former.

I imagine 11-year-old Kate waving goodbye to her Uncle John before heading to St. John's German Catholic School, her long, dark brown hair neatly braided. She enjoyed the peaceful walk after the hectic morning at the crowded Ebner house on Vigo Street. Mr. Schaller waved from his bakery, filling his window with fresh loaves of bread. She thought about asking for a warm cinnamon schnecken, but her aunt would find out and scold her when she got home. Next door to the bakery, Uncle Jacob was sweeping out his saloon and muttering to himself. She definitely wouldn't ask about his problems. That could take all day. She knew everyone she passed on the way to school—and everything about them. As she turned the corner onto 6th Street, she saw Mrs. Laugel pinning wet laundry to her clothesline. Mrs. Laugel was such a nosy parker! Kate avoided causing gossip. As an extra in the Ebner household, her reputation was precious. She had much to lose.

As she walked the last few blocks to school, she saw some children walking to the public school. She didn't know them well. They weren't Catholic. She straightened her spine. She was a child of Mary. She loved the sweet and serene nuns, their round faces framed by black veils edged in white, flowing over their long black robes. That afternoon, Sister Agnes planned to read to them during Fancywork, which was much more fun than Plain Sewing. Anyone could hem a pillow slip. Sister Agnes had a pinched face and liked to smack hands with her ruler. But Kate loved listening to her read while the girls sat at a long table, embroidering linen vestments for altar servers. Next week, they were going to knit. She wanted to knit a shawl in blues and greens. And wonders of wonders, her aunt had complimented her on her darning and turning buttonholes. She smiled, sighing. It was a fine morning, after all. Even the morning classes on Christian doctrine and recitation might be interesting. She whispered a quick prayer to help her against her worst sin, pride. She saw Father Merz, who gave her his special smile. She heard a thief had broken into his poultry yard and stolen a dozen of his hens. Pshaw!

Uncle John read in the newspaper that her school was providing an excellent education under Father Merz. Half of the classes were in

English, and the other half were in German. Unlike her male cousins, who were expected to take over the family business, she knew her schooling would soon end. Her aunt told her that an education would only make her unhappy. Kate needed to learn skills to attract a good husband, be a good mother, manage a household, and get along with neighbors. Although it seemed Kate had more advantages growing up in the wealthy Ebner household than her sisters, her clearly defined role was to marry and raise children in the Catholic faith—or become a nun, as her older sister did.

In winter, Kate watched horses pull massive plows across the frozen Wabash River, breaking through ice that was ten to twelve inches thick. Men used handsaws, chisels, dip nets, scrapers, or any tool capable of breaking the ice into blocks for the Ebner Ice Company. At the foot of an elevator, two men with long-handled hooks grabbed two or three blocks of ice at a time. Other men pulled them off at the top of the elevator and guided the blocks down a 100-foot chute to the icehouses, where the ice was packed in sawdust for summer use. One man broke his leg when his pants got caught on the iron hooks, twisting his leg. It took seventy-five men and teams to harvest the ice, but they were rewarded with a hearty meal and beer every day at 9:30 am and 3:15 pm. By 1889, the Ebner Ice Company had shifted to manufacturing artificial ice from distilled water.

In Vincennes, telephone subscribers turned a crank and asked the operator in the Odd Fellows building to connect them to the party they wanted to reach. Mule-drawn streetcars appeared in 1883; water and electrical services were installed in 1886. Every town calculated time by the sun. Located due south of Chicago, Vincennes followed Chicago time, nineteen minutes ahead of St. Louis and twenty-three minutes behind Cincinnati.

Near the river was the Laugel Cooper Shop which made barrels; a starch factory with a brick smokestack so large that a horse could be ridden into it; a woolen mill; Schaller's Cooper Shop; and E. Bierhaus and Sons Packing Plant, which processed 12,000 to 20,000 hogs annually. St. John's Hotel stood on the corner of Church Street, where Mary, Kate's sister, lived and worked, and across the street was the Sleet and Company's flour mill. On Main Street was Francis Thuis' harness store; Jacob Cassell, grocer; George Fenrich, cigars; Frank Horsting, grocer; Schaller & Ohnemus, bakers; Henry Thuis, confectionery; I.H. Liepshutz, clothing; Smith & Sons, stoves and tinware; J. Fred

Harsh, jewelers; more grocers; a millinery; shoemakers; saloons; a meat market; and other businesses—many owned by members of St. John's Catholic Church. Stone for the new courthouse was cut and shaped on-site, leaving the whole block inches deep in broken stone. The news was spread by three newspaper offices and two telegraph companies, Western Union and B. O. Telegraph. Outside of town were a couple of woolen mills and two more flour mills.

The society page reported that Katie Kuhn attended dances and game parties or traveled out of town with a girlfriend or cousin to visit friends. This social butterfly could have been our Katie Kuhn or her cousin, also named Katie Kuhn, who was a year older and the daughter of her father's brother, John Kuhn. Regardless, neither girl spent time in one of Vincennes' forty saloons, where men could buy a large glass of beer for a nickel and get a free lunch. Whiskey was self-serve, with three drinks for a quarter; the smallest glass held two ounces.

While teenage girls enjoyed themselves, adults worried about the periodic fires that burned down downtown businesses. A fire started at McGinsey's Livery Stable on Third Street and spread to a furniture store on Second Avenue on December 28, 1885. McGinsey lost 40 horses, and the Grand Hotel was destroyed, resulting in a $60,000 loss. In 1886, a Black man, arrested for killing a Green County farmer, was dragged from jail and hanged by a mob of 20 to 30 masked men from Green County, wielding sledgehammers and cold chisels. The citizens of Vincennes watched, but no one stepped in to stop the hanging.

The 1890s recession was marked by labor unrest and strikes. In 1892, the president of Vincennes National Bank took his own life while sitting on his daughter's grave. A week later, businessmen were shocked to learn that the former bank president had been in debt, and the bank's financial condition was much worse than they had thought. The bank closed, and a meeting with the bank's stockholders was quickly scheduled.

Kate's first cousin to marry was Lena Ebner, who wed Joseph Schmidt at St. John's Catholic Church in 1878. He was an Austrian cigar manufacturer in Vincennes. "The bride was elegant and perfect in every particular," in the morning ceremony.

Mary Ebner married Herman Wissing in 1884 at St. John's Church, surrounded by friends and family, making her the second cousin to marry. Kate and her sister Mary presented the newlyweds with a parlor lamp. They departed on the noon train for their honeymoon, traveling through various Eastern cities and visiting friends and relatives along the way. A beautifully furnished cottage at the corner of 9th and Broadway awaited them upon their return. Sadly, their happiness was brief. Herman died three years later from winter fever at age 28. Mary quickly moved back into her parents' home on Vigo Street with her four-month-old son and his two-year-old brother.

The marriages of her male cousins were expected to benefit the family business, just as they were expected to run it. Her oldest cousin, John Jr., attended the Catholic school in Vincennes, followed by St. Meinrad College in Spencer County, Indiana, and St. Joseph College in Illinois. He joined the Eagle Brewing Company as a bookkeeper and junior partner. John Jr. and his brother Joseph expanded the Ebner Ice Company (which replaced the brewery in the family's fortunes) beyond the small-town company their father had established. However, John Jr.'s involvement with the family company was brief. He built an Eastlake-style home for his bride in 1886, paying $1500 for the lot. Unfortunately, less than a year later, his wife died of brain fever before they had a chance to live in the house. Then, a friend accidentally shot him in the neck with a pistol, the bullet narrowly missing his jugular vein. John survived the gunshot only to become ill with consumption (or tuberculosis, as it is known today). He took a prolonged trip through the East, spending the winter of 1889 in Asheville, North Carolina, where he enjoyed the mountain air and reported feeling better. But he died the following year at age 31. Mourners at his well-attended funeral at St. John the Baptist Catholic Church described him as universally liked and remarkably generous. He left his two nephews $2,000 each, his siblings $1,000 each, his cousin Reverend Claude Ebner, O.S.B., $500, and $500 to his cousin Kate, among other bequests. After his death, his mother sold his dream house for $3,250. It remains the best example of Eastlake architecture in Vincennes.

Like his older brother John, Joseph was educated in the German Catholic schools of Vincennes. He attended college—similar to our high school—for a year under the guidance of the Franciscan Fathers. At seventeen, he left school and became his father's assistant in the ice business. At the social event of the year, Joseph married Katie Raben, the daughter of one of the wealthiest men in southern Indiana. Kate was a bridesmaid. The names of prominent guests and their gifts were printed in the newspaper. A year after their marriage, Joseph traveled to Alsace with two other Vincennes citizens to visit their parents' childhood homes. But after a brief seven years of marriage, Katie died of nervous exhaustion, leaving behind three small daughters.

Joseph Ebner

Joseph, described as a man who shunned publicity because of his modest and reserved nature, served as president of the Ebner Ice and Cold Storage Company, vice president of the Vincennes Milk & Ice Cream Company, a member of the board of directors at First National Bank, and a nineteen-year member of the Vincennes Board of Trade - a prominent figure in the Vincennes business community. Before his death at age 51, he sued an insurance company that had refused to issue him a $20,000 life insurance policy after he was diagnosed with a leaky heart valve. He died of heart disease.

Kate

Laurence, Kate's youngest cousin, began working as the bookkeeper at Ebner Ice Company in 1883 and became the company's president in 1930. He was 5'8", with brown hair, brown eyes, and a slight build, typical of the family. He was also known as the wild one. As Kate later testified in court, Aunt Catherine gave her the thankless task of dragging Laurence home after he spent the night carousing. His mother eventually decided that her youngest son needed a change of scenery. He applied for a passport in May 1894, at age 22, to participate in a two-year training program in Europe to become a coal trader. Instead, he traveled through Europe with his oldest sister Lena, her husband, and a friend, Joseph Kiefer. They sailed from New York City on the steamer LaTouraine. Years later, Laurence, who loved traveling, sailed in 1925 with his wife, Mamie, on the SS California from Havana, Cuba, to Key West, Florida. In 1929, he also sailed from New York to San Juan, Puerto Rico.

Ebner Ice Company was frequently involved in litigation, keeping lawyers busy. Stockholders of a rival company, Citizens Ice and Cold Storage, filed a lawsuit, claiming that Joseph and Laurence (who somehow managed to get appointed to the board of the rival company) had ruined their business by altering the bylaws and appointing themselves General Manager and Assistant Manager. The brothers were accused of undercutting prices, selling horses, wagons, and harnesses, and damaging the company's machinery, which ultimately led to the company's closure. The lawsuit alleged a clear conflict of interest since Ebners owned the only other ice company in town.

Kate grew up to be a petite brunette with large brown eyes in the cosmopolitan Ebner family, with whiskey on the sideboard, fine paintings adorning the walls, and weekly trips to the confessional. Her uncle, likely her protector, died in 1889. She left her aunt's home three years later when she turned 20. She may have moved to St. Louis or stayed in Vincennes, as she had relatives in both cities. Somewhere, she met a well-dressed man from Chicago who captivated her with tales of beautiful gardens and left her awestruck by his future plans. John Gabler was a German Catholic, a well-traveled landscape gardener, and Kate saw the promise of a good life.

John (baptismal name Johann) Gabler was the son of a tailor and the grandson of a gardener from the village of Pfaffendorf, across the Rhine River from the historic city of Koblenz, Germany, about 300 miles north of where Kate's parents were born. He probably spent his childhood watching barges move up and down the Rhine beneath an ancient Roman fortress on a high promontory. On the other side of the river stood the Electoral Palace, which governed the Prussian Rhine Province from 1824 to 1945 and remains a historic landmark. I visited Koblenz in 2015 and 2018; it's a beautiful town where the Moselle River flows into the Rhine. During World War II, German troops blew up the bridges, and nearly 80 percent of the city was bombed by the Allies, including the Catholic church where John's parents got married. (It has since been restored.)

In his late teens, John likely finished a two-year apprenticeship in landscaping, where he studied botany, forestry, and design. As part of his education, he probably visited many of Europe's famous gardens. John later mentioned the Palmengarten in Frankfurt and the Duke of Devonshire's Chatsworth House Gardens in England, as if he had been there. He claimed to have traveled extensively across two continents. Once in America, he joined botanical societies and published well-written papers in English. He never called himself Johann—always John.

John reported on the 1900 Census that he emigrated to America in 1878 at age 20. However, there is no record of him until 1884, when he wrote a letter published in the Missouri State Horticultural Report, describing how to graft the dog rose (Rosa Canina) and the best way to glaze a greenhouse.[137] He may have returned to Pfaffendorf for his father's death in 1881 and then returned to the U.S. in 1882. A John Gabler, age 24, immigrated in September 1882 aboard the Scardian from Liverpool to Quebec. This might have been our John Gabler, because a year later, his older sister, Theresa, her family, and their youngest sister immigrated through Quebec. Theresa, her husband August Sprengnether, their four young children, and her sister, Francisca, age 22, crossed the Atlantic via Liverpool to Quebec en route to St. Louis, Missouri, in 1883.[138]

Professional gardening opportunities for John in Missouri were slow to develop. Around 1886, he moved to the Bay Area of California and arrived at the bustling terminus of three transcontinental lines at the Oakland Pier: the Southern Pacific, Western Pacific, and San Francisco railroads. He likely felt energized by the carnival-like atmosphere of the train station, with its busy travelers, peddlers hawking everything from fruit to motion sickness remedies, accident insurance solicitors, newsboys, hotel runners, and salesmen offering investment opportunities in western farmlands and mines. Surely, he believed he could pursue his profession in the Golden State.

He stayed at the Union Hotel in Oakland and traveled south to Santa Barbara, where he lodged at the Western Hotel on February 22 and June 6, 1888. He was a founding member of the California State Floriculture Society in San Francisco, which aimed to improve floral culture, introduce new plant varieties, import bulbs and seeds, and promote the study of plant propagation. Most society members were prominent horticulturists from universities and gardening publications. The society covered a broad range of topics, from selecting the California poppy as the state flower to officially requesting the Police Chiefs of Oakland, San Francisco, and Alameda to take action against the theft of flowers and shrubs from private gardens and floral offerings in cemeteries. It also organized public flower and plant exhibitions, followed by evening concerts.

John was invited to present at least two papers he had written: "Landscape Gardening" (1888) and "Rockeries and the Plants Suitable for Them" (1890). "Landscape Gardening" suggested a European education as he wrote about how the Anglo-German free picturesque style replaced the French geometric landscaping approach. He asked a fellow member to read his "Rockeries," which provided excellent tips for constructing rock ornamentations in gardens, the best plants to use, and how to grow and arrange them. He also suggested using rocks to construct hothouse interiors instead of the shelving nurserymen typically use for compact plant arrangements.[139] He was selected to represent the Society at the 1888 state fruit-growers convention in Chico, California, where he was to present a paper. However, John's name was not mentioned in the convention's official record. His co-delegate, Emory Smith of San Francisco, presented his paper "The Future of Floriculture in California" and answered questions. It's unclear whether John even attended.[140]

John displayed landscape gardening and labyrinth designs at the 1889 State Floral Exhibition in San Francisco, where he received a medal, like most exhibitors. He began to be described as an essayist and as a horticulturist. California Florist & Gardener published one of his letters, "Culture of Holland Bulbs," about Crocus, Freesia, Narcissus, Anemone, Ranunculus, Amaryllis, Gladiolus, and Lilies. He stated, "The climate of California is so kind that a man of small means may have a garden which elsewhere can only belong to people of wealth. Besides the technical knowledge required by the landscape gardener, he should have traveled much and should have the genius which would enable him to see his work as it will appear in after years." He was also quoted as saying, "A landscape gardener was born, not made. To be a good landscaper gardener, a man must have traveled considerably and seen much. Above all, he must be a man of taste, patience, and practical energy."

Despite his self-confidence and abilities, his professional dreams did not come to fruition. He left California for St. Louis, where he was listed in the 1891 St. Louis City Directory as a gardener, living at 1835 Linn, before moving on to Chicago, Illinois. John had filed his Declaration of Intent to become a U.S. citizen in Alameda County, California, on August 5, 1890, the so-called "first papers." Two years later, in Chicago, on August 31, 1892, the day after his wedding, he completed the petition to become a citizen, the "second papers." He promptly registered to vote, stating he had lived in Cook County, Illinois, for 14 months. Citizenship laws left room for manipulation. One judge in Monterey County, California, disregarded the legally required waiting period between the first and second papers and traveled 75 miles south to a rural area to naturalize nearly 100 people, whom he registered to vote on the same day, likely to increase his vote count. Manipulating laws is nothing new.

Marriage

Catherine Mary Kuhn and John A. Gabler were married on August 30, 1892, by Father Merz, who had known Kate all of her life.[141] Kate was 25; John was 34. "A Chicago Florist Weds a Vincennes Maiden. A quiet but very elegant wedding occurred here Tuesday morning. Mr. John Gabler of Chicago and Miss Katie Kuhn were married at St. John the Baptist German Catholic Church at 7 am, with Reverend Father Merz officiating. Attendants were Mr. Henry Raben, Miss Theresa Ebner, Mr. Jake Kuhn, Miss Mattie Gaal, Mr. John Bey, and Francisca Gabler. A few immediate relatives and intimate friends witnessed the ceremony. The bride wore a light gray traveling suit and carried a bouquet of white roses. The bridesmaids were tastily attired in dotted Swiss, each carrying pink and yellow roses. The groom and groomsmen wore conventional suits. After the wedding ceremony, a sumptuous wedding breakfast was served at the palatial residence of Mrs. John Ebner, corner of 5th and Vigo streets. Mr. and Mrs. Gabler left for Chicago, their future home. They were the recipients of a large number of very costly presents. The guests from abroad were Miss Gabler of St. Louis, Miss Raben of Mt. Vernon, and Miss Gaal of St. Louis. Mr. Gabler's home is in Chicago, where he is doing a prosperous business as a florist. The bride is a niece of Mrs. Ebner. Her home was in Vincennes."[142]

Wedding attendants, Jake and Theresa, were Kate's cousins; Francisca was John's sister, who traveled from St. Louis for the wedding. Mattie Gaal of St. Louis, soon to become Mrs. Hintersteller, was Kate's best friend. Kate's cousin hosted a party for wedding guests still in town the following weekend, including Mattie Gaal of St. Louis and Lizzie Raben of St. Wendells. After dancing and games, elegant refreshments were served.[143]

The newlyweds took the train to Chicago to begin their life together, but six months later, their plans were interrupted by the death of Kate's father. Andrew Kuhn's body was transported by train back to Vincennes and laid in his sister's parlor. Catherine Ebner may have felt it was her duty to host her brother's viewing, but she did not pay for his funeral, nor did his daughters contribute. He only had enough money to cover his modest funeral costs—$12.00 for the hearse and services, 75 cents for candles, and $3.00 for digging the grave. He left behind three grown daughters: Mrs. Gerhard Recker of Vincennes, Mrs. Gabler of Chicago, and Victoria, a nun.[144]

John and Kate found Chicago to be a massive city of one million immigrants, failed homesteaders, industrialists, and those filled with hope and optimism. A city famous for anarchists and labor strikes, Chicago was recovering from the Haymarket Affair when a bomb exploded after a labor demonstration in 1886. Construction had begun on the 28-mile Sanitary and Ship Canal, and the Chicago World's Fair and Columbus Exposition to celebrate the 400th anniversary of Christopher Columbus's discovery of America. Chicago Fair organizers commissioned landscape architect Frederick Law Olmsted to design the fairgrounds. Horticultural groups and merchants, including florists, nursery owners, and members of the public who owned greenhouses, viewed the fair as an opportunity to promote the city's gardens and floricultural industry. John, the Chicago florist, got a job landscaping the fairgrounds.

The Chicago World's Fair, a Gilded Age extravaganza, showcased the modern industrial city of Chicago. A 50-cent admission introduced fairgoers to a wondrous illuminated city, brightly lit for the first time with electricity and Edison's Tower of Light. During its six-month run, twenty-seven million visitors were awed by a new engineering marvel called the Ferris Wheel, standing 264 feet high with 36 passenger cars, each capable of holding up to 60 passengers. They nibbled on a new snack made from peanuts and popcorn, mixed with a syrupy concoction, later marketed as Cracker Jack.

John knew his employment at the World's Fair was only temporary. Ads were placed in Chicago newspapers for a German gardener and florist seeking a position. This person had several years of practical experience growing flowers and vegetables, as well as caring for private and commercial greenhouses, hotbeds, and hot frames. A person who understood horses. Spoke English.

Operating a small truck farm in California or working as a florist or landscape gardener did not bring John the success he craved. With no employment offers in Chicago that suited him, John and Kate visited Springfield, Missouri, in September 1893, even before the Fair closed. John described himself to Springfield dignitaries as "the head landscape gardener who supervised the preparations of the Chicago World's Fairgrounds and brought flattering recommendations from the World's Fair Commission." John was shown throughout the town and introduced as an experienced nurseryman who had traveled extensively on both continents. He wanted to establish an art nursery and had arrived at the conclusion that there was "no more suitable location than Southwest Missouri." He was looking for a farm near a stream. He advocated planting dwarf peach trees in hedge rows that would bear when two years old and not be injured by frost.[145]

Horticulture magazines claimed that propagating fruit trees could make a grower wealthy quickly. Railroads promoted "Ozarks, the Land of the Big Red Apple" by mailing free maps, timetables, and promotional materials. Apple trees in Springfield, Missouri, became productive four years earlier than in Germany, and they could be planted at a density of 40 trees per acre. Nicknamed the "Royal Fruit County," Springfield had an excellent railroad hub for shipping young nursery stock nationwide and branded itself as "Just watch our smoke." Kate packed her expensive wedding gifts to display in a new home in Springfield.

John and Kate probably traveled comfortably in beautifully appointed Pullman cars that traveled directly from Chicago to St. Louis without having to transfer trains. Perhaps they stopped briefly in St. Louis to visit John's sisters and Kate's cousins before continuing on to Springfield. A pregnant Kate bought 10 acres of land near Springfield on October 18, 1893, for $700. The deed did not list John.[146]

While John advertised fruit trees for sale in national publications, Kate gave birth to their first two children. Laurence (my grandfather) was born on February 24, 1894, and Eleanor was born on April 21, 1897; both children were baptized at St. Joseph Catholic Church in Springfield. A German neighbor, who would later partner with John in a mining venture, and his wife became Laurence's godparents. The ten-acre farm and three-room cottage were a far cry from the Ebner mansion in Vincennes.

John sold one-year-old pear trees for $2.50 each (a dozen trees for $25.00) and several varieties of apple trees for $1.00 each. He introduced the Ozark pear, a competitor of the Bartlett. The Ozark pear tree was touted as entirely blight-proof, bearing large, delicious pears annually. He sent Kate's cousins in Vincennes "fine specimens of Ozark pears of delicious flavor and great producers. They grow in clusters and are shaped like an apple."[147]

Before his death, John Ebner Jr. developed an interest in growing, storing, and shipping apples as the ice company expanded to include apple storage. His brothers Joseph and Laurence continued his interest in fruit. John Gabler and Joseph Ebner purchased 80 acres of land outside Springfield on January 18, 1900, for $1,000, assuming a $400 encumbrance. They may have intended the land to become an orchard, but they apparently didn't keep it long. Laurence Ebner tried to interest apple growers in sending an apple to every soldier in World War I. In another promotion in 1924, he gave apples away to celebrate Apple Week.

John's day brightened when he received new orders for trees, letters commenting on his published articles, or correspondence from experts. He experimented with New Zealand, Hungarian, and Russian apple varieties sent to him by pomologists in Washington, D.C. "For about 15 years, we have been experimenting with Russian varieties, and it has been established that they are a failure in our variable climate," wrote John Gabler in Rural World. "It takes years of time and labor for such experimenting, but it is a great charm to see something new coming forth." He concluded that the New Zealand apple varieties were best for Springfield's climate. Newspapers across the country picked up the article.

Telephones became available to Springfield residents in the fall of 1899, and the first automobile appeared in April 1900. Concerns about train robbers, politics, and diseases brought back by the Spanish-American War military troops dominated the headlines. Whites blamed a smallpox epidemic on Blacks and closed colored schools to prevent its spread. The City Council voted by a narrow margin to fence the "colored burial ground" at Hazelwood Cemetery, making it more difficult for Blacks to bury their dead in the rear section of the cemetery. During the months of panic, Black Springfield residents had to carry their dead around the fence on overgrown tracks through cornfields and brambles to reach their final resting place. Rumors circulated about new cases of smallpox, driven more by hysteria than fact.

Kate's husband asked the Springfield City Council for $15.00 to repair his wagon after it was damaged when his horses became frightened by a volley of gunfire from the Springfield Rifles during a parade. In a similar incident in July or the same incident, John presented a claim to the city council for $35.00 for damages caused by runaway horses startled by a volley fired by the Springfield Rifles. The horses upset Mr. Gabler's wagon, throwing him out and injuring him slightly.

In 1898, Gablers' neighborhood was assessed for street repairs to install Macadam pavement. Their share of the special tax was $12.44. John bought 79.22 acres outside Springfield on March 23, 1900, for $1000, and on the same day, sold two lots in Springfield for $500.

(And this could be the same acreage that he bought with Joseph Ebner in January 1900).

Mining became John's next big idea to get rich. Enamored with risky ventures, John started a mining operation in his orchard. The Springfield paper ran a front-page article detailing how John Gabler and William Plum finished sinking a 20-foot shaft on the Gabler farm on Melville Road, one and a half miles northwest of the Eisnmayer Mills. "Mr. Gabler will start a shaft about 200 yards from the other and prospect it actively in hopes of striking 'pay dirt.' He says mining experts pronounce the specimens taken from the first shaft exceptionally fine and believe the two prospectors are on the right road to wealth."[148] Many in Missouri believed that the products of a mine were more profitable than those of a farm.

After mining with William Plum for a year, they suddenly struck mineral deposits, making them believe they had a fortune in sight. In a 100-foot shaft, John found disseminated copper in a stratum of magnesian limestone. In another shaft farther away, he struck silver ore. Having already spent $2,000, he was eager to "work his find for all it was worth." John and his neighbor, William Plum, were the only men in the 1900 North Campbell Township census district whose occupations were listed as miners; everyone else was a farmer or had a job related to the railroad.

In 1900, John was 42; Kate was 33; Laurence (later he exchanged the "u" for "w" and spelled his name Lawrence) was six years old, and Eleanor was three. John and Kate owned their farm outright.

John's mining operation and fruit trees did not bring him wealth. In 1902, John, Kate, and their two children left their orchard and mine shafts near Springfield to move to St. Louis. The orchards around Springfield, Missouri, peaked at 540,000 fruit trees, but by 1940, that number had fallen to 100,000 due to diseases, competition from West Coast fruit, and aging trees.

They arrived in St. Louis just before Kate gave birth to their third child, Joseph, who was born on October 21, 1902, at John's sister's home. Theresa, widowed for six years, lived in Dutchtown, a German neighborhood anchored by St. Anthony of Padua Catholic Church. Space was made for John, Kate, their two children, and the new baby in a house crowded with Theresa's five children, aged 12 to 25, and probably her sister, Frances. From Theresa's home, the children could see the House of Refuge, an institution that served both as an orphanage and a jail. They knew that children went there if they misbehaved.

Kate could now walk to Mass instead of enduring a bumpy wagon ride. She had missed electricity, cakes with raspberry filling, and her cousins and sisters-in-law. John advertised their three-room cottage in Springfield for sale in June 1902 and then again in December 1903, possibly renting it out in between. "$950 will buy my 10-acre garden land, one mile northwest of the city on Melville Road, with running water all year, a three-room cottage, fine trees, and more. John Gabler, 4411 Norfolk Avenue, St. Louis." By then, Gablers had a new address in St. Louis and no longer lived with John's sister and her family.

Kate was probably excited to shop at Stix, Baer & Fuller Department Store just as she had before her marriage. Raised in the fashionable Ebner household and married to a tailor's son, she knew how to dress in fine-quality fabric if she had the means. St. Louis was bustling with streetcars and rushing pedestrians, amid the stench of horse droppings and the heat of politics. The city was the nation's fourth-largest, after New York City, Philadelphia, and Chicago. Damage was still visible from the 1896 tornado, one of the deadliest and most destructive in U.S. history: over $10,000,000 in damages ($4.35 billion today), 255 people dead, and over a thousand injured. More than 5,000 were left homeless, losing all their possessions. The tornado destroyed some schools and caused extensive damage to others, which were already overcrowded. Saints Peter and Paul German Catholic Church was destroyed; the cemetery of which will soon hold the remains of John, his sister, and his brother-in-law.

After a violent streetcar strike in 1900, during which tracks were blown up, electrical lines were cut, and men on both sides were killed, St. Louis upgraded its streetcar and rail service in preparation for the 1904 St. Louis World's Fair and the 1904 Summer Olympics, the first Olympics held in the Western Hemisphere. The Fair, celebrating the centennial of the Louisiana Purchase, was constructed in the western section of Forest Park, which covered 1,240 acres of uneven, clay soil and had previously been used as a dump. Five hundred workers were hired to turn the rough, debris-filled hills into smooth lawns and flower gardens, framed by waterfalls and canals. Gablers' new address on Norfolk was within walking distance of the site. According to family stories, John was a landscape architect who designed the plantings on a bowl-shaped slope surrounding a pond below what is now the St. Louis Art Museum.

Instead, John was a popular labor foreman. In October 1903, just as John was about to receive a recognition gift in front of the crews, he was unexpectedly fired. Several days later, eight union workers were also dismissed. The union demanded reinstatement, but when that was denied, a strike was authorized, supported by the Central Trade and Labor Union of St. Louis and the Teamsters Union. On October 28, 800 men from the landscape, engineering, and railroad departments of the World's Fair walked off the job. John Gabler, identified as the former general foreman of the landscape department, claimed the strike was called because of his own discharge and that of other union men. He said that the Director of Works and other Fair officials were hostile to the unions, and that the men were fired for their union activities.[149] It's unknown if John was rehired. A week later, he traveled to Springfield on business, describing himself as a general foreman in the landscape department of the World's Fair. It's also unclear how long the strike lasted or if the other men were rehired, but by the next spring, thousands of workers were working double shifts for weeks to get the grounds ready. John's leadership role representing the disgruntled laborers may have been righteous, but it seems somewhat rash, as he was the sole support for Kate and three children, and Kate was pregnant.

John placed ads in St. Louis newspapers in June 1904 and May 1905 as a landscape architect and gardener specializing in artistic landscape designs that imitate natural rockeries. John had an office in Room 210 of the Temple Building on Broadway in 1904, but by the next year, his business address had become his home at 4347 Kennerly. The one-story, four-room frame cottage on a 25' × 145' lot was soon listed for sale at $1,500. Once again, a professional life was not working out for him, and, as a result, not for Kate either.

April 30, 1904, marked the opening of the St. Louis World's Fair, which drew 187,793 visitors. An astounding crowd of nearly 20 million attended from April 30 to December 1, 1904 (excluding Sundays when it was closed). Adult tickets cost 50 cents; children's admission was 25 cents. Visitors included Teddy Roosevelt, Geronimo, Helen Keller, and John Phillip Sousa. The country celebrated its acquisition of the Philippines, Puerto Rico, Guam, and the Mariana Islands from the Spanish-American War. The classic movie "Meet Me in St. Louis," starring Judy Garland, captured the excitement of a family visiting the St. Louis Fair, with women wearing wide-brimmed hats decorated with feathers, ribbons, and flowers, wrapped in tulle and net, and men in long-sleeved shirts with starched collars.

Riding the 265-foot-high Observation Wheel, introduced a decade earlier at the Chicago World's Fair, offered visitors a view of the exhibition palaces. The Pike, an amusement area, starred Jim Key, the world's smartest horse, who could solve math problems, spell names, and express his political preferences. Exhibits ranged from historical French fur-trading posts to Eskimo and Filipino villages, showcasing authentic villagers. The Cascades of the Grand Basin sparkled, with 45,000 gallons of water per minute cascading over its three falls, symbolizing man's mastery over nature. New technology was displayed, including infant incubators, while young women pounded away on new Underwood Typewriters. The fair even popularized ice cream cones, iced tea, Dr. Pepper, hamburgers, and hot dogs served with French's mustard.

"Help yourself to an apple" was the theme of the Missouri Horticultural Exhibit, where apples of uniform size were featured from most states and Cecil Rhodes's farm in South Africa. Due to advancements in cold storage, the apples from South Africa arrived looking as if they had been freshly picked. Apple growers' goal was to change the public perception that eating raw apples was unhealthy. John Gabler and the Ebner brothers may have enjoyed the publicity surrounding apples, but John's infatuation with apples ended with their move from Springfield to St. Louis.

Weeks before the fair opened, their second daughter, their fourth child, was born on March 12, 1905, at their new address at 2809 North Taylor. The baby did not live long.[150] In her grief, Kate probably walked to Mass in a long dark skirt and a starched white shirtwaist, her head bowed, her wide-brimmed hat covering her dark hair, and a crocheted shawl draped over her shoulders.

She may have distracted herself from her daughter's death by sewing. Patterns for shirtwaists cost 25 cents, and a fashionable five-gored skirt pattern, available in sizes for waists of 22, 24, 26, 30, and 32 inches, sold for 10 cents. Store-bought women's clothing was believed to be made from poor materials, whereas men's ready-made clothing was not. At the May Company, a well-tailored suit for John ranged from $12.50 to $20.00.

Fortunately, the trend of extremely tiny waists for women was fading. A fifteen-cent corset from Penny & Gentle's clothing store no longer needed to be tightly laced. The unnatural posture caused by the high-fashion, tightly laced S-curve silhouette corset—with its flat front compressing the waist, pushing the chest forward, and forcing the hips back—led to fractured ribs, collapsed lungs, liver displacement, and uterine prolapses. Women could not lift their arms above shoulder height. In England, fashionable women wore as much as fourteen pounds of undergarments under even their heaviest gowns. This weight was reduced to about seven pounds, mainly by removing the corset, which was so harmful to women's health. But women accustomed to the constricting corset felt untethered, as if their insides would rattle and fall out. They were unlikely to embrace the rational dress movement of the late Victorian era, with its practical and comfortable clothing—no high heels, no heavy skirts, and no corsets.

Corsets became even looser when steel stays were needed for World War I production. Eventually, women switched to girdles and bras and wore dresses that ended above the ankle, with roomier waists allowing the female body greater freedom of movement. Women could take invigorating strolls without long, full skirts entangling their legs and restricting their steps to little mincing ones. And with ankles exposed, high-button boots became fashionable. Times had changed since lifting a skirt was considered a sexual invitation.

John, meanwhile, was actively pursuing schemes. He persuaded the president of the Tamm Glue Company in St. Louis to allow him to search for natural gas on the company's property. The newspaper headline read: "St. Louis Man Locates Gas Wells with a Magic Stick—Indian Learned Him."

> A well of natural gas was discovered yesterday afternoon on the premises of the Tamm Glue Company, Sarpy and Vandeventer Avenues. John Gabler of 4347 Kennerly Avenue located it. Having prevailed on Max Tamm, the president of the company, to allow him to attempt to locate the gas, which he was convinced was on the premises, Gabler produced a stick covered with black cloth. With this extended in front of him, he walked about the yard until the stick suddenly and apparently of its own accord took a sharp downward turn. Pointing to the spot, Gabler exclaimed dramatically, "There's your gas." He added that the gas would be found about 600 to 700 feet below the surface in a stratum of hard rock. Gas was located after drilling 750 feet below the spot indicated. Thirty feet down the drillers came across a bed of rock which extended apparently to a limitless depth. How this scientific act of Gabler is performed is a mystery to all except himself,

and even he confesses that he cannot wholly explain it. When asked about it, he said: "Fifteen years ago, I was in California carrying on my business as a market gardener. In Santa Barbara County, I saw an Indian locating oil fields by means of some kind of stick, which seemed to be attracted to the oil. I became very interested in this and prevailed upon the Indian to allow me to try my hand. To my surprise, I found that the stick would obey me. Occasionally, however, I was at fault. I determined to find out why I sometimes failed. For fifteen years, I have been trying to find out where that stick was at fault and have at last succeeded in perfecting the instrument. I can only say it consists of a stick of a particular kind of wood, to the end of which certain chemicals are attached. Such is the instrument, but it will respond only to a very few. I cannot explain it, but there seems to be some magnetic attraction between the man and the stick," Mr. Gabler added that the gas that has been so far located in St. Louis is only from a side vein, the main body of which he declares runs through Jefferson County. The principal vein of all he believes is located in southeastern Kansas.[151]

Natural gas was discovered at the Tamm Glue Company at a depth of 750 feet, and it erupted into a 25-foot-high column of fire, threatening nearby buildings. The gas pressure was estimated at 500 pounds per square inch. The fire required a half-hour's work before the flames were stopped by means of an iron cover. Neighbors in the West End of St. Louis were astonished to see the sky light up. Some thought it was a brilliant sunset, but others believed it to be a huge fire. John Gabler, identified as "the engineer who discovered and sank two wells, predicted that St. Louis would be well supplied with natural gas." He claimed to have struck a vein that ran southeast from St. Louis to Kansas, containing enough gas to supply power and light for the city for years to come.[152]

For nonbelievers, Max Tamm posted a small newspaper notice stating that John Gabler and E.H. Sublette had found oil and gas on his property at Sarpy and Maxwell. According to the U.S. Geological Survey, the Tamm Glue Factory did indeed have a natural gas well that temporarily yielded a considerable amount of gas before it filled with water.[153]

In the 1904 St. Louis City Directory, John listed his occupation as a laborer; in 1905, he upgraded himself to architect, and the following year, his occupation was a cryptic "gas." Five months after his discovery of natural gas, John was dead at 48 years old. After 13 years of marriage and three surviving children, Kate's husband suddenly and unexpectedly died on April 5, 1906. Lawrence was 12, Eleanor turned 9 two weeks after her father died, and Joseph was 3. John, the great persuader and self-promoter who joined professional organizations, experimented with orchard stock, championed laborers, used a diving rod to locate minerals and natural gas wells, had fallen ill with appendicitis, and died. Kate lost her husband—the sole wage earner, the wavering flame of a candle—who tried his hand at landscape gardening, writing, raising fruit, mining, and natural gas exploration. And then the candle blew out. John was buried at Saints Peter and Paul Cemetery in St. Louis in a plot purchased by his sister, Therese Sprengnether, next to Therese's husband, August.

Widowhood in St. Louis

Dressed in black, Kate lost the safety and protection her marriage offered. Attractive and youthful at 40, women may have seen her as a threat to their own marriages. Socially, she was not a lady. Ladies pursued education and personal interests, while Kate needed a job to support her family. Despite all of John's grandiose schemes, Kate and the children were not left well-to-do. In three years, her occupation will be listed as a servant.

Kate and the children moved to 2601 North Taylor Ave, above Taylor Pharmacy. Their flat was near her uncle, Andrew Shasserre, who owned a grocery store at 2401 North Taylor. In the Elleardsville neighborhood, Shasserre Grocery advertised for German-speaking clerks and for good, honest German boys to deliver groceries and care for the horses. One horse was advertised for sale in 1908, as the era of horse-drawn delivery wagons was coming to an end.

Kate had always been close to the Shasserres, who left Vincennes for St. Louis in 1883 to build houses. The Shasserre marriage, however, faced problems that no nails could hold together. Kate's aunt and uncle experienced a marital rift so profound that when their son Jacob died in 1904, his mother and all his siblings were listed in his obituary, but his father was not. Their permanent separation divided the children's loyalties. The children supported their mother, except for Kate's cousin, Andrew, who worked at his dad's grocery store on Taylor Street and eventually owned it. As good Catholics, Kate's aunt and uncle never divorced.

Kate's uncle was probably charming but hot-headed. As a 78-year-old, he got into hand-to-hand combat in the Home for the Aged carpenter shop, operated by the Little Sisters of the Poor. A fight broke out when his old friend of forty years tried to open the shop window to let in a breeze. The argument went back and forth. Finally, Shasserre threatened, "I'll break your head if you don't leave that window alone." One man pulled a knife; the other grabbed a hammer. Spectators from the Home for the Aged took sides. Riot police were called. Kate's uncle ended up with severe wounds to his neck, face, and head. Both men were charged with assault and battery. Scolded by the judge, they shared a plug of tobacco and, using their canes, limped out of court arm in arm.[154]

Kate was woefully unprepared to support herself and her children. Although she had an eighth-grade education and was a skilled seamstress, thanks to the Nuns, job opportunities for women were scarce. Her struggle was further complicated by the Panic of 1907, when banks failed and the economy slowed dramatically. The family story is that Dr. George H.M. Goehring misdiagnosed John's appendicitis, which led to his death. To make amends, he offered to train Kate to become a nurse. John's death certificate states he died of bronchial pneumonia, complicated by bowel congestion.

Nursing became an accepted career choice for women largely because of Florence Nightingale's efforts. During the Crimean War, she improved nursing standards and earned respect for women providing care. Nurses were no longer viewed as prostitutes, laundresses, or camp followers offering inconsistent and often unsanitary healthcare. Kate soon identified herself as a nurse, likely learning nursing skills through informal on-the-job training. Formal licensure and educational requirements for Licensed Practical Nurses (LPNs) were not fully established in St. Louis until 1920.

In 1909 and 1910, Kate and her three children lived at the Missimore home, located at 4869 Page Boulevard. The unmarried Missimores—two brothers and a sister—worked as a physician, a police officer, and a stenographer at a flour mill. Although she was listed as a servant, Kate may have gained nursing experience by helping the doctor. However, when the doctor married a widow, Lucille, on October 5, 1910, Kate was ready to leave. Lucille accused the doctor of ranting and cursing. He struck her, bruising her eye, when she refused to make coffee for his sister. They separated after five months of marriage, on May 6, 1911.

News arrived from Vincennes that Kate's aunt Catherine Ebner, the family's Grande Dame, had died of dropsy. John Ebner's widow was 76 and passed away at 428 Vigo Street. Her obituary described her as "a good Christian woman, well-liked and highly respected by all who knew her," a devoted member of St. John's Catholic Church, and a participant in the St. Ann's Society in Vincennes. Catherine left substantial Ebner cash and property to her children and the church, but, unpardonably, nothing for Kate, whom she had raised. Although Catherine's will confirmed she did not entirely trust her children, Kate was excluded despite being the sole support for three children. She had never been "one of the family."

> Estate Divided by the will of the late Catherine Ebner. Joseph Ebner was appointed executor. To her son Joseph Ebner, $5000 paid by her son Laurence Ebner; to her daughter Lena Schmidt, the sum of $5000 to be paid by Laurence Ebner, Mary E Wissing, and Theresa Ebner; to Laurence Ebner, part of the lots in Old Town, provided he pays Joseph $5000 and Lena $3000 within one year. To Mary Wissing, a lot in Old Town and other lots, provided she pays Lena $1000. To Theresa (now Mrs. George Schaller), lots and all household and kitchen furniture, fixtures, and goods owned by the estate, including wearing apparel, jewelry, etc. She is to pay Lena Schmidt $1000 within a year. To Rev. Father Claudius Ebner, $500, and in case of his death, his portion to the Abbot of the Abbey of St. Meinard. To Rev. Agid Merz or the successor of St. John's Roman Catholic church, the sum of $1000. Residue and remainder of estate and properties, to Joseph L., Laurence, Lena, Mary, and Theresa.[155]

After Aunt Catherine's death, Kate resumed her visits to Vincennes. Had she and her aunt fallen out over John Gabler? Did Catherine quickly see through John Gabler as a man full of schemes, dreams, and promises of wealth and social status, realizing that his stories were all make-believe?

Trips to Vincennes opened up social opportunities for her children and herself. On a trip there in August 1911, Kate's teenage son Lawrence attended a Friday evening party with a group of young people from St. John's parish. Two days later, Lawrence attended another party. Eleanor attended a masquerade party held in her honor by Mary Ebner on December 31, 1912, at the family home on Vigo Street. When Joseph Ebner's daughters, Vivian and Laurine, married the Glover brothers in a splashy society wedding in 1916, the Gablers attended. Eleanor was invited to pre-wedding events at the Vincennes Union Depot and Hotel, the city's hub. Their visits filled the Ebner family home, which was already crowded with Kate's widowed cousin Joseph, his three daughters, her widowed cousin Mary, and her two sons.

In St. Louis, Kate's children attended school through the eighth grade, just as she had. Lawrence, her oldest son, did odd jobs for Mina Myers, a divorced florist, from 1910 to 1912. In 1913, he worked as a clerk for Meyer Brothers Coffee and Spice Company. Three years later, Lawrence married a girl from St. Louis named Hannah Bartram, slipping over the border to Tennessee, most likely without Kate's approval. He was 22, and Hannah was 20. After their marriage, they rented a room in Mrs. Minnie Trenkle's residence in Rolla, Missouri, where Lawrence was a salesman for Gildenhaus Buffing Company. Hannah visited relatives in St. Louis in the summer of 1917. Lawrence registered for World War I military duty and was reclassified from Class 4 to Class 1A, but never served.

From 1913 to 1925, Kate worked as a nurse for private families and rented 1825 North Taylor for $25 a month. North Taylor was a busy street lined with long, narrow, shotgun-style brick buildings featuring commercial space on the ground floor, an apartment in the rear, and an apartment upstairs. Kate's flat was described as having seven rooms, including a bath and a furnace.

Kate's son, Joseph, drove his car into the North Taylor alley at 6:20 pm in 1925. He discovered a fire in a garage attached to a tin shop at the back of their building and sounded the alarm. The tinner had been pouring gasoline from one can into another when the fumes exploded, likely from a spark from his pipe or from a match he struck to see better, costing him his life. The fire caused minimal damage. Nine years earlier, at 1 a.m., a motorman and passengers on a passing Taylor Street streetcar saw flames coming from another building near Kate's. They woke the eight people sleeping in two apartments and saved their lives from a fire believed to have started in the downstairs shop. Due to a fear of fire, most buildings and homes in St. Louis were built of brick, as the city had an abundance of high-quality red clay, earning the nickname "Brick City."

The growing feminist movement advocating for women's voting rights faced open hostility in St. Louis. In the fall of 1913, a parade of 60 automobiles heading to a downtown suffragist rally was heckled by boys who yelled, "Who's going to do the dishes?" The 1911 Missouri Homemakers' Conference entirely omitted the word "suffrage," but members openly discussed the importance of registering births, reducing infant mortality through breastfeeding, promoting food safety, and marketing farm products such as butter and hams. Suffragists, mostly white upper-class women who supported women's rights and economic independence, were surprised to discover that lower-class and immigrant women also needed help. They established the Voters' School Committee in 1914 to teach women about their rights in English, German, and Yiddish.

Efforts to reduce alcohol consumption grew alongside protests for and against American involvement in World War I. Emotionally charged posters linked German American breweries and the German tradition of drinking a daily beer to German militarism. Drinking beer was viewed as unpatriotic, almost treasonous. The St. Louis Post-Dispatch speculated that a quarter of the city's 2,100 licensed saloons might close. Already, laws closing Sunday beer gardens had been enacted, depriving German American families of a beer and bratwurst while they sang, socialized, and conducted business. By January 1918, beer's alcohol content was limited to 2.75%. The U.S. government declared that corn and grains were needed to prevent starvation in German-occupied Belgium, rather than to feed the U.S. beer industry, which German Americans operated. Anheuser-Busch Brewing shifted to war production and diversified its operations, producing truck bodies, refrigerated cabinets, diesel engines for Navy submarines, and police vehicles used to catch bootleggers. It also introduced Bevo, a non-alcoholic malt beverage, which became popular after the passage of the Eighteenth Amendment in 1919, banning alcohol sales. This amendment stayed in effect until 1933.

Ethnic Germans faced attacks fueled by anti-German war propaganda. Kate's parents were born in French Alsace-Lorraine, which Germany had annexed, while the Gablers were born in the Rhineland. They lived in ethnic German neighborhoods in St. Louis. German American art, literature, and music became objectionable. Popular

Turner Hall gymnastic clubs, shooting clubs, and singing societies were viewed with suspicion. German-language newspapers were considered sympathetic to Germany. German Americans were accused of bribing corrupt union leaders to stage strikes and suspected of disrupting ammunition production. Rumors spread that Germany was planning a coup in Mexico. President Wilson heightened paranoia by warning in a speech that Americans with foreign roots were poisoning American life. He created the Committee of Public Information (CPI) as a propaganda tool. Wilson stated that all loyal Americans must defend U.S. interests, regardless of their ethnic background. Consider this: criticizing the U.S. government became illegal, publications were banned and labeled unpatriotic, the German language was no longer taught in schools, and German food and beer were viewed as subversive. Sauerkraut was renamed liberty cabbage, and frankfurters became liberty sausages. Posters depicted Germans as evil ogres and mocked their accents. Streets in St. Louis were renamed, including Kaiser, Von Versen, Hamburger, and Bismarck. Berlin Avenue was renamed Pershing Avenue to honor the Missouri-born general. The Kaiser-Huhn grocery, the oldest in St. Louis, was rebranded as the Pioneer Grocery Company after its delivery drivers were pelted with stones.

By early 1917, it was clear that the United States would not remain neutral in the Great War. Germany violated its promise not to attack U.S. naval ships by sinking seven U.S. Merchant Marine vessels. President Woodrow Wilson responded by declaring war on Germany on April 2, 1917. St. Louis shop owners faced arrest for hoarding or price-gouging sugar and other foodstuffs. Housewives were morally obligated to conserve food and reduce waste, and encouraged to turn vacant lots or backyards into Victory Gardens. Ammonia could not be wasted because one pound of ammonia made twenty hand grenades. Cutting back on wheat, meat, and sugar led to meatless Mondays and wheatless Wednesdays. Gasless Sundays, heatless Mondays, and lightless Wednesdays saved fuel for the war effort. With many men volunteering, farms lacked field workers, and factories faced staffing shortages. Women stepped in to fill these roles, covering their hair with headscarves to harvest vegetables and work in manufacturing plants and munition factories.

At the end of World War I, the Vincennes post office announced that mail service had resumed to about 60 villages in the disputed areas of Alsace. Citizens had been loyal French citizens for 200 years before the Treaty of Frankfurt ceded Alsace to Germany following the Franco-Prussian War of 1871. Even Kate's uncle, John Ebner, was quoted in 1878 lamenting the despotism of Bismarck's iron rule, which his poor countrymen endured. Kate probably made it clear she was of French, not German, descent.

The euphoria after the war was short-lived. Women were expected to resume their pre-war roles of domestic life, abandoning the independence that jobs and wages granted them. Factories that made bullets, uniforms, and meals for the army laid off workers. Job seekers joined shell-shocked men with missing limbs in search of employment. Postwar celebrations, suffrage protests, and the return of soldiers were blamed for the Spanish flu epidemic. Citizens were required to wear gauze face masks and follow curfews. Schools, libraries, theaters, movie houses, dance halls, churches, ice cream parlors, and soda shops were temporarily shut down—an unsettling echo of the COVID pandemic. Warning signs appeared on the homes of infected residents. Hospitals became overcrowded. Streetcars, considered breeding grounds for infection, were ventilated and cleaned, and passenger capacity was limited. In St. Louis, infections spiked the day before Thanksgiving, prompting shoppers to avoid streetcars and sick passengers. Parents hung camphor balls, onions, or garlic in cheesecloth bags around their children's necks for protection.

Kate continued working as a private nurse and living with her children, Eleanor and Joseph. She couldn't help but notice the changes happening around her: the dreadful corsets with whalebone stays disappeared, flapper girls exposed their knees, and women demanded the right to vote. When the Nineteenth Amendment was ratified in 1920, women across the country finally gained the right to vote. Kate and Eleanor registered, listing their address as 1825 North Taylor. Kate was 53, and Eleanor was 23. They had lived in the precinct for eight years, in the city for eighteen years, and Eleanor had lived in Missouri her whole life, while her mother had lived there for twenty-eight years.

Eleanor became a clerk at Laclede Gas Light Company in 1918, as women entered the workforce as stenographers, clerks, and secretaries, sporting hairstyles such as the Marcel and the finger wave. Joseph became an optician at age 18. He may have apprenticed with a cousin on his dad's side, Adolph Sprengnether. Lawrence still lived in Rollo with his wife, where he worked as a grocery salesman before becoming a Frisco salesman—an organization of traveling salesmen.

Kate and her daughter Eleanor

In a 1920 photograph, Kate sits demurely in a canoe, wearing a long cotton dress and a straw hat, while Eleanor is dressed in a swimming costume. Influenced by women's suffrage, appropriate clothing became necessary for the 'new' woman who bicycled, swam, bowled, golfed, and played tennis. The bicycling craze challenged fashion norms. Corsets were discarded as they restricted breathing. Lead weights were added to the hems to prevent the wind from billowing skirts and accidentally exposing the calves. More daring women wore divided skirts or even bloomers because, even with lead weights, long skirts interfered with pedals and gears. Society fretted about women becoming over-exerted and bicycling alone.

In the Roaring Twenties, women were accused of being too masculine, mimicking men by wearing trousers, smoking, drinking, and socializing in saloons and public houses, while bobbing their long hair to just below their ears. Psychic mediums and religious cults appealed; gramophones and radios were purchased, lipstick was applied, and movies were attended. Wild girls drove their automobiles with the same flair as girls who burned their bras in the 1970s.

People ate as much lard as chicken. Cold cereal made its debut with the introduction of cornflakes, shredded wheat, and puffed rice. Thirty percent of Americans owned a telephone, less than twenty percent had an electric kitchen range, and very few owned a refrigerator. Little had changed for Kate in the 1920s. She still worked as a nurse, Eleanor remained employed by the Laclede Gas Company, and Joseph was an optician for Arthur P. Thursby.

The invention of the typewriter created two skilled jobs: stenographer and typist. Women poured into the workforce (2.6 million in 1880 grew to 7.8 million thirty years later), yet 60 percent of women were stuck in poorly paid domestic work, such as laundry or housecleaning, or labored in garment factories and mills. These jobs were viewed as temporary means to earn money before marriage, rather than as long-term careers. The prevailing attitudes believed that single women like Eleanor were entitled to a career only if their fathers could not afford to care for them. A man was permitted to replace a working woman because he was responsible for supporting his family, while she was not.

While women's jobs were changing, Kate's old neighborhood of Elleardsville was undergoing changes as well. The St. Louis Post-Dispatch in 1911 listed Kate's old address, 4347 Kennerly, for rent under "For Colored People" for $15 per month. The neighborhood, soon shortened to the Ville, was no longer a mix of Negroes, Irish, and Germans. By 1910, the Ville was 13 percent Black, which evolved into 98.8 percent Black as most Whites fled to the townships, leaving behind a neighborhood with high unemployment, no services, and uncaring landlords of buildings that eventually got bulldozed, becoming an example of urban decay.

As my flight crossed the Mississippi River, I spotted the St. Louis Arch and a vast green space that I initially thought was a big park. After landing, I realized what I thought was a park was really overgrown, empty fields that used to have houses, stores, trees, and people in Kate's old neighborhood. From potholed streets and acres of weeds, occasionally dotted with a building or a tree, I only had to cross one boulevard to reach a vibrant modern neighborhood of landscaped condos and restaurants. Well-dressed professionals sat at sidewalk tables, sipping coffee. Stores displayed upscale linens and wooden toys for sale. The transition between neighborhoods was shocking, abrupt, and dramatic.

Kate also moved out of the Ville, closer to John's sisters. Theresa, two years older than John, came to America with her husband, August, their four children, and her sister, Frances. Theresa had two more children in St. Louis; one son died at age ten, and another at 31 from tuberculosis. August was a music teacher and an organist for the Catholic Church. He likely attended the 25th annual National Sängerfest in St. Louis in 1888, where forty-two German choirs from across the U.S. gathered for the national singing festival. At the train station, visiting choirs were greeted by oom-pah brass bands and escorted to the Central Turner Hall. After four days of singing complex four-part German folk songs and other music, the festival ended with a stunning display of Japanese fireworks.

Theresa, like Kate, was widowed with young children when August died, but unlike Kate, she remarried. The St. Louis Post-Dispatch published an amusing article, although Theresa wouldn't have found it funny. The headline read: "Krey Wedding Outvoted. His Son and Daughter Oppose; Woman's Four Children Approve Plans." John Krey had been widowed for only three months when he married Theresa, a longtime family friend. His son, who took over the family business of Krey Packing Company, even refused to attend the wedding. Despite his children's objections, John and Theresa married at St. Anthony of Padua Catholic Church—the Dutchtown neighborhood church.[156] John Krey died five years later.

John and Theresa's sister, Frances, who attended her brother's wedding in Vincennes, never married and worked as a seamstress, maid, or cook in St. Louis. She lived with her sister unless her job provided room and board. After Theresa was widowed for the second time, the two sisters moved in with Theresa's daughter, Anna. Anna's husband was an architect and part of a family firm that specialized in designing Catholic churches—churches described as giving pleasing unity through matching bricks and finely shaped terracotta moldings. Anna's brother-in-law was also a priest. Theresa's daughters adored their Aunt Frances.

One of Frances' jobs was cooking at the St. Louis San Francisco Hospital, better known as the Frisco. The hospital treated Frisco railroad employees and passengers suffering from on-the-job injuries, train wrecks, or illnesses far from their family physicians. While employed there in 1910, Frances worked with Albert Wagner, a retired engineer for the Frisco Railroad. Albert was 74, and Frances was 47. Albert purchased a double cemetery plot for $48.00 at Saints Peter and Paul Cemetery, a Catholic cemetery in St. Louis, where he was buried in 1917. Although Albert was married and had children, Frances was buried beside him when she died in 1928.

The Gabler family gathered for Frances' funeral procession. Theresa Sprengnether Krey rode in the first limousine with her two daughters and granddaughters. More Sprengnethers followed in the second car with a Mrs. Born. Kate Gabler, Martha Hintersteller (the daughter of Kate's best friend), and three other women filled the third car, with Martha driving. Kate's son Joseph, daughter Eleanor, and Eleanor's husband rode in the last car. Joseph served as a pallbearer.[157] Kate's other son, Lawrence, was far away in Portland, Oregon.

During the Great Depression of the 1930s, 182 banks collapsed in Missouri, and 115,000 people lost their jobs. The number of women employed in the U.S. increased only because they were hired for positions that paid lower wages than those for men. St. Louis offered free food to one out of every ten families. Kate, 64, rented an apartment at 796 Aubert Avenue in St. Louis with her son Joseph for $35 a month. The neighbors were working-class: mail handlers for the railroad, department store stock clerks, streetcar motormen, and a truck driver. Two Jewish families lived nearby. One was a tailor; the other, a Russian Jew, owned a laundry. A Greek neighbor worked as a busboy in a hotel. After Joseph married Edna Obergoenner, Kate lived with them at 1865A Kosuth Avenue in 1931 and 4846A Farlin Avenue in 1932. Joe worked as an optician with George D. Fisher and Company.

In Vincennes, Kate's cousin Laurence Ebner became the head of the family after his brother died in 1914. By 1920, Laurence was living with his wife, an eleven-year-old girl listed as a niece, and a servant. Ten years later, only Laurence, his wife, and a cook remained in his mansion at 404 North 4th Street, now valued at $20,000. The Ebner Ice and Cold Storage Company had expanded to an annual capacity of a million tons of ice, with cold storage facilities large enough to store 135,000 bushels of apples. Kate often visited Vincennes and accompanied her widowed cousin Mary to social events. They attended Mass, drank a little wine, avoided political discussions, and laughed at others' foibles. Her female cousins frequently won bridge games as members of the Cathedral's Social Club. Kate attended a Watch Party on New Year's Eve in 1921 with most of the Ebner relatives, some of whom had traveled from Indianapolis. She was also a guest of Mrs. John Hall in Mt. Vernon, Indiana, along with her cousin Mary. Guests competed to see who could piece the best quilt block at a birthday luncheon in

February 1931. Mary won first prize. Kate also attended a party at the mansion where the room was described as "decorated with tall pink tapers that cast a soft glow upon a low art bowl of pink roses and foliage resting on an exquisite lace banquet cover, where additional beautiful appointments of silver and china added to the alluring scene."

Kate nursed her Ebner cousins in Vincennes from 1933 to 1935. She cared for Laurence's wife, who died of heart disease in February 1933, attended her cousin Theresa, who passed away from cancer in September 1933, and then looked after her cousin Laurence, who also suffered from heart disease like his brother Joseph. Theresa left $50 to the pastor of St. Francis Xavier Church, $25 to her cousin Kate Gabler, $25 to her sister-in-law, and the rest of her estate to her daughter.[158]

Laurence quickly remarried after his wife's death. Kate helped the new couple look for luggage keys to their two trunks before they left for a Mediterranean honeymoon cruise. Upon their return, Laurence died of a fatal heart attack on January 1, 1934. His funeral was held at the Old Cathedral, with a cluster of priests in attendance. He left a large estate.

Four months later, Kate became involved in one of the biggest scandals to hit Vincennes. Three individuals claiming to be Laurence Ebner's illegitimate children challenged his will during a three-week trial. The front page of the Vincennes newspaper printed the testimony verbatim each day. A crowd, mostly women, filled the Knox County Circuit Courtroom, with many standing along the walls for hours. Some brought lunches and ate in the courtroom to hold their places. The courtroom crowd thinned out, however, on the day of the annual Pioneer Parade.

Mrs. Marie Curtis and Elmer Manning claimed they were born out of wedlock to Laurence and his first wife, Mamie. Mamie was the daughter of a poor farmer, while Laurence was the son of a wealthy businessman. His family found her unacceptable. Although Laurence and Mamie eventually married when Laurence was 24 and Mamie was 26, they never had any children during their marriage, nor did they claim any children born before their marriage.

The first plaintiff, Marie, was raised by Laurence's sister, Lena Schmidt, and her husband. She cried on the stand, recalling a quarrel she had on the playground with another child who tormented her by saying her father was Laurence Ebner. She went home upset and testified, "Father Schmidt called me aside and said it was true."[159] Over the years, Marie attended social events hosted or attended by Ebner family members, such as a New Year's party in 1920. She testified that she went to Laurence, whom she believed was her biological father, for business advice when she owned a bakery. In August 1933, just before Theresa's death, Marie hosted a dinner at her home, inviting Kate, Theresa, Theresa's daughter, and Mr. and Mrs. John Wissing. When Theresa was dying of cancer in the hospital, Marie and a friend went to Laurence's house to inform him. His girlfriend, Aline, who later became his second wife, was holding a bottle of liquor. Laurence told her to go into the kitchen and make the girls highballs. Marie testified that Laurence had always treated her as his daughter.

Elmer Manning, the second plaintiff, was adopted from an orphanage by a local family. While Laurence and Mamie never publicly acknowledged Marie and Elmer's parentage, the trial revealed the townspeople had always suspected, especially regarding Marie.

Margaret Lee, the third person involved in the suit, claimed that Laurence was her father and that her mother was a half-sister of Marie and Elmer, making Laurence's first wife, Mamie, her grandmother. Before Mamie gave birth to Marie and Elmer, whom Laurence allegedly fathered, she had a daughter by a neighbor boy when she was very young. Mamie's parents raised this daughter as their own. When she came of age, she started working in Ebner Ice Plant's office, where Laurence was the manager. During her employment, she had a child, Margaret Sweazey, allegedly fathered by Laurence. Margaret lived with Laurence and his wife in 1920 and was listed as a niece. Laurence's will named Mrs. Margaret (Sweazey) Lee as a "niece," but Elmer Manning and Mrs. Marie Curtis were not mentioned. The judge threw his hands up when confronted by the convoluted relationships.

The court was tasked with validating Laurence Ebner's will, written on October 17, 1933, and determining whether he was of sound mind and good morals at the time of its execution. Testimony suggested that he was known to chase women, drink excessively, curse, have a temper, play with dolls, believe in questionable medical practices, rely on horoscopes, and follow an unhealthy diet of only vegetables. Accusations reverberated through the courtroom. The plaintiffs' attorney claimed that Laurence had been with his girlfriend in a roadhouse while his wife lay at home ill and that he was drinking whiskey with the same girlfriend while his sister, Theresa, lay dying in his home. After the funeral of his wife, Mamie, Laurence was criticized for throwing a lavish party filled with alcohol. He responded, "Mamie liked a lot of people around. She enjoyed the big show. I'm putting her away with a big bang." Testimony also revealed Laurence became angry when asked to pay medical costs for his dying sister, Theresa. He claimed that she had money and had squandered it. It was insinuated that Laurence rushed from his first wife's funeral to marry his girlfriend. Yet, business associates testified they considered Laurence to be of sound mind: honest, moral, and a shrewd businessman. The trial featured contradictory portrayals of Laurence Ebner, sordid stories about the parentage of Mrs. Marie Curtis and Elmer Manning, and the cross-complainant, Mrs. Margaret Lee. Counsel for the plaintiffs repeated Bible quotations. It was a sensational scandal for the good folks of Vincennes—enough shocking gossip for a lifetime. One trait both sides agreed on was that Laurence had quite a temper, known as the "family temper."

It's clear from the transcripts that Kate wasn't happy to be called to testify. Newspaper accounts of the trial named her simply as Kate Gabler. She testified that Laurence's mother and father reared her, and she moved out when she was about 20. She recounted the history of the Ebner family in detail, naming all the sisters and brothers and specifying their death dates. She had been visiting the Ebner home in August 1933 and then returned on October 16, 1933, the day before Laurence wrote his will and left on his honeymoon with his second wife, a trip his doctor warned him against.

Q: "Did Mrs. Ebner have you get up at night and hunt for Laurence when he was a young man?"
A: "Never late at night. I have gone out early in the morning to find him, however."
Q: "Did Laurence have a temper?"
A: "Laurence had an uncontrollable temper."
Q: "Did he curse and call you names?"
A: "I don't think he meant it."

When asked to repeat the names Laurence had called her, Kate replied that she just couldn't. She admitted she knew the words but would rather not say them. She also testified that the night before Laurence and Aline left for a honeymoon cruise, they had company until 11 pm. She had one glass of wine. She talked to Aline the following day, who mentioned she had a hard time getting Laurence up the stairs, implying he was drunk. They laughed about it. When Laurence and Aline returned home from their honeymoon cruise, the day after Thanksgiving, Laurence went straight to bed.

Marie Curtis testified in court that she stopped by the Ebner home before Laurence and Aline left for their European trip. She found everyone excited. Aline, Mrs. Gabler, and Laurence were searching for papers. Months later, after Laurence Ebner's death on January 1, 1934, several witnesses testified that they saw Kate frantically searching the house for Laurence's will.

Kate

The jury found that Laurence Ebner was not of sound mind, thereby rendering his will invalid, and that his children were Marie Curtis, Elmer Manning, and Margaret Lee. However, the judge disagreed with the jury's verdict, stating it was not supported by sufficient evidence and that the jury had acted on sentiment. A new trial was set for June 18. The first trial had already disrupted the court's schedule and cost $694.10, including $2.50 per juror per day and mileage of 5 cents per mile for travel from home to court and back. The June date was postponed to December, and by October 30, 1935, the Ebner case was settled out of court. Marie Curtis and Elmer Manning compromised their claims and kept the terms secret. Margaret Lee had already been mentioned in the original will as a "niece" with a bequest of stock shares.[160]

Laurence bequeathed stock and cash to various institutions and individuals. St. Meinard's College received 60 shares of preferred Ebner stock, with the income designated for the education of Roman Catholic secular priests. His second wife was granted the house. According to court testimony, Laurence collected art, spending between $5,000 and $6,000 on oil paintings and Oriental rugs. The value of his personal property was assessed at $55,840.39. He also left behind two homes, a two-story office building, income from two life insurance policies, and all his shares of common stock. And all of this during the Great Depression! He did not mention his cousin Kate Gabler in his will.

In 1935, Kate was 69 years old. She had severed ties with her son Lawrence, who struggled with alcoholism and had divorced, violating the sacrament of marriage. She was troubled by her son Joseph's rejection of the church, which he criticized as always begging for money. Kate felt closest to her daughter Eleanor, who shared her strong attachment to the teachings of the Catholic Church.

Joseph built a career as an optician. He demonstrated an eye-photographing machine to the Police Board, which captured detailed images of the intricate patterns of blood vessels and optic nerves in the retina.[161] He also made weekly trips to an eye clinic in Illinois, accompanying two doctors and a nurse. His role was to assist the doctors in preparing or adjusting the glasses made for patients seen the previous week. However, on a trip on September 15, 1938, at 6:45 am, Joseph was instantly killed along with the other people in the car in a collision with an Illinois Central Railroad passenger train. The impact was so severe that the car's motor landed near the intersection, and the automobile was pushed 650 yards down the tracks. The nurse was tossed into a ravine 200 feet away. From the position of the dead men in the car, it appeared as if Joseph was driving. He was the vice president of Clarke & Gabler Inc., Opticians, located at 822 North Grand, St. Louis. The company announced in the newspaper, "In respect to our beloved partner, our store will be closed tomorrow."[162]

Joseph Gabler

Joe's daughter, who was seven years old when her father was killed at age 35, remembered that Kate and Eleanor did little to support her mother. She still harbored bitterness when I spoke with her by telephone 70 years later. Kate was angry about Joe's disenchantment with the church. Unfortunately, her judgment affected any hope of a future relationship with her daughter-in-law and grandchildren.

A month after Joe's death, Kate was again in Vincennes, visiting her cousin Joseph's daughter and other relatives. In 1940, the newspaper reported that Mrs. Kate Gabler of St. Louis had visited "upon numerous occasions with relatives and friends and was well known."[163]

Early in February 1939, Kate's oldest sister, Victoria (Sister Laura), died. Kate had outlived all her siblings and all of her Ebner cousins. Kate moved in with her daughter, son-in-law, and their three children at 4938 Bancroft Avenue, St. Louis. She lived in a rented upper flat with them for 20 years until shortly before her death. They lived near the Church of the Magdalen, where Kate's grandchildren attended school, and the family attended Mass. Always a devout Roman Catholic, Kate attended Mass several times a week. Eleanor asked one of the children to walk their grandmother to church when she became frail. I asked Jim if he resented this, and he replied, "No, not at all." He was an altar boy and was on the verge of taking final vows as a Jesuit priest before realizing that religious life was not for him. By his admission, he said with a grin, he liked women too well.

Kate Gabler

Jim remembered his dad was delighted when rents were frozen during World War II. There was plenty for him to do while growing up—most activities he described as "strictly forbidden." He and his buddy hopped on a narrow-gauge railroad that ran down an alley beside their apartment, crossing Kingshighway to a clay mine and back again. By age 9 or 10, he got a job at the Avalon Theatre, scraping gum off the bottoms of the seats. It earned him a little money, and he saw a lot of movies. He remembers his grandmother as a terrific cook and pie maker.

Kate fell on April 24, 1960, fracturing her left femur. The Hogans could no longer provide adequate care as they were working full-time (Eleanor as a seamstress for the Famous-Barr Department Store and her husband as co-owner of an auto parts store). She was cared for at the St. Louis State Hospital, located at 5400 Arsenal, for two months until her death. Constructed in 1869, the hospital was originally the Female Hospital (previously known as the Social Evil Hospital, which cared for prostitutes) and was located adjacent to the Poor House. Jim remembered his grandmother lying in a long row of beds on the first floor.

Catherine Mary Gabler, nee Kuhn, died on July 23, 1960, at the age of 93. She was buried in Resurrection Cemetery in St. Louis, where her daughter, Eleanor, and son-in-law were later buried.[164] Her granddaughter, Eileen, who shared a bedroom with Kate while growing up, asked that her ashes be buried with her beloved grandmother. Kate had been widowed for 54 years when she died. Still, her obituary noted that she was the beloved wife of the late John Gabler, dear mother of Lawrence Gabler, Mrs. Eleanor F. Hogan, and the late Joseph Gabler; dear mother-in-law, grandmother, great-grandmother, and aunt in her 93rd year. She was also a member of the Mary and Martha Sodality, a parish group dedicated to devotion, reverence, and filial love toward the Blessed Virgin Mary.[165]

My grandfather, Lawrence, and his first wife, Hannah, moved to Portland, Oregon, in 1926, where he worked as a Prudential Insurance salesman. Hannah divorced Lawrence on August 22, 1929, citing desertion. A month later, Lawrence married Beatrice Hemsworth, my grandmother, who was 16 years younger, taller, larger, and pregnant. Lawrence joined the merchant marine and rarely saw his children: Frank, born on March 13, 1930, and Eleanor, born on the same day two years later. My mom faintly remembered riding "seahorsey" on his leg, using his belt for reins. When he drank, he was a mean drunk and at least once sent Bea to the hospital when their children were small. She divorced him on the grounds of cruelty.

I saw my grandfather when he was sober. From our farm in the Oregon Coast Range, my dad drove to the highway to pick him up for Christmas visits, where the Greyhound bus dropped off passengers. He brought us a shopping bag filled with small toys, like balsa wood airplanes. He was quite different from my dad and uncles, who were tall, lanky loggers dressed in jeans and blue chambray work shirts. Grandpa Gabler always wore a white shirt and a tie. His false teeth clicked at the dinner table, making my father nervous. He weighed 150 pounds most of his life and stood 5'6" with brown eyes and brown hair. I remember him living on the top floor of a house in Portland, above where Interstate 5 freeway was constructed. He drove a laundry delivery truck. His kitchen cupboards held tin cans of potatoes and gravy. I was shocked to find out potatoes and gravy even came in cans. At home, I got real potatoes from a bin in the fruit room, and my mother made the gravy.

Grandpa developed bleeding ulcers but continued to drink, exacerbating the problem. We visited him in a hospital where the nurses were nuns. My mom hoped that because he was raised Catholic, he would be respectful to the Sisters. When we entered his room, there was a collective gasp, and I was hustled out the door before I saw him. Whatever was going on, it obviously wasn't for my eyes.

He moved to a small cottage on the Oregon coast with curled-up linoleum and a mildewy shower, with a woman he called his housekeeper. I loved visiting so I could play on the beach. I remember him fondly because the adults around me protected me from his alcoholism, but I know my mother suffered. He was a belligerent binge drinker with periods of sobriety.

I grew up believing Kate had cut off contact with my grandfather forever. However, much to my surprise, I discovered that my grandpa had visited his mother in St. Louis in the 1950s. Jim Hogan remembered his mother explaining that her brother was coming to visit and that he was a drinker, but Jim was to be polite. Jim was astonished to learn his mother had brothers! After his mother's warning, he found my grandfather soft-spoken and fun.

Kate's long life left a tiny footprint in a journey that began with her birth in Vincennes and ended in 1960 in St. Louis. She faced trials: the early deaths of her mother and husband, the struggle to provide for her children, and challenges as a Roman Catholic and German-American. A sense of not belonging shaped her—as the replacement child in the Ebner family, marriage to a man who yearned for fame and riches, and as a widow for years. Her uncle's insistence on the 1880 census that she was "one of the family" indicates that he knew it wasn't true for everyone in the family. Her aunt and cousin Laurence did not mention her in their wills. She was the poor relative who was taken for granted. She was expected to find a teenage Laurence when he was out all night, to nurse the sick, and to raise her children without support. That Kate could recite the dates of her cousins' deaths when she testified in Laurence's trial was significant. Those confident in their place in a family do not feel the need to memorize every detail.

Kate may have believed John Gabler would provide the sense of belonging she craved, but he got sidetracked by his next grand scheme. Instead of becoming comfortably wealthy, she ended up poor. Her sense of belonging came from the church. True, she was rigid in her beliefs and judgmental, rejecting her sons because she felt they didn't follow the church's teachings, but the church was always there to comfort her. Because I overheard some malicious gossip between my grandmother (her former daughter-in-law) and her mother, I thought my great-grandmother Kate was a witch: ugly, stern, cold-hearted, and unforgiving. Whenever my St. Louis great-grandmother was mentioned, it was always coupled with a reference to the Catholic Church and was consistently unfavorable.

Kate left her grandson Jim with cherished memories of her faith, kindness, humor, and excellent cooking. She would quietly tell Jim's dad to stop yelling at his children when he had gone too far, especially toward his sons. Jim found that amazing because his dad would actually cease his tirade. He remembered his father obeying no one else.

Jim and I study family pictures and connect the dots of our genealogy—of Kate and her parents, Andrew Kuhn and Mary Maschino, who immigrated from Alsace-Lorraine; her husband, John Gabler, from Koblenz; and her children.

Minnie's Family

Wilhelm Friedrich Wohlfeil
born: March 25, 1847, Zigahnen, Marienwerder, West Prussia
immigrated: 1870
married: Catherine Radke, August 16, 1874, Green Bay, Wisconsin
married/lived with: Wilhelmine Rosenau
died: October 4, 1924, Portland, Multnomah, Oregon
parents: Karl Wohlfeil (1814–1898) and Louise Henkelmann (1816–1895)

Wilhelmine Rosenau
born: October 17, 1865, Klein Bandtken, Marienwerder, West Prussia
immigrated: 1886–1887
died: July 18, 1923, Portland, Multnomah, Oregon
parents: Michael Roseau (1823–1883) and Ernestine Justine Dombrowski (1825–1869)

The children of Wilhelm Friedrich Wohlfeil and Catherine Radke
Albert Herman Wohlfeil, 1875–1951, m. Ruby Beck
Ida T. Wohlfeil, 1876–before 1880
William Fred Wohlfeil, 1878–1963, m. Anna Ava Sandberg
Martha Malvine Wohlfeil, 1880–1952, m. Jacob Nicholas Smith
Charles Otto Wohlfeil, 1882–1978, m. Mary Sylte

The children of William Fred Wohlfeil and Wilhelmine Rosenau
Mary, 1887–1920, m. James McClellan Luther, 4 children
  Minnie Teresa, 1891–1968
    m. Frank Wesley Hemsworth, November 24, 1909, 4 children
      Beatrice Helen Hemsworth, 1910–1984
      Lyda Riley Hemsworth, 1911–1970
      Frank Wesley Jr. Hemsworth, 1912–1912
      Robert Wesley Hemsworth, 1915–1976
    m. Dellon Olds, November 16, 1929, 2 children
      Edwina Olds, 1932–2023
      Warren "Bud" Olds, 1933–
Bertha Wohlfeil, 1893–1998, m. Frank Archibald McKever, 2 children

Minnie Wohlfeil Hemsworth Olds
(1891–1968)

My strongest memory of visiting my grandma's house is eavesdropping on the morning coffee klatch. Three generations of women—my mother, grandma, great-grandma, and usually a neighbor—gathered around grandma's kitchen table, drinking coffee and smoking cigarettes, talking, laughing, and sighing about the lousy, unreliable men they missed. Usually, my grandma or my mom ended up weeping. My great-grandmother, Minnie, clicked her tongue in disapproval at the tales of woes but kept listening. With less than 20 years between generations, I learned early on that in my matrilineal world, women stumble through life, hope for the best, but expect the worst.

My great-grandma lived a block away from my grandma in Cornelius, Oregon. Sometimes, Minnie would give us a slight smile or, more often, a disapproving frown, but never a hug. She was intimidating and unapproachable. My grandma was much friendlier. She welcomed us at her door with wide-open arms. I loved being squished into Grandma's soft, flowered housedress. However, it was best to play outside afterward to avoid her yelling.

Minnie Theresa Wohlfeil was born on May 31, 1891, near Laurel, a small farming community south of Hillsboro in Washington County, Oregon. On the edge of the fertile Willamette Valley, their land resembled the rolling farmland of the old country. Her parents were German-speaking Lutheran immigrants from Marienwerder, West Prussia, a region east of the Vistula River, now part of Poland. Her father, Wilhelm Friedrich Wohlfeil, emigrated with his parents and siblings in clusters between 1869 and 1872 to Green Bay, Wisconsin. Fifteen years later, Minnie's mother, Wilhelmine Rosenau, emigrated and joined her older brother and his family in Green Bay, where she met Wilhelm. They soon moved to Oregon, followed a year later by Wilhelmine's brother, and three years later by her sister. Minnie grew up with many cousins in Oregon, about whom I knew nothing when I began researching my great-grandmother's life.

Visit to the Old Country

In the thirteenth century, a Polish prince mistakenly invited the knights of the Teutonic Order to eradicate pagan Slavic tribes. Initially, a religious order that offered charity and care for the sick during the Holy Land's Third Crusade, the Germanic order had grown into a fierce and powerful military force. The Teutonic Knights turned against the Polish prince and seized the region for themselves. They built fortresses along the Vistula River, stretching from the Baltic Sea southward to defend their conquests. German settlers migrated from crowded areas further west to establish villages around the fortresses. German tradesmen and craftsmen joined farmers who cultivated wheat and grains in the fertile floodplain of the Vistula River. These waves of German colonists transformed Eastern Europe, pushing the boundary of the German-speaking world hundreds of miles eastward.

My ancestors lived for generations in the district of Marienwerder under a succession of Grand Masters who led the Teutonic Knights in battles against the Swedes, Poles, Slavic tribes, and the French. Poland was wiped off the map in 1795 when it was partitioned among Austria, Russia, and Prussia. It reappeared on maps after World War I, except for the Marienwerder district. In 1920, the citizens voted overwhelmingly to remain in the German Reich, creating a political anomaly right in the heart of northern Poland. Maps from that period depict Marienwerder as a circle between Warsaw and Gdansk, whose laws and government still originated in Germany rather than Poland. Remarkably, the district remained German from 1233 to 1945.

The Marienwerder Fortress is a Gothic castle-cathedral complex built by the Teutonic Knights. It has been used over the centuries to defend the district, shelter the court system, and serve as a school for Hitler Youth. In 2008, archaeologists unearthed the crypt of three

14th-century Grand Masters. Thanks to DNA analysis, researchers have determined their names, ages, and hair colors (two were gray, and one was a redhead). Their bodies draped in silk, one Grand Master is believed to have worn nine costly silk shirts to stay comfortable in the afterlife.

By January 1945, despite Hitler's orders for all militia units to "stand and fight," Germany had essentially lost the war. Merciless Russian soldiers advanced from the east, bringing tanks, the whine of rockets, and artillery fire. The ethnic Germans of Marienwerder began fleeing westward. They pushed exhausted horses toward Berlin through deep snow or crowded into the few trains still running. Suffering frostbite, exposure, and starvation, some Germans fled toward Danzig (today's Gdansk) to escape on ships to German or Danish ports. Many were swallowed up in battles and nameless massacres. In 2008, during hotel construction, workers found a World War II-era mass grave believed to contain the nude bodies of 1,800 German men, women, and children who disappeared during the Soviet Army's march to Berlin.[166]

I visited Marienwerder in 2015. All place names were changed from German to Polish after German rule ended in 1945. I tried to visualize the chaos of a forced exodus in the middle of winter for families with roots dating back to the 13th century. They were forced to leave their businesses, homes, farms, Lutheran churches, and cemeteries with what they could carry. I saw photographs of the town taken before the war. Streets were lined with businesses bearing German surnames. There were Lutheran churches and a Jewish synagogue. But after the exodus, the German existence was obliterated. Today, the capital, Marienwerder (the same name as the district), is Kwidzyn, a Polish town with a Polish name, a partially destroyed Teutonic Fortress, and several Catholic Churches.

A guide drove me to the villages where my ancestors lived. The first village we visited was Licza (Littchen in German), six miles east of Kwidzyn. My great-grandmother's aunt had lived there before she immigrated to Oregon. I saw a red brick two-family home with a decorative black brick design and a thick orange tile roof. The guide identified the house as built by the Prussians before the Communist rule from 1945 to 1989. She said disgustedly, "The communists never built houses and barns as well as the Prussians and never added decorative touches."

The village's Manor House had been restored into a high-end retirement home for seniors. The owner was pleased to show us around the retirement home her husband had remodeled, pointing out the tile stoves in the corners and the intricately carved wood stairway. Much to my delight, the original painted floor, featuring a pattern of scrolls complete with a Latin blessing, had been reused as the foyer ceiling.

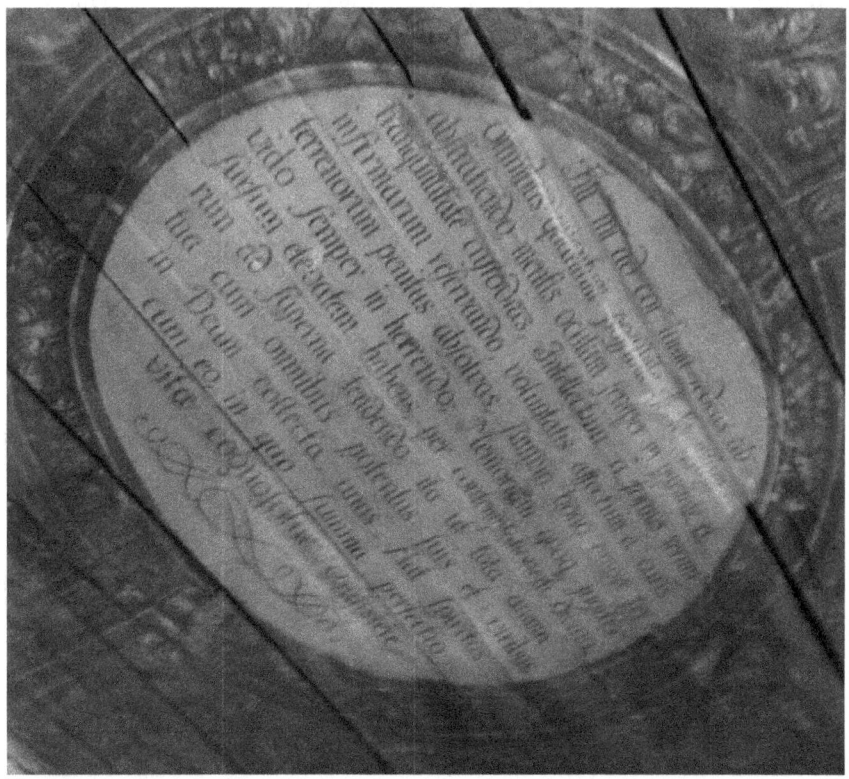

Outside, we saw long brick Prussian-built barns adorned with Gothic follies or crenellations of cattle that were once part of the manor's estate—and where my ancestors had toiled. After the ethnic Germans disappeared, Poles, Lithuanians, and Ukrainians (forced to move by the Soviets and taking no pride in ownership) moved into the abandoned Prussian houses, even converting barns into homes. The guide described her mother as prejudiced against those living in the manure-smelling Prussian-built barns, considering them shiftless and lazy.

I was incredibly excited to see the next village because Wohlfeils had lived in Zigahnen at least since the early 1600s. I found Cygany (or Zigahnen in German) in worse shape than Licza. The village, divided by a highway, had a small grocery store and houses on one side, abandoned Soviet barracks, and a run-down manor house on the other. Two young men were outside the manor, cutting wood pallets for firewood in the muddy, overgrown yard. One of them told my guide that twelve families lived in the manor, including his wife, baby, and parents. I asked if any Wohlfeils still lived in the village in hopes of finding cousins, temporarily forgetting the expulsion of all Germans in 1945. My guide had to correct my pronunciation of Wohlfeils, making it sound like "villheld" so he could understand. He looked surprised and shook his head no.

The former manor house in Cygany

The Protestant cemetery in Cygany had only a few broken headstones, none of which bore the name Wohlfeil. A historical activist recently inspired the community to clean up the cemetery by clearing the brush and installing a sign that explained its historical importance as an evangelical cemetery. My guide considered the volunteer effort quite remarkable. Still, it looked very different from the landscaped Catholic cemetery I could see across the highway, with its tidy graves decorated with flowers and mementos.

We drove to the market town of Gardeja (Garnsee in German), along a road lined by large trees. In the 18th century, Prussian rulers mandated the planting of trees along every road in the realm to provide shade for carriages on the way to church. Today's drivers zipping by in their cars along the narrow county roads, sometimes impaired by alcohol, often crash into the now substantial trees, receiving serious injuries.

Gardeja, located between two small lakes, once had an Evangelical Lutheran Church where generations of Wohlfeils were baptized and married. But the town was 90% destroyed during World War II, and the church, manor house, and cemetery no longer exist. The guide pointed to a sloping lawn of a city park as the site of the former Protestant cemetery.

I had heard many news stories about genocide in Cambodia, Serbia/Croatia, and Africa, as well as the systematic killing of Jews in World War II, but ethnic cleansing felt like an abstract concept. I didn't fully realize that I was related to people who either participated in the Nazis' extermination of Jews, Poles, and others or did nothing to stop it. At the end of the war, those who had suffered under the Germans retaliated, expelling them from Marienwerder to almost certain death. The shock that my ancestors participated in genocide scatters my genealogy files across the floor of my life.

Life in Marienwerder

The American branches of the Rosenaus and Wohlfeils distanced themselves from the language and customs of their homeland, which were scarred by anti-German sentiments stemming from World War I and World War II. When their relatives were expelled from Marienwerder in 1945, they had already been living in the United States for 70 years. My great-grandmother's sister showed me a German-language Bible in which she had written her parents' and siblings' birthdates when she was seven, sitting at the kitchen table. When I asked if she could read German, she clicked her tongue, shook her head in disgust—just like I remember my great-grandma doing—and told me it was "old country."

Under Prussian feudalism, the Teutonic Knights granted estates to Junkers, a term derived from the High German Juncherre, meaning "young noblemen." Adding "von" to their names came to signify Prussian aristocrats (as in Otto von Bismarck). The oldest son inherited the family manor, while the younger sons pursued careers in the military or government. Daughters received a dowry and were expected to marry well within their aristocratic class. They were utterly confident of their place in the universe.

The Rosenaus and Wohlfeils were less sure of their place in the social order. They scrubbed the manor's kitchen, mucked out the barns, plowed the fields, and produced little workers for the estate. Junkers exercised law enforcement powers and patrimonial jurisprudence. When the infant survival rate increased, Junkers (who were obligated to house and feed everyone on the estate) forbade marriage among their workers.

The manor's aristocratic family owned the village of a few hundred inhabitants, multiple barns, and the largest land area. In a poor country where the aristocracy was nearly bankrupt, they managed to survive by squeezing the peasantry for all they could get. Most of their income came from their fields—primarily grains for the markets. The manor house was the head of each village. This is a typical village layout (x representing houses):

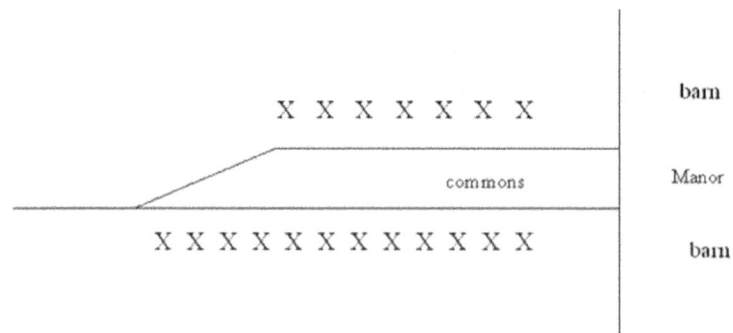

A Junker's manorial farm had these kinds of workers:

- Small farmer who had hereditary tenure on the estate land,
- Farm servants who worked on an annual contract,
- Day Laborers, and
- Village craftsmen, including millers, blacksmiths, tailors, weavers, and tavern keepers, who enjoyed the highest degree of freedom but still needed the Junker's permission to live on his estate.

The Wohlfeils were small farmers. Land reform laws enacted in the early 1800s enabled peasants to purchase small parcels of land. Johann Wohlfeil (1747–1831) was a "Bauer und Einsasse" (farmer and owner).[167] He had four sons and two daughters. The oldest became a coachman; the next son, a farmer; followed by one who became a tailor, another who was a farmer; and two daughters: one married the village blacksmith, while the other married a soldier who became a smith. With a combination of skilled craftsmen and farmers, Johann's family belonged to the middle class—a relative term in a poverty-stricken area. During the Napoleonic Wars in 1806, a British diplomat described Prussian peasants as desperately poor. His party of eight rented two miserable rooms for sitting, dining, and sleeping in a filthy beer house in Marienwerder. They made their beds by spreading a little straw over the dirty floor and using their cloaks as coverlets. There was hardly any meat, the water was terrible, and there was no possibility of obtaining wine as a corrective. The area was filled with wretched barns that passed for houses, and stepping outside meant landing in mud up to their ankles.[168]

I descend from Johann's second son, Gottfried, who, like most small farmers, paid rent to the Junker in grain and unpaid labor, often three days a week. They were allowed to live in one- or two-room houses with outbuildings and a garden plot. Oxen were "rented" from the Junker to plow long, narrow fingers of farmland radiating from the village for cash crops such as rye, barley, oats, and potatoes. The "commons" provided pasture for a cow or geese and was shared by the village. A pig was a godsend; it could supply hams, sausage, bacon, feet for pickling, blood for puddings, and, most importantly, lard for cooking. Gottfried fathered 14 children in two marriages, ten of whom were sons. When inheritance made the long, narrow fields shaped by heavy, unwieldy Prussian plows unable to support a family, Wohlfeils were forced to emigrate.

Rosenaus, Minnie's maternal ancestors, were probably estate servants—plowing fields, herding animals, or working in the dairy, flour mill, distillery, or manor house. They received food, drink, a new set of clothes, possibly shoes made in the village, and sometimes a small amount of money each year. They slept in the manor house or paid rent to a small farmer, such as Wohlfeils, happy to earn extra income. The attic of the manor house was cold, and sharing space with the farmer, his wife, their children, and other laborers was cramped. In winter, the farmer kept his animals inside. It was more important for the cow to stay healthy than for the family to be comfortable. Besides that, animals added warmth to the house during bitterly cold winters and manure for the garden in early spring.

Village celebrations and weddings were lively, accompanied by Prussian firewater, a blend of grain alcohol and honey. In the fall, everyone gathered for the harvest of the manor's fields. The reapers went first, followed by women who gathered the cut grain into bundles, then men who stacked the sheaves to dry. Children brought baskets of food and bottles at noon. Everyone worked until dark each day. Once the harvest was finished, the butchering, brewing, and baking for the harvest festival began, a time when everyone wore their best clothes. People sang, told stories, and made jokes, though not always kindly. One joke involved a cross-eyed boy who looked at the potatoes but picked up the onions instead. Children were bathed monthly in a large wooden tub of tepid water heated over open fires. Adults washed their hands and faces about as often. Clothes were seldom changed.

Life was a continuous dance of luck, danger, and magic. A charm might be hung over the doorways to invoke God's blessings, so the family wouldn't have to sell the cow because of a poor harvest. Children listened to fairy tales about clever heroes who married princesses or disturbing, brutal stories of shapeshifting witches who lured children into the forest to kill them. Births, christenings, confirmations, marriages, and deaths were recorded in the Evangelical Lutheran Church parish records. Small farm owners like Wohlfeils had the best seats in the parish church. Behind them, also separated by gender, sat the landless laborers, like the Rosenaus. The village midwife sat near the door to ensure the service was not disturbed if she was needed.

Learning to read was essential so the Prussians could read the Bible and understand God's holy laws and commandments. In 1836, an impressive 75% of West Prussians were literate. Children attended school once a week (more often in winter when work was slack). Church records dating back to 1607 indicate that children typically attended school until the age of 13 or 14, or until they were confirmed in the church. After confirmation, the Junker could require mandatory service for children on the estate for up to three years. This service was a good step between childhood and marriage, especially for non-inheriting children. Boys worked on the farm or as apprentices, while girls served as milkmaids and domestic workers at the manor.

Girls were expected to fill their wedding chests with a complete set of household linens: bed and table covers, hand-sewn underwear, and a shroud—all handwoven, hand-spun, embroidered, and embellished with crochet stitches. Wives were destined to support their husbands and bear children. Marriages were not based on romantic love but were viewed as business agreements. The marriage contract included gaining inheritance rights, the wife's dowry, gifts from both families, the right for the husband's parents to retire and live with them, and payments to disenfranchised siblings. Marrying a first cousin was a practical choice because it kept the land within the family—after all, marriage was a business deal. A fortunate girl married someone she could grow to love. However, the high mortality rate among mothers led men to recognize the need to remarry quickly within their social class. No one married outside their social class. The daughter of a Prussian servant would never marry the son of the manor.

Social and political reforms of the nineteenth century gradually led to the decline of the manorial farm system. Fewer servants were needed. The Rosenaus fell into deeper poverty. As day laborers, they had no right to inherit, no chance to acquire land, and could be hired and fired at any moment. When my great-grandmother's aunt was baptized, the parish church had to cover half of the baptism fee because the family was impoverished.[169] And since the church supported the destitute, those without employment were not welcome to stay in a village. This caused the Rosenaus to live a transient lifestyle. For example, Minnie's uncle's residence changed with each child's baptismal record, in stark contrast to the common practice of spending one's entire life in the village of one's birth.

Families were large, communities small, and there were no secrets. One was inescapably part of the village, where everyone was constantly judged. Disapproval could lead to complete ostracism for those who failed to follow the strict, structured code of conduct. Children learned the Prussian concept of authority, which emphasized a duty to the church and the government, to their estate, and ultimately to their parents. This policy aimed to transform peasants into loyal subjects, regular taxpayers, and capable soldiers.

Immigration to Green Bay

Those who had already immigrated wrote encouraging letters from Green Bay, Wisconsin. America was a land of free thought, free speech, a free press, and the freedom to choose one's work. Men earned between $25 and $30 a month in the sawmills. Railroads were seeking workers. Land was affordable! Eighty acres of woodland in Wisconsin sold for $100 to $150. Growing a crop was easy: dig a hole in the ground with an old ax, drop in a corn seed, press it down with your foot, and celebrate. Settle near neighbors for a helping hand and advice. America lacked social classes, a king, and an excess of high officials to irritate people. It would be their last time bowing to anyone. One could escape the rigid Prussian social class system and become somebody. Women were more respected and expected to only work in the home and garden. Fieldwork for women was considered disgraceful and could lead to husbands being ridiculed by other men.

Spring, under a new moon, was considered the best time to immigrate and a good omen. Winter storms had passed, and the seas were less frigid. Aggressive travel agents urged the discontented to leave their homes and farms, promising safe transportation all the way to America. Travelogs, guides, promotional pamphlets, brochures, and broadsheets were passed from family to family until the paper became soft and the words blurred. Some proved helpful; others were not.

A sturdy ship with an honest captain who would not cheat passengers was essential. Letters from America advised packing sheepskins and clothes, as much linen as possible, and a few kitchen utensils.[170] Don't bother packing cotton sheets and shirts because they are inexpensive and readily available. Instead, bring a warm, well-stuffed feather bed packed in a strong, laced-up bag. Retrieve the wooden chest from the attic, inspect it, scrub it, and pack it with the following:

- Tools
- Gun, powder horn, and shot pouch
- Knitting needles, sheep shears, sewing needles, and thread
- Woolen and linen clothes
- Bridal quilt
- Bedclothes with sheets sewn into big sacks
- Knapsack with cups, eating tools, wooden bowls
- Food basket with smoked sausages, rye and barley loaves, honey, cheese, coffee, sugar, dried apples, and small bags of salt and pepper
- Bible, hymnbook, and almanac
- Soft soap, salve for lice, and camphor

As the Franco-Prussian War escalated, Wohlfeils decided to emigrate to Green Bay. They longed for the opportunity to sleep in their beds without fear and express their beliefs freely. They gathered the necessary documents: a certificate issued by the parish pastor confirming that their financial obligation to the church had been met; the Junker certifying that their debts were paid, no criminal charges were pending, and the men had completed their military duty. Lastly, authorities issued a government visa to leave the country.

Military obligations were taken seriously in Prussia. Wars and rumors of war made a standing army necessary since 1717. Soldiers were needed for the First Schleswig War (1848–1851), the Second Schleswig War of 1864, the Austro-Prussian War of 1866, and the Franco-Prussian War of 1870–1871. Before 1871, the nobility, often seen as stiff, formal, and humorless, was responsible for providing military training to farmers like Wilhelm Wohlfeil. However, after Germany's unification in 1871, military training was conducted under the first Emperor of the German Reich, Kaiser Wilhelm I.

Ordinary Prussian men were required to serve a mandatory seven-year military enlistment from the age of 20 until the beginning of their 28th year: three years in the regular army, followed by four years in the reserves. Afterward, they served for 5 years (aged 28 to 33) in the Landwehr, or militia. During this time, men participated in occasional drills to remain "military ready." Until age 42, they were members of the Landstrum (Home Guard).[171] Regiments were assigned to different districts. A biannual poll tax and Hibernen (winter bread money), an extra tax levied on citizens, provided wages. Soldiers were sometimes quartered in homes or barracks, overwhelming towns and creating a racket of drum rolls, trumpet blasts, marching boots, and shouted commands.

Crossing the ocean in 1870 took two weeks, reducing the passenger death rate to 0.5%. Shipowners realized that the emigration of thousands of Germans could benefit their companies. They pressured ship captains to improve passenger care and reduce complaints about food. The spread of railroads across Europe allowed Wohlfeils to purchase a ticket voucher with a specified departure date and schedule from a shipping company office in Marienwerder and board a train to the port city, knowing when their ship would depart. If the embarkation point was Bremen, they could almost step directly from the train onto their boat—the city had railroad tracks leading straight onto the docks. Ships making regular trips from European ports became routine, much like a city bus on its route.

Carl and Louise Wohlfeil, along with their nine children and other relatives, emigrated over a span of four years, much like knots on a rope. Some left from Hamburg, others from Bremen. Their oldest son, Frederick Wilhelm, was the first to leave, sailing with his wife and her parents on the ship Liebig in May 1868. A son-in-law followed in April 1869, and their son Carl and his wife traveled in July 1869. Another son, Wilhelm Frederick (Minnie's father), arrived in America in August 1870. In June 1871, their daughter Caroline, with her two children, a 17-year-old brother, and a 17-year-old cousin, joined her husband, who had immigrated earlier. Wohlfeils united in Green Bay when their parents, Karl and Louise Wohlfeil, arrived on April 4, 1872, with three more of their children: Justine, age 22; Hermann, age 15; and Ferdinand, age 12, on the ship Smidt from Bremen to New York. The ship's manifest also listed their son-in-law, Carl Behrend, age 25; their daughter, Wilhelmine, age 26; and their 11-month-old son, Carl.[172]

Navigating the North Sea, with its storms and towering waves, was dangerous at any time. Steerage passengers were allowed to go up a steep, slippery staircase to the deck only in good weather to enjoy the fresh air. Below, people were injured by falling bags and flailing arms and legs as the ship rolled. Pieces of canvas were hung to create sections: one for married couples and children, another for unmarried men, and a third for unmarried women. A foul smell from poor sanitation filled the air. Passengers ate at simple tables or on food boards; otherwise, they played cards, prayed, slept, smoked, and waited. In the weekly food rations, a family received a half gallon of water for drinking and washing, along with bread and biscuits, salt pork and beef, rice and barley, peas, thirteen ounces of flour, six ounces of sugar, and syrup poured into their own containers. Immigrants found that potatoes boiled in their skins were easier to pick up when the ship rocked and twisted through the waves. Some people ate fish and then hated it for the rest of their lives because it reminded them of seasickness.

Rays of sunlight filtered through the main hatch until the light faded, then a few faint, smoky kerosene lanterns were lit. The cacophony of steerage—a hundred diverse snores, the sobs of babies, and the occasional retch as the ship rode from swell to trough—was nerve-wracking. But once they reached solid, dry ground, heartfelt prayers were offered to God, and hymns were sung.

Arriving on American shores introduced the Wohlfeils to a new culture, language, and unfamiliar country. They feared being preyed upon by hotelkeepers, money changers, and land speculators, not to mention the usual thieves and scoundrels. They were overwhelmed by the smell of rotting fish and fried oysters, with everyone shouting at the top of their lungs. They were stunned to learn that Americans feared immigrants brought diseases. What nonsense!

Minnie's father, Wilhelm, probably traveled to Chicago by rail in the fall of 1870, then by boat north to Green Bay. Or he might have sailed the Hudson River to Albany, then west on the Erie Canal to Buffalo to reach the Great Lakes and down the finger of Green Bay from Lake Michigan. Although his name has never been found on a ship's passenger list, he stated on his naturalization application, dated November 5, 1872, that he arrived in August 1870 through the port of New York.[173]

The anniversary of Wilhelm's first year in Green Bay was marked by forest fires raging in Minnesota and upper Wisconsin. Drought-stricken pine forests were burning, exacerbated by decades of slash piles left from logging, farmers burning stumps to clear land, and railroad crews clearing brush from rights of way. Word trickled into Green Bay that the fires 100 miles to the north were beginning to behave strangely—burning underground, hurling embers, and leaping creeks. Fires burned uphill, downhill, and sideways, jumping canyons, outrunning horses, and hiding in smoldering tree roots. By early October, conditions were right for a vast firestorm on the peninsula, so named because fire could flow like water in any direction and generate its own weather.[174]

On the same day as the Great Chicago Fire (when Mrs. O'Leary's cow is rumored to have kicked over the lantern), fires broke out simultaneously on the west shore of Green Bay and the southern half of the Door County peninsula. Named for the mill town that suffered the most significant loss of life, the Peshtigo Fire expanded into a sixty-mile front and became the deadliest forest fire in American history. Roaring swirls of flame plumes resembling tornadoes raced through wooden sidewalks, buildings, and shingle mills, forcing citizens to jump into wells or creeks to escape. Most people were burned alive, even those who hid in wells, because the fire consumed all the oxygen. Survivors described a wall of flame a mile high, traveling faster than a speeding locomotive, with winds that tossed railroad cars and houses.

An estimated 1,200 people died, and over a million acres burned. The death toll will probably never be known. No one knew exactly how many loggers were in the woods, how many transient workers there were, or even how many recently arrived immigrants were around. The firestorm jumped across Green Bay but did not quite reach downtown, leaving a panic-stricken city thick with smoke. Mills blew warning whistles. Terrified men formed bucket brigades, and fire trucks with bells clanging were pulled by brave horses. Gray ash dusted the hats of citizens. The air was suffocating, filled with the smell of charred pine and burned haystacks mixed with the stench of horse manure. Barns, livestock, fences, houses, cords of firewood, and mills were reduced to piles of ash on the outskirts of Green Bay. Tracks burned, the telegraph was down, wooden bridges were destroyed, and charred trees blocked roads. Severely burned people began arriving by boat from the north (the only available transportation) with unbelievable horror stories. As the casualties increased, trainloads of supplies meant for fire victims in Chicago were diverted to the north. Committees were quickly formed to collect food, clothing, shoes, boots, and tools for those who had lost everything and needed to prepare for the Wisconsin winter. By Christmas, there was little cause for celebration. Nearly 7,200 people were left homeless and destitute in a cold wilderness. Weather-beaten children stood vacantly, and timber wolves crept about in search of young pigs.

Recovery from the forest fire was followed by the Panic of 1873. Even so, there was more food and money than back home in Prussia. Green Bay and Fort Howard, located across the Fox River from each other, boasted over 100 saloons, 28 hotels, and three banks, with a combined population of 10,000. Steamers and sailing vessels crowded the docks; long lines of farm wagons piled high with produce supplied the markets, and three shifts of workers kept busy at the railyards, choked with lumber and shingles. Millions of hand-shaven and milled shingles were loaded into freight cars and schooners for distribution in Chicago and elsewhere, briefly making Green Bay the shingle capital of the world.[175]

Wohlfeil men found jobs as railroad laborers or in sawmills. Cousins married at the First Evangelical Lutheran Church, where services were conducted in German. Minnie's father, Wilhelm, married Catherine Radtke, a girl from back home, in 1874. They had three boys and two girls and lived in Green Bay before moving across the river to Fort Howard. They likely watched skaters cross the frozen Fox River during Green Bay's snowy winters, planted a kitchen garden in spring, and dodged loose livestock and cow pies in the streets during the summer.

But something was wrong in Wilhelm and Catherine's home. Catherine's behavior drew the attention of law enforcement. She may have become depressed after the death of her daughter. Maybe she imagined things. Perhaps Wilhelm's Aunt Eleanora heard the children screaming next door while their mother stared at the river. Whatever the reason, Catherine was admitted to the Northern Hospital for the Insane in Oshkosh in 1883.[176] Wilhelm was left alone with four children, aged eight, five, three, and one year old. His aunt, who had been widowed in June, probably tried to help Wilhelm with the children, but she never had children of her own and did not have much practice.

After spending two years among the more than 500 residents at the Northern Hospital for the Insane, Catherine Wohlfeil and five other women were transferred by the sheriff to the Brown County Asylum on March 5, 1885.[177] The most common diagnosis for women at the time was "female hysteria," which in modern terms could mean anything from postpartum depression to psychosis. Experts believed that female health, both mental and physical, was closely linked to a woman's reproductive organs. As a result, puberty, menstruation, pregnancy, childbirth, and menopause all played a role in her mental health. Blame was also placed on excessive use of tobacco, reading novels, domestic difficulties, desertion by a husband, and poverty and neglect. Psychiatric care was dismal, cold, and impersonal. Even strong women who dared to live outside society's strictly defined gender roles of home, children, and faith could be judged mad. A visitor to an all-female school in 1858 worried that teachers were preparing girls for the lunatic asylum by teaching them to think.

The Brown County Asylum was remodeled in 1889 at a cost of $2,500 to separate the insane from the poorhouse inmates. It was regarded as the best asylum in Wisconsin, with a capacity of 100 beds. The County Board installed a heating system and considered renovating the attic for activities such as dancing, card games, dominoes, and checkers; however, the attic likely remained unchanged. The Board's main responsibility was to pay bills for the Insane Asylum and the Poor House. John Cryan served as superintendent for 21 years and was succeeded by his nephew, Fred Loftus, who was 28 years old and had completed one year of high school. Fred's mother served as matron because his wife was busy with their children. The staff never exceeded eight people, most of whom were Irish. The doctor visited the inmates weekly to provide basic healthcare and to sign death certificates.[178]

Doctors believed that asylums should mirror the social classes of the outside world. Wealthy white women with charming manners and deportment were viewed as the sanest, occupying the best wards and dining at tables covered with white linen with strawberry shortcakes for dessert. Poor immigrant women were considered vulgar and obscene, perceived to have low intelligence, and were housed accordingly. The Brown County Asylum had few patients of color, but they were assigned to the worst wards. Seen as therapeutic, patients—likely including Catherine—worked without pay in various capacities, such as sewing, farming, laundry, and kitchen work, to help make the institution self-sufficient.

It soon became apparent that Catherine would not return home. Wilhelm may have turned to his aunt and sisters-in-law to find a girl to help with the children. Letters were mailed to Marienwerder. He wanted a good, clean girl willing to watch his children and cook his supper. A girl from the old country, accustomed to living in primitive spaces with few rooms, little privacy, and never-ending work, would be impressed by his simple dwelling in America.

A girl was found. She was 20 years old and came from Klein Bandtken, a village ten miles from Wilhelm's village of Zigahnen. Wilhelm probably never met Wilhelmine Rosenau, for that was her name. Besides being 18 years older, Wilhelm grew up in a different Lutheran parish, although he may have known her brother.

Wilhelmine had little reason to stay in Marienwerder. Her father and stepmother had died two years before the letters from America arrived. She had no assets and slim prospects of a job in the manor's barns or marriage in Klein Bandtken. Mustering all the courage she possessed, she chose to emigrate, knowing she would never dance at another village wedding or weep at another funeral, forsaking her parents' graves and turning her back on everything she had ever known.

Her best chance to reach America was to hitch a ride on a farmer's wagon to travel the rough roads to the district town of Marienwerder, home of the fortress built by the Teutonic Knights 400 years earlier. There, she could catch a train to Danzig (today's Gdansk), likely the first train journey of her life. She passed dense forests, white dots of sheep and cattle, wheat fields, villages with tall church steeples, and cities with ornate buildings and factories. At the docks by the Baltic Sea, the smell of the sea air mixed with the stench of the streets. She saw countless ships and all kinds of strange people—some staring, others ignoring her: sailors with bare, tattooed necks and hands tucked into wide, low trousers; grain haulers in blouses and knee breeches made of glazed linen; wagon drivers waiting to unload their cargo; soldiers marching in step; servant girls in aprons and heavy striped skirts carrying large market baskets over their bare forearms; women selling fish and vegetables; middle-class shopkeepers rushing out on errands without their hats; sons serving apprenticeships in offices run by their fathers; schoolboys with book bags walking past noisy, dingy taverns.

With money sent to her from America, inherited from her father, or what she had saved, she bought a steerage ticket to America. I have never found Wilhelmine listed on a ship manifest. It's highly unlikely that she traveled alone and unescorted, but she may have. Most emigrants leaving German ports—Hamburg, Bremen, and others—travelled to Hull, England, on steamships that operated like modern ferries. After disembarking in Hull, Wilhelmine probably took a train to Liverpool to board a ship bound for North America—roughly the same route Wilhelm had taken over a decade earlier.

Before Wilhelmine boarded, a doctor likely examined her hair, checked her mouth, and listened to her heart by pulling open her coat. The sea looked dark green and smelled of rotten fish and burning coal. It was not the blue sea from her father's stories. Closing the hatch during stormy weather in the North Atlantic made life below deck miserable amid the squalor of her fellow passengers. On deck, the air was refreshing, even though it was bitterly cold. She wore all her clothes. Her rough leather shoes, made for walking across fields, slipped on the deck.

Men carried water in large buckets so women could scrub, scour, and wash clothing to hang out to dry, only to discover that wool didn't wash well in seawater. There were disputes about who took more than their fair share of food. Women avoided depraved men who tried to molest them. But on good days, passengers told stories and sang songs to counter the monotonous motion of the ocean. At first, they spoke about home bitterly, but as the days passed, their conversation about home shifted to one of longing.

Boarding a coal-powered steamship in Liverpool, Wilhelmine probably arrived in the United States about ten days later through U.S. or Canadian ports, likely via Castle Garden in Lower Manhattan, New York. Perhaps her brother warned her not to rub her eye or scratch her head out of fear she would be sent back. Castle Garden had a railroad ticket office, a hospital, a foreign currency exchange, and women's washrooms with stone troughs of cold water, soap, and large, clean towels on rollers. After giving her name, birthplace, and destination, a "booker" clerk handed her a printed slip with information on where to safely exchange money, protecting her from swindlers and scam artists who might try to sell her a fake ticket or steer her to a disreputable rooming house. She was warned in German to be careful of pickpockets. She stayed close to another family, as some women weren't allowed to leave Castle Garden without a male relative. Names were called out for people who had a letter with money or instructions waiting for them. Faint from hunger, she may have bought brown bread and a sausage from a man with thick, shaggy whiskers. Outside, she found her bag waiting for her after being frisked by the lady inspector, who had not discovered her hidden pocket in her dress with her secret money.

She might have traveled by train to Chicago and then taken a steamship across Lake Michigan to reach Green Bay. Only shame and gossip awaited her if she returned to the old country. Her brother Carl's wife was expecting another baby to add to their already crowded household, and, as in Prussia, Carl was looking for work. There were too many hungry children around her brother's soup pot. She needed a job that provided room and board. She likely felt desperately homesick and cried to sleep, missing her sister, her friends, and her lost home.

Perhaps Wilhelmine immediately began caring for Wilhelm's children, cooking his supper, and cleaning the house. She was pregnant. Whether this child was Wilhelm's or if she arrived in Green Bay already pregnant remains a mystery. When her daughter Mary was born in Green Bay in July 1887, the German Lutheran pastor recorded the birth as illegitimate in the church's records, leaving a blank space as if the father's name might be added later. Her brother Carl's wife was named as the godmother. Illegitimate children were not uncommon in the old country, and immigrants found the attitude toward illegitimacy surprising in America.

Ultimately, Wilhelm's legal wife, Catherine, was diagnosed as chronically insane. Her children never visited or maintained any relationship with her for the rest of their lives. On his marriage application, Charles believed that his mother's first name was Martha rather than Catherine and was unaware of her maiden name. Martha's death certificate states "no record" on the line reserved for her mother's name. However, when their brother William died in 1963, his wife knew the name of his birth mother.

Catherine spent the next 40 years confined as an inmate at the Brown County Insane Asylum. To keep patients subdued and tranquil, caretakers could legally control them by virtually any means available, including forced restraint and immersion in cold water. If Catherine was not insane when admitted, she soon became so. In the late 1800s, mental health facilities were not for the faint of heart. Conditions reportedly improved with reforms. In 1906, the Brown County Physician reported that patients were cared for, but could benefit from a piano to provide music. In 1916, the Brown County Committee on Insane and Sanatorium requested $375 for a laundry mangle to assist the women patients with washing clothes. Patient populations fluctuated due to new admissions, deaths, and the small number of patients granted a leave of absence. For example, there were 92 patients in 1890 and 133 in 1906. Catherine was always present 365 days a year.[179]

Records of farm production were meticulously maintained to prove the asylum's self-sufficiency.[180] The county also pursued the assets of inmates. Beginning in 1892, the County Board of Supervisors recommended seeking guardianship of Catherine Wohlfeil, who was deemed incompetent. She owned property that could be sold to support her. Wilhelm had purchased a lot in Fort Howard in 1875. In April 1897, the Chairman petitioned the court for permission to use the property of insane individuals to cover their maintenance costs. The County Clerk was appointed as Catherine's guardian and gave temporary guardianship to Leonie Befay. A judgment in the case of Leonie Befay, Plaintiff, versus William Wohlfeil, Defendant, ordered William (Wilhelm) to pay the plaintiff costs of $57.75 and the remaining value of the property to the county as part of Catherine's dower interest.[181] In March 1899, the guardians of Catherine Wohlfeil were discharged.[182] There is no record whether Catherine was present at the hearing or if William, who was far away in Oregon, paid the costs or participated in the court case. When Catherine died in 1920, her niece provided accurate details on her death certificate regarding her name, age, place of birth, parents' names, and that Catherine was the wife of Wilhelm Wohlfeil.

West to Oregon

Wilhelm and Wilhelmine arrived in Oregon sometime between Mary's baptism in Green Bay on August 21, 1887, and the purchase of property in Albina on November 25, 1887. No one in Oregon knew Wilhelm had an insane wife back in Green Bay. Everyone in the congregation of St. Paul Evangelical Lutheran Church of Green Bay knew: his parents, brothers, sisters, and cousins—the Wohlfeils, Bensels, Henkelmanns, and Olschefskis. Even poor, crazy Catherine's sister attended the church. Wilhelm, accompanied by a pregnant Wilhelmine, had been a scandal. The congregation had not forgotten he was married to Catherine. No wonder Wilhelm fled to Oregon. Three of Wilhelm's nephews also moved there; two stayed, and one returned to Wisconsin. Gradually, family ties to Wisconsin began to fade.

In Oregon, Wilhelm Frederick, who went by William Fred, and Wilhelmine lived together as husband and wife until their deaths. If he was a bigamist, it was never mentioned. They always told the census taker they had been married since 1886.

William and Wilhelmine Wohlfeil, along with the children, probably traveled west to Oregon by train. Upon arriving in Portland, William purchased Lot 16 in Block 3 in the Railroad Shop Addition in Albina from Van DeLashmutt and his wife, Maria, for $600.[183] The deed, recorded in William's name only, was witnessed by DeLashmutt's son and John M. Pittenger, a local real estate developer and notary public. The property was near the corner of Sellwood Street (later renamed Graham Street) and Williams Avenue. Today, this property is part of Legacy Emanuel Medical Center. William listed his occupation as a laborer.

William was one of three men who filed incorporation papers for the St. Johannes German Evangelical Lutheran Church in 1888. The church was located on the east side of Williams Avenue, south of San Mateo Street. The morning service was conducted in German, while the evening service was in English under the guidance of Reverend A. Dietrich, the pastor. Sunday School took place at 2 p.m. William's oldest son, Albert, was confirmed at St. Johannes in 1890.[184]

Annexed by Portland in 1891, Albina was a community primarily of German and Polish immigrants. It offered amenities like electric lights, city water mains, and soon-to-be-improved streets. Houses were sold on installment plans. It was roughly divided into three areas along the Willamette River. Lower Albina served as the terminus for transcontinental railroads in the Northwest, handling 900 railcars daily in 1909.[185] The central commercial strip was perched atop a bluff along streetcar lines, while the residential area sat on low hillsides to the east. German bands marched on holidays, saloons sold children a pail of beer for Papa, and housewives bought German and Polish sausages.

William repaired passenger and freight cars at the Northern Pacific terminal. Thirty saloons lined the street from the ferry slip in Lower Albina up the hill to the corner of Russell and Union Avenue, a span of ten blocks and just two blocks from William and Wilhelmine's house. On Sundays, they could catch a streetcar to cross the Willamette River to downtown Portland to watch bicycle races or see Chinese peddlers with large wicker baskets of vegetables hanging from poles balanced on their shoulders. Statues of wooden Indians, with feather-decorated heads, cigars in one hand, and a tomahawk in the other, stood on plank sidewalks. Frequent rain showers failed to wash away the stench of coal-fired railroad engines, musty old rotten timber, ship tar, spoiled vegetables, and foul fish. Iron-shod horses pulled heavy wagons with iron-rimmed wheels that rang across cobblestone streets. Light wagons and buggies added to the noise and congestion. Streetcar warning bells, shouts and curses from horse-drawn wagons, the snap of long blacksnake whips, and yelling and carryings-on from the many saloons added to the chaos. Piles of horse droppings, missed by sanitation workers, froze in winter and, in the rainy spring, mixed with mud, turning into thick clouds of dust in summer.

William and Wilhelmine (listed as Minna) sold their property at Sellwood and Williams Avenue on August 9, 1890, to Charles Lundberg and his wife for $1,250. Three years earlier, they had bought it for $600.[186] They purchased 40.33 acres near Laurel, Washington County, Oregon, from Henry Dilberger and his wife on September 8, 1890.[187] Taxes were paid on their 40-acre farm, valued at $300 in 1890 and $350 in 1891.[188] Their home was probably a box house with two rooms upstairs and two downstairs, heated by a wood-burning stove.

Before moving to the farm, Wilhelmine's brother Carl (known as Charles) and his wife Wilhelmina (known as Marta) and their children arrived in Portland sometime between the birth of their daughter Louise in Green Bay on August 24, 1888, and their purchase of property in the Albina neighborhood in January 1889. Charles and Marta settled at 307 Failing Street, where they lived for the rest of their lives.

Their sister Caroline soon joined them. Caroline arrived in Portland in 1892 with her second husband (the brother of her deceased husband), two daughters from her first marriage, and a daughter from her second marriage. They departed from the German port of Bremen and arrived in Baltimore on December 4, 1891. Caroline had six children during her first marriage, but only two daughters survived. Three of her sons died in 1889, including twins who were kept in a warm oven in an unsuccessful attempt to keep them alive. August died on May 25, 1889; Gustav on July 14, 1889; and Carl on September 17, 1889. This appalling rate of child mortality was not unusual. Prussian records indicate that about a third of children died before the age of ten. Disease accounted for most of these deaths. Tuberculosis was common, along with periodic epidemics of smallpox, dysentery, typhoid, cholera, and diphtheria.

It was considered good luck to name children after Prussian royalty. Even a poor squatter could name a daughter Wilhelmine and a son Friedrich Wilhelm. To complicate genealogical research, every family seems to have a Caroline, Karl, Herman, Augusta, and, especially, Wilhelmine or Wilhelm. And to add to the confusion, if a child died, the next baby was often given the same name as the deceased. Naturally, nicknames were used. People also anglicized their names in the new country. Karl/Carl became Charles; Wilhelm became William; Friedrich became Fred.

Caroline (known as Carrie) and her second husband, Gottfried Franz Reichwald (who became Frank Richwold), rented 301 Failing from Charles before moving around the corner to 871 Cleveland. In this German neighborhood, Jacob Smith, whose son married Martha, Minnie's half-sister, in 1901, lived nearby. Frank grew roses in his front yard and worked as a longshoreman on the docks, then as a grain handler, and later, operated a freight elevator for Retail Drugs. Carrie, like her sister Wilhelmine, spent her days in the kitchen wearing her flour-streaked apron, kneading dough, slicing vegetables, braising meats, and cleaning up the mess. Her grandson remembered Carrie as having a round, doughy face, wrinkled like a dried apple, but with kind, twinkling eyes. His younger cousin frowned, overhearing this description, but Caroline likely resembled her sister, Wilhelmine, with the same round face and a fat bulb of a nose.

The families of Carrie and her brother Charles attended the German Trinity Lutheran Church, where their children were baptized and confirmed, and the Albina Homestead Public School, where students recited Santa Claus' Wife in 1895. Samples of classroom exercises completed by two of Frank and Carrie's daughters as fifth graders at Albina Homestead School were displayed at the Oregon Educational Exhibit in 1909. Dorothy Richwold's examples included an itemized grocery receipt where she carefully totaled purchases of 3 ½ pounds of walnuts at 16 cents per pound, 3 1/3 pounds of pickles at 48 cents per pound, crackers, prunes, 1 ½ pounds of chocolate, tea, and sugar; long-division problems of varying difficulty from zero to three; and a page demonstrating her ability to add fractions. Edna, a year younger at 11 but in the same grade, corrected common grammatical errors and showed her skill at reducing fractions. According to the Oregonian, approximately 400 "foreigners" seeking to learn English were enrolled in the Albina Homestead Night School, but with very few women among them. The Richwold sisters, first-generation immigrants, did not continue their education beyond 8th grade, but at least received some recognition for their grasp of English grammar and mathematical skills.

The Roseuau siblings' reunion was overshadowed by the Panic of 1893, which slowed down the lumber, manufacturing, and shipping industries. In Washington County, many families never recovered and were forced to sell their farms. In June 1894, the Willamette River flooded, reaching a high-water mark of 33.5 feet, inundating 250 square blocks of downtown and knocking out public utilities, warehouses, and docks.

Two drawbridges were stuck open, restricting travel between Portland's east and west sides. Businesses sold merchandise from their second-floor windows or from boats. The Union Pacific Railroad was forced to suspend service, laying off workers from the Albina neighborhood.

Wilhelmine and Caroline should have been worried about their sister-in-law, Marta. She had as many as 17 pregnancies while Charles worked stints for the railroads or as a watchman, a laborer, or a warehouseman on the docks—even working from home as a shoemaker. Their first child was born three months after their wedding, and the babies never stopped coming. Her last two babies died in 1892 and 1894 (one daughter lived two days; the other a week). On a pleasant September day in 1898, Marta reached into a cupboard, grabbed the bottle of carbolic acid, and drank it.[189]

The coroner estimated it took her 15 minutes to die. Ingesting carbolic acid caused second to third-degree burns in her mouth and esophagus, followed by respiratory distress and fluctuating blood pressure, leading to shock and ultimately her death. It was a sweet-smelling, clear liquid commonly used as a wound antiseptic and disinfectant for cleaning. It was also the preferred poison of the despondent at the turn of the century. Did her six children living at home, the youngest only eight years old, witness her suicide? Did seven-year-old Minnie, living on the farm in Washington County, overhear a discussion of her aunt's suicide? Or was nothing said?

Charles filed a lawsuit to recover $850.00 in insurance that his wife had through the Female Auxiliary of the Grand Lodge Degree of Honor of the Ancient Order of United Workmen (A.O.U.W.), a year after her death. The A.O.U.W.'s constitution specified that only Caucasians could be members. It was amended in 1893 to expel members who sold intoxicating liquors.

Six years later, on September 29, 1904, Charles was working for the Oregon Railroad and Navigation Company. (OR&N Co.) at the Albina docks when he fell, striking his head on rocks and breaking his neck. He was pronounced dead when the doctor arrived.[190] He left nine children, five of whom were married and four of whom were living at home. The children received a $600 settlement from OR&N for their father's death, along with $20 of his pay on March 7, 1905. Their attorney advised them to accept the settlement because "it might be shown that the deceased was guilty of contributory negligence." Deductions from Charles' estate included a grocery bill of $11.30 to

Walter & Greggory, funeral costs of $129.25, County Clerk filing fees, costs for newspaper notices, $2.00 a day paid to appraisers, and an attorney fee of $125. Each heir received $40; their attorney withheld $160 for the minor children—John, Fred, Lizzie, and Otto.[191]

Marta's probate closed on October 30, 1905, after her husband's death, even though she had died in 1898. She owned two frame houses at 301 and 307 Failing Street. The house at 301 Failing was rented for $7 a month, while the house at 307 Failing was rented for $9. Charles had "been a tenant by courtesy" at 307 Failing. He purchased the property for $550 from JE Bennett and his wife on January 25, 1889.[192] Three years later, he sold the property to his wife for $1.00.[193] Marta's estate owed $13.80 in taxes for 1904, $7.65 for insurance premiums, and $193.20 for street improvements on Failing Street. The property was offered for sale at the Multnomah County Courthouse on May 29, 1905. The highest bid was $1,025 for a property appraised at $1,000. Each child received $66.82, with their attorney receiving money for Fred, John, Otto, and Louise (Lizzie).

None of the older Rosenau children wanted to provide lodging and board for their younger siblings. They couldn't even agree on an administrator. Attorneys complained to the Multnomah County Court that several conferences were held with the children to explain the necessity and advisability of having an administrator. An agreement was finally "thrashed out," as the "children were young and had no understanding of business practices." A brother-in-law, Charles V. Jennings, reluctantly agreed to be the administrator, protesting that he was busy with his job at the City Messenger Company. His wife, Lena, also reluctantly agreed to look after her younger brothers, stating it was a "very unprofitable bargain," even though she could keep the rents from 301 and 307 Failing as compensation. However, she received very little rent: seven dollars for 301 Failing, eight dollars for 307 Failing from "some night school that paid for two months for the use of the basement," and "some woman" who paid $4 (no explanation given). William Keller was paid $9 for painting and repairing 307 Failing on March 6, 1905 (perhaps in lieu of rent), as he paid $10 in rent on April 6, 1905.[194]

Among the minor children, John, aged 20, became a helper in a pretzel factory; Fred, aged 17, quickly found a job that allowed him to support himself; Louise (Lizzie), aged 15, resided at the Magdalen Home; and Otto was 13. The Magdalen Home was a charitable Catholic institution located at East 20th and Irving Street, where public officials and county courts sent incorrigible girls and destitute children. Girls who "fell from the pinnacle of chastity and virtue to the depths of debauchery and shame" could be detained, redeemed, cared for, and educated. Once released, Louise worked a grueling ten-hour shift as an ironer in the steam-heated American Laundry and lived in a boarding house. With their dangerous boilers, mangles, and irons, laundries were among the first workplaces women attempted to unionize, seeking shorter hours and safer conditions. Too many young women were burned, fainted from the heat, or lost a hand.[195]

Otto joined the "Malvern Troupe," a Portland-based ensemble that toured show circuits across America. In an interview years later, he described himself as an orphan, reminiscing about his time in Vaudeville as a member of an acrobatic troupe and about meeting performers who later became motion picture stars. By age 20, he had grown too tall for acrobatic acts, so he returned to Portland and became a plumber's apprentice.[196]

The graves of Charles, Marta (Wilhelmina), and a grandson are marked with a monument in Lone Fir Cemetery in Portland. The stone reads, "Charles Rosenau, Sept. 29, 1904, 52 years; Wilhelmina Rosenau, Sept. 23, 1898, age 44." It was noted in the Multnomah County Coroner's report that members of Eureka Lodge A.O.U.W. buried Marta following her suicide.[197] The 1904 report for Charles stated that relatives buried him.

Immigrant parents probably pulled their hair out over their children's behaviors. Minnie's cousin, Edith, was sent to the Multnomah County Poor Farm. Her condition, stated on her admission, was pregnancy. She was voluntarily discharged on January 5, 1903, with the note "Baby adopted by friends." Minnie's uncle, Frank Richwold, reported his 16-year-old daughter to the police for coming home late every night for a week. One night, she didn't come home at all. Lizzie was described as 5'4", 120 pounds, with a light complexion, and stooped slightly when walking.[198]

Neighbors caught four teenage Polish boys stealing from vegetable gardens in 1910. The boys had constructed a ten-foot-square shack lined with burlap and building paper, furnished with discarded furniture, in the gulch at Morris and Delay, where they played cards and shot craps. When confronted, the boys brandished a hand axe and a ten-inch hunting knife and shouted profanity. The neighbors called the boys' parents and the police. Consequently, a strict 8 pm curfew was enforced to prevent similar incidents. Raising children in Portland was far different from the old country, where village eyes and ears missed nothing.

Minnie's siblings and cousins never completed more than eighth grade. The boys found jobs on the docks or in factories, such as sack sewers, bottle washers, or helpers. The girls got jobs in laundries or as maids. As technology advanced, they secured positions as telephone operators and clerks. They were part of a workforce of immigrant girls, aged fourteen to twenty, who were single and lived in urban areas. Their employment was seen as temporary until they married and had children.

Succeeding generations drifted apart. No stories or memories about Minnie's siblings, parents, or grandparents were discussed around my grandma's kitchen table. I had no idea that Rosenau—or Wohlfeil, for that matter—was even a surname in my family tree. When I started researching, I discovered Minnie had a sister named Bertha. During a visit, she told me that their mother, Wilhelmine, had moved to Portland to join her sister, Caroline Richwood. I later discovered that Wilhelmine had arrived in Oregon first, and her sister's married name was Reichwald, anglicized to Richwold—not Richwood.

Caroline's descendants have remained connected, especially the grandchildren of her second daughter, Marie, who married Paul Smith. After he was killed on the Willamette River pilings in 1915, she married his younger brother George Smith, continuing the tradition of marrying a brother-in-law when widowed, just like her mother had done. Caroline's grandchildren were only vaguely aware that their grandma had siblings who settled in Portland. Charles' grandchildren were completely unaware he had any sisters in Portland. It took several years of genealogical research by descendants to confirm that Charles, Caroline, and Wilhelmine were siblings. The proof was eventually found in the Evangelical Lutheran Church records of baptisms, marriages, and burials of Klein Bandtken, Marienwerder, West Prussia. And my DNA test revealed that I am a close match to Caroline's grandchildren.

Birth of Minnie

My great-grandmother, Minnie, was born in Washington County, Oregon, in 1891. Mary had just turned four. Her sister Bertha, born in 1893, joined Minnie, Mary, three half-brothers, and a half-sister on the farm. The boys completed the equivalent of a fifth-grade education, while their sister Martha finished eighth grade before working in Portland. Mary didn't miss a day of school in the spring of 1898, earning recognition for attending every day from April 11 to June 7 without being tardy. Whether William was Mary's biological father became irrelevant, as she was raised as part of the family with her older half-siblings and younger sisters.

William probably divided his time between working on the farm and repairing railcars for the Union Pacific Railway in Portland during the year Minnie was born, earning money to get them through the winter. His teenage children also worked in Portland, sending money home to their father and stepmother. In 1895, 15-year-old Martha was employed as a domestic maid for a businessman, and 17-year-old William worked as a laborer. They boarded in the same neighborhood where Wilhelmine's siblings lived.

The Southern Pacific West Side Line, powered by an old steam engine, ran the 20 miles from Portland's Fourth Avenue to Hillsboro on a regular schedule for 65 cents. No matter how homesick Martha felt, she probably didn't go home very often. She needed the fare and her big brother to go with her. After getting off the train, they had to carry their grips a long seven miles south or catch a ride in a neighbor's horse-drawn wagon across muddy streets and roads to see how big their half-sisters were getting.

Martha was one of two chambermaids in 1899, while her brother, William, worked as a waiter at the Hotel Zur Rheinpfalz located at 253 Front Street. The hotel had a diverse clientele, including several gold prospectors, a music teacher, a capitalist, a fruit peddler, a cigar maker, sailors, laborers, and railroad workers, totaling 151 guests. Their brother Albert drifted around doing farm work, while Charles lent a hand on the farm. Wilhelmine likely kept cows and poultry, selling the milk to the creamery and trading cheese, butter, and eggs for essentials. William may have taken trips to Portland to sell their farm produce or sent it with a storekeeper who made regular journeys to bring back supplies for his store.

Hay was mowed, raked into windrows, and left to dry before being hauled by wagon to the barn in late June. A threshing crew moved from farm to farm to thresh the harvested grain during July and August. Many families picked hops during a three-week season in late August and early September. The Willamette Valley was known as "The Hop

Capitol of the World" at the turn of the century. Hops were sold to Portland's Henry Weinhard Brewing Company for ales and lagers, and shipped to the Midwest and overseas, including Great Britain, the largest importer of American hops. Families brought camping tents and earned a dollar for every 100 pounds of hops they picked. It was like a paid vacation, but gloves or old socks were needed to cover their hands to avoid a skin rash.

Fourteen-year-old Charles got into a fight with a neighbor boy. He was walking past the McClarkin farm when words were exchanged, leading to a brawl involving dirt clods and clubs. Young McClarkin's father, James McClarkin, and his older stepbrother, Clyde Finn, became involved. Finn and James McClarkin were arrested. Mr. McClarkin was found not guilty, but his stepson was fined $10 plus other costs.[199] The McClarkins were recent immigrants from Ireland, while the Wohlfeils were Prussian. Prejudice was alive and well over a hundred twenty years ago, too.

After farming in Washington County for 13 years, William and Wilhelmine sold their 40.33 acres for $1900 to fellow Germans Fred and Fredricka Goetter on December 10, 1903.[200] They joined others who left rural communities for towns and cities, lured by better employment opportunities and transportation. However, cities came with gambling, drinking, prostitution, overcrowding, clanging streetcars, rumbling wagons, and smoky air. Removed from the racket of downtown, William Wohlfeil purchased three adjoining lots in the upper Albina neighborhood on December 5, 1903, for $375. Charles was probably stuck leading the family's milk cow the twenty miles to Portland, a distance that was murder to prod a tired cow that wanted nothing more than to lie down and rest.

Mary was 16 and already working as a domestic, Minnie was 12, and Bertha was 10. Their half-brother Charles sometimes lived with them or stayed in boarding houses with William or Martha. At 1012 East 11th Avenue, Minnie's world transformed from fields to a rutted street lined with scattered houses, tall firs, stumps, vegetable gardens, fruit trees, wandering cows, and the occasional runaway horse. Hammers pounded nails into houses made from kits sold through Sears or Montgomery Ward catalogs. Everyone had an outhouse. Wires for electricity were being connected, a magical source of light that wouldn't burn paper. But the garishness of a single electric bulb hanging from the ceiling was too shocking for tidy housewives, exposing a coating of years-old dust and cobwebs in the corners.

Minnie initially didn't understand the word "suffrage," but soon learned it meant women gaining the right to vote. Abigail Scott Duniway occasionally gave lectures in Portland. However, throughout her life, Minnie showed no interest in politics or issues like women's rights, poverty, education, healthcare, or social improvement.

From August through November, enormous piles of slab wood were delivered to homes and stacked on sidewalks or curbs for heating and cooking. It may have been Minnie's job to fill the wood box with kindling each morning while her mother started the coffee, dropping an eggshell into the pot to settle the grounds. School lunches were carried in folding tin boxes lined with a cloth napkin. Monday morning was wash day in the neighborhood, and by afternoon, lines full of clothes fluttered in every backyard. In winter, clothes were dried on ropes crisscrossing the back porch.

The 1905 Lewis and Clark Centennial Exposition was in the planning stages, and business was booming. The population had grown from 90,500 in 1900 to 207,000 in 1910. Nearly three-quarters of this increase was due to immigrants. Schools were bursting at the seams. Minnie's neighborhood school had 250 pupils crowded into four classrooms. In March 1903, the foundation was completed to expand the school to ten rooms and an assembly hall connected to the old classrooms.

Minnie's father was 56 years old when he quit farming. During the Panic of 1907, when socialism spread among the unemployed, he worked as a laborer for the Portland City Water Department. He reported being unemployed for 26 weeks in 1910, but always seemed to find work. He labored on the street railroads (streetcars) and served as a watchman at a machine shop. He also worked as an expressman or drayman, driving a wagon hauling freight. He may have worked with Jacob Smith, whose son married Martha in 1901. Two tough old men in their sixties and seventies could load and unload freight better than most, but both died from hernia problems. Jacob's express wagon collided with a jitney bus at Williams Avenue and Beech Street during the evening rush hour in 1915. Witnesses reported that the express wagon's lights were on, and the collision occurred under a streetlight. Luckily, no one was injured, but the wagon was badly wrecked.[201] Two years later, William was sitting on his wagon enjoying a midday nap at the corner of 10th and Hoyt when an automobile sharply turned to avoid a woman and a small boy crossing the street. The vehicle hit the rear end of his express wagon, throwing William to the ground and causing his horse to run away. Newspaper headlines read "Siesta Disturbed by an Auto Collision." William F. Wohlfeil was taken to the Emergency Hospital, where a head wound and a few minor bruises were treated.[202] William probably met steamboats at the docks or trains at the depot, hauling baggage and freight to customers' destinations. He would have kept his horse stabled at the nearest livery stable, paying extra for hay and water. German draymen were known to haul anything—even coffins during funerals. Horsepower essentially built the streets of Portland, delivering groceries, fuel to heat homes, and ice for kitchen iceboxes.

As technology improved, tractor-driven road graders replaced draft horses, and automobiles replaced horses and buggies. Similarly, streetcars declined as people began driving their cars to work. In 1905, there were 218 automobiles in Oregon, with forty in Portland. The speed limit was eight to ten miles per hour, but increased to 15 miles per hour farther out. Henry Ford introduced his popular Model T in 1908 and sold fifteen million nationwide over the next two decades. A single-cylinder Cadillac runabout, recently painted and in good running condition, equipped with skid chains and lights, was listed for sale for $200 at William and Wilhelmine's address, complete with a phone number.[203] Since William earned a living hauling freight in a horse-drawn wagon, the two-seater horseless carriage with its single-cylinder engine (rated at 6.5 horsepower) likely belonged to one of his sons. Minnie's father probably didn't think much of those automobiles, which were noisy, unreliable, and smelled bad. They couldn't compete with a strong team of horses through Portland's rain and mud. Mein Gott!

It took time for streetcar drivers, bicyclists, pedestrians, and horses to adjust to one another. Some individuals also made poor decisions. Minnie's uncle, Frank Richwold, was walking home from his job as a longshoreman for Albers Brothers Mill when he tried to jump onto the crowded rear platform of the Williams Avenue streetcar on the Steel Bridge, despite a warning from the conductor. He became trapped between a steel girder and the moving streetcar. Fortunately, passengers held on to him, preventing him from falling under the wheels, but he still broke four ribs and suffered numerous contusions and lacerations.[204]

Adapting to the new modes of transportation caused some women to become hysterical, either screaming in public or fainting. This kind of behavior only reinforced the unfortunate idea that women were the weaker sex. Someone reportedly shouted that a drawbridge was open, triggering panic on the Williams Avenue streetcar. Minnie's sister-in-law jumped, badly spraining her ankle and sustaining several scalp wounds. Another woman also sustained injuries. Both women were hospitalized for several days.[205]

Minnie's oldest half-brother, Albert, found work in Washington's Yakima Valley, while his brother William bottled whiskey for H. Varwig and Son at 231 Front Street in Portland. The Varwig family created a popular rye whiskey called "VIM," followed by R. Bond Whiskey. Later, William and Charles worked for the Oregon Railroad and Navigation Company (OR&N) in the Albina rail yards. They lived in boarding houses at 77 Morris and 572 Delay, before moving to 571 Mississippi in the heart of Albina from 1911 to 1914. Charles was a blacksmith helper at the railyard before becoming a teamster. He left Portland in the 1940s to farm near Seal Rock, Lincoln County, Oregon, and married at 54. William built a career with Portland streetcars, retiring as a bus driver for Rose City Transit. He married at 44, gaining a stepson. Their sister, Martha, described as a warm and loving woman, became everyone's favorite aunt. Her husband, Jacob Smith, worked as an engineer for the railroad and built a few houses in Albina. From 1910 to 1918, Jacob and Martha lived in a five-room bungalow that he had built at 252 Cook Street. In 1912, they sued the Proebstel Land and Adjustment Company for ownership of Lot 1 in Block 3 of the Albina Addition. The decree, issued in 1914, confirmed that the plaintiffs held a good and valid title.[206] They also attended the Spanish-American War Boys, Wives & Sweethearts Banquet, where Oregon's Governor was the guest of honor. Martha hosted card parties for the members of the Club of Queen Elizabeth Review, an affiliate of the Independent Order of Odd Fellows. She also served as treasurer for the Ladies' Altar Society of St. Mary's Parish in Upper Albina, as the Smiths were Catholic rather than Evangelical Lutheran. Sometimes her brother, Charles, boarded with them.

Of William Fred's four children with Catherine, only the oldest son, Albert, had children, and he had three. His first two children died in infancy, and the third he left at a children's home after his wife's suicide by drowning in the Yakima River in 1910. Albert left his 3½-month-old son at the Washington Children's Home in Seattle, choosing not to leave him with his in-laws in Yakima or with his sister Martha, who had been married for nine years and had no children, nor would she ever.

Albert drifted south to Southern Oregon and raised cattle. He was one of four men who sued a real estate company in 1914 to recover money. He also claimed payment for appearing as a witness for the state. In 1920, he worked as a hired hand for Phillip Duncan's stock farm in Poison Creek, nine miles south of Burns. Ten years later, he owned a farm on Poison Creek with a cabin valued at $100. In the winter of 1951, when Albert was 76, he suffered severe frostbite on both feet, which turned gangrenous, as if he had fallen in bad weather. His condition worsened due to bronchial pneumonia. He never recovered and was buried in an unmarked grave in Burns Cemetery.

Minnie grew up at the L-shaped house at 1012 East 11th Avenue in Portland. The triple lot had plenty of space for apple trees, dairy cows, a chicken coop, and a garden.[207] The lots were individually valued at $190 in 1908, rising to $250 each in 1909, and then to $305 in 1910. The following year, the assessed value was $350 per lot, plus $600 for improvements, for a total of $1,650. A butcher shop was near a corner grocery store, where candy was displayed in glass jars. Customers waited for the lyrical call of the Italian peddler who stood on the rear step of his wagon to weigh fruits and vegetables from a hanging scale.

Minnie got a job as an operator for the Western Mantle Company at 28 Front Street with her cousin, Minnie Richwold. The company made silk mantles for lanterns and lamps. The girls took a streetcar for a nickel or walked to work. They were careful to avoid the heckling bullies in the Scandinavian, Irish, or Polish neighborhoods who loved to yell insults. Likely dressed in a long navy flared skirt, a loose blouse with a sailor collar called a middy, her waist cinched by a corset, and her long red hair styled into a pompadour topped with an 18-inch brimmed hat secured by two deadly hatpins (she believed her red hair was her best feature for the rest of her life), she wasn't intimidated. When Minnie started wearing a corset and her hair up, she was a woman!

When news of the 1906 San Francisco earthquake arrived by telegram, Minnie had a new job as an operator for the Pacific Telephone and Telegraph Company. The switchboard lit up as the news spread among the 25,000 subscribers who owned telephones. By the afternoon of April 18, the headline of the Oregon Daily Journal declared, "San Francisco in Ruins, 2,000 Dead in Earthquake, Flames following shocks threaten to destroy entire city." In fact, 3,000 were dead, and 200,000 were left homeless. Portland bakeries sent 36,000 loaves of bread. Doctors and nurses headed south. Women formed committees to send blankets and medical supplies, all of which had to be transported by train to Oakland and ferried across the bay. Three days after the quake, 1500 refugees arrived in Portland for temporary lodging in private homes, the YMCA, or boarding houses. Local restaurants offered free meals.

The Pacific Telephone and Telegraph Company offered Minnie better pay and working conditions than most other jobs. Female operators earned $1.00 per day, rising to $1.10 after a 2-month training period. Their voices were considered more soothing than those of male operators; however, male operators still received higher wages. New labor laws limited Minnie's workday to 8 hours, including 15-minute breaks. She could buy her lunch from the company lunchroom, which provided warm meals at cost. Nearly three-fifths of women in Portland earned less than $10 per week, which was regarded as the minimum weekly wage necessary for any self-supporting female wage earner in the city.

Perhaps Minnie had a nickel to go to the Nickelodeon with a cousin. Nickelodeons were set up in downtown storefronts, featuring machines that resembled vending machines. Minnie could insert a nickel in the slot, then press her face against a peephole to watch a show for a few minutes, like a cops and robbers show or a romantic love story. But she had to add another nickel to see the next scene. Other Nickelodeons had chairs or benches facing a canvas sheet that repeatedly showed one- to ten-minute films, mostly boxing matches and vaudeville skits. Popular among the working classes, her parents would have worried about the lack of fire escapes and the questionable reputation of the films. Silent films were first shown at the new theater on 6th Avenue in 1907, and were more entertaining. A nickel could also take her on a trolley to Oaks Park, the top of Council Crest (where, on clear days, she could enjoy a stunning view of Mount Hood, Mount St. Helens, and Mount Adams), Jantzen Beach, Cadenza Park near Estacada, or Chautauqua in Gladstone. Oaks Amusement Park opened on May 30, 1905, and it became so popular that by 1907, the railroad company added 15 long open trolley cars to run to and from the park every five minutes. From downtown, at First and Alder, Oaks Park was a 15-minute trolley ride away. By 1909, 30,000 people rode to Oaks on Sundays and holidays. Women and children were admitted free until 6:30 p.m. every day except Sundays. I imagine Minnie screaming on the most popular ride, Shoot the Chutes. She had to climb 70 feet of zigzagging wooden stairs to a platform. Twelve riders gripped the handrail and faced forward in backless seats in a flat-bottomed open boat. The boat was then pushed onto greased rollers down the chute, splashing into a shallow pond and drenching the riders. There were also winter amusements, including a heated saltwater swimming pool, a bowling alley, a dancing pavilion, and a skating rink. In the summer, a band concert was held every evening and twice on Sundays.

In 1907, Minnie's mother purchased Lots 14 and 15 of Block 4 in the Oakhurst subdivision from J.C. and Alice H. Ainsworth for $400, as Mina Wohlfeil, a married woman. She did not list her husband on the deed. The lots might have been used as investments or for pasture for her cows. By 1914, Portland had 1,004 licensed dairies along with many small, unlicensed ones. Cows roamed the neighborhoods during the day, prompting neighbors to demand that the City Council take action because of the inconvenience and unsanitary conditions. No one wanted dried cow pies in their street or their shrubbery destroyed. Wilhelmine (or her daughters) probably milked the cows in a milk shed in their backyard, selling milk, cream, butter, and cottage cheese (known as Dutch cheese). Milk rooms were required to be kept spotless, with a concrete floor and drainage into a cesspool. No manure piles attracting flies were acceptable. Wilhelmine first saw housewives pasturing their cows in the neighborhoods of Green Bay. Over 400 to 500 cows damaged streets, disrupted traffic, and destroyed flowerbeds until Green Bay passed a "cow" ordinance in 1882, warning the public in brochures printed in German and English. By the 1920s, Portland's small dairies had disappeared because of the many rules and complaints. A decade later, Minnie will milk cows and sell cream and cottage cheese in Oak Grove.

Wilhelmine sold Lot 15 on May 3, 1918, to her daughter Bertha and son-in-law Frank McKever for $1.00 and other valuable considerations. The deed was corrected on May 15, 1918, to include Mina's husband, F.W. Wohlfeil.[208]

Frank Hemsworth

Minnie met Frank Hemsworth, whom she probably believed was the most exciting man alive. He had that charming "bad boy" appeal. He was a tall man, six feet two and a quarter inches, older than Minnie by 11 years, and divorced. Frank was the youngest in his family and a bit of a troublemaker with a juvenile record. He was first arrested for stealing chickens as a "mere boy" in 1894.[209]

The next year, he was arrested with two other boys while burglarizing an Albina store. The robbery was his idea, but he quickly blamed the other boys, choosing to appear as a witness for the state to reduce his consequences. The three boys, all 15 years old, faced burglary charges in municipal court. Due to their ages, they were allowed to plead guilty to petty larceny and were fined $50. The sentence was suspended, and they were placed with the Boys' and Girls' Aid Society, pending good behavior. They were allowed to return home on parole but had to report to the Society every Saturday morning. Failure to do so could result in sentencing. The Society offered a temporary home for homeless, neglected, and abused children and tried to save juvenile offenders from serving time in penal institutions.

The lessons didn't stick with Frank. He was charged with highway robbery when he held up a man in Albina, threatened to kill him, and stole three dollars. Unable to make the $300 bond, he went to the county jail.[210] A week later, the grand jury indicted him. On February 24, 1896, Frank was transported to a reform school. He was 15 years old and the tallest man at the school without exception.[211]

Probably because a judge strongly suggested he enlist in the military, Frank enlisted as a private and served in the Spanish-American War with the Second Oregon Volunteer Infantry from May 15, 1898, to June 12, 1899. His father had served during the Civil War and may have thought military life was just the thing to straighten Frank out.

Once discharged, Frank became a fireman. One of the Portland theaters offered free passes until it was discovered they couldn't hear the alarm bell from inside. They were fined $2 for missing roll call. Frank got married (which lasted three years) and then, surprisingly, became a Portland police officer despite his juvenile record. Frank's name often appeared in the newspaper, at least monthly, from 1903 to 1908. Perhaps his father bragged to the crime beat reporters who frequented his coffee shop, a few blocks from the police station.

Frank captured a rattlesnake that had escaped through a drugstore transom from a window display. He shot an ex-pugilist in the leg who tried to run away after being caught in an opium den on Second Street. The ex-pugilist was greatly incensed over Patrolman Hemsworth shooting him and sued for $1000, finally settling for $580. Frank chased men trying to sneak into a house's basement in the early morning hours, shot at men robbing a saloon's till, marched behind President Theodore Roosevelt during his visit, arrested a man who hurled a torrent of profane language at his wife, and broke up their home with a four-foot club. He kept the peace between the union and non-union painters at the Weinhard Building and broke up fights. A logger came in from the woods with $80, bought a $20 suit to visit a songstress from Blazier's First Street Variety Theater, and then claimed she robbed him of $50. Frank arrested her. He also stopped wagons hauling open garbage barrels, in violation of a city ordinance. Each hauler was fined $5 upon conviction.[212]

However, more than just his capture of a rattlesnake made the news. He was fired for patronizing saloons while on duty and talking with the women who frequented them; he was reinstated and fired again. He was hired by the Fire Department, which was the focus of an inquiry into intoxication, fighting, or ungentlemanly conduct among firemen while on duty. F.W. Hemsworth, the ladder man of Fire Truck No. 1, voluntarily resigned.[213]

Frank then worked as a special police officer for seven years. The Portland Special Police operated in a gray area between traditional police officers and security guards. They were paid by businesses but had the authority to make arrests. Patrolmen wore dark blue uniforms with shiny badges, tall, rounded helmets, capes for cold and rainy days, and carried billy clubs used liberally on unruly citizens. Frank's beat covered the district bounded by 18th and 23rd Avenues, between Washington and Marshall Streets. Late-night wanderers were warned to stay within the bounds of the law on Patrolman Hemsworth's north end beat, as he enforced the after-hours ordinance with an iron fist and did not tolerate loafers after the clock struck 1 am. Frank arrested Robert Gardiner, B. Roop, and J. Dooligan early one morning, as they could not account for themselves. Roop and Dooligan were each fined $10, while Gardiner, an ex-convict, was sentenced to 15 days.[214] In 1906, an elderly pedestrian, mistaking Patrolman Hemsworth for a highwayman, pointed a revolver at him while Hemsworth, who was over six feet tall, leaned against a telephone pole and considered the incident a joke.[215]

Patrolman Hemsworth's law enforcement career was marred by his frequent visits to saloons and oyster houses. He insisted he

Patrolman Hemsworth on the left

had never drank while on duty, claiming he only went in to get a meal or to see the proprietors. At the turn of the century, police standards in Portland were somewhat lax. In 1903, a patrolman was caught drunk, sitting in a cigar store and spinning tales. He was simply sent home to sober up. But Frank tried to get away with more. When caught talking to a woman of the streets while on duty, he claimed to have known her from school and was trying to persuade her to return to her respectable parents. Despite his evangelical leanings, Hemsworth threatened to reveal unflattering information about the police department when facing termination. He later denied making such threats and even wrote a letter to The Oregonian asserting his innocence. He was again in trouble for talking to women on Second Avenue, claiming they were seeking a doctor and he was trying to help. Frank was well-known around town, and everyone had an opinion on whether he was a hero, a bully, or a blackmailing coward.

Frank was assigned to patrol the 1905 Lewis and Clark Centennial Exposition, an event when Portland's city fathers wanted the city to look its best. The mayor ordered weather-beaten and dingy houses to be painted, dilapidated buildings torn down, old fences repaired, and lawns and grounds cleaned up. Roses were planted along the streets to enhance the city's appearance. Enthusiastic children collected tin cans, old scraps, and garbage. However, beneath Portland's glitter was the grime of gutter politics, vice, and sporting girls. Gambling and prostitution were rampant, with bawdy houses and cribs. The "Red Light District" extended along Fourth Avenue. Prostitutes called out to potential customers from windows flush with the sidewalks, with names above the doors like Jennie, Lulu, The Favorite, or Rosie. The "sporting girls" lived short and brutal lives. Loggers, sailors, railroad repair gangs, and farm workers who wintered along Portland's waterfront spent their wages on women, alcohol, or gambling in one of Portland's 200 saloons and ended up sleeping in flophouses where flimsy half-walls and chicken wire partitioned tiny spaces. The 1912 vice report showed that in the City of Roses, 25% of all diseases treated by the town's physicians were venereal. This report noted that this was a "conservative" figure as it did not include the number of people who used quacks or self-dosed with home or drugstore remedies.

Young women who came to Portland seeking jobs were considered to be in sexual danger. This view led to reforms, such as the closure of saloons, bowling alleys, billiard rooms, and skating rinks on Sundays.

These closures left respectable young women and men with little to do on their day off except spend their time on the streets. In 1908, Portland took the remarkable step of hiring a woman for the police force, making her the first policewoman in the nation. Mrs. Lola Baldwin's role was to protect the moral welfare of young women and girls, and for the next dozen years, she would do so with exceptional zeal and skill. Minnie had a good idea of the future for impoverished pregnant girls and saw their lives as cautionary tales.

But Minnie willingly overlooked Frank's checkered past. Likely against her parents' wishes, she traveled to San Francisco in November 1909 to marry that rascal, Frank Hemsworth. Properly married by a minister, their relationship with organized religion seemed to end, except for their insistence that their children attend Sunday School, a decree passed down through the generations.

Frank bounced between Portland and San Francisco, working on the docks as a longshoreman but never staying in any job for long. The year before he married Minnie, he lived at 421 Julian Street in Santa Clara and worked as a teamster. He returned to Portland six months later to testify before a grand jury. An intoxicated woman had gotten out of her car when it stopped running and was killed by a hit-and-run driver. The driver who allegedly caused her death was out for the night with another man's wife and was reluctant to come forward. Frank testified that he recognized the hit-and-run driver and his passenger after seeing their picture in the newspaper, as he had served them drinks while moonlighting at the Lakeview Inn. He was even sent to the county jail to identify the couple. However, the jury was instructed to disregard his testimony when it was proven that the couple was nowhere near the roadhouse.

Married life with Frank proved to be exciting, though a bit uncertain. Frank and Minnie moved frequently to a dizzying array of addresses in the San Francisco Bay Area. From 1910 to 1911, he worked as a laborer in San Francisco and lived at 1628a Sutter in a building that housed apartments and businesses. Frank was a fireman when my grandmother, Beatrice Helen (Bea), was born on Halloween, October 31, 1910. Bea was followed 10 months later by Lyda, born on August 27, 1911. They resided at 707 Utah Street, San Francisco, where Frank worked as a stevedore. Their third child, Frank Jr. born 10 months after Lyda, tragically died choking on his vomit at six weeks of age. They lived at 1734 Palou Avenue, where Frank continued working as a stevedore. I grew up overhearing warnings never to lay babies on their backs because they might choke and suffocate.

After having three children at 10-month intervals, Minnie had a break until Robert Wesley was born on October 1, 1915, while the family lived at 340 North 11th in San Jose. Two weeks later, Frank attended the 74th birthday celebration at the Eureka Hotel for a veteran driver of the San Jose Ice Company, where Frank was employed as a driver. No women were listed among the long list of guests. I bet the alcohol was flowing. By 1917, Frank and Minnie had moved to 212 Fox Avenue in San Jose, where Frank worked as a teamster.

Minnie became skilled at moving, washing diapers, and dodging bill collectors. Frank's paychecks disappeared in saloons. She turned his frayed collars over and used flour sacks as dish towels and underwear, but it was never a skill she boasted about. Flour came in 49-pound sacks, stitched on three sides. A single snip of the scissors would unravel the stitching, leaving sturdy cotton fabric that wore like iron.

I visited Bertha, Minnie's younger sister, in 1977. She looked like my great-grandmother and clicked her tongue in disapproval, just like I remembered her sister doing. Bertha remembered visiting Minnie in San Francisco and taking little Bea (my grandmother) by the hand to fetch Frank from the saloon to come home for dinner.

Frank's father died in 1911 while he and Minnie lived in the Bay Area. (His mother passed away in 1905, probably before Minnie met Frank.) His father left an estate consisting of cash and three lots in Portland to be split equally among his four children. Unlike his siblings, Frank borrowed from the estate before it went into probate. In December 1912, a bill collector from San Francisco petitioned the court for $96.70 of Frank's inheritance from his father's estate. Since Frank had already received an advance of $200, the bill collector was paid $90.65 directly from the estate. Frank, as one of the heirs of John W. Hemsworth, attempted to sell the three Portland lots to Deitrich Henry Otto of San Francisco for $10 on September 6, 1913. Minnie's name was included in the deed as well.[216] Frank must have been drunk. He knew he couldn't sell the lots without his siblings' consent. Moreover, one lot in the Vernon subdivision alone was worth more than $10. It had been his father's residence at the time of his death.

Working on the docks was labor-intensive and hazardous for Frank, with few safeguards in place for the teams loading and unloading cargo from ships. And West Coast longshoring was rife with anarchists and labor strikes. Although the Clayton Anti-Trust Act of 1914 provided a slight reprieve by legalizing strikes, boycotts, and peaceful picketing, it did little to improve working conditions. On June 1, 1916, 10,000 longshore workers walked off the job in a major West Coast strike that lasted 11 days. Members sought a closed-shop agreement (limited to hiring union members in good standing), overtime benefits, and increased wages. African Americans were brought in as strikebreakers against White trade unionists, creating a no-win situation for everyone. On April 6, 1917, Congress declared war on Germany, and the United States entered World War I. Suddenly, shipyards were busy day and night building ships and loading them with war materials and Oregon timber, wheat, and other foodstuffs. There was plenty of work, yet members of the International Longshoremen's Association (ILA), including Frank, groused that ship owners were getting rich from their hard labor. To boost their image and link their work to patriotism, the ILA adopted their initials as the slogan, "I Love America."

Posters asking, "Are you 100% American?" were displayed in grocery stores and barbershops. A Portland Special Policeman uttered a remark considered disloyal to the United States and was forced to resign immediately.[217] Portland flour miller J. Henry Albers received a three-year prison sentence for singing German songs while drunk. The library withdrew from circulation all books considered pro-German or otherwise objectionable.[218] The Espionage Act, signed by President Woodrow Wilson shortly after the U.S. entered World War I, was applied to German Americans. The Sedition Act made it a federal offense to use disloyal, profane, scurrilous, or abusive language about the Constitution, government, military uniforms, or the flag. Five hundred thousand men and women were questioned about their loyalty to the United States.

German heritage and language were seen as barriers to American unity. The Portland City Council changed the names of streets with German-sounding names: Frankfurt became Lafayette, Bismarck became Bush, and Karl became Haig. Signs in German were removed from the German churches. It marked the end of the German-language press, the Turnverein gymnastic and sharpshooting (Schützen) clubs, and German-language sermons in Portland. Germans or people with German names were restricted from Portland docks and forbidden to be within half a mile of the Armory on NW 10th Street or any federal or state fort, camp, or naval vessel. Hamburger became known as Salisbury steak; sauerkraut as liberty cabbage. Boys played army, shooting the "Germans" with toy guns. Women were urged to sign the pledge to save and conserve food. The slogan "food will win the war" appeared everywhere. Seditious behaviors allegedly included refusing to sign food-conservation pledge cards or participating in Liberty Loan drives, the campaign to sell government bonds to finance the war.

Minnie looked, dressed, and sounded as American as Frank, whose ancestor was a British Redcoat who deserted in New York City during the Revolutionary War. She likely refused to admit that she could speak German. However, she held onto her lifelong prejudices. She despised those who spoke Low German (Plattdeutsch), believing that High German (Hochdeutsch) was associated with a higher social class.

Frank and Minnie moved back to Portland in 1918 with Bea, 8, Lyda, 7, and Robert, 3. Despite citizen protests claiming that the military draft violated American individualism and democracy, Frank registered. He was 38 years old, supported a wife and three children, and had served in the Spanish-American War. He was described as tall and slender, with brown eyes and brown hair. He was employed as a longshoreman for the San Francisco and Portland Steamship Company at the Ainsworth dock and lived at 282 Margin. A flat at 282½ Margin Street was advertised in the Oregonian newspaper as a modern five-room flat, newly painted and papered, at the foot of Halsey Boulevard, a ten-minute walk from the Union Train Depot, and three blocks south of the Broadway Bridge. It was advertised for rent again on July 6, 1921, for $32.50 a month.

Frank was elected President of Local 6 of the ILA in December 1919. He had already been serving as the advisory board's chairman. One in five American workers participated in strikes, including the United Mine Workers, steelworkers, Boston police, machinists, ironworkers, butchers, and longshoremen. A strike on the Portland waterfront from April to late June 1922 was nearly the final straw for the ILA. Portland longshoremen walked out when the union contract expired. In a crucial innovation, management brought in an old steamship, the F.J. Potter, and moored it at the dock, allowing strikebreakers to live on board, which eliminated their need to cross picket lines to work. The ILA fought to regain control over working conditions and hiring practices. Frustration erupted in fistfights, head-bashing, and outbreaks of violence. The mayor got angry, and approximately 500 men, likely including Frank, were arrested. The West Coast longshore industry became known for kickbacks, blacklists, goon squads, wage cuts, and staggering accident rates. Some ship owners had a "vigilante committee" whose members would storm the court to influence the verdict in their favor. They threatened to lynch a judge whom they saw as insufficiently sympathetic to their side.

Frank continued to work as a longshoreman, earning a dollar an hour, interspersed with stints as a driver and general laborer. He applied for reinstatement as a Portland patrolman on February 15, 1918, but was denied by the police chief, who cited Hemsworth's questionable record. The chief reopened the case about Frank's shooting of a man in the leg in 1904, which had been approved at the time as in the line of duty. However, when the alleged victim sued the city, Frank resigned and refused to testify against the man. Fourteen years later, the chief still believed something was fishy.

A soldier heading to Texas for training in the fall of 1918 fell ill and checked into a Portland hospital. He was diagnosed with the Spanish flu. The Oregon State Board of Health ordered all public gathering places statewide to shut down. Parades were canceled. Churches suspended services. Restaurants sat empty. Dance halls fell silent. Ice cream parlors and soda shops closed. Citizens were advised to keep their feet dry, eat more onions, and keep windows open. People wore garlic pouches tied around their necks. On October 17, the newly dedicated Civic Auditorium was converted into a city hospital. Slogans like "Don't wear tight clothes or tight shoes" or "Chew your food carefully" appeared. People wore gauze masks. Portland churches held a Grand Reunion Service on the Sunday after Thanksgiving to celebrate the end of the flu, but it was premature. The epidemic lingered a little longer. Before it was gone, 3,500 Oregonians died. Then, Minnie received word that Frank had been hurt in an accident.

On a winter night, Frank was riding the streetcar home, perhaps from his job with the Oregon Auto Dispatch Company, when the Williams Avenue streetcar lost its brakes and collided with a parked car on the northwest corner of Third and Glisan Streets. He would have been better off drunk that night. Frank and the conductor were badly injured. An ambulance responding to a sick call witnessed the accident and transported the two men to Good Samaritan Hospital. Frank's ear was torn off, and he sustained lacerations to his face, head, and hands.[219] He was patched up and sent home to their rental at 265 Holladay Avenue on the corner of Larrabee. Rents for houses in the neighborhood began at $15 a month. It's where the Portland Trail Blazers play basketball today.

After the Great War, prohibition, the automobile, and motion pictures sparked new social trends and challenged old moral codes. Silent films provided entertainment and a means of escape from reality. Women embraced cigarettes, drank more in the sinful atmosphere of Prohibition, found psychic mediums and religious cults appealing, listened to gramophones, applied lipstick, and wore trousers. Minnie was probably too stout to fit into a straight skirt hemmed just above her ankle, revealing her scuffed boots. Perhaps she cut her lovely red hair into a bob and later regretted it.

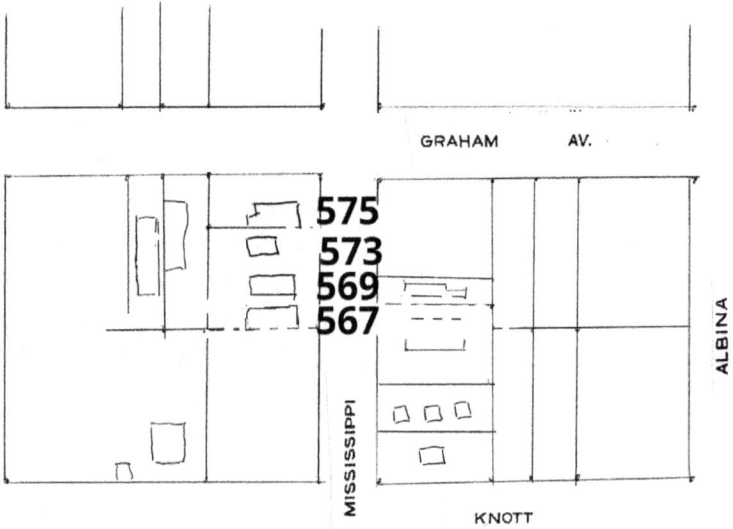

The 1920s was tarnished by the Ku Klux Klan spreading racial hatred and religious prejudice, fueled by the silent film *Birth of a Nation* and its sympathetic portrayal of the Klan. The so-called Red Scare intensified fears of radicals, labor unionists, and communists. Racial tensions rose sharply. The KKK burned crosses from the hills and buttes around Portland to protect White Protestant America from immigrants, Bolsheviks, Blacks, and Catholics. Portland's 15,000 KKK also attempted to shut down all of Oregon's Catholic schools.

Socially prominent women formed reform groups, including temperance leagues, suffrage movements, and moral reform societies. They discovered they could improve public healthcare, help impoverished immigrants, secure state support for education, and protect women from labor abuses. Minnie wasn't interested, particularly in the temperance league, as Frank was likely making and selling bathtub gin.

Although Oregon adopted an amendment granting women the right to vote in 1912, most women were slow to change their attitudes. In January 1922, nine women were called to jury duty. When asked by a reporter how they felt about being among the first women to serve on a Portland jury, most responded with a version of, "I'll have to ask my husband."[220] Rumors and innuendos swirled. A petticoat government was feared. Women would stop cooking if they had the right to vote. But Minnie never registered. Her half-siblings, Martha, Charles, and William, faithfully registered to vote. Their father, a naturalized citizen and therefore eligible to vote, registered in 1910, when he was 63.[221]

Minnie's parents sold their house at 1012 East 11th North for $2,350 on May 10, 1919, after living there for 16 years. Oskar and Elizabeth Eisenhurst signed a private contract and received the deed on July 17, 1922.[222] William and Wilhelmine briefly rented 917 Williams Avenue before moving to 569 Mississippi near their son Charles, who lived at 571 Mississippi Avenue. Charles had previously lived at that address with his brother, William. Minnie and Bertha, along with their families, lived next door at 567 Mississippi in what likely was a 22-foot-by-45-foot building with an apartment upstairs and one downstairs. The family was back in the familiar neighborhood of Lower Albina—except for Mary. Mary had died on April 14, 1920. Her three sons lived with their father, while her daughter, Bernice, lived with Martha and her husband, Jacob. After Martha died in 1952, Jacob legally adopted Bernice, by then a 44-year-old married woman. Her adoption changed her maiden name from Luther to Smith and legally made Jacob her father, giving him grandchildren.

Frank and Minnie moved to their own place around the corner from Mississippi Avenue on Knott Street. It was advertised as a seven-room, furnished, move-in-ready house with a monthly rent of $20, including water.[223] Mary's oldest son lived with them for a short time after he turned 17. Kennard and Adams Department Store was a few blocks north on Williams Avenue, where overcoats were priced between $29 and $39 but could be bought "on time" as Americans discovered the installment plan. A new Victrola phonograph ranged from $135 to $275. Ball-bearing roller skates for Bea and Lyda, aged nine and ten, cost $2.39 per pair, while a toy wagon for five-year-old Bob was more affordable, ranging from 39 cents to 59 cents. Jefferson High School hosted a jitney dance, a pay-per-dance scheme to raise money for the football team.

Minnie might have taken her children to the Albina Branch Library, a short walk up the hill. I doubt it, as I never saw any books at Minnie's or her daughter Bea's houses except TV Guides. In the 1920s, libraries served as community centers, hosting Americanization classes, Boy Scouts, Campfire Girls, Red Cross activities, and political meetings. The reference and reading rooms at the Albina Branch Library became crowded once the cold weather set in, despite concerns about the spread of germs. A student with smallpox at Washington High School was part of 251 reported cases, of which thirty were admitted to the contagion hospital at Kelly Butte. During the smallpox outbreak, all students were required to be vaccinated before returning to school. One school closed because of scarlet fever.[224]

Mississippi Avenue ran through a diverse neighborhood of houses, shops, and saloons. To the north, there were dry goods stores, meat markets, drug stores, grocery stores, a tailor, second-hand shops, and a smoke shop selling candy, cigars, and popular magazines. The Tivoli movie theater, located at Russell and Williams, showed a different silent film every night, but the Gay Theater was closer to their homes. The talkies arrived in Portland in 1926. People began driving to Welches on Mt. Hood. Martha learned to drive an automobile but collided with a streetcar in 1922. She sustained severe lacerations on her left arm, and her leg was slightly injured. She was taken to St. Vincent Hospital.[225]

The old Albina neighborhood underwent significant changes in the 1950s and 1960s with the construction of Interstate 5. The neighborhood was further changed by the building of the Fremont Bridge and the ongoing expansion of Legacy Emanuel Hospital. Properties on Mississippi Avenue in Lower Albina, where the Wohlfeils once lived, were demolished. Run-down and neglected, the northern part of Mississippi Avenue has been transformed into a trendy neighborhood, with shops and restaurants that feature an eclectic blend of Victorian and modern architecture.

Minnie's mother was ill. She signed her will on July 17, 1923, while in the hospital. She died the next day from colon cancer. Minnie claimed her mother developed cancer after being kicked in the stomach by a cow. This was a common misconception at the time. Stomach and other cancers were often attributed to being kicked in the stomach by a cow or mule.

Wilhelmine's executor and trustee was her son-in-law, Frank McKever, to whom she granted full powers to care for her husband. She described William in her will as "fast becoming feeble both in body and mind and is no longer able to care for himself, and desiring to provide for his care and comfort as best I can, and confident that my son-in-law, Frank McKever, of Portland, Oregon, will to the best of his ability care for and look to the comforts of my husband, during the remainder of his life." Frank was to act without "direction, order, interference or intervention, and that he may not be required to answer to anyone." She bequeathed $100 each to her stepdaughter, Martha, and her oldest grandson. Her stepsons, daughters, and Mary's other three children were each bequeathed $5.00 to be paid after the death of her husband, with Frank McKever receiving the remainder of her estate.

Her estate totaled $2,073.50, including cash on hand, loans to Frank McKever and Frank Hemsworth, and Lot 14 in Block 4 in Oakhurst, assessed at $350. Frank McKever paid off his loan, including interest, while Frank Hemsworth paid $100 of his $150 loan. Disbursements of $461.50 included a doctor's fee, $50 for a lot in Rose City Cemetery, and $274 to the funeral director. (For comparison, a simple burial in Portland in 1920 cost $27.00, including an $18.00 casket.) Two individuals received $7.50 and $10 for providing unspecified funeral services. Three dollars were paid to the doctor who witnessed her will, while the other witness, an attorney who handled her case, never charged the estate for his services.

Frank McKever requested that Multnomah County Court authorize additional expenditures for William Wohlfeil's care that winter. Besides being "overcome by lapses of memory and other mental disorders during which he was irresponsible, obstinate, stubborn, and hard to care for," William fell ill on November 11, 1923. A special nurse was needed around the clock for four weeks after surgery at Emanuel Hospital. The hospital bill for 19 days was $68; the surgeon was $185; private nursing care was $60 per week; and two trips in the Arrow Ambulance were $11 each. To share the care and responsibility of their father, the children agreed to take him from time to time and care for him in their homes for $42 per month. The court approved.[226]

William Fred Wohlfeil died on October 7, 1924, at Emanuel Hospital at age 77 due to a bowel obstruction complicated by old hernia scarring. His obituary listed his children: beloved father of Albert Wohlfeil of Burns, Oregon; William Wohlfeil, Mrs. J.N. Smith (Martha), Charles

Wohlfeil, Mrs. F.W. Hemsworth (Minnie), and Mrs. F.A. McKever (Bertha), all of Portland. William was buried beside his wife at Rose City Cemetery in Portland.

After William's death, Wilhelmine's estate could be settled; he left no estate. It seems she had managed the finances for years. Her estate received $50 from Frank Hemsworth's loan, $140.75 from Metropolitan Insurance Company, $5.45 from Portland Gas Company, and a $2.50 refund from Emanuel Hospital. Expenses after William's death included $19 paid to a Christian Science Practitioner, medical costs of $511.92, and payments to William's daughters for his care. Martha cared for her father for about 5 months, Bertha for 4 months, Minnie for 5 months, and the hospital for approximately 1 month. Minnie was also reimbursed for clothing and medications. Martha and Bertha were close neighbors. Martha lived at 1139 Garfield, and Bertha at 1355 Garfield. Minnie still lived in Lower Albina.

However, Frank McKeever found he was unable to close the estate because legal guardians had never been appointed for Wilhelmine's grandsons after their mother, Mary, died. Since James Luther was the minors' father and natural guardian, he received $110 and distributed it accordingly among his sons: Harold ($100), James ($5), and Earl ($5). The probate was finally closed on December 7, 1926.

During this period, Frank Hemsworth applied for military pension benefits because of his rheumatism. His father had been hospitalized during his three-year Civil War service due to rheumatism, which worsened after contracting smallpox and pneumonia. Running a boarding house in Missouri and Oregon, as well as Pap's Coffee House on Yamhill Street for 20 years, hadn't improved his health. With each pension application, John Hemsworth's weight increased from 240 pounds at age 52 to 273 pounds by the time he was 62.[227] He was finally awarded $6.00 per month in 1902. He also didn't tolerate disrespect. When a restaurant customer complained that John gave him skimmed milk instead of cream for his coffee and refused to discount the 20-cent meal, John rapped the customer on the knuckles with a stick and crushed his hat. The customer decided he could live with the bruised knuckles, but the destruction of his only hat, which cost him $5.00, was too much.[228]

Six weeks after her father's death, Minnie's life changed dramatically. Frank died unexpectedly on November 24, 1924. Her tall, lively, life-of-the-party husband passed away from a burst appendix (acute peritonitis) at St. Vincent Hospital at age 44. He was working as a piano mover for Sherman and Clay. Frank was buried under the auspices of the Loyal Order of Moose at Rose City Cemetery, the same Portland cemetery where his in-laws were laid to rest. His oldest daughter, Bea, wept when recalling her dad's death for the rest of her life. She named her son Frank.

Minnie might not have felt an emotional loss for Frank, but his death was a financial disaster. His siblings were less than sympathetic to Minnie's struggles as a widow—perhaps justifiably so. James Riley, Frank's oldest brother, had lived at 725 Vancouver for years and occasionally partnered with their father in the restaurant business. Now, he worked as a salesman for Olds, Workman, & King department store, was separated from his wife, and owned a new Dodge every other year. Although he probably lost patience with Frank years ago, he stepped in to help Minnie settle Frank's estate. Frank's other brother, William, had done well as a railroad engineer. His sister Lyda also had money, but Minnie thought she was uppity—a judgment my mother remembered years later. Lyda paid for a handsome obelisk in Portland's Lone Fir Cemetery to mark the graves of her parents and a brother who died at 18. One side was engraved for her father, one for her mother, and the third for her brother. Frank could have been memorialized on the fourth side, but he was instead buried in Rose City Cemetery without a headstone. Even in death, he wasn't welcome in the family plot where his brother James Riley and sister Lyda, along with her husband, would later be buried. No one was willing to pay for Frank's tombstone. To this day, Frank still doesn't have a headstone marking his grave.

Bea was 14, Lyda was 13, and Bob was nine years old when their father died. Minnie had few options, with three kids to feed and no income. First, she told Bea to quit school and find a job. She hadn't made it past eighth grade and saw no reason her daughter should either. Bea was a big, tall girl who looked older than her age, so she lied and said she was 18 and got a job at Portland Cracker Company, which later became Nabisco. Her wages went to her mother, just as Minnie had turned her wages over to her parents.

Secondly, Minnie applied on May 25, 1925, for a widow's pension based on Frank's military service during the Spanish-American War. Frank's original pension application was complicated by his inability to accurately report his marriage date and his children's birthdates, including misspelling his daughter Lyda's name, which was also his sister's name. He had entered the military in 1898, using a false birthdate of

June 21, 1877, which made him appear three years older than he was. When he applied for his military pension in January 1923, he stated that he was born on June 21, 1874, and claimed to be 49 years old, when in fact, he was born on June 21, 1880, and was therefore 43 years old. Minnie encountered a similar issue with dates on her application for a widow's pension; she had to include an affidavit correcting her marriage date and the birthdates of her two daughters.[229] Minnie became well known for fudging her date of birth to appear younger than she was. For example, her tombstone lists a birthdate of 1892, when she was born in 1891.

There was a third option for Minnie for financial support. By 1919, 39 states had established a Mothers' Pension (also known as Mothers' Aide), an early effort to create a social safety net that provided cash assistance to help widows with minor children stay home. The assistance was limited to widows of good character with children aged up to 14 or 16, depending on the state. Mothers' Aide was not free, however, from moral judgments. If you were a "proper woman," you deserved help. Oregon passed a Mothers' Pension Bill in 1913, allowing $10.00 per month to mothers with one child and $7.50 per each additional child. However, Oregon mothers could be rejected for not attending church, living in an immoral neighborhood, smoking or drinking, or taking in male lodgers. In 1914, the bill was amended to favor women with young children and set a maximum allowance of $40 per month.

Minnie likely had never earned wages after her marriage. The idea of working-class women earning wages was hotly debated in the 1920s. Some acceptance existed in traditionally female-dominated fields, such as nursing, teaching, clerical jobs, or social work, but men still dominated payrolls, from factories to political leadership. Besides her experience as a telephone operator twenty years earlier, Minnie's options were limited. She was a competent cook and baker (her favorite activity), and she had hands-on experience with cleaning, crocheting, washing clothes, milking cows, and caring for chickens. She still needed an income to survive.

Her last option was to sell illegal alcohol. Her neighborhood, Lower Albina, was well known for liquor sales. She had learned a lot from Frank, who had gained extensive knowledge from the shadowy worlds of police, vice, and roadhouses. Her grandchildren remember being fascinated when she showed them how to cheat at cards.

The only time Minnie got her name in the newspaper, aside from obituaries, was on September 23, 1925: "Women held as Bootleggers. Two alleged moonshine dens operated by women were raided by members of the vice squad under the leadership of Sergeant Oelsner yesterday. At 101 Knott Street, nine pints of liquor were found, and Minnie Hemsworth was arrested and charged with possession and sale. Officer Robertson claimed to have purchased a pint of liquor for $2.50. At 665 Larrabee Street, two and one-half pints and one quart of moonshine were found, Anna Geisy being arrested."

I nearly fell out of my computer chair when I read this online newspaper article. I remember my great-grandma as a stern yet respectable woman, dressed in a printed housedress and a warm wool coat, clucking her tongue in disapproval. I couldn't imagine her getting arrested. Did Minnie's run-in with the law threaten her eligibility for Mothers' Aide with its morality judgments?

In the Albina neighborhood, whiskey cooks competed with the monthly meetings of the Albina Christian Temperance Union. Odds favored the temperance union when the Police Morals Squad arrested the bootleggers. In 1922, Mrs. Gottlieb Reigart threw whiskey mash out the window when the police knocked on her door. She claimed she had thrown out prunes, raisins, and potato scraps. Her husband was fined $50.00, even though he had less than a teaspoon of mash left after she was done. Emil Schiller, who also lived on Mississippi Avenue, was arrested with 40 gallons of whiskey and pleaded guilty to bootlegging. He was fined $500.[230]

There was a popular jingo at the time:

Mother is in the kitchen/Washing out the jugs,
Sister is in the pantry/Bottling the suds,
Father is in the cellar/Mixing up the hops,
Johnny is on the front porch/Watching for the cops.

The Volstead Act prohibited the production, sale, transportation, and possession of alcoholic beverages, depriving Portland's German community of its favorite beverage. Six German-owned breweries and a third of the German-owned saloons closed. Although Prohibition (1920–1933) did lead to an overall decline in alcohol consumption, it also spurred the growth of a black-market alcohol industry run by bootleggers like Minnie.

It took Minnie 18 months after Frank's death to file for probate in Multnomah County, Oregon. The estate of Frank W. Hemsworth had no personal assets but included real property valued at $3,000. The estate's annual income did not exceed $300.[231] The property, inherited from Frank's father's estate, was shared by four siblings: Frank, James, Lyda, and William. Each held a quarter interest in three parcels of property: Lot 13, Block 42, in the Vernon neighborhood, and Lots 25 and 26, Block 7, in the Mansfield Addition. When James died in 1932, the properties remained undivided according to his probate, properties that Frank once tried to sell for $10 in San Francisco. James may have helped Minnie with Frank's estate, but he left his own estate of $16,234 to his brother and his sister without mentioning his widowed sister-in-law. Minnie never completed Frank's probate, despite the court having unsuccessfully contacted her six years later. When I requested a copy of Frank's probate nearly 100 years later, the Multnomah County clerk was startled to find it was still pending.

Minnie continued living at 101 Knott Street in 1925. In 1926, she briefly moved to the Woodstock neighborhood at 600 Martins Avenue, which was rented for $50 a month in 1921. Located one block from the Sellwood trolley line, it was a seven-room furnished home with a piano, a full basement, a furnace, and wash trays. Her daughter Lyda was 16 and working as a maid when the family moved to 984 East Stark. The next year, they moved again to 743 East 33rd, which was advertised in 1920 as a three-room furnished house with a sleeping porch and a full cement basement on a 100 × 100 lot with fruit trees and bearing bushes near the Woodstock streetcar line.

Lyda married Harold Hotchkin in October 1928 when she was 17. Harold was 12 years older than Lyda, but their marriage lasted until Lyda died in 1970. Minnie lived with her daughter, Bea, and son Robert at 1200 Union Ave North, conveniently near the streetcar line that took Bea to Overall Laundry.

Bea worked as a laundry sorter when she married Lawrence Gabler on September 18, 1929. He was 16 years older, a divorced Catholic, and an alcoholic. She was pregnant. The month before, he had received his final divorce decree from his first wife, Hannah Bartram. I was told Bea met Lawrence when he visited her father's basement speakeasy in Albina. Since Bea was only 14 when Frank died, she might have met Lawrence when he came to see her mother, Minnie, to buy booze.

Bea's marriage lasted long enough to produce two children born two years apart on the same day. Bea named her oldest child Frank after her cherished father. Lawrence named their daughter (my mother) Eleanor Katherine after his mother and sister. Bea never met her mother-in-law or sister-in-law, who lived in St. Louis, but she knew they disapproved of her marriage and divorce.

Dellon Olds

Minnie married Dellon Olds at the Clackamas County Courthouse, with a judge related to Dellon officiating, two months after Bea's wedding. Dellon was a year younger (although she claimed to be the same age or younger), had never married, and lived with his parents, brother, and sister-in-law, who had married the year before. Dellon's leg was crushed in a mill accident on September 4, 1915, and he walked with a noticeable limp. He spent months recovering from surgery in the hospital in 1916 and again in 1921. It was noted that he was 6'1", 175 pounds, but he was considered disabled due to scarring on his right leg when he registered for the World War II draft.

The Olds family lived in a large farmhouse built by Dellon's father in 1904. It had a large front window, allowing him to remove a boat he had built in the living room. The farm was situated at the corner of River Road and Center Street (now Oak Grove Boulevard) in Oak Grove, a small town between Portland and Oregon City. Dellon's parents were of German descent, creating a familiar environment for Minnie. Moreover, her marriage spared her from homelessness during the difficult times of the Depression.

But she also lost her widow's pension of $36 a month when she married. She reapplied on January 22, 1930, for her minor son, Robert. Jacob Smith, Martha's husband, and her sister Bertha made sworn statements in an attorney's office in downtown Portland that "Minnie Olds was formerly the wife of Frank W. Hemsworth, deceased: that a son of said marriage in the person of Robert W. Hemsworth, is the only son of Frank W. Hemsworth under the age of sixteen years on November 16, 1929, the date of the marriage of its mother, now Minnie Olds; that said son is now living and is in the custody of the mother." The $30 monthly pension lasted until December 21, 1931, when Robert turned 16.

A month after their marriage, Minnie's father-in-law, Edwin Olds, died, hopefully after he removed his boat from his living room to the nearby Willamette River. The following year, the household included his widowed wife, 64-year-old Alice Olds, their son Orval, and daughter-in-law Mary Alice, both 34; their son Dellon Warren, age 37; daughter-in-law Minnie Theresa, age 36 (actually 38); and Minnie's son Robert Hemsworth, age 14. The farm on River Road was valued at $6,000. Like his father, Orval worked in bridge construction, and Dellon was employed in a furniture factory.

The kitchen likely felt tense with three Mrs. Olds—mother and two daughters-in-law. Minnie had controlled her kitchen for twenty years and probably wasn't used to sharing space. Her fiery redheaded temper might have led to some pots and pans flying. There probably wasn't much room for Minnie to escape either, since her mother-in-law's older brother, Joseph Colosky, lived nearby with his daughter and son-in-law, who owned a neighborhood grocery store.

Dellon and Minnie had two children early in their marriage. Edwina was born in 1932, followed by Warren (Bud) in 1933, just 13 months apart, in the farmhouse their grandfather had built. Edwina was born a month before Minnie's oldest daughter, Bea, gave birth to my mother. Bea filed for divorce from Lawrence Gabler in 1938 on the grounds of desertion. With two children, Bea struggled during the Depression and often left them with neighbors in Portland's Creston neighborhood.

While her children were farmed out, Bea took the streetcar to her mother's house in Oak Grove to stay for a while. Edwina recalled that Bea would move in when she was angry at the world and leave when she was happy. Minnie and her daughter, Bea, had a contentious relationship; visits to Oak Grove often ended in screaming matches. My mother never forgave her grandmother for throwing her wicker doll buggy off the porch, breaking it into smithereens during a heated exchange between the two.

Minnie also had a fractured relationship with her daughter, Lyda. Lyda inherited the alcoholism that so plagued her father. Yet, despite the problems, Minnie's children tried to support one another. Bea helped Lyda after the birth of her last baby, believing that having a daughter would lead her to stop drinking. But she did not.

Minnie milked six to eight cows twice a day in Oak Grove, likely just like her mother had done in Portland. A milk truck collected the cream and cottage cheese. It was hard and tedious work for Minnie to clean the stainless-steel separator used to separate the cream, keep the cream at the right temperature, and boil, wash, and hang the cheesecloth to dry after making the cottage cheese. The leftover milk was dumped. She also sold eggs.

Minnie and her daughter Lyda

They moved into a $10-a-month rental at the end of Railroad Avenue, near the Teresa Station streetcar stop and close to the Olds family home. The rental had two bedrooms—one for the parents and one for Edwina. Warren slept on the couch. He didn't sleep in a regular bed until he got a job with the Milwaukie Fire Department while in high school.

One side of the enclosed back porch had an oil barrel and a shelf where Minnie kept the milk separator. On the other side were cupboards. When I was about seven years old, I was shown a big black .44 revolver and brass knuckles kept on a high shelf that belonged to Frank Hemsworth. I never forgot that big, scary black gun. It certainly makes me wonder why Minnie kept her first husband's revolver and brass knuckles thirty years after his death. Warren kept the gun for years before passing it on to Gale Hemsworth, since it belonged to his grandfather. The brass knuckles got lost.

There was a small barn for the milk cows, a chicken coop, a pig pen, a rabbit hutch, and an orchard of apple, cherry, and walnut trees. Dillon took care of the garden, planting snap peas, green beans, tomatoes, corn, onions, and strawberries. Minnie wasn't known for pulling weeds in the garden, but she canned all the produce. Minnie rarely had to use her ration coupons for sugar, coffee, and red meat during World War II. She had plenty of butter, milk, and eggs for cooking. She loved to bake. Her specialty was apple pie. Fewer pies were baked when each household was limited to 15 pounds of sugar, plus an additional 15 pounds a year for canning from 1945 through 1947. When the Japanese bombed Pearl Harbor, my mother remembered her mother crying and her grandmother stoic. My mother thought the world was coming to an end. She also recalled the same emotional response from her mother and grandmother when President Franklin Roosevelt died in April 1945.

Minnie loved to fish. The family scooped buckets of smelt from the Sandy River. Some people ate smelt without cleaning them, but Edwina spent hours with her mother cleaning each fish. On the Oregon coast, they caught rockfish and dug clams. Minnie especially loved digging razor clams and invited her daughter, Bea, to join her. There was no daily limit. Later, the limit was changed to 36 clams per person, and now it's 15 clams per person per day. Cleaning 15 clams takes time. I can't imagine cleaning as many clams as people wanted to dig. Warren remembered his stout mother digging clams with her back to the ocean when a big wave knocked her down, billowing her house dress and drenching her from head to toe. But she didn't stop digging and still got her clam.

Dellon worked as a sawyer in a lumber mill, but later he took shifts at the Hawley Paper Mill at Willamette Falls in Oregon City, just like his stepson Bob Hemsworth. They caught the streetcar near their house and rode it to the end of the line to go to work. They finally bought an old Model T with bald tires, but barely made it home from a trip to the coast. Minnie never got her driving license, but she was excited about electricity: cooking meals on an electric range, washing laundry in a wringer washer, and using an electric iron.

They lived a few blocks from the Oak Grove drug store, a variety store, Pfennings Meat Market, Buy Rite Grocery, and a school on a street lined with chestnut trees. Once a month, Dellon would take Edwina and Warren to the drugstore for a soda and let them pick a piece of red or black licorice. When they were sick, the pharmacist, not a doctor, prescribed medication. The pharmacy had a liquor store in the back that sold a different kind of medicine. Dillon helped himself to Minnie's egg and milk money and bought a jug of wine, making it last the month until it was time to dip into her egg money again. The house was Minnie's domain. Any drinking Dellon did was in the shed out back.

Edwina and Warren were kind enough to answer my questions about their parents when Edwina was 90 and Warren was 89. Edwina believed her father was responsible for discipline. He was fond of switches. In contrast, Warren told me that his mother enforced the discipline. His father was always working at the paper mill. He remembered his older half-brother Bob as more of a father figure than his dad. Bob lived at home until he married in 1936 and moved a few houses away.

Bea and her formidable mother, Minnie (on the right)

Neighbor women came over for morning coffee—some that Minnie liked and some she did not. Edwina became skilled at hiding under the large kitchen table to eavesdrop, bringing along her crocheting or knitting. There was gossip about infidelities, ungrateful children, babies who arrived seven months after the wedding, and how a nice girl couldn't find a decent husband. Warren, Edwina, and Bea (then an adult with fostered children) played a trick on an old neighbor woman who smoked a pipe by tapping on her window one evening and running away. Edwina had to stifle her giggles from her spot under the table the next morning when the neighbor complained about the harassment.

Family fights were legendary. During family dinners, Minnie would slyly criticize something, upsetting everyone. I heard Minnie mutter that my grandma was too big and tall to be attractive. Even as a kid, I knew this wasn't her first time criticizing her daughter. She could be inconsiderate and dismissive. At age 13, Edwina wanted to surprise her mother with a cake. When Minnie got home after shopping with a neighbor, she took one look at Edwina's batter and dumped it down the drain. Edwina never forgot that incident. My mom took us on the streetcar to visit when we were babies. After standing on the front porch for 30 minutes listening to her grandmother's complaints, my mother took her fussy kids back to the streetcar station. Minnie yelled after her, "Why aren't you staying for dinner?"

Minnie lived nearly 12 years after Dellon died. I remember she rented a house a block from my grandma or stayed with Edwina or Warren. I stayed overnight with her when there wasn't enough space at Grandma's, sleeping upstairs in a clean room with bleach-smelling sheets. The next morning, Minnie cooked me oatmeal before we headed back down the street to Grandma's. I heard her telling my grandma that I must have been scared because I didn't say a word. And I was.

Minnie and Bea appeared to get along as neighbors, unlike the yelling and screaming I heard about when they were younger. But Bea had a car, and Minnie loved to go places. During a drive through the countryside, Minnie tried to find her parents' farm in Washington County, where she had lived as a child, but she couldn't remember exactly where it was.

The three Wohlfeil sisters, Mary, Minnie, and Bertha, reached adulthood at a surprisingly young age—perhaps too young. In the old country, girls didn't marry until they finished hand-embroidered linens for their marriage chests, earned enough money to help their parents, and learned to manage a household, usually marrying in their mid-twenties. Mary married at 17 to a man 22 years her senior in 1906. She was likely pregnant or had just given birth to a son. Her husband was a harness maker during a time when demand for harnesses was declining. They lived with her parents at their family home, 1012 East 11th North, at least for the first year of their marriage, before moving on to run boarding houses. By age 23, Mary had four children, with the last three born 13 months apart. She tragically died at age 32 of peritonitis, an infection the doctor noted on her death certificate was caused by a self-induced abortion.

Minnie married at 17, likely without her parents' blessing. During the first six years of her marriage, she gave birth to four children. Her first three children were born a remarkable ten months apart. Bertha married five days after her 16th birthday to a 21-year-old steamfitter. Although she was young, Bertha seemed to have chosen a better husband than her sisters. Frank McKever was gainfully employed as a steamfitter and gradually transitioned into the plumbing business. They had two children born five years apart. Bertha was widowed at 48 and lived with her daughter and son-in-law in Camas, Washington, past her 106th birthday.

Their mother's pregnancies occurred every 18 to 24 months, allowing for a nine-month pregnancy and at least nine months of nursing. Wilhelmine lost a baby between Mary and Minnie, but three daughters survived. Wilhelmine was only 28 when Bertha was born in 1893, and she had no more children. Wilhelmine's sister, Caroline, had two children survive out of six during her first marriage and six children with her second husband. Wilhelmine and Caroline's sister-in-law, Marta, had an unknown number of pregnancies. She committed suicide, possibly triggered by the death of her last two baby girls.

Learning how Mary and Marta died was upsetting for family genealogists. Vonnie Kauffman wrote a fictionalized account of the struggles her grandmother, Wilhelmina (Marta), and her oldest daughter, Anna. In her book, *Anna's Waltz*, Marta endured at least 17 pregnancies, with Anna helping to deliver some of her siblings. Anna was forced by her father to marry a man she did not like and whose children she did not want.[232]

This was at a time when Marie Equi, a Portland birth control advocate, Margaret Sanger, Marie Strope, and others tried to distribute birth control information and help women facing unwanted pregnancies. They ran afoul of the 1873 Comstock Law, which made it illegal to mail contraceptive information through the U.S. mail. Women in my family could have benefited from some frank conversations around the kitchen table. They could talk at length about giving birth, but were mum on what caused pregnancy.

Circumstances compelled Minnie's immigrant mother to become resilient to survive. Wilhelmine had to develop thick skin to ignore the criticism she likely faced while living with William in Green Bay and giving birth to Mary. She also likely controlled the finances, buying property in her name. She left an estate, while her husband did not. Her will stipulated that William be cared for, but was it out of obligation? Wilhelmine was forced to control her destiny, and Minnie learned from her example.

Minnie, and certainly her daughter, Bea, treated men like unwelcome houseguests. Bea was married several times, but eventually she became a housekeeper for an older man, whom she married. In my memory, he was banished to the back bedroom. Bea washed his clothes and cooked his meals, but always called him the "old man."

The coffee group that huddled around my grandma's kitchen table spoke of their miscarriages, their stillbirths, and their curdled insides. Men were unreliable and more trouble than they were worth. The women grumbled about skimpy paychecks that never made it home, the cost of groceries, betrayals, and double crossing, always circling back to death. Deep in shared suffering and misery, cradled with coffee, cigarettes, and gossip, my matrilineal world of women sent me outside if they caught me listening. Serious conversations always took place at the kitchen table.

Minnie died on March 4, 1968, while sitting in an armchair at her youngest daughter's home in Joliet, Illinois. She was buried beside her second husband in Mountain View Cemetery in Oregon City. My mother described Minnie as a run-and-hide type of grandma, not the warm and hugging type. Edwina portrayed her mother as self-centered and someone who never talked about her past. Yet, one grandson remembered her as very kind. I remember her in perfectly starched and ironed house dresses stretched across a substantial bosom, black square-heeled shoes with hook-and-eye black laces, dyed red hair, and fibbing about her age like Jack Benny. Once, when my great-grandma and grandma were bemoaning their swollen ankles, mushrooming over the tops of their shoes, they explained to me that "they had too much water in the basement." They both died of congestive heart failure. I am reminded of that often as I look at my thickening ankles.

Taken in the summer of 1960, Minnie looks dour and sour-faced as she stands by Bea, who is smiling. Between my grandma and my great-grandma is Uncle Ed, kneeling, and from left to right, me, my brother, and my sister. I remember posing for a similar photograph of four generations; great-grandma and grandma teasing me that the picture would have five generations if I had a baby. I was indignant. It was one of the only times I remember Minnie laughing.

Resurrecting My Great-Grandmothers

At the turn of the twentieth century, women gradually emerged from a cocoon that had kept them wrapped for centuries. Changes began to unfold rapidly as the Victorian Age gave way to the Progressive Era. The nation swelled with pride and technological confidence. The New Woman, as the press called her, no longer accepted being treated like fragile china and considered intellectually inferior to men. Telephones, motor cars, flying machines, and talking pictures revolutionized culture. Outhouses became obsolete, and bathtubs turned into status symbols. With their long hair rolled and twisted under wide-brimmed hats, covered from neck to ankle to wrist by clothing, and squeezed into corsets, women were ready to cut their hair, hem their skirts, and pitch the corset. Yet, for Kate, Minnie, Cora, and Texanna, my great-grandmothers, these societal shifts barely touched their lives. They remained poor, undereducated, overworked, and reliant on men. Their stories are nuanced tales of resilience, hope, and adaptability.

My great-grandmothers found comfort in Catholic Masses, revival meetings, and gossip over coffee. Kate and Minnie were first-generation German Americans: Kate's Catholic parents emigrated from Alsace, now part of France, while Minnie's Lutheran parents came from Marienwerder, now part of Poland. Kate faithfully attended Mass, and Minnie enjoyed digging for clams on the Oregon coast. Although they never met, their children married briefly and had two children before divorcing; their daughter was my mother. My paternal great-grandmothers, Cora and Texanna, were Southern girls raised in Tennessee and Texas. Cora's son married Texanna's daughter in the Texas Panhandle before catching a train for a wilderness adventure in Oregon. This adventure eventually faded into a farm in the Coast Range and five children, including my father.

Photographed with mouths as straight as Bible verses, the harsh realities of farm life deeply affected their physical and mental health. They fought depression, silence, and resentment and became gray women, emitting no light of their own. They endured isolation, poverty, and limited medical care. Accidents from axes and sharp knives, burns from long hair or skirts catching fire while cooking, gunshots, or being kicked or thrown by horses, mules, or cows took their toll. Letters and diaries of nineteenth-century women complain of physical ailments such as poor eyesight, toothaches, headaches, fevers, cysts or growths, malaria, and the constant fear of childbirth. Literate women wrote letters to their family back home, requesting dress patterns or recipes, and begging them to come visit. Immigrant women remained trapped in their communities by their accented English. Regardless, during long days from dawn to dusk, they all cared for their children, homes, and gardens; fed the chickens, milked the cows, hauled water, gathered fuel, and helped with traditionally male tasks like harvesting and hunting—often while pregnant or nursing. From delivering babies to washing the bodies of the dead, these women had a deep connection with life and a profound understanding of the invisible line dividing life and death.

Death was life's most constant event—it touched them every day. Parents, husbands, and children died in wars, of disease, or in their own beds. Women found comfort in their Christian faith, a reminder that all lives were guided by God, who embodied eternal love and wisdom. Everyone knew that death carried their loved ones to glory and everlasting life.

Faith

Looking through my prism of the twenty-first century, my great-grandmothers had more faith in the Almighty than I do in my little finger. Whether fundamentalist Evangelical or Roman Catholic, their belief in an omnipotent and omnipresent God shaped their lives. Cora found salvation in the austere, conservative Primitive Baptist Church. Kate's faith was sustained by the teachings and rituals of the Catholic Church, with its ornate gilt altar and stations of the cross. Texanna likely saw the hand of God in spring wildflowers on a windy Texas prairie and heard hellfire preaching from circuit-riding Methodist preachers. Minnie defined her religious duty as sending her children to Sunday School. But they all believed in sin and the concept of redemption. Bibles written in German or English were found in every home. Cora likely memorized entire chapters of the Bible and quoted scriptures.

It was a time when men held leadership roles in churches as guides and protectors. They administered the sacraments, wrote the prayer books, preached the sermons, and made the decisions. Women arranged the flowers, swept the church, played the piano, organized fundraisers, and, most importantly, set the congregation's moral standards. Women were expected to devote their time to selfless Christian charity, to embody the Golden Rule, to forgive transgressions, and to ease suffering. Their hearts and minds were to be filled with the truth and love of the gospel. God's spirit enveloped their world.

Hidden beneath my great-grandmothers' faith was their belief in superstitions. Although the village church and its pastor wielded the greatest social authority, belief in the old spells persisted. The ancient Celtic belief in omens and charms, brought to the Appalachian Mountains, influenced Cora and Texanna, while Minnie and Kate were shaped by the folklore of medieval Germanic tribes, where unexplained events needed explanations. Only fools failed to nail a horseshoe above doorways for good luck.

Legal Rights

As part of our colonial heritage, women's rights were virtually nonexistent. A wife had no claim to her wages, property, or even her own body. She could not initiate contracts, execute wills, sue in court, vote, serve on a jury, or hold public office. She could not control her biological reproduction; even distributing information about contraception was illegal. She had no rights to her children if she divorced or left her marriage. She did not even own the clothes on her back. From birth, a female was under the guardianship of her father or a male relative; marriage only shifted control to her husband. Her dower was her only protection, allowing her a portion of her deceased husband's estate.

Some women defied societal norms by using their wit and courage to navigate challenges. Fiercely rejecting men's controlling behavior and dominance, they were accused of lifting their long skirts to behave like men, damn the consequences. Some wives wouldn't let their husbands through the door if they didn't vote as they were told. Mothers advised their daughters to obey their husbands for the first year, then decide who was truly in charge. One woman wrote to *The Farmer's Wife* magazine in 1910, "If your husband slaps you, slap him back. Keep on being mean until he changes. It might take a year to break him."

Progress plods along in tiny steps, hindered by setbacks. Women continue to fight for fundamental rights, and the battle for true equality persists. Today, women constitute the largest group of welfare recipients, earn the lowest wages, are the least educated, and possess fewer real estate assets, including land and home ownership. Women still blame themselves or minimize incidents of sexual assault and harassment, believing that breaking the silence can be just as harmful as the abuse.

The Equal Rights Amendment (ERA) outlines long-denied fundamental rights for women. These rights are:

- To live free from violence and discrimination
- To be educated
- To own property
- To vote
- To earn an equal wage

Even during my lifetime, opening a bank account, applying for a loan, or obtaining a credit card was challenging for women. Prejudiced attitudes further humiliated women: married women who used their maiden names were ridiculed; women who traveled alone for business were seen as prostitutes; women who wore trousers were considered subversive, rude, or immoral. Activists faced accusations of emasculating their husbands by refusing to cook dinner or by taking men's jobs. The Civil Rights Act of 1964 promised equality. But the traditional view of the home-oriented, dependent wife, with its strict definitions of class and gender, persists in many ways. White women, and even more so women of color, continue to wait for full and complete parity with men. Beneath the idealized June Cleaver frilled apron lies an oppressively conformist and sexist world.

I wish my great-grandmothers could have seen Kamala Harris on television in a white pantsuit, honoring the suffragette movement and acknowledging her place in history as the first female vice president of the United States. The contentious 2020 election created a deep national divide between the two recliners in my living room. But when I saw the joy on Kamala's face, tears streamed down my cheeks as I thought of the restricted lives of my great-grandmothers: my grandmother in her flour-streaked apron, standing in the kitchen doorway during meals in case one of the "boys" needed anything; my mother who couldn't get a checking account without my dad's signature; and the day my first credit card arrived in the mail. I traced the raised letters of my name with my thumb, marveling at my financial independence.

Marriage, Children, and Widowhood

Starting in adolescence, my great-grandmothers were socialized to marry, create a happy home, and have as many children as the Lord saw fit. Fifteen-year-old girls spent hours daydreaming about who they would marry and how many children they would have. Marriage was the cornerstone of their lives. Well-chosen marriage partners could forge political, business, and social ties. While romantic love was desired, security was more important in an uncertain world. In Vincennes, Indiana, Kate married a man who promised a bright future; Cora married her double first cousin, strengthening close kinship ties in Gravel Hill, Tennessee; Texanna married an educated man who was a respected breeder of Norman horses in Gainesville, Texas; and Minnie defied convention, likely disappointing her parents by eloping. Kate, Cora, and Texanna were born around the time of the American Civil War, whereas Minnie was born 30 years later. They were raised to act as "true" women: passive, obedient, pious, and pure. Reinforced by sermons, newspapers, and magazines, the cult of womanhood defined the "true" woman as religious and reverent, free from immoral acts, content in her home, and submissive to men. Men were expected to display the masculine traits of ruthlessness, strength, bravery, and daring, to perform feats of physical difficulty, and to make the tough decisions in life. A woman's role was to be devoted to her faith, husband, and children.

To fulfill their destiny of a good marriage, girls were expected to remain chaste and guard their virginity. Only wicked, foolish girls gave themselves before marriage. Girls were warned to avoid being lifted on or off a horse, sharing a book with a male, or being too close in narrow spaces. Even thoughts about men were treated with a "wholesome dread' since they could lead to "entanglements" and "snares." The virgin bride was then expected to reverse her frigid behavior and approach her husband with "wholesome joy." It was quite an emotional leap and did nothing to dispel the myth that women had little sexual feelings. After all, their only role was to become pregnant, ideally with sons.

A marriage could make a woman the saddest fool God ever made or His luckiest angel. Abuse, violence, neglect, and unhappiness followed marriage to the wrong man. After years of relentless struggle, only a grimly silent wife remained; one who seldom spoke, her words short and snapped, with displeasure underlining every sentence.

Motherhood was characterized by continual cycles of pregnancy. Cora was pregnant or nursing from age 20 to 46. She had a baby roughly every two years: pregnant for nine months, nursing until the baby could drink from a cup, then pregnant again, giving her "stairstep" children. Kate gave birth to four children, three of whom survived. Minnie's first three children were born in less than three years. Complications from childbirth probably caused the deaths of Texanna, her mother, and Kate's mother. Even in the twenty-first century, despite medical advances, giving birth remains the most life-threatening experience for any woman.

Women who failed to conceive were considered unblessed in an era when preachers and priests held the greatest influence over people's lives. Unblessed were also those who failed to marry and were then expected to care for the elderly and infirm. And those blessed with only one child were suspected of having female problems, as if males bore no responsibility. Women who started having babies at a young age were more likely to have even more children, decreased only by the number of children who died before age five. Older women who had outlived their childbearing years were expected to help care for their grandchildren, thus increasing their daughters' productivity. Large families were encouraged because children were seen as economic assets—they helped on the farm and at home, and as teenagers, they earned wages from factories or domestic work. However, large families also affected the health of mothers, the earning potential of fathers, and the overall well-being of each child. My great-grandmothers experienced the heartache of feeding too many kids from a small soup pot.

Options for an unwanted pregnancy were limited: an illegal abortion (which risked infection and even death), a hasty marriage, or adoption. Raising a child alone could quickly lead to prostitution and illness. Minnie's sister, Mary, sadly died from a failed abortion. Her 17-year-old cousin was admitted to the Multnomah County Poor Farm in 1902; her "disease" was pregnancy. She was voluntarily discharged two months later, with a note added to her record: "Baby adopted by friends."

None of my great-grandmothers celebrated as many wedding anniversaries as I have. Cora was married for 46 years when she died; Texanna didn't live to see her sixth wedding anniversary; and Kate was married to John for 13 years before he died. Minnie, widowed twice, was married to Frank for 15 years and Dellon for 27 years. Frank died on their 15th wedding anniversary. Ironically, Kate and Minnie's husbands died from appendicitis in their forties, a preventable death with modern medical practices. My life could have been very different if not for modern medicine, too. My husband almost died at age 28 from bacterial endocarditis, and although not as severe, I fought anemia. I would have been described like Texanna as not "strong." How miserable my life would have been without medical fixes.

When husbands died, their wives faced a devastating loss of financial support. Gravel Hill widows, including Cora, could keep a year's supply of food based on the value of their husbands' estates. Kate and Minnie were left to care for their minor children without a pantry full of food. With only an eighth-grade education, their opportunities were limited. They never had a chance or any encouragement to pursue education beyond that point. Kate worked as a servant in a volatile household to gain rudimentary nursing training. Minnie was arrested for selling bootleg liquor, which was far more profitable than her Mothers' Aide payments. The program was available to Kate in St. Louis in 1911 and to Minnie in Oregon in 1913. However, welfare laws were never free from moral judgments, making distinctions between the "deserving" and "undeserving" poor. Proper women deserved assistance, while women of color and those involved in criminal activities, like bootlegging, were considered undeserving.

Kate and Texanna were so young when their mothers died that they probably had no memories of them. Did they receive a keepsake belonging to their mothers? Or did their distraught fathers burn all of their mothers' belongings? Kate's father entrusted his motherless daughters to the care of godparents. Texanna likely depended on her older half-sisters to help raise her, and when she died, her children were cared for by their paternal relatives. Resentment still lingers in Gravel Hill over the decision to place Cora's orphaned husband with his wealthier uncle, while less fortunate relatives raised two other brothers. The same might have been true for Kate and her sisters, as Kate was raised by "rich" relatives, while her sisters were not.

My great-grandmothers' highest expectations for their daughters were to marry. Education beyond eighth grade was not considered essential and was seen as a shortcoming. Mothers taught their daughters to care for younger siblings so they would be good mothers, trained them in household chores to become good wives, and expected them to support the family with their wages earned as teenage domestic helpers or factory workers. While most girls married in their twenties, my maternal Prussian ancestors married young. Wilhelmine's three daughters married at 16. Her great-granddaughter, my mother, married my dad two weeks after her sixteenth birthday. Her mother, Bea, shrugged and asked, "Why not?" Only my paternal grandmother noted in her diary that she was deeply worried about such a young daughter-in-law.

My cousins and siblings, third-generation descendants of Minnie, Cora, Texanna, and Kate, are college-educated and self-supporting, breaking the cycle of generational poverty caused by undereducated daughters marrying too young. My paternal grandmother, who valued education, would be very proud.

Legacies

When I told my niece I wanted to write the stories of my great-grandmothers, she got excited, thinking we would find independent women liberated from the female stereotypes of faithfulness, humility, and subservience to men. However, I discovered they were not rebels or trailblazers but ordinary women whose lives were shaped by grit, determination, and quiet strength. They were sensible, conventional women who worked hard, attended church, lived frugally, and remained wary of public displays of emotion or foolishness of any kind. Not wealthy in a material sense, they had no pension or retirement benefits. They cared for their families and never betrayed them to outsiders. They sacrificed so that the lives of their husbands, children, and grandchildren would be easier than their own. Poverty, lack of education, and change to limited exposure to sophisticated culture slowly but surely robbed them of self-confidence, pride, ambition, and imagination.

I enjoy an independent lifestyle that my great-grandmothers never imagined: the convenience of having a bank card, a reliable car, a secure retirement, medical advances that keep me healthy, the freedom to travel for pleasure, and access to technology. I have more free time to occasionally spend a morning working on a jigsaw puzzle or getting lost in a novel. Yet, I also juggle the demands of household, family, work, volunteering, and friendships, never fully meeting the crazy quilt of expectations. There is still a "be careful" warning that limits us, whether we are climbing a ladder or not.

I was so jealous of the 1970s superwoman: impeccably dressed, confident, with a degree from a prestigious university, her best-selling novel in her bulging briefcase, her sandwich made from wheat bread she baked in her sparkling kitchen, supported by a loving, cooperative husband and well-behaved children. It took me longer than I care to admit to realize that such an idealized image of womanhood was a myth. I envied successful women who seemed to do it all until I finally saw the cracks in their lives: nervous breakdowns, unhappy children, messy kitchens, and broken marriages. Beneath the myths are ordinary women trying their best—from 1880 through 2025 and beyond.

Hundreds of internalized factors diminish, marginalize, sexualize, and stigmatize women. I suspect Cora was a quiet woman who felt uncomfortable around strangers. Kate was the most cosmopolitan, while Minnie was the most streetwise, familiar with criminal activity. Cora followed her husband to Texas but returned with him to Gravel Hill—a man who hurt her feelings with his insensitive teasing and insisted that his family work "like horses." Minnie followed her first husband, Frank Hemsworth, from job to job and rental to rental in the Bay Area of California and Portland, Oregon, while Kate seemed to tolerate John's next get-rich-quick scheme. Descended from generations of women who survived wars, scattered corn to poultry, washed the bodies of the dead, simmered pots of soup, and struggled to keep babies alive, the identities of my great-grandmothers were shaped by their class, religion, and community—communities filled with relatives and near relatives who knew everyone's business down to the identity of the girl who sassed her mother.

We women navigate life in similar ways: learning to paddle to avoid drowning while grasping passing branches, constantly adjusting to the river's current to stay afloat. Over the years, my great-grandmothers scraped away any softness, becoming rigidly pragmatic, fighting to be strong as they carved out paths to survival. They learned to unstitch themselves and sew themselves back together like Raggedy Ann dolls. They were women I have known all my life: stoic women, their bodies stiff and unyielding, nursing their resentment, with little tolerance for whimsy and daydreaming, as they wipe kitchen drainboards with strong strokes using sore arthritic fingers. Women who began their day by putting on their apron from the nail by the back door.

A woman leaves her legacy on a tombstone: beloved wife, mother, grandmother. Cora raised ten children to adulthood, and they all gathered at her deathbed to honor her, except for a daughter who had died and my grandfather, who lived too far away and whose wife was about to give birth. Cora's stone is engraved with the inscription, "Cora, wife of J.C. Springer, 1858–1924." She is buried beside her husband in Gravel Hill, Tennessee. Texanna's short life ended in 1890 before her children started school. She lies buried in Springbrook Cemetery in Cooke County, Texas. Widowed, Kate worked as a nurse to support herself and her children, later rejecting her sons for not being good Catholics. Her stone is engraved only with her name, Catherine M. Gabler, and is shared with her daughter, son-in-law, and granddaughter in a Catholic cemetery in St. Louis, Missouri. Minnie created a nest of sharp sticks that her children carefully navigated to avoid being poked and jabbed, but she died peacefully in a recliner at her youngest daughter's home. She lies beside her second husband under a stone that reads, "Minnie T. Olds, 1893–1968, Mother," in Oregon City, Oregon. All four women left behind children, laughter, and disappointment. They finished one chore after another, doing what had to be done in a world of things to mend and mind with never enough time. Through hard work, they carefully organized, stitched, and pressed many small quilt squares to create a stunning pattern, repairing it as best they could when it ripped. I am part of that pattern.

As the mist, smoke, and fireworks cleared from my great-grandmothers' lives, they were exhausted from caring, worrying, and solving problems. Their journey spanned from birth to death, from innocence to wisdom, and from ignorance to knowledge. Remembering their names and stories keeps their legacy alive. Pieced together from hearsay, newspaper articles, photographs, and vital records, they saw themselves as ordinary and might have been puzzled (or, in some cases, offended) by anyone who thought their stories were important. Some chapters may have stayed with them forever; others were quickly discarded. Their stories are fragmented, incomplete, misinterpreted, or flawed by my memory. I discovered some of the facts, but not what they dreamed of in their sleep. It's not much of an epitaph to say, "She made a good apple pie, or got more milk from the cow, or gathered more eggs from the chickens." There must be more to her story. All our great-grandmothers deserve to have their stories told.

Endnotes

1. The 1880 Census asked participants where their father was born. Of Phillip's children still alive, some did not know, and others recorded that he had been born in North Carolina. Only his son James M. Huggins recorded his father's place of birth as Maryland.

2. Dan and Katherine Donnell Page, The Descendants of Phillip Huggins, born about 1765, North Carolina, 2001, Arkoma, Oklahoma, page 9.

3. Jane's maiden name and the date of her marriage were found in a family Bible in an old shed in McNairy County, Tennessee, by Nancy Kennedy, an amateur historian of McNairy County.

4. 1800; Census: Morgan, Buncombe, North Carolina; Series: M32; Roll: 29; Page: 173; Image: 118; Family History Library Film: 337905

5. Ancestry.com. North Carolina, Land Grant Files, 1693-1960 [database online]. Provo, UT, USA: Ancestry.com Operations, Inc., 2016.

6. F.A. Sondley, A History of Buncombe County, North Carolina, 1930, Buncombe County Court Minutes 1794-1795, January Term 1801 and Chapter XVI, page 460.

7. Bureau of Land Management, General Land Records, Lauderdale County, Alabama, Township 1 South, Range 10 West, Section 8. History.Geo.com. A section equals 1 square mile or 640 acres.

8. Lauderdale County Deed Record, Book 4; Lauderdale County, Alabama Day Book, 1825-1827, FamilySearch Film #1022631, item 3.

9. James Montgomery Huggins was appointed Constable March 3, 1823, resigning March 7, 1825; serving as Justice of the Peace from March 25, 1825, to April 10, 1828, and from March 18, 1829, to February 20, 1830. Lauderdale County, Alabama, Civil Register of County Officials, 1819-1832, Volume 1.

10. Lauderdale County, Alabama Deed Book A7, page 127.

11. Lauderdale County Court Records 1829-1839, Natchez Trace Traveler, Volume 10, Number 2, May 1990, page 73; Volume 16, 1996, pages 43, 96.

12. Adjutant General's Office of Alabama. Register of Officers, 1820–1863. Alabama Department of Archives and History, Montgomery, Alabama, Ancestry.

13. "Alabama, United States records," images, FamilySearch: Aug 7, 2025, image 4523 of 4930; Image Group Number: 008704011

14. White County, Tennessee Deeds, Book E, page 75, FamilySearch Microfilm 8150957, image 583.

15 Joseph Robertson, Probate Record Packets, 1800-1920, Alabama. Probate Court, Lauderdale, Alabama.

16 Tennessee Land Grants McNairy County: James M. Huggins, Grant #3346; 37.5 acres June 26, 1847; Book 4A page 382; Grant #12504 for 427 acres October 15, 1851; Grant #15056, 131 acres, December 1, 1854, Book 19, page 556; and James & L.M. Huggins, Grant #15053, 200 acres, December 1, 1854, McNairy County Book 19, page 553.

17 Tennessee Land Grant, Western Tennessee District, McNairy County, Grant #12503.

18 Owens, Loulie Latimer, Taproot of the South Carolina Baptist Back County: Fairforest Baptist Church, 1980, pages 10-11.

19 Union, South Carolina, United States records, FamilySearch, August 7, 2025, image 236 of 661. Image Group Number: 008152071

20 Union, South Carolina, United States records, FamilySearch, August 7, 2025, image 87 of 515. Image Group Number: 008152072

21 Second Creek Primitive Baptist Church, 1830-1930, Lawrence County, Tennessee, Minutes, Natchez Trace Traveler, Volume 4, Number 4, 1984, pages 155-156.

22 John B. Boles, Religion in Antebellum Kentucky, 1976, University Press of Kentucky, pages 27-28. Jerking was a fast and spasmodic movement of the body and limbs. Barking was probably a natural grunt elicited by the jerks. Stories have circulated of demented Christians barking up trees – "treeing the Devil."

23 Second Creek Primitive Baptist Church, 1830–1930, Lawrence County, Tennessee, Minutes, Natchez Trace Traveler, Volume 4, Number 4, 1984, pages 155-156.

24 Ezekiel Springer Lien to Alston Hatley, McNairy County, November 14, 1842.

25 McNairy County, Tennessee, FamilySearch Film #008264383, Deeds, Book D, pages 489-490, accessed August 23, 2023.

26 McNairy County Circuit Court 1860-1870, page 43., McNairy County Deed Book K, 1871-1873, I 302-303, Family Search Film 008477446, Deed Book I, K646-649, #008477447, accessed August 22, 2022.

27 Nancy Wardlow Kennedy, A Brief History of McNairy County, Tennessee.

28 June Bullard, Corinth, Mississippi, Reflections: A History of McNairy County, Tennessee 1823-1996, compiled and edited by the Reflections Committee for the Tennessee 200 Bicentennial Celebration, 1996. Heritage House Publishing, Marceline, Missouri.

29 Nancy Wardlow Kennedy, Confederate Guerrillas Terrorized McNairy County, Excerpts from the diary of Narcissa Black and Circuit Court Records, 2020, pages 95–101.

30 Larry Watson, Reflections: A History of McNairy County, Tennessee 1823-1996, compiled and edited by the Reflections Committee for the Tennessee 200 Bicentennial Celebration, 1996. Heritage House Publishing, Marceline, MO 64658.

31 Nancy Wardlow Kennedy, Looking Back I, www.mcnairy.history.com.

32 Nancy Wardlow Kennedy, Looking Back III in McNairy County, Tennessee, 2005.

33 Eddie Wayne Shell, Evolution of the Alabama Agroecosystem: Always Keeping Up, but Never Catching Up, New South Books, 2013, page 313.

34 Nancy Wardlow Kennedy, The Churches at Gravel Hill, undated.

35 McNairy County, Tennessee, Estate Inventory, 1865-1931, FamilySearch, pages 547-550, accessed August 15, 2020.

36 McNairy County Settlements 1865-1877, FamilySearch Microfilm, page 63, assessed 29 August 2022.

37 McNairy County Year's Support, Homestead and Dower, 1857-1915, FamilySearch Microfilm, pages 147, 163, 274, accessed August 22, 2022.

38 McNairy County History of Tennessee, Goodspeed Publishing, 1887, page 5.

39 McNairy County Independent, August 27, 1915.

40 The Commercial Appeal (Memphis, Tennessee), December 4, 1915, page 10.

41 Grover Cleveland, Second Presidential Inaugural Address, March 4, 1893.

42 Cooke County, Texas Land Records, #77744238, Warranty Deed, filed September 27, 1902, Book DR, Volume 83, page 114; Grantor RF and Martha Jenkins; Grantee JC Springer, #77718607, December 8, 1902, Grantor Deed of Trust, Book DT, Volume 26, page 482.

43 Cooke County, Texas Land Records, #77746107, October 24, 1903, Book DR, Volume 86, page 335; Warranty Deed, Grantor: J.C. Springer and Cora C., Grantee: McCary, C.V.

44 Widow's Indigent Pension: Tennessee Military Records, 1908. FamilySearch image 1389 of 2401. Elizabeth Huggins. Letter written July 30, 1911.

45 McNairy County Independent, August 31, 1917, image 1.

46 McNairy County Independent, November 30, 1923, Gravelhill News.

47 The Commercial Appeal (Memphis, Tennessee), March 17, 1919, page 8.

48 McNairy County, Tennessee County Court, FamilySearch, image 524 of 644, accessed August 27, 2020.

49 United States Census (1850 Slave Schedule) FamilySearch, Microfilm #444861, James Huggins, McNairy County, line 42.

50 Letter by Burton Springer, March 1978.

51 Letter by Mollie Springer, Claude's widow, 1978.

52 McNairy County Independent, April 11, 1913, image 4; McNairy County Independent, October 8, 1921, image 2.

53 Nancy Wardlow Kennedy, Looking Back, III, in McNairy County, Tennessee, 2005, page 24.

54 Ellen Schmacher, copied from Independent Appeal, Summer of 1994.

55 Jersey County, Illinois Marriage Records Index, October 1839-1876. Family Search Film #00761975, image 9 of 230. Barch and Nancy were married by George H. Pegues, Justice of the Peace.

56 This quote is attributed to Nancy's aunt, but it was a common saying. Memorial page for Joseph Bach Klepper, Find a Grave Memorial, ID 1994574, citing Old Plano Cemetery, Plano, Collin County, Texas.

57 Texas Land Abstracts: Grantee: Baurch Cantrell. Certificate #443, Patentee James Thomas. Patent Date 5 July 1854, 557 acres, Dallas County. Grantee: Baurch Cantrell. Certificate #443, Patentee Abraham Hart. Patent Date 5 July 1854, 83 acres, Dallas County. Colony Certificate No. 443, Volume 2, Filed 20 April 1850. Dallas Quarterly, Volume 33, number 2, June 1987, number 3, September 1987.

58 Larry Drake et al to A.H. Fortner, Dallas Daily Herald, March 18, 1883, page 7; 200 acres for $3600, Dallas Weekly Herald, Volume 30, number 17, March 22, 1883. W.D. Salisbury to Frank Winfrey and wife, Dallas Daily Herald, November 11, 1883, image 2.

59 Patillo et al. vs. Thompson, appeal from Fannin County, and Thompson vs Evans, Fannin County, Fort Worth Gazette, May 1, 1884, page 3.

60 Maude Ella Cantrell stated her father was born at Plano and was 34 when she was born on March 10, 1882. Texas Probate Record of Births.

61 Anderson County, Texas Land Sales, Book "E," page 364.

62 Brothers Elisha Cantrell and Hazel Green Centrell and nephews James Elisha and John Calvin "Jack," sons of Stephen, and William C, son of Elisha. Marion Day Mullins, compiler, Republic of Texas Poll List for 1846. Genealogical Publishing Company Inc., 1974, page 236. Nieces Nancy Cantrell Evans, Sarah Cantrell Elkins, and Isabell Cantrell Blansett, daughters of Stephen.

63 Anderson County, Texas Land Sales, Book "E," page 537.

64 The 1853 Pre-emption Act was available to anyone who settled, lived on, and made improvements for three consecutive years. Married men were entitled to 160 acres; Single men to 80 acres. They paid the Texas General Land Office $0.50 to $2.00 per acre in Austin. The pre-emption grant was changed in 1853 to be an outright gift.

65 Leah See Survey, patented to Burch Cantrell, September 16, 1859, Patent Number 483, Volume 26, Parker County, Texas. Barch's name is recorded as Burch; Leah's name as Leah See or Leah Lee. A land patent is a legal document that grants ownership of a piece of public land to a private individual.

66 Austin Weekly Statesman, October 27, 1892, image 1.

67 Dennis Owens, Captain W.G. Veal, Waxahachie High School, 1979, accessed January 22, 2021.

68 Henry Smythe, Historical Sketch of Parker County and Weatherford Texas, 1877, page 102.

69 Ft. Worth Genealogical Society Vol. 61, No. 2, May 2018, page 85. Old-Timer Recalls Thrills of Early Days.

70 Dallas Herald, July 15, 1860, page 1. History of Dallas County, Lewis Publishing Company, 1892, page 293.

71 Plano, Texas: the Early Years, Friends of the Plano Public Library. Second Edition, 1996, page 197.

72 Johnson County, Texas, Deed Record Book D, Filed October 26, 1864; recorded March 18, 1865, pages 728-729

73 Texas Deeds, Brazos County, Book I, page 90.

74 Texas Deeds, Brazos County, Book I, pages 351, 471, 489, 519.

75 Texas Deeds, Brazos County, Book K, pages 1, 6, 77.

76 Texas Deeds, Henderson County, Book P, pages 192 and 193.

77 1870 United States Federal Census, Athens Precinct, Henderson County, Texas, Film no. 553090.

78 Dallas, Texas, United States records, FamilySearch image 622 of 2409; Dallas Genealogical Society (Texas). Image Group Number: 005781998

79 Dallas County Civil District Court Case Papers, Heirs of B. Cantrell vs David Bowser et al, 1875. Case Number 2828. FamilySearch images 415-462 of 1897. Dallas County Court Minutes 1877-1879, FamilySearch Film 008504729, images 273-274 of 777.

80 Cantrell Heirs give Power of Attorney to Ira C. Mitchell of Collin County, Texas. dallas.tx.publicsearch.us, volume. 29, pages 139-140. This court document is the only record naming Texanna's mother and documenting Barch's second marriage.

81 The Frontier Echo (Jacksboro, Texas), Volume 3, Number 41, April 26, 1878; Volume 3, Number 47, June 7, 1878; Volume 4, Number 3, August 3, 1878, and Denison Daily Herald, Volume 1, Number 195, May 20, 1878, Portal to Texas History.

82 Galveston Daily News, December 14, 1884, page 2; The Dallas Daily Herald, October 3, 1884, page 5; Austin American-Statesman, October 4, 1884, page 2; Fort Worth Daily Gazette, October 28, 1885, page 4. Fort Worth Daily Gazette, February 21, 1886, page 1.

83 Austin American-Statesman, August 19, 1887, page 8.

84 R.T. Crist et al. vs. M.J. Cantrell et al. Dallas County, Texas, Court Case files, number 3864, FamilySearch film 008505529, image 903-926 of 1,144.

85 Dallas County Probate Case 2246: Compton, Nancy et al (Minors), legal document, 1883-05-02/1898-11-07, accessed March 6, 2024, University of North Texas Libraries, Portal to Texas History.

86 Charles E. Heare, The Heare Family Genealogy, Bolton, Missouri, 1980.

87 Gladys Powelson Jones, The American Family Powelson Virginia Branch, 1988.

88. Gainesville Daily Hesperian. (Gainesville, Texas), Vol. 11, No. 81, Ed. 1 Tuesday, February 25, 1890. The ad ran in the newspaper as early as Feb. 6, 1890.
89. Texas Deeds, Cooke County, 1889-1890, image 241-243 of 326, pages 472-475; image 261 of 325, pages 516-518.
90. Fort Worth Daily Gazette, December 28, 1884, image 3.
91. The Covington Crescent, Andalusia, Alabama, July 20, 1889, page 2. Transcribed by Heather Holley.
92. Cooke County History: Past and Present, Cooke County History Book Committee, 1992, page 22.
93. Cross Timbers Genealogical Society Newsletter, December 2010.
94. Gainesville Daily Hesperian, February 16, 1890.
95. Gainesville Daily Hesperian, Volume 11, Number 81, Edition 1, February 25, 1890.
96. Galveston Daily News, April 20, 1890. Hessian fly is a pest of cereal crops.
97. Fort Worth Star Telegram, January 18, 1983, page 16.
98. Cooke County, Texas Land Deeds, Book DR, volume 78, page 596. Heare, Bonnie, minor estate.
99. Cooke County, Texas, birth records 1860-1986, image 412, FamilySearch, checked March 20, 2020.
100. Dallas County, Texas Court Case Files 1889-1892, Civil Case papers #7500, FamilySearch Film #008505603, image 580–598 of 1780.
101. Frank P. Heare petitioned for Charles Elizabeth Roberts, widow, and her minor children as they were beneficiaries of Policy of Insurance No. 158600 issued by Knights of Henor through their lodge at Plano, Collin County, Texas, for $2,000. Cooke County Probate Records, Petitions for Guardianship. FamilySearch, Heard in Court April 16, 1890, image 588 of 904. Final Records, Volume 7, image 195-196, pages 383-384. Cooke County, Texas, Probate Records, 1849-1982, FamilySearch, accessed December 13. 2023, Entry for Mary E. Roberts, 1907, File #1011, image 263-422 of 1,110 images.
102. Hubbard Madison Smith, M.D., Historical Sketches of Old Vincennes, 1903, page 121.
103. Indiana, Marriages, 1780-1992, FamilySearch, accessed 13 January 2020, Andre Kuhn, 1856.
104. Dwight and Pamela Cook, The Immigration of the Maschino, Manginot, Maginot, Maschinto, Marchino, Musteno, Moginot, Marchive, Mashino, Maschin, Mangin, Marginot Families to the United States, Mill Stream Press, 2008, pages 13-18, 27, 135-136.
105. Euronews, https://www.euronews.com/2021/04/13/life-is-a-bitche-for-french-town-after-facebook-page-removed-in-error, accessed June 7, 2022.

106 Furchhausen, Cavern Canton, Bas-Rhin (Lower Rhin), Alsace, France, 1831 and 1841 Census. Civil Register, Archives of Bas-Rhin, France. Archives bas-rhin.fr, assessed July 24, 2016.

107 Passenger Lists of Vessels Arriving at New Orleans, Louisiana, 1820-1902, NAI Number 2824927, Record Group Number 85, The National Archives at Washington, D.C.

108 Paul Simpson, Old Virginia Bound, Clippership Press, 2019, pages 14, 28 to 31.

109 Jack Sievers and Kitty Frey Deckard, John the Baptist Catholic Church 150 Years (1847-1997), Ewing Printing, pages 12, 55.

110 Under the act of February 10, 1855, an immigrant woman instantly became a U.S. citizen at the moment a judge's order naturalized her immigrant husband. Her proof of U.S. citizenship was a combination of the marriage certificate and her husband's naturalization record. Marian L. Smith, Women and Naturalization, ca 1902-1940, Prologue, Summer 1988.

111 Turner Halls, or Turnvereins, were a popular German institution. These gymnastic clubs may have included libraries, shooting clubs, singing societies, and trade, labor, and craft associations.

112 The Vincennes Weekly Western Sun, March 12, 1859.

113 The Vincennes Weekly Western Sun, August 4, 1860. September 26, 1860.

114 Shrine of St. Joseph German Catholic Church, 11th & Biddle, St. Louis, Missouri, FamilySearch Microfilm #1870933, Baptism 1853-1861.

115 French Catholic Records for St. Louis (Drouin Collection), Ancestry, accessed December 26, 2023.

116 United States, Census, 1860, FamilySearch, Entry for Andw Cohn and Mary Cohn, 1860.

117 James W. Covington, The Camp Jackson Affair, 1861, Missouri Historical Review, 1961, page 198.

118 Civil War draft registration: Kuhn, Andrew, age 42 as of July 1863, laborer, born in Germany and lived at Number 1, 12th Street, 2nd Sub District, 5th Ward, St. Louis, Missouri.

119 Kuhn, Andrew, Teamster with T.A. Buckland, right corner 15th and Market; Kuhn, Michael, Teamster with T.A. Buckland, corner of Market and 13th; St. Louis City Directory, 1864.

120 St. John the Baptist Catholic Church Parish registers; Marriage, Baptism, Death Records, 1847-1947. FamilySearch Film 1433368.

121 Peter Maschino Sr. Probate Records, 1869, Knox County, Indiana, Box 79.

122 Vincennes Weekly Western Sun, January 15, 1876.

123 Vincennes Weekly Western Sun, June 23, 1877, page 2.

124 Vincennes Weekly Western Sun, November 6, 1885.

125 Sisters of St. Joseph of Carondelet, St. Louis, Missouri, information from Sister Patricia J. Kelly, Archivist, April 25, 1988.

126 Charlotte Observer, (Charlotte, North Carolina), April 8, 1901, page 7. Boston Globe, April 16, 1901, page 7. Indianapolis News, April 6, 1901, page 3. Savannah Morning News (Savannah, Georgia, April 6, 1901, page 11. Phillipsburg Herald, (Herald, Kansas) Newspaper Archives, April 9, 1901, page 6. Richmond Tiles, (Richmond, Virginia), April 6, 1901, page 6. Semi-Weekly Messenger, (Wilmington, North Carolina) April 12, 1901, page 3. Birmingham Age-Herald (Birmingham, Alabama), April 6, 1901, page 2. Dillon Tribune (Dillon, Montana), April 12, 1901, page 5.

127 Laura of Mary Kuhn, buried at Resurrection Cemetery, Section 23, Row 2, Lot 004.

128 Vincennes Daily Commercial, May 24, 1887.

129 Vincennes Commercial, July 23, 1910, pages 1, 4.

130 Mary Recker, Kansas, age 79y 5m 1d, died June 2, 1938. Gardner, Vault, Sacred Heart, Service: St. John. Mt. Calvary Cemetery, Vincennes, Indiana, Vol. 1 Interments 1907-1938.

131 Vincennes Commercial, April 15, 1915, page 4; Western Sun, April 16, 1915, page 3.

132 The Cincinnati Enquirer, March 5, 1868.

133 The Indiana Herald, February 15, 1868, page 1.

134 Sullivan Democrat (Sullivan, Indiana), August 10, 1865.

135 St. John the Baptist Catholic Church Parish registers, Marriage, Baptism, Death Records 1847-1855, FHL US/CAN Film 1433368.

136 Vincennes Weekly Sun, November 14, 1873, page 4.

137 Missouri State Horticultural Society Annual Report, 1884, volume 27.

138 August and Therese Sprengnether, their children, and her sister, Frances, are listed on the Hamburg Passenger lists to America via Liverpool, 20 April 1883. They were on the Retford, a steamboat from Hamburg to Grimsby (Liverpool). Departure from Hamburg 20 Apr 1883. Sprengnether, August, age 36 (Laborer/Gardener); Theresa, 27; Francisca, 4; Anna, 3; August 2; Karl, 1/2; and Francisca Gabler, age 22. Residence: Ehrenbreitstein. Destination: Liverpool. Ship Name: Retford, Captain Seaton. Staatsarchive Hamburg; Volume: 373-7 I, VIII B 1 Band 054; Seite: 447; Microfilm Number: S13141. Ancestry.com. Canadian Passenger Lists, 1865-1935. Provo, UT, USA: Ancestry.com Operations Inc, 2010. From Liverpool to Quebec, Canada, in steerage on the "Buenos Ayrean," arriving in Quebec on 10 May 1883. Family Search film #00808976, image 136 of 1290 says the Buenos Ayrean sailed from Glasgow 25 April; Liverpool, 26 April; Galway 27 April; and arrived Quebec 10 May 1883.

139 Daily Alta California, v. 83, No. 12, July 12, 1890. Oakland Tribune, July 12, 1890.

140 State Board of Horticulture of the State of California, Official Report of the Fruit Growers' Convention of the State of California Held Under the Auspices of the State Board of Horticulture at Chico, Butte County, Commencing Tuesday, November 20, and Ending Friday, November 23, 1888.

141 John Gabler of Chicago, Illinois, married Catherine Kuhn of Vincennes on August 30, 1892. Her parents were Andrew and Mary Kuhn. Witnesses: Jacob Kuhn, John Bey, Theresa Ebner, and Francisca Gabler. St. John the Baptist Catholic Church Parish registers, Marriage, Baptism, Death Records 1847-1855, FHL US/CAN Film 1433368, 1892, #12.

142 Vincennes Commercial, August 31, 1892, page 3.

143 Sunday Commercial, September 4, 1892, page 5.

144 Duesterberg Funeral Home Records March 3, 1887 – March 28, 1893.

145 The Springfield Democrat, September 10, 1893, page 6.

146 Greene County, Missouri Deeds, Ed O'Day to Kate Gabler, Book 133, page 163.

147 The Springfield Republicans, Springfield, Missouri, August 24, 1897, page 8; American Gardening, page 428, Rural Publishing Company, 1894.

148 The Springfield New-Leader, November 9, 1900, page 3.

149 St. Louis Globe-Democrat, October 28, 1903, page 6.

150 Missouri Birth Registers 1904-05, Missouri State Archives, indexed as John and Kate Gubler, daughter born February 12, 1905.

151 The Coffeyville Daily Journal (Coffeyville, Kansas), October 14, 1905.

152 St. Louis Post Dispatch, November 11, 1905, page 7; St. Louis Globe-Democrat, November 12, 1905, page 30; St. Louis Globe-Democrat, November 26, 1905, page 14

153 Geological Survey Bulletin, U.S. Govt Printing Office, 1911.

154 St. Louis Post-Dispatch, September 20, 1910, page 1, October 6, 1910, page 1.

155 Vincennes Commercial, May 15, 1908, page 1.

156 St. Louis Post-Dispatch, July 5, 1909, page 2.

157 St. Louis Post, December 10, 1928, page 33; Gebken's Chapel Funeral Home records.

158 Vincennes Sun-Commercial, October 2, 1933, page 2.

159 Vincennes Sun Commercial, March 14, 1935.

160 Vincennes Sun Commercial, October 30, 1935, page 1.

161 St. Louis Globe-Democrat, November 9, 1935, page 6.

162 Edwardsville Intelligence, (Edwardsville, Illinois), September 15, 1938. St. Louis Post-Dispatch, September 18, 1938, page 8.

163 Vincennes Sun-Commercial, May 20, 1940, page 3.

164 Catholic Cemeteries of the Archdiocese of St. Louis.

165 St. Louis Globe-Democrat, July 26, 1960, page 9.

166 Reuters, January 14, 2009, Poland Unearths 1,800 Bodies in WW2 Mass Grave.

167 Bauer und Einsasse (farmer and owner) in Zigahnen, Kreis Marienwerder in 1808. www.westpreussen.de/einwohner/index, checked June 19, 2014.

168 The Diaries and Letters of Sir George Jackson, K.C.H., R. Bentley & Son Publisher, 1872, page 51.

169 Klein Bandtken, Marienwerder, FamilySearch Microfilm Number 245635.

170 Adapted from Myron Guenwald's Two Worlds for our Children, 1885, pages 30-32, as printed in the Die Pommerchen Leute, Volume 36, Issue 1, page 9.

171 Min-19th Century Prussian/German Army: Organization and Sources, by Joyce Rohloff-Gardner, Die Pommerchen Leute, Volume 35, Issue 3, page 6.

172 Germans to America. List of Passengers Arriving at U.S. Ports, Volume 26, October 1871 – April 1872, page 328.

173 Brown County, Wisconsin Naturalization Records, Box 6, Folder 3, Family Search. Assessed February 1, 2023.

174 Denise Gess and William Lutz, Firestorm at Peshtigo: A town, its people, and the deadliest fire in American History, 2001.

175 Jack Rudolph, Birthplace of a Commonwealth (A Short History of Brown County, Wisconsin), Brown County Historical Society, 1976.

176 Green Bay Press-Gazette, November 29, 1883, December 5, 1883, page 2.

177 Green Bay Press-Gazette, March 28, 1885, page 4.

178 Post Crescent, May 7, 2007, Susan Squires, reporter.

179 De Volkstem (DePere, Wisconsin) December 24, 1890; February 6, 1907; June 14, 1916.

180 In 1892, the asylum's farm yielded 35 tons of hay, 20 bushels of beans, 30 bushels of onions, 900 heads of cabbage, and 1800 pounds of butter. Also tallied was the number of livestock consumed by inmates. Green Bay Weekly Gazette, December 15, 1892, page 2. In 1906, the asylum had one driving horse, one pony, 24 cows and calves, and 46 pigs. The farm produced hay, corn, potatoes, carrots, beets, cabbage, and 300 bushels of mangelwurzel beets. De Volkstem (DePere, Wisconsin), February 6, 1907, page 3.

181 Brown County, Wisconsin, Deeds, 1895 – 1899, Number 664a, page 589, FamilySearch #008695211, Image 1394 of 1397.

182 Green Bay Weekly Gazette, March 17, 1897, page 1; March 13, 1897, page 5; March 17, 1897, page 1; March 18, 1897, page 1; April 21, 1897, page 5.

183 Multnomah County, Oregon Deeds, Book 100, page 410.

184 Statesman Journal, Salem, Oregon, May 9, 1888, page 3; Weekly Oregon Statesman, Salem, Oregon, May 11, 1888, page 5; 1889 and 1890 Portland City Directory, Albina. Oregonian, April 12, 1890.

185 History of the Albina Plan Area, Winter 1990, Comprehensive Planning Workshop, Portland State Department of Urban Studies and Planning, pages 7-8.

186 Multnomah County, Oregon, Deeds, Book 142, page 465.

187 Washington County, Oregon, Indirect Deed Index July 1, 1888 – June 31, 1891, line 36, volume 26, page 459.

188 Washington County, Oregon Tax Rolls 1890-1891, The Genealogical Society of Washington County.

189 Death of Wilhelmina [Marta] Rosenau, duration of last illness 15 minutes. Suicide by carbolic acid. Aged 44 years, 9 months, 18 days, born in Germany. Office of the Corner. Portland, Multnomah County, Oregon.

190 Charles Rosenau died 29 Sept 1904 at the age of 52 years 6 months 0 days at the O.R. & N. dock of a skull fracture. He was born in Germany. J.P. Finley was the Coroner and the Undertaker. Index of Coroners' Inquests, page 412, Oct. 5, 1904. Oregon Death Index, Certificate 1969. Morning Oregonian, September 30, 1904.

191 Multnomah County Probate File 5542, Charles Rosenau Estate, 63 pages, closed May 23, 1905.

192 Multnomah County, Oregon, Deeds, Book 114, page 23.

193 Multnomah County, Oregon, Deeds, Book 187, page 86.

194 Multnomah County, Oregon, Probate File 5549, Wilhelmine Rosenau Estate, 28 pages, closed October 30, 1905.

195 In 1907's Muller vs. Oregon, regarding the working hours of women in Oregon Laundries, Louis D. Brandeis, later U.S. Supreme Court Justice, argued that "women are fundamentally weaker than men in all that makes for endurance; in muscular strength, in nervous energy, in the power of persistent application and attention." His arguments against the injurious effects of long hours on their feet are hardly open to serious challenge. Eleanor Flexner, Century of Struggle: The Woman's Rights Movement in the United States, 1970, page 215.

196 Oregonian, January 30, 1985, page 94.

197 Oregonian, September 26, 1898.

198 Oregon Daily Journal, December 13, 1908.

199 Trial for Assault, Hillsboro Argus, October 28, 1897, image 3.

200 Washington County, Oregon, Deeds, 1850-December 1907, 1901-1904, line 12, column 56, page 170, Section 7 T2S R2W; Hillsboro Argus, December 17, 1903, image 2.

201 Oregon Daily Journal, February 3, 1915, page 5.

202 Morning Oregonian, July 25, 1917, image 18. Oregon Daily Journal, July 24, 1917, page 4.

203 Oregonian, January 28, 1912.

204 Oregon Daily Journal, February 13, 1909, page 16.

205 Oregonian, June 26, 1917.

206 Cook's Addition to Albina, Abstract of Title, 1919, Portland, Oregon.

207 Highland School House Addition Lots 4, 5, 6, of Block 3, Section 23, Township 1 N Range 1 E.

208 Multnomah County, Oregon, Deeds, Book 752 Deed 148, Book 755 Deed 235.

209 Oregonian, March 24, 1894, page 8.

210 Oregonian, February 11, 1896.

211 Daily Capitol Journal, Salem, Oregon, February 24, 1896.

212 Morning Oregonian, May 21, 1903, image 6; Morning Oregonian, July 17, 1903, image 14; Oregon Daily Journal, July 28, 1903, page 3; Oregon Daily Journal, July 30, 1903, page 7; Oregon Daily Journal, August 29, 1903, page 7; Oregon Daily Journal, September 1, 1903, page 9.

213 Morning Oregonian, November 3, 1905, page 9.

214 Oregon Daily Journal, October 19, 1903, page 3.

215 Oregonian, March 9, 1906, page 3.

216 Multnomah County, Oregon, Direct Deeds, F.W. Hemsworth to D.H. Otto, September 6, 1913, Book 631, Deed 391. Lot 13, Block 42, Vernon and Lots 25 and 26 of Block 7, Mansfield Addition.

217 Oregonian, April 7, 1917, pages 1, 9.

218 Wayne A. Wiegand, Oregon's Public Libraries during the First World War, Oregon Historical Society, Spring 1989, volume 90, pages 55-57.

219 Morning Oregonian, October 21, 1918, image 1.

220 Oregonian, January 25, 1922, image 1.

221 Multnomah County Voting Registration, 1910.

222 Multnomah County, Oregon, Deeds, Lots 4, 5, Block 3 Highland School House Addition, Book 892, Deed 74.

223 Oregonian, August 22, 1922.

224 Morning Oregonian, January 20, 1920, page 9.

225 Oregonian, July 15, page 20.

226 Multnomah County, Oregon, Probate, Wohfiel, Minnie, Case Number 22899, 37 pages.

227 Military Pension record for John W. Hemsworth.

228 Morning Oregonian, March 19, 1908, page 12.

[229] Military and Pension record for Frank Wesley Hemsworth, Spanish-American War, Company L, Second Oregon Infantry.
[230] Morning Oregonian, April 28, 1922, page 7, image 7.
[231] Frank W. Hemsworth Estate, Multnomah County Probate, filed June 24, 1926.
[232] Vonnie Kauffman, Anna's Waltz, 2009, AuthorHouse.

Selected Bibliography

Braude, Ann, *Sisters and Saints: Women and American Religion*, Oxford University Press, 2008.

Carrington, Evelyn M., editor, *Women in Early Texas*, Texas State Historical Society, 1994.

Childs, Lydia Marie, *The American Frugal Housewife*, 1936.

Cook, Dwight, and Pamela, The Immigration of the Maschino Families to the United States, Mill Stream Press, 2008.

Crowley, John G., *Primitive Baptist of the Wiregrass South, 1815 to Present*, University of Florida, 1998.

Decker, Doug, "Alameda Old House History," https://alamedahistory.org/

Donlon, Regina, "Go West and Grow Up With the Country": A Study of German and Irish Immigrant Communities in the American Midwest, 1850–1900. (Thesis 2014). RIAN.

Faulk, J.J., *History of Henderson County*, Texas, 1929.

Fogle, Mary Katherine, *Through a paper looking glass: Reality and mythology in the personal identities of pioneer women, 1860–1930*, 2012, Texas Woman's University, viewed February 1, 2021.

Foster, Pearl O'Donnell, *Trek to Texas 1770–1870, History of early Texas Pioneers: Tarrant—Denton—Cass and other counties*, 1966.

Gess, Denise and William Lutz, *Firestorm at Peshtigo: A Town, Its People, and the Deadliest Fire in American History*, Henry Holt and Company, 2002.

Goetz, Henry Kilian, "Goin' West: Kate May's Trip to Old Greer County," *The Chronicles of Oklahoma*, Number 3, Fall 1994.

Hall, Roy F. and Helen Gibbard, *Colin County: Pioneering in North Texas*, 1975.

Heare, Charles E., *The Heare Family: A Genealogy*.

Historical Map of Bryan, College Station, and Brazos County.

Hodge, Roger D., *Texas Blood: seven generations among the Outlaws, Ranchers, Indians, Missionaries, Soldiers, and Smugglers of the Borderlands*, Alfred A. Knopf, 2017.

Hybarger, Courtney, Cooking in the 1800s, originally published as "When Dinner Wasn't Quick and Easy," reprinted with permission from Tar Heel Junior Historian, Spring 2007, Tar Heel Junior Historian Association, NC Museum of History, accessed October 5, 2018.

Jeffrey, Julie Roy, *Frontier Women*, Hill and Wang, 1998.

Johnson, Kari, *"Sweet spirit hovering around me": Texas Methodist women face the Civil War*, Baylor University, 2020, accessed February 26, 2021.

Jones, Gladys Powelson, *The American Family Powelson: Virginia Branch*.

Jones, Mary Ellen, *Daily Life on the 19th Century American Frontier*, Greenwood Press, 1998.

MacNamara, L. T., *Birth Control and the Good Life in America, 1900–1940*. (Doctoral Dissertation 2015). Columbia University, accessed February 27, 2021.

Maranto, Samuel Paul, *A History of Dallas Newspapers*, thesis, June 1952; Denton, Texas, accessed February 3, 2021, University of North Texas Libraries, UNT Digital Library.

Miller, Rick, *Texas Ranger: John B. Jones and the Frontier Battalion, 1874–1881*, 2012.

Mills, Betty J., *Calico Chronicle: Texas Women and Their Fashions 1830–1910*, Lubbock, Texas Tech Press, 1985.

Mock, M., *The Modernization of the American Home Kitchen, 1900–1960*. (Thesis 2011). Carnegie Mellon University. Accessed February 26, 2021.

Mooberry, Lester C., *The Gay Nineties*, 1957, Binford and Mort, Portland, Oregon.

Moynihan, Ruth B., Susan Armitage, and Christine Fischer Dichamp, Editors, *Too Much to Be Done: Women Settlers on the Mining and Ranching Frontier*, University of Nebraska Press, 1990.

Plano, Texas: The Early Years, Friends of the Plano Public Library, Henington Publishing Company, 1985.

Poor, Agnes Blake. *My Four Great Grandmothers*, 1919, Forgotten Books, 2018.

Pruitt, Wade. *The Bugger Saga*, Vine Press, 1982.

Serbulo, Leanne Claire, "Women Adrift, Sporting Girls and the Unfortunate Poor: A Gendered History of Homelessness in Portland 1900–1929" (2003). *Dissertations and Theses*. Paper 741. Accessed February 27, 2021.

Stites, Russell, *Creating the Character of North Texas: Demographics and Geography, 1841–1861*, thesis, December 2019; Denton, Texas. Accessed February 4, 2021, University of North Texas Libraries, UNT Digital Library.

Strasser, Susan, *Never Done: A History of American Housework*, Henry Holt & Company, 1982.

Sutherland, Daniel E., *The Expansion of Everyday Life, 1860–876*, Harper & Row, 1989.

Sager, Robin, *States of Suffering: Marital Cruelty in Antebellum Virginia, Texas, and Wisconsin*. Rice University, viewed February 1, 2021.

Thompson, Jesse R., *Reconstruction in Collin County, Texas, 1865–1876*, thesis, August 2015; Denton, Texas. Accessed February 3, 2021, University of North Texas Libraries, UNT Digital Library.

Utley, Robert M., *Lone Star Justice*, 2002, Berkley Publishing Group.

Ware, Susan, *American Women's History: A Very Short Introduction*, Oxford University Press, 2015.

Watkins, T.H., *The Great Depression: America in the 1930s*, Little, Brown and Company, 1993.

Watts, S. S., *Gemütlichkeit Verboten: The Influence of World War I Anti-German Sentiments on Prohibition*. (Master's Thesis 2020). University of North Dakota. Accessed February 28, 2021.

Yellin, Emily, *Our Mothers' War: American Women at the Front during World War II*, Free Press, 2004.

Ziegelman, Jane, *97 Orchard: An Edible History of Five Immigrant Families in One New York Tenement*, Harper, 2010.

Index

Albina, Oregon, 237, 248, 262
Alsace-Lorraine, 144
Anderson County, Texas, 90, 108
Brazos County, Texas, 98
Buncombe County, North Carolina, 5, 7
Cantrell, Barch, 88, 92, 106
Civil War, 32, 40, 81, 164
Collin County, Texas, 97, 105
Cooke County, Texas, 64, 118, 123
Dallas County, Texas, 88, 94, 134
Ebner, John, 157, 160, 170–173
Gabler, John, 180, 183, 189
Gravel Hill, Tennessee, 26–27
Green Bay, Wisconsin, 225, 229
Heare, Franklin Pierce, 117–118
Hemsworth, Frank, 225
Henderson County, Texas, 100
Huggins, James Monroe, 31, 37, 53
Huggins, James Montgomery, 14, 17, 33
Huggins, Phillip Jasper, 15, 48
Kuhn, Andrew, 144, 165
Lauderdale County, Alabama, 9, 24, 34
Marienwerder, West Prussia, 216, 221
Maschino, Peter, 152, 165
Nineteenth Amendment, 78, 199
Parker County, Texas, 96, 113
Peters Colony, 87, 106, 134
Robertson, Joseph, 16, 19
Spanish-American War, 186, 189, 252
Vincennes, Indiana, 143, 161

World War I, 146, 197, 257
World War II, 217, 271

www.ingramcontent.com/pod-product-compliance
Lightning Source LLC
Chambersburg PA
CBHW070611030426
42337CB00020B/3753